Nevertheless, We Persist

Nevertheless, We Persist

A Feminist Public Theology

ROSEMARY P. CARBINE

ORBIS BOOKS
Maryknoll, New York 10545

Founded in 1970, Orbis Books endeavors to publish works that enlighten the mind, nourish the spirit, and challenge the conscience. The publishing arm of the Maryknoll Fathers and Brothers, Orbis seeks to explore the global dimensions of the Christian faith and mission, to invite dialogue with diverse cultures and religious traditions, and to serve the cause of reconciliation and peace. The books published reflect the views of their authors and do not represent the official position of the Maryknoll Society. To learn more about Maryknoll and Orbis Books, please visit our website at www.orbisbooks.com.

Copyright © 2023 by Rosemary P. Carbine

Published by Orbis Books, Box 302, Maryknoll, NY 10545-0302.

All rights reserved.

Scripture quotations are from New Revised Standard Version Bible: Catholic Edition, copyright © 1989, 1993 National Council of the Churches of Christ in the United States of America. Used by permission. All rights reserved worldwide.

Cover: "Companion: Mary Magdalene with Joanna and Susanna (The Succession of Mary Magdalene)," Triptych, First Panel. Copyright 2008 by Janet McKenzie, www.janetmckenzie.com, Collection of Catholic Theological Union, Chicago, IL.

Permissions listed at the end of this book represent an extension of this copyright page.

No part of this publication may be reproduced or transmitted in any form or by any means, electronic or mechanical, including photocopying, recording, or any information storage or retrieval system, without prior permission in writing from the publisher.

Queries regarding rights and permissions should be addressed to: Orbis Books, P.O. Box 302, Maryknoll, NY 10545-0302.

Manufactured in the United States of America

Library of Congress Cataloging-in-Publication Data

Names: Carbine, Rosemary P., author.
Title: Nevertheless, we persist : a feminist public theology / Rosemary P. Carbine.
Description: Maryknoll, NY : Orbis Books, [2023] I Includes bibliographical references and index. I Summary: "Examines the impact of feminist and womanist theologies on public theology"—Provided by publisher.
Identifiers: LCCN 2023023441 (print) I LCCN 2023023442 (ebook) I ISBN 9781626984776 I ISBN 9781608339396 (epub)
Subjects: LCSH: Public theology—United States. I Feminist theology—United States. I Womanist theology—United States. I Feminist criticism—United States. I Feminists—United States.
Classification: LCC BT83.63 .C37 2023 (print) I LCC BT83.63 (ebook) I DDC 230.082—dc23/eng/20230824
LC record available at https://lccn.loc.gov/2023023441
LC ebook record available at https://lccn.loc.gov/2023023442

Contents

Acknowledgments   vii

Introduction   xi
    An Impoverished Public   xi
    Cracking Publics   xiv
    Creating a Feminist Public Theology   xvii

Chapter 1. Defining Feminist Public Theology: Ekklesial Work   1
    Public Theology and Public Engagement:
       Creating Community   5
    Reclaiming the *Ekklesia* of Wo/men   19
    Ekklesial Work: Constructive Vision
       and Critical Principle   25

Chapter 2. Doing Ekklesial Work: Practices   41
    Rhetorical Practices   43
    Symbolic Practices   53
    Prophetic Practices   58

Chapter 3. Poverty, Personalism, and the Catholic Worker   68
    The Catholic Worker   70
    Women, Public Theology, and a Praxical Christology   85
    Revolutionary Love Project   96

Chapter 4. Racism, Nonviolent Collective Action,
       and the Civil Rights Movement   113
    Freedom Movements in the Obama Era   116
    The Civil Rights Movement   124
    The Poor People's Campaign   144

Chapter 5. Ethno-nationalism, Community Organizing,
       and United Farm Workers   155
    Poetry and/as Public Theology   155

v

United Farm Workers Movement   158
The New Sanctuary Movement   180

Chapter 6. Militarism, Pacifism, and the Plowshares Movement   192
Doing Eco-public Theology in *Laudato Si'*   194
The Plowshares Movement   208
Green Nuns   221

Chapter 7. Doing Ekklesial Work in Intersectional,
Interfaith Ways   227
The Vatican, the Nuns, and the US Bishops   228
The Sacramentality of Ekklesial Work   233
NETWORK and Nuns on the Bus   237

Permissions   249

Index   251

Acknowledgments

All books come to fruition through supportive and sustaining networks, both professional and personal. I am indebted in so many ways to various presses and publishers, institutions, colleagues, students, family, and friends for participating in theological conversations and in many other ways creating the conditions which made possible not only my research culminating in this book but also the more just future religio-political vision it proposes. Robert Ellsberg, Tom Hermans-Webster, and various departments at Orbis Books have so generously guided this project to completion. I am grateful for their careful attention at each stage of the process.

My research in public theology was initiated in my dissertation about feminist theological anthropology and theological education for public theology and ministry at the University of Chicago Divinity School, guided by Kathryn Tanner, W. Clark Gilpin, and the late Anne E. Carr, and funded in part by a fellowship from the Pulpit and Pew Project at the J. M. Ormond Center at Duke Divinity School. My research into feminist public theology was further endorsed and encouraged by two residential research grants at the Center for the Study of Religion (now renamed the Center for Culture, Society, and Religion) at Princeton University and at the Women's Studies in Religion Program at Harvard Divinity School. I owe particular thanks to Robert Wuthnow and Jeffrey Stout at Princeton as well as Ann Braude and Elisabeth Schüssler Fiorenza at Harvard for the opportunity to further expand my research, and to my colleagues in those years at Princeton (especially Anthea Butler) and at Harvard, whose engaging comments and conversations in weekly fellows' meetings inspired new multidisciplinary horizons for my research and publication in this field. I was also privileged to present my research to colleagues and students at both Harvard and Yale Divinity Schools during my residence in Cambridge, which laid some fruitful foundations for my further publication in this field. I am also indebted to the collegial conviviality and longtime friendship of women theologians in a writing group with which I connected at Boston College, especially Colleen Griffith and Nancy Pineda-Madrid.

vii

viii   *Nevertheless, We Persist*

Earlier publications which shape and are significantly modified in parts of this book are gratefully used with permission from presses and publishers. My research and publication in this field have stemmed from my conference papers, presented at the American Academy of Religion and at the Catholic Theological Society of America annual meetings. My special thanks for the collegial and stimulating conversations in these venues, especially in the AAR's Christian Systematic Theology Unit, Ecclesiological Investigations Unit, Ethics Unit, Feminist Liberation Theologians Network meeting, Feminist Theory and Religious Reflection Unit, Roman Catholic Studies Unit, Teaching Religion Unit, Theology and Religious Reflection Unit, Theology of Martin Luther King Jr. Unit, Women and Religion Unit, and in the CTSA's Topic Session in Theological Anthropology. My presentations and conversations at other conferences have also enhanced this book, especially on the Future of Catholic Systematic Theology at Fairfield University, on Catholic Feminist Movement Building sponsored by Call to Action and the Women's Alliance for Theology, Ethics, and Ritual, on Theological Anthropology at Katholieke Universiteit Leuven, on Vatican II at Saint Mary's College, as well as on various topics in the Workgroup on Constructive Christian Theology and in the New Voices Seminar. Colleagues in these professional societies, workgroups, and seminars have engaged with me on different aspects of this project and have promoted my thinking about it, particularly Susan Abraham, Sarah Azaransky, Rachel Bundang, Laurie Cassidy, Min-Ah Cho, Shannon Craigo-Snell, Nancy Dallavalle, Teresa Delgado, Mary Doak, Kristin Heyer, Jeannine Hill Fletcher, Hilda Koster, Jennifer Owens-Jofre, Elena Procario-Foley, Shelley Rambo, Michele Saracino, and Karen Teel. In addition, many mentors in these professional societies, workgroups, and seminars have enabled and fostered my theological praxis at different important moments: Maria Pilar Aquino, Don Compier, Shawn Copeland, the late Paul Crowley, the late Kathleen Dolphin, Mary Fulkerson, Diana Hayes, Mary Catherine Hilkert, Mary Ann Hinsdale, Mary Hunt, the late Ada María Isasi-Díaz, Serene Jones, Paul Lakeland, Chuck Mathewes, Joy McDougall, Stephanie Mitchem, Diann Neu, Susan Ross, Cynthia Rigby, Joerg Rieger, Victoria Rue, the late Rosemary Radford Ruether, Kathleen Sands, Don Schweitzer, Mark Taylor, John Thiel, and Sharon Welch. From this cloud of witnesses, I will strive to pass on the wisdom which they have shared so generously with me about liberationist, feminist, and womanist theological commitments and thriving in the church, academy, and society.

My students over the years have validated my research with their keen interest in seeing and seeking new and renewed religio-political

Acknowledgments ix

engagement for justice. My courses on comparative women's liberation theologies, religion and social justice, and religion and politics, which inspired this book and have been integrated in it, were offered under different titles and different iterations at each institution where I have been privileged to advise and teach so many wonderful students engaged in interdisciplinary studies of gender, theology and religion, and social justice movements, namely Saint Mary's College, College of the Holy Cross, Harvard Divinity School, and Whittier College. One of these courses at Holy Cross was initially supported by teaching and research grants for early career undergraduate faculty from The Wabash Center for Teaching and Learning in Theology and Religion. Moreover, since joining the faculty at Whittier, Professors Joe Price, Wendy Furman-Adams, Rebecca Overmyer-Velázquez, and Michelle Switzer have provided listening ears at particularly pivotal moments, and as a result they have enriched this project.

"Love never fails." Throughout my graduate studies and career, my mother in our weekly conversations has edged forward my career as a teacher-scholar. Also, my life-partner and spouse Jake Carbine has shown unfailing love, care, and compassion, by urging in varied ways my perseverance with this project, particularly amid the multiple professional, teaching, health, and socio-political challenges during the COVID-19 pandemic, as well as by taking on domestic diva tasks and other household economy duties during his own sabbatical year to ensure my well-being and sufficient time for the book's completion.

Art imitates and guides life—and theology! Artist Janet McKenzie's work graces the cover of this book, titled *Companion: Mary Magdalene with Joanna and Susanna (The Succession of Mary Magdalene) Triptych, First Panel* (Copyright 2008 by Janet McKenzie, www.janetmckenzie.com), held in the collection of Catholic Theological Union, Chicago, IL. This image theologically testifies to and emphasizes the expansive agency and roles of diverse women in heralding and proclaiming renewed life and possibilities, which this book similarly highlights. This book articulates a feminist and womanist-informed public theology and then applies it to reinterpret various US faith-based social justice movements, asserting and affirming the often overlooked women who play central and catalyzing roles in these movements. I am ever grateful to the artist for permitting me to reproduce this image. In this way, from the first, this book signals the salient roles of diverse women in co-creating alternative more just worlds, in history and in our own day. Nevertheless, we persist!

Introduction

> What do we do when our leaders have lost their moral voice? When our leaders are silent or endorse hateful attitudes? ... What do we do when our religious leaders are not voicing moral truths? To whom can we look amid these civic and moral crises? ... We have reached a point at which it is clear we ourselves must take responsibility. We are the leaders we have been waiting for!
>
> —Sr. Simone Campbell, *Hunger for Hope*

An Impoverished Public

In the early 2000s, the links between conservative Christianity and US American politics began to become unhitched. The Religious Right and its influence on reproductive, sexual, and bioethics started to decline in US public life. Certain Catholic bishops outlined and advocated moral guidelines for Catholic political candidates and voters about abortion, embryonic stem cell research, human cloning, same-sex marriage, and euthanasia. Often equated with US episcopal politics and institutional church statements regarding the so-called non-negotiable beginning and end-of-life issues, Catholic public theology was further reduced to gender, sexual, and reproductive politics. Many bishops lobbied for a broader focus on economic justice, immigration, and climate change, and questioned these limited priorities that effectively discouraged healthy debate and discernment as well as falsely separated moral issues from social justice issues in US political discourse and policy. Catholic public engagement is often limited to the ways in which official church leaders shape US public discourse and policymaking through discursive practices of rational argument about this narrowed scope of Catholic socio-political issues, advocated since the 2004 US presidential election to coalesce the mythic monolithic Catholic vote. Nonetheless, the institutional Catholic Church may not enjoy a wide hearing as a moral

xi

and socio-political critic in US public life, given mainly left-leaning Catholic voting.[1]

Taking these religio-political trends as an illustrative index of the current US political climate, US public life itself is impoverished, endangered, and eviscerated, as anger mixed with anti-intellectualism and anti-truth now play a major role in growing ideological religio-political divides in US public life. How else might we imagine the relationship between Christianity and US public life, especially with regard to multiple pressing issues, such as poverty and racism amplified by the COVID-19 worldwide pandemic, immigration, war, and the climate crisis?[2] Religion frequently forms a major basis of and motivates faith-based social justice movements to challenge and change our prevalent unjust public life. Religion possesses in its beliefs, symbols, and traditions the "capacity to mobilize, promote and abet social movements—organized efforts of challenger groups to promote . . . social change through disruptive means" that critically contest an unjust socio-political order as well as creatively construct a more emancipatory future vision.[3] What might the history of US Christian social justice movement praxis around such issues suggest about another alternative justice-seeking relationship between religion and politics? What insights do feminist and womanist theologies[4] hold to critically clarify that relationship? These guiding questions shape this book, which aims to reclaim public theology as well as amplify critical and creative religio-political witness in US public life by constructing a feminist public theology that proposes a new way of understanding the purposes and practices of religio-political engagement during a time of rich radical democratic possibilities for emerging alternative political visions to revivify and to renew the common and public good.

This book examines intersections of religion and US public life by exploring the impact of feminist and womanist theologies on public theol-

---

[1] Several studies aptly analyze and debunk the mythic monolithic Catholic vote: Clarke E. Cochran and David C. Cochran, *The Catholic Vote: A Guide for the Perplexed* (Maryknoll, NY: Orbis Books, 2008), esp. chap. 2; Bernard F. Evans, *Vote Catholic? Beyond the Political Din* (Collegeville, MN: Liturgical Press, 2008); and Kristin E. Heyer, Mark J. Rozell, and Michael A. Genovese, eds., *Catholics and Politics: The Dynamic Tension between Faith and Power* (Washington, DC: Georgetown University Press, 2008), esp. chaps. 2–3, 6.

[2] Robert Wuthnow, *Why Religion Is Good for American Democracy* (Princeton, NJ: Princeton University Press, 2021).

[3] Christian Smith, ed., *Disruptive Religion: The Force of Faith in Social Movement Activism* (New York: Routledge, 1996), 1.

[4] In this book, "feminist" and "feminist and womanist" are not intended to reinforce or reproduce white privilege or false solidarity, but rather counteract any potentially totalizing term that occludes or obscures different methods, contexts, and struggles in and among African American, Asian American, Latina/x, and Anglo women's liberation theologies.

Introduction *xiii*

ogy, a subfield of Christian theology that addresses the interrelationships between religion and the US public or political order. Although public theology is often located and treated within the field of Christian social ethics, this book engages in critical and constructive theological interpretation of the significance of the term *public* in doing public theology itself. This book offers a feminist theological perspective on public life, on the kind of socio-political community imagined and enacted via practices of religio-political engagement. In addition, this book combines public theology, feminist and womanist theologies, and Catholic social thought, among others, to yield creative and constructive insights into how to effect socio-political change and transformation and how to redefine both a more just vision of public life and practices of religio-political engagement to realize that vision. Furthermore, it articulates and advances an innovative theological framework to visibilize and interpret different modes or practices of public theology, of religious engagement at the everyday level in US public life about multiple social justice issues, especially at a time when US scholars and everyday folxs critically reconsider how religion is intertwined not only with Washington politics but with US public life more generally.

Beginning with the concept of the *ekklesia* of wo/men introduced by Elisabeth Schüssler Fiorenza as a theological starting point, this book creatively conceptualizes, articulates, and elaborates an innovative feminist theological approach to the praxis of public theology as ekklesial work. I contend that purpose and praxis of public theology aim to create, sustain, and actively hope in a more inclusive and just as well as justice-seeking public life. In this book, I interweave major figures in public theology with feminist and womanist theologies as promising and potent theological resources to reshape the field of public theology and to inspire rich theological reflection as well as ground constructive theological engagement with US public life.

I distinguish ekklesial work as a new framework to illuminate a new vantage point and sources that influence and affect public theology. My main claim is that the *ekklesia* of wo/men affords a fruitful theological perspective to critically interpret and analyze as well as to constructively reshape and reimagine public theology, both its vision of political community as well as its practices of public engagement to better realize that vision.[5] Redefining US public theology as ekklesial work sharpens its

---

[5]Women's liberation theology "embraces an alternative vision for humanity and the earth and actively seeks to bring this vision to realization" (Sandra Schneiders, *Beyond Patching: Faith and Feminism in the Catholic Church* [New York: Paulist Press, 1991], 15). Doing constructive

shared but oftentimes implicit or sidelined task—to remake and reshape a public, to re-create and sustain community, to imagine, enable, and struggle to enact a more just, egalitarian, and inclusive common life. Thus, this book breaks new ground in public theology and opens up the possibility to redefine public theology as well as outline some profound implications for its practices. It focuses *less on* prevalent views of public theology that introduce religious claims into a multireligious public square in a widely intelligible way and instead revolves *more around* how religio-political participation reimagines, reshapes, and remakes an all-too-often exclusionary US society as well as signifies and realizes a more just vision of common life via religious claims, symbols, and prophetic praxis.

Cracking Publics

Religion figures prominently in contemporary US public life, as demonstrated in the increasing analyses of faith in any presidential, congressional, or judicial candidate's political viewpoints and in the continued lobbying by religious groups to inform and influence public policymaking on a variety of locally and nationally significant issues. Christianity has been especially entangled with and harnessed by US Republican Party ideology and the Religious Right since the 1980s to solely support a conservative religious agenda in public discourse and policy. Such limited and limiting religio-political engagement both de-centers the church's social justice teachings and advocacy and further divides rather than bridges different groups in an already highly polarized political and ecclesial setting—thereby contradicting the role and goal of religion in public life to shape consensus about public policy and the shape of common life.[6]

Furthermore, some institutional church leaders may not be equipped to

---

feminist theology involves a threefold method that criticizes patriarchal claims, structures, symbols within religion and society; recovers alternative liberative sources in scripture, tradition, and critical theories of women's experiences; and reconstructs those claims, structures, and symbols in light of such alternative sources for the well-being of women, all humanity, and the earth (see Elizabeth A. Johnson, *She Who Is: The Mystery of God in Feminist Theological Discourse* [New York: Crossroad, 1992], 28–33, and Anne E. Carr, "The New Vision of Feminist Theology," in *Freeing Theology: The Essentials of Theology in Feminist Perspective*, ed. Catherine Mowry LaCugna [San Francisco: HarperSan Francisco, 1993], 5–29). This book applies this shared method to do public theology, that is, to criticize multiple intersectional injustices, to reclaim alternate sources for theological reflection and action, and to actively construct an alternative vision—in this case, of US public life.

[6]Margaret Farley, "The Church in the Public Forum: Scandal or Prophetic Witness?" *CTSA Proceedings of the Fifty-Fifth Annual Convention* 55 (2000): 87–101, esp. 90, 94–95.

Introduction   *xv*

engage in rigorous civic debate about reshaping contemporary US public life. Since 2001, the Catholic Church damaged and undermined its own credibility during the mishandling and cover-up of the US clergy sexual abuse of children that erupted in the Archdiocese of Boston, spiked in major eastern and western cities like Philadelphia, Washington, DC, and Los Angeles, and occurred alongside the church's increasing litmus tests for ensuring religious orthodoxy, silencing of theologians, and so on.[7] Although Catholic bishops are regarded as authoritative arbiters of faith and morals and are thereby recognized as the church's official political actors and representatives, the US bishops increasingly lack credibility with Catholics and non-Catholics alike, since approximately fifty bishops have been implicated or accused in clergy sexual abuse scandals. Moreover, the institutional church's political advocacy for human dignity and rights, especially the right to political participation, contrasts sharply with its own institutional structures that increase episcopal control of ecclesial, theological, and moral discourse and that lead to a less than fully inclusive participatory church. If public discourse aims through argument to build community and eventually consensus, then the Catholic Church's structures and processes should (but often do not) reflect an ability to achieve a (con)*sensus fidei*, an agreement among "the body of the faithful."[8] In sum, this so-called "Evangelical crackup"[9] in the Religious Right ironically cracked open a new theo-political space for critical reflexivity on the purposes of religion in US politics.[10]

Unfortunately, this newfound religio-political space was filled by "three dominating, antidemocratic dogmas" of free-market fundamentalism, militarism, and authoritarianism,[11] fueled by white supremacist and Christian nationalist movements that unleashed anti-Black racist

---

[7]Farley, "The Church in the Public Forum," 94–98. Cf. Marie Keenan, *Child Sexual Abuse and the Catholic Church: Gender, Power, and Organizational Culture* (New York: Oxford University Press, 2012); Gerard Arbuckle, *Abuse and Cover-Up: Refounding the Catholic Church in Trauma* (Maryknoll, NY: Orbis Books, 2019); Pew Research Center, "Americans See Catholic Clergy Sex Abuse as an Ongoing Problem," June 11, 2019; Elizabeth Dias and Jason Horowitz, "Pope Defrocks Theodore McCarrick, Ex-Cardinal Accused of Sexual Abuse," *New York Times*, February 16, 2019; and Shelley Murphy, "Defrocked Cardinal Theodore McCarrick Charged with Sexually Assaulting Teenager in 1970s," *Boston Globe*, July 29, 2021.

[8]Mary E. Hines, "Ecclesiology for a Public Church," *CTSA Proceedings of the Fifty-fifth Annual Convention 55* (2000): 25–26, 38–40, and Richard R. Gaillardetz, *By What Authority? A Primer on Scripture, the Magisterium, and the Sense of the Faithful* (Collegeville, MN: Liturgical Press, 2003).

[9]David D. Kirkpatrick, "The Evangelical Crackup," *New York Times Magazine*, October 28, 2007.

[10]E. J. Dionne Jr., *Souled Out: Reclaiming Faith and Politics after the Religious Right* (Princeton, NJ: Princeton University Press, 2008).

[11]Cornel West, *Democracy Matters* (New York: Penguin Books, 2004), 3–8.

xvi   *Nevertheless, We Persist*

backlash against US President Barack Obama and a simultaneously rising multifaith, multiracial, multicultural American society. In both the 2008 and 2012 US presidential campaigns, Obama was relentlessly stereotyped as a terrorist, socialist, communist, atheist, Muslim, Hindu, non-US citizen, and in multiple other ways, signifying an increasing racially and religiously polarized US public life. Portraying Obama as a threatening other and outsider both reasserted dominant racial and religious marks of personhood in a post- 9/11 era that rendered Obama an allegedly unfit candidate for embodying a ma(i)nly white and Christian iconic ideal of political subjectivity and agency symbolized by the White House, and also epitomized xenophobic caricatures of "others" who presaged a radically changing racial, cultural, and religious American landscape.[12]

"Republicanity" aptly characterized the resurging far right and its Christian conservative restorationist political theology, composed of a religio-historical revisionist myth of America's Christian origins and a literal and moral exegesis of American sacred texts, to take back and protect a so-called lost theocratic way of life and divine providentially anointed leaders.[13] In this same religio-political vein, President Donald Trump violently fused race, religion, and politics to foment white Christian nationalist movements.[14] Elected by rising national and global influences of anti-democratic and neofascist movements, Trump promoted American autocratic militarism, nationalism, and exceptionalism, and asserted isolationist notions of US identity and citizenship that led to hypermilitarized border walls, deportation policies, incarceration camps, and immigration bans, among other policies, all induced by white nationalist, racist, and economically driven xenophobic fears and anxieties. Trump also mobilized Westcentric Christian neocolonial hegemony and its associated ma(i)nly WASP-ish iconic ideals of race and class-privileged political subjectivity and agency, exemplified by his photo-op with an upside-down Bible in front of St. John's Episcopal Church after he invoked militarized crowd-

---

[12]Donald Cunnigen and Marino A. Bruce, eds., *Race in the Age of Obama* (Bingley, UK: Emerald, 2010); Gastón Espinosa, ed., *Religion, Race, and the American Presidency* (Lanham, MD: Rowman & Littlefield, 2011), chaps. 9, 11; and Adia Harvey Wingfield and Joe R. Feagin, *Yes We Can? White Racial Framing and the 2008 Presidential Campaign* (New York: Routledge, 2010).

[13]Gary Laderman, "Republicanity—The GOP Transformation Is Nearly Complete," *Religion Dispatches*, July 17, 2011. Cf. Pauline Maier, *American Scripture: Making the Declaration of Independence* (New York: Random House, 1998) and *Ratification: The People Debate the Constitution, 1787–1788* (New York: Simon & Schuster, 2010); Andrew Romano, "America's Holy Writ," *Newsweek*, October 25, 2010; and Simon Schama, "The Founding Fathers, Unzipped," *Newsweek*, July 4 and 11, 2011.

[14]Michelle Goldberg, *Kingdom Coming: The Rise of Christian Nationalism* (New York: W. W. Norton, 2006).

Introduction *xvii*

control forces to violently disperse Black Lives Matter protesters who were galvanized by anti-racist uprisings in the wake of the Minneapolis police murder of George Floyd.

Stoked by a religio-political media culture of repeated lies and other unsupported claims about a stolen 2020 US presidential election in which Democrats won control of Congress as well as the US presidency, white nationalists vented their religio-political anger during the January 6, 2021, insurrection at the US Capitol. Nationwide threats of secession after the 2012 election radically morphed into a white Christian nationalist seditious riot that tried to obstruct the certification of US presidential election results. The Capitol siege was rooted in religious events and groups associated with rising white Christian nationalism alongside neo-Confederates, Nazis, fascists, the Klan, and multiple anti-government alt-right militias such as the Proud Boys and the Oath Keepers. The insurrection's redemptive violence to cleanse the nation and restore white Christian dominion through prayer and violence (including the intended lynching of US congressional leaders as radically symbolized by the gallows erected at the Capitol) was incited and sanctified by racism, nationalism, and religion. Religious iconography and imagery from the Capitol siege and its parallel nationwide events show this significant role of white Christian supremacy and nationalism. For example, a huge cross was erected at the Michigan capitol surrounded with US and Trump flags as well as signs that read "Jesus is My Savior. Trump is My President." Prayers offered by insurrectionists in the stormed congressional chambers in the US Capitol reveal that these groups engaged in this sacred religio-political violence in the name of Christ to rebirth the nation.[15]

Creating a Feminist Public Theology

This book initially introduces and develops ekklesial work, and then subsequently applies it to identify and interpret theological symbols and

---

[15]Randall H. Balmer, *Bad Faith: Race and the Rise of the Religious Right* (Grand Rapids, MI: Eerdmans, 2021); Anthea Butler, *White Evangelical Racism: The Politics of Morality in America* (Chapel Hill: University of North Carolina Press, 2021); Andrew L. Whitehead and Samuel L. Perry, *Taking America Back for God: Christian Nationalism in the United States* (New York: Oxford University Press, 2020); and Sarah Posner, *Unholy: How White Christian Nationalists Powered the Trump Presidency, and the Devastating Legacy They Left Behind* (New York: Random House, 2021). Cf. Emma Green, "A Christian Insurrection," *The Atlantic*, January 8, 2021; Mallory Simon and Sara Sidner, "Decoding the Extremist Symbols and Groups at the Capitol Hill Insurrection," CNN, January 11, 2021; and Drew Griffin, *Assault on Democracy: The Roots of Trump's Insurrection*, CNN Special Report Aired June 20, 2021.

xviii   *Nevertheless, We Persist*

claims (e.g., *imago Dei*, Christology, eschatology, and ecclesiology) as well as to describe and distinguish practices of public engagement (e.g., rhetorical, symbolic, and prophetic practices), exemplified in salient twentieth- and twenty-first-century US Christian and multifaith social justice leaders and movements. It examines too often overlooked—at least in the field of public theology—social justice movements and their constructive contributions to redefine our shared common or public life, to re-symbolize its values, as well as to reshape its practices that emerge from these movements' struggles that imagine and instantiate new compelling alternative horizons for the flourishing of life as well as cultivate religio-political agency, relationships, and community. These social movements reimagine an alternative theological vision and practice of common or public life that motivates and is enacted by their practices of public engagement to insist on community building. Social movements consist of interrelations between individuals, groups, organizations, and events around a common cause of public significance and common goals or commitments, such as worker, immigrant, and human rights, racial, gender, and sexual justice, environmental justice, peace, and so on. Social movements engage in collective political action on the public stage, such as protests, marches, rallies, sit-ins, boycotts, and other kinds of demonstrations with purpose and meaning to support social change, to build a new more just collective political identity. These movements depend on networks of shared material and other resources among various individuals and organizations, to negotiate and mobilize action with allies. More than the sum of their political allies and actions, social movements articulate a common purpose or commitment and recognize their links to others in that common purpose to foster a new shared collective identity.[16] Challenging and seeking to change unjust US socio-political cultures and structures consists of participating in struggles and social movements to resist them and of re-thinking organizing norms, visions, and practices that undergird them.

Rethinking theological understandings and symbols of the human person as *imago Dei*, Christology, eschatology, and ecclesiology can help reclaim and regain the religio-political agency and humanity of women and men in doing public theology. Although women have figured prominently in recent twentieth- and twenty-first-century US faith-based political activism for social justice, women are often not recognized as public theologians. Catholic public theology is often equated with US episcopal politics, or institutional church leaders' or spokespersons'

---

[16]Donatella Della Porta and Mario Diani, *Social Movements: An Introduction*, 3rd ed. (Hoboken, NJ: Wiley-Blackwell, 2020).

Introduction *xix*

statements about the so-called non-negotiable beginning and end of life issues for Catholic voters, at times further reduced to gender, sexual, and reproductive politics, which mostly do not regard women as doing public theology. Recent histories of Catholic public engagement recount a mainly clerical-patriarchal tale of prominent US bishops and their differing strategies to influence US government and policies.[17] This book will offset such a predominant clerical-patriarchal paradigm in public theology by creating a feminist public theology, which enables and empowers women to recover their rightful place as the church's political actors and agents. Initial chapters engage in part with Catholic theological understandings of the presence and practices of the church in US public life, based on the anthropology, Christology, and eschatology that underlies the church's self-understanding of its socio-political mission. These chapters critically analyze dominant Christic and related anthropological symbols in magisterial theologies that limit women's active political presence, and then reconstructs those same symbols based on Vatican II's eschatology in *Gaudium et Spes*, the constitution on the church's public role. Revisioning public theology in a feminist and womanist perspective provides a meaningful eschatological way for women to baptismally reclaim doing public theology and proclaim a sacramental sign of the body of Christ in public based on multiple types of praxis.

Each subsequent chapter examines a rich range of historical and contemporary faith-based movements, such as the Catholic Worker, the Civil Rights Movement, United Farm Workers, and The Plowshares Movement, that (1) wrestle with different social issues, e.g., poverty, racism, ethnonationalism, militarism, and ecocide, that fragment US public life, and (2) fuse religion and politics through various theological claims, symbols, and practices in order to engage in world-making,[18] that is, to reimagine and rebuild US public or common life oriented to social, economic, racial, immigrant, and ecological justice and peace. Each chapter also features a contemporary social movement that extends and radicalizes an earlier movement but in more multifaith ways to redress the increasing fracture of US public life in our time as a result of the rise of white Christian supremacists and nationalists and thereby reconstruct our current socio-political imagination and way of life—movements such as the Revolutionary Love Project, Poor People's Campaign, New Sanctuary Movement,

---

[17] Mark A. Noll and Luke E. Harlow, eds., *Religion and American Politics: From the Colonial Period to the Present*, 2nd ed. (New York: Oxford University Press, 2007), esp. chaps. 11 and 15.

[18] Laurel C. Schneider and Stephen G. Ray Jr., eds., *Awake to the Moment: An Introduction to Theology* (Louisville, KY: Westminster John Knox, 2016), 105–111.

xx   *Nevertheless, We Persist*

and Green Nuns. The book's concluding chapter offers a contemporary case of feminist intersectional and interfaith justice, with insights from Nuns on the Bus to future feminist public theology in ways that create community, that construct public life in more expansive ways beyond single perspectives, issues, and religions.

Chapter 1, "Defining Feminist Public Theology," and Chapter 2, "Doing Ekklesial Work," engage with and interweave multiple theological perspectives to offer a feminist theological approach to doing US public theology as ekklesial work, that is, the work of convoking, creating, forging a public, a community, a common life. Constructing this approach involves critically reclaiming feminist theological concepts and praxis associated with the *ekklesia* of wo/men (coined by Elisabeth Schüssler Fiorenza to criticize and redress dehumanizing and unjust practices within contemporary democracy), Vatican II's Constitution on the Church in the Modern World (especially its Christology and its eschatological understanding of the public church), and predominant figures in public theology, both Protestant and Catholic. These chapters also elaborate three practices for doing ekklesial work, that is, a community-building public theology: rhetorical, symbolic, and prophetic practices. This feminist theological perspective redefines and sharpens a central task of US public theologies: what makes public theology "public" consists in the ability to create a public, a shared public life, that is, to actualize eschatological views of the good society and then imagine and incarnate—to envision and begin to enflesh—communities of justice and peace, to evocatively witness in various ways to and generate glimpses of new future possibilities for public life. Ekklesial work thus expands the field or broadens the scope of public theology to include often neglected faith-based agents and activism in social movements as exemplary of public theology's eschatopraxis of community building, of convoking community, of building a more inclusive and justice-seeking public life.

Each subsequent chapter mobilizes and galvanizes this approach to public theology as ekklesial work to interpret and analyze US social justice movements, focusing on the kind of public envisioned and enacted by various practices of their faith-based political engagement. Each chapter identifies and interprets shared practices of community-creating or ekklesial work in select US social movements. Engaging in and reshaping new visions of public life in these social movements take place through a wide range of shared rhetorical, symbolic, and prophetic practices. Each chapter also continues to leverage feminist and womanist theologies to

Introduction xxi

further reflect on and elucidate each movement's symbolic practices to reclaim and rearticulate theological symbols of the *imago Dei*, Christology, eschatology, and ecclesiology.

Chapter 3, "Poverty, Personalism, and the Catholic Worker," examines and emphasizes illustrative parts of Dorothy Day's life, writings, and activism to theo-politically unpack a personalist approach to social justice, and to suggest how world-making through love is activated across Catholic and other religious contexts to produce a more just world. Day's approach to social change and social justice pivoted around rhetorical practices of journalism and autobiography (as popular outreach and education); of innovating theological symbols such as the *imago Dei* (e.g., all life co-creates itself in relation to dispel and combat loneliness), Christology (e.g., a personalized and politicized love is rooted in voluntary poverty, the works of mercy, etc.), and ecclesiology (the Catholic Worker's houses of hospitality, farms, and solidarity all introduced and reshaped new visions of community, of common life); and of nonviolent anti-war prophetic protests—all to criticize poverty, militarism, and racism. Day integrated rhetorical, symbolic, and prophetic practices of public engagement in founding and forwarding the Catholic Worker Movement and its three-pronged approach to socio-political change, i.e., the newspaper, houses of hospitality, and farms. Writing to rouse public engagement around poverty, worker rights, and pacifist responses to multiple impending wars figured centrally in the newspaper and in her autobiography. In addition to Christological claims based on the works of mercy and the Sermon on the Mount, the theological symbol of the mystical body of Christ—or the interdependence of all life in the reality of God—formed a theological and moral basis for the houses of hospitality. Finally, prophetic practices such as marches, hunger strikes, and other forms of public demonstrations characterized Day's public religious activism, particularly demonstrated in the 1950–1960s public protests against Cold War drills. Such drills alienated people and fomented fear of enemies, while prophetic protests in public parks reclaimed not only public space but also community and love amid nuclear wartime policies. In our time, the contemporary Revolutionary Love Project reclaims and amplifies the Catholic Worker Movement's praxis of world-making through love in ever broader justice-seeking ways to heal the increasing fracture of US public life by white nationalist movements. This chapter thus expands on love as a religio-political ethic of justice based on the Sikh activist Valarie Kaur's life and founding of this new multifaith, multicultural, multiracial movement. Kaur stresses a trifold notion of love as seeing no stranger, tending personal and socio-political wounds, and breathing and pushing together to birth a new more just world through a variety of practices.

Chapter 4, "Racism, Nonviolent Collective Action, and the Civil Rights Movement," points to significant parts of Martin Luther King Jr.'s as well as Ella Baker's life, writings, and activism that articulate and advance a nonviolent approach to racial justice. Their racial justice advocacy centralizes what I name the trifold practices of ekklesial or community-creating work: rhetorical practices of speeches, letters, and sermons or addresses in mass meetings in churches as well as prayer, ritual, and song; symbolic practices that innovate new theological views of the *imago Dei* (e.g., we are all God's children endowed with full humanity), Christology (a theology of suffering in solidarity), and ecclesiology (e.g., the beloved community); and prophetic protest to build solidarity (e.g., alliance politics) against systemic racism, poverty, and militarism as well as for civil and global human rights. Both King and Baker appealed to democratic and humanist principles of human dignity to garner broad public solidarity against systemic racism, and engaged in nonviolent direct action (sit-downs, sit-ins, marches, rallies) as well as mass mobilization campaigns in different civil rights organizations. Both King's and Baker's praxis aimed to reimagine and more fully realize both the theological notion of the beloved community and a more just, radical participatory democracy. The contemporary Poor People's Campaign, restarted in 2018 on its fiftieth anniversary, centers the activism of Rev. William J. Barber II and Rev. Liz Theoharis. Multifaith leaders with Barber and Harris reignited this Civil Rights Movement campaign to practice what King called alliance politics or what the PPC terms moral fusion coalition building. Their ekklesial work and rhetorical, symbolic, and practices encompass sermons, speeches, local and national listening sessions assemblies, and congressional hearings; theological empowerment of economically marginalized folxs (impacted by racism and anti-immigration policies) as the body of Christ focused on the renewal of the US body politic; and local and national rallies, tours, nonviolent direct action (protests and sit-ins at congressional offices) and civil disobedience—all channeled to constructively criticize the dominant national narrative, to energize religio-political spaces, and to realize the liberative possibilities and policies that rehumanize a viable US public life.

Chapter 5, "Ethno-nationalism, Community Organizing, and United Farm Workers," explores and engages with significant parts of the life, writings, and activism of César Chávez and Dolores Huerta; they feature a community-based approach to farmworker and immigrant justice. In

Introduction xxiii

my view, ekklesial work and its characteristic community-creating praxis in the UFW interrelates rhetorical practices of speeches and statements in conjunction with fasts and marches, prayer vigils and masses, and US congressional hearings; symbolic practices of innovating theological symbols like the *imago Dei* (to promote human dignity), Christology (to emulate Jesus), and ecclesiology (expressed through the union's community organizing, pilgrimage, and multifaith solidarity); and prophetic practices of nonviolent protest (strikes, picket lines, and boycotts)—all to build solidarity against ethnonationalism, or the interlocking injustices of racism, nationalism, poverty, and so on, as well as to enable a this-worldly view of the eschaton, the reign of God or a more just flourishing vision of society and public life. The contemporary New Sanctuary Movement for immigrant rights and justice showcases multifaith leaders' activism to extend faith-based hospitality in the form of humanitarian, legal, pastoral, social, and spiritual aid to immigrants facing detention, deportation, and family separation. Tracing its heritage to religious activists that sheltered and supported Central American civil war refugees in the 1980s, the NSM aims to raise public awareness about immigration rights and reforms through multiple rhetorical, symbolic, and prophetic practices of ekklesial work: immigrant testimonies and educational literature, prayer vigils and religious rituals, and most importantly giving hospitality to immigrant families, particularly women, in the form of sanctuary in participating US religious institutions—all to recognize the *imago Dei* or the shared humanity and consequent inalienable human rights that transcend (traverse and transgress) social, political, and nation-state borders.

Chapter 6, "Militarism, Pacifism, and the Plowshares Movement," features significant aspects of Philip Berrigan's life, writings, and activism alongside Elizabeth McAlister and multiple women and men in the movement. As this chapter shows, nonviolent direct action to construct a disarmed pacifist society employs ekklesial work's rhetorical practices of testimony (education through public protest and court); symbolic practices of innovating theological symbols such as the *imago Dei* (rooted in life), Christology (pertaining to church-state relations), and ecclesiology (the kin-dom of God); and of nonviolent prophetic protest (provocative direct actions). As a leading figure in Catholic pacifist movements, Berrigan and Plowshares activists combined these rhetorical, symbolic, and prophetic practices in nonviolent direct action to resist militarism, racism, and poverty as well as to communicate an alternative view of our common life, symbolized by the kin-dom of God. Courtroom testimony among other practices provided a rhetorical means to gain voice for the *xxiv* *Nevertheless, We Persist*

victims of war, racism, and poverty. Theological symbols, such as hammers, blood, Christology and the kin-dom of God, formed a major basis of the Plowshares movement and its active interference with militarist production of weapons of mass destruction. Prophetic acts of creative and dramatic ritual protest—which involve breaking into military facilities and symbolically inspecting as well as disarming nuclear weapons with hammers and blood—condemned and disrupted war-making societies and at the same time imagined an alternative peaceful society. Plowshares actions take their theological directive to "beat swords into plowshares" by hammering and pouring blood on weapons, signifying both their death-dealing purpose as well as the new community with all life in Christ. More contemporary Plowshares eco-actions and Green Nuns feature lay-women and vowed women religious in the broader religious eco-justice movement who resist ecocide by sustaining life, by advocating a biocratic view of democracy that emerges from Christology, especially emulating the purpose of Jesus' life and ministry to establish the body of Christ. A more interdependent, interconnected sense of community with all of life emerges, which especially includes environmental justice for vulnerable communities in the climate crisis.

Chapter 7, "Doing Ekklesial Work in Intersectional, Interfaith Ways," focuses on Nuns on the Bus, which marked NETWORK's fortieth anniversary, and continues to impact NETWORK's ministries as it celebrates its fiftieth anniversary. Nuns on the Bus inspires, motivates, and exemplifies a critical and constructive feminist approach to doing public theology today, through its rhetorical, symbolic, and prophetic practices. Crisscrossing the US in ways reminiscent of the 1961 Freedom Rides, the 2012–2018 tours challenged federal budget proposals, immigration policy, voting and tax policy, and encouraged political education during the Pope's 2015 US visit and during the Democratic and Republican Conventions. The tours spotlighted sisters' social justice ministries, and most importantly centralized hearing and sharing stories of the most negatively affected and vulnerable peoples in our current US economy, health care, immigration, voting, and other systems and structures. The nuns' prophetic praxis—the tours themselves and the solidarity they built—re/imagine and re/create community, or generate and bring to birth new possibilities for a US shared public life that flows from the political notion that we the people are all in this society together, or, in terms of theological symbols, we the people constitute one body as well as accompany and ally with God's persistent presence for a future world of love and justice.

This book, in sum, outlines possible prospects for the transformation of

Introduction   *xxv*

US public life from the perspective of a feminist and womanist-informed approach to public theology, called ekklesial work. It introduces this critical and constructive approach to doing public theology, and then leverages that approach to interpret US Catholic, Christian, and ultimately multi-faith social justice movements and their rhetorical discourse, symbols, and prophetic praxis of public engagement—which aim to critically articulate, envision, and enact more inclusive, transformative, and justice-seeking lived visions of US public life, of the common good. Doing public theology as ekklesial work turns from an institutional clerical-patriarchal paradigm, and instead democratizes this field or broadens the scope of who and what constitutes and counts as public theologians and practices. Doing ekklesial work, doing public theology, is neither limited to the institutional church or its official, clerical, or designated representatives, nor characterized as a single-man movement constituted by charismatic theologians. This long-standing paradigm can occlude and obscure many religio-political agents and activities in US public life, thereby diminishing their religio-political agency. Thus, ekklesial work undermines patriarchal public theology and turns from its laments for the loss of theological giants or singular charismatic figures in the US public square to ask, "How do we, as a nation and in religious sectors, summon energies, inspiration, resources, will, and potential constituencies so new sets and types of leaders with new tactics and messages can emerge?"[19] Building on this use of "we," doing public theology recast and rearticulated as ekklesial work is neither restricted to singular, solitary theologians nor limited to institutional church leaders or their representatives.[20] Thus, this book offers and constructs a broader theological view—under the rubric of ekklesial work—that democratizes the doing of public theology to include women and men, lay and ordained, individuals and groups, activists and movements, and so on, who rightfully claim their religio-political agency and activism as they strive to shape their lives in a performative imitation of the life and ministry of Jesus and other religious leaders as well as to reenvision and reconfigure US common life in more inclusive and just ways. Doing public theology as ekklesial work widens to incorporate community organizations and social movements that organize and mobilize to realize a more justice-based and justice-seeking political order from a faith-based perspective. Further,

---

[19]Martin E. Marty, "Remembering William Sloane Coffin," *Sightings*, April 17, 2006. Cf. Marty, "Under Many Influences," *Sightings*, February 14, 2005, and Charles Curran, "Where Have All the Dominant Theologians Gone?" *National Catholic Reporter* 41 (February 4, 2005).

[20]Hines, "Ecclesiology for a Public Church," 36–39.

xxvi   *Nevertheless, We Persist*

ekklesial work lends theological legitimacy to other modes of public/political engagement beyond deliberation and debate, thereby enriching and expanding the theological tradition of who and what is regarded as public theology, or theologies that contest and undo the exclusionary and unjust cultural and political logics and systems of US public life as well as imagine and construct new more just possibilities for the common good. Ekklesial work is leveraged here to reconceptualize various practices of public engagement—including and beyond the rhetorical—as expressed and embodied in progressive Christian and multifaith social movements. Public theology as enacted in these movements consists of rhetorical, symbolic, and prophetic practices, which include but go beyond addressing the public to create and transform the public itself in more just ways.

Moreover, ekklesial work sheds new light on the locus and efficacy of public theology, based on sociological and theological insights. Ekklesial work refers primarily to a public theology that is located at the interstices of multiple groups for the purpose of community building, for weaving those groups together into a more just social fabric of common life. From a sociological perspective, mediating structures occupy the civil society sphere or middle space that stands between different personal and community groups, on the one hand, and the public sphere or impersonal political or economic institutions, on the other hand. These mediating structures provide both metaphysical and actual goods for meeting and sustaining human needs to flourish amid oppressive systems related to race, class, gender, sexuality, culture, religion, national identity, language, ability, and so on.[21] From this vantage point, public theology entails more than being simply situated between discrete, distinct spheres of life, between church and world. Following womanist studies of the Black Church in the twentieth-century African American women's movements and in US Black Catholicism,[22] ekklesial work plays an inter/mediatorial, or what I will elaborate as an interstitial, role that eschatologically bridges an existing kyriarchal political order and a more egalitarian, emancipatory future political order, by reclaiming and re-creating all sorts of institutional, theological, moral, organizational, and practical resources to promote religio-political engagement, to mobilize for and effectuate social justice

---

[21]Peter L. Berger and Richard John Neuhaus, *To Empower People: The Role of Mediating Structures in Public Policy* (Washington, DC: American Enterprise Institute for Public Policy Research, 1977), 26–28.

[22]Evelyn Brooks Higginbotham, *Righteous Discontent: The Women's Movement in the Black Baptist Church, 1880–1920* (Cambridge, MA: Harvard University Press, 1993), 7–13, and Diana L. Hayes, *Forged in the Fiery Furnace: African American Spirituality* (Maryknoll, NY: Orbis Books, 2012).

Introduction **xxvii**

in the present, and to begin to realize that alternative more just future. Doing public theology, then, means occupying a middle space between different communities to envision and realize an alternative more just world or common public life in US society. Doing public theology also means inhabiting a middle space between an unjust present and a more just longed-for future.

Fulfilling this interstitial and eschatological role, public theology may certainly entail but exceeds gaining majority media attention; influencing US congressional debates, legislation, and votes; empowering citizens to influence the political process by writing to political leaders; and so on. Such measures of political efficacy may reduce the vision of the public to political representation and limit the practices of public engagement to rational debate, thereby too narrowly construing religio-political actors, access, and agency. From a feminist and womanist theological perspective, political efficacy—the power to motivate and at least begin to effect meaningful political change—has to do with fulfilling the church's mission, "to be in the world creating the signs of the realm of God."[23] It has to do with the consonance of public actions with "the narrative shape of [Jesus'] compassionate, liberating life in the world, through the power of the Spirit."[24] Doing public theology as ekklesial work is effective on theological terms, even if appearing to fail on conventional political terms, when imagining and trying to realize eschatological ideals of the reign of God, namely equality, justice, and peace. To do ekklesial work, then, entails promoting and providing (1) a rhetorical counterspace that enables marginated men and women to find and reclaim a public voice; (2) a site for rethinking theological imaginaries and symbols for their broader socio-political implications about the norms and shape of public life; and (3) a struggle to enact prophetic practices that open up and embody new theo-political possibilities to bring about or birth that alternative future. Ekklesial work, in short, lifts up feminist and womanist public theological praxis for co-creating and ushering in the reign of God. When reframed as ekklesial work, public theology consists of everyday personal, social, and political practices to imagine a new more just, more peaceful public life, practices which both image and enact through voice, symbol, and prophetic protest that ever-coming future.

---

[23]Mary E. Hines, "Community for Liberation—Church," in *Freeing Theology: The Essentials of Theology in Feminist Perspective*, ed. Catherine Mowry LaCugna (San Francisco: HarperSanFrancisco, 1993), 166.

[24]Elizabeth A. Johnson, "The Maleness of Christ," in *The Power of Naming: A Concilium Reader in Feminist Liberation Theology*, ed. Elisabeth Schüssler Fiorenza (Maryknoll, NY: Orbis Books, 1996), 313.

xxviii   *Nevertheless, We Persist*

When women publicly act for racial, gender, social, economic, and sexual justice, as well as for broad civil and human rights, they are interrupted, rebuked, silenced, criminalized, and politically disenfranchised as nonpersons; nevertheless, they persist. On February 7, 2017, Senator Elizabeth Warren incorporated into her speech on the US Senate floor a 1986 letter and statement from Coretta Scott King to oppose then attorney general nominee Senator Jeff Sessions. Then Senate Majority Leader Mitch McConnell interrupted her speech, citing a Senate rule about inappropriate speech that impugns another senator. In exchange with McConnell, Warren protested excluding King's words, witness, and testimony from the Senate's deliberative debate. "She was warned. She was given an explanation. Nevertheless, she persisted," said McConnell. After Warren was silenced and barred from participating on the Senate floor during the rest of the Sessions debate, Warren finished her speech, including King's full letter and statement, on Facebook. Warren's savvy strategy created an alternative more inclusive and just counterspace for political discussion and debate to continue, as well as galvanized further racial and gender solidarity not only about women's political participation but more so about civil and human rights. Paraphrasing her mother who linked women with saving the soul of the nation, Bernice King thanked Warren on Twitter for being the soul of the Senate. Warren critically and creatively—innovatively—turned a rebuke into an intersectional feminist and justice-seeking rallying cry: nevertheless, she persisted.

Where is women's socio-political praxis for intersectional justice-making carried on, continued, persisting in creative and dynamic ways? Women have paved and are still charting new paths for such particularly faith-based praxis, for doing political and public theology today. This book attends to the ekklesial work especially but not only of women within some significant historical and contemporary social movements to offer glimpses of an alternative possible world that offsets the deeply fractured and oppressive public life in which we currently live, move, and have our being in the US, politically speaking. Nevertheless, we persist!

1

Defining Feminist
Public Theology

Ekklesial Work

> If Christian the*logy wants to proclaim the domination-free
> alternative world of G*d effectively and to continue such
> proclamation in the future, it has to engage intentionally in
> the process of religious and ethical world making.
> —Elisabeth Schüssler Fiorenza, *Transforming Vision*

This chapter provides one map of the terrain in public theology. Public
theology consists of one major and multivalent field of theo-praxis regarding the mutual interplay between religious and public life, between church
and world, between the body of Christ and the body politic in a religiously
diverse and politically polarized society. This chapter examines important
contributions from some of this field's major figures and then emphasizes
the significance of the term "public" to reconceptualize public theology's
task from feminist and womanist perspectives. It critically analyzes and
challenges predominant discursive definitions of public theology and
opens up the possibility to redefine public theology and its associated
practices of public engagement as ekklesial work, or advancing, creating, and sustaining a more inclusive, just, and liberative political vision
and public life. Pathbreaking work by feminist and womanist theologies
reframes public theology as theological reflection on public life itself
and on the kind of public that is created and sustained through various
practices of religio-political participation. In my view, the feminist notion
of the *ekklesia* of wo/men holds promising theo-political implications for
understanding and engaging this perennial task of public theology: to
re/create an inclusive, egalitarian, and just community with and for diverse

1

2   *Nevertheless, We Persist*

groups in US public life, or what this and the next chapter define and elaborate as ekklesial work.

Taking the term "public" to signify this theological field reveals a shared but often sidelined task of its theological praxis (a mutually critical, imbricated, and cyclical relationship between theological reflection and socio-political action), namely to theologically reimagine and actively re-create the public itself. From this feminist and womanist-informed theological starting point, public theology pivots around a theological vision of the public or common good and sheds new light on specific practices of public engagement that actively aid, contribute to, and realize that vision. Prominent US public theologians mainly portray a discursive vision of public life and describe public engagement through associated discursive practices of political inquiry, deliberation, and decision-making. Public theology tends to advance rhetorical norms and practices of rational argument or reasoned debate in a deliberative democracy that ultimately seeks consensus about public policies to shape and sustain the common good. However, US public life often fails to realize its egalitarian vision of communicative practices in civil society. Public theology—when primarily defined as a rhetorical practice of giving and exchanging reasons in a broadly intelligible way about socially significant issues—insufficiently criticizes deliberative democracy. Deliberative democracy often trades on and perpetuates exclusionary logics, discourses, and practices related to idealized essentialist definitions of humanity that continue to re/produce multiple modes of injustice. It often excludes marginated peoples who do not fit privileged race, gender, class, ethnic/cultural, religious, sexual, and other ideological social constructs of US political subjectivity and agency, which mutually determine what is considered rational discourse, who counts as a political actor, and what defines the common good.[1] As feminist theorist Judith Butler queries, "Who counts as human? Whose lives count as lives?"[2]

The *ekklesia* of wo/men signifies and exposes such deeply entrenched and divisive contradictions between egalitarian ideals and exclusionary practices in US public life. This chapter elaborates on the *ekklesia* of

---

[1]Feminist criticisms of deliberative democracy and its damaging limits include Seyla Benhabib, *The Claims of Culture: Equality and Diversity in the Global Era* (Princeton, NJ: Princeton University Press, 2002), and *Democracy and Difference: Contesting the Boundaries of the Political* (Princeton, NJ: Princeton University Press, 1996); Valerie Bryson, *Feminist Political Theory: An Introduction*, 2nd ed. (New York: Palgrave Macmillan, 2003); Nancy Fraser, *Justice Interruptus: Critical Reflections on the "Post-Socialist" Condition* (New York: Routledge, 1997); Iris Marion Young, *Justice and the Politics of Difference* (Princeton, NJ: Princeton University Press, 1990), and *Inclusion and Democracy* (New York: Oxford University Press, 2000).

[2]Judith Butler, *Precarious Life: The Powers of Mourning and Violence* (New York: Verso, 2004).

Defining Feminist Public Theology

wo/men, amplifies some of its significant features, and explores its community-creating praxis, or what I call ekklesial work, that is, the task to envision and enable a more just possible world. Developed by Elisabeth Schüssler Fiorenza, the *ekklesia* of wo/men carries multiple theological meanings for feminist biblical interpretation[3] or feminist ritual practice.[4] In my view, the *ekklesia* refers to the critical reconstruction of kyriarchal religion and politics in the struggle for a more egalitarian and emancipatory church and society.[5] It aptly describes an alternative, more just theological vision of common life against which to critically judge kyriarchal public life. It also signifies a site of religio-political struggles and prescribes practices of socio-political engagement to reconstruct and transform public life in light of that vision and to bring about that vision. As this chapter will show, the *ekklesia* of wo/men illustrates an eschatological orientation of public theology because it exemplifies a future participatory, egalitarian, and just vision that is already underway but not yet fully actualized in a seemingly intransigent kyriarchal society.

Imagining and enacting the *ekklesia* of wo/men as an alternative religious reality is already well theologically argued and practiced through the notion of the "discipleship of equals."[6] This chapter focuses on imagining and actualizing the *ekklesia* of wo/men as an alternative political reality. Here, I retrieve and reclaim the not-yet adequately analyzed and actualized

---

[3] Elisabeth Schüssler Fiorenza, *But She Said: Feminist Practices of Biblical Interpretation* (Boston: Beacon, 1992), 52–76, 131–132; *Wisdom Ways: Introducing Feminist Biblical Interpretation* (Maryknoll, NY: Orbis Books, 2001), 93–98. 151–161, 179.

[4] Rosemary Radford Ruether, *Women-Church* (San Francisco: Harper & Row, 1985), and "Women Church: An American Catholic Feminist Movement," in *What's Left?* ed. Mary J. Weaver (Bloomington: Indiana University Press, 1999), 46–64. Cf. Schüssler Fiorenza, *But She Said*, 125–128; Marjorie Procter-Smith, "Feminist Ritual Strategies," in *Toward a New Heaven and a New Earth*, ed. Fernando F. Segovia (Maryknoll, NY: Orbis Books, 2003), 498–515; Teresa Berger, ed., *Dissident Daughters: Feminist Liturgies in Global Context* (Louisville, KY: Westminster John Knox, 2001); and Dianna L. Neu, *Stirring Waters: Feminist Liturgies for Justice* (Collegeville, MN: Liturgical Press, 2020).

[5] Rather than a sex/gender system of dominance that circumscribes all women into a sex/gender-differentiated identity, patriarchy in feminist critical theory problematizes social, cultural, and political constructions of women's relative privilege and power in different social locations and contexts. It emphasizes the intersectional injustices of gender, race, class, culture, religion, sexuality, ability, nationality/geopolitical identity, and so on that legitimate and justify a complex system of power relations, as well as ultimately idealize an elite, white, male, heteronormative, able-bodied Western Christian paradigm of personhood. To better capture this complex interstructured system of dominance and marginality, Schüssler Fiorenza renames patriarchy as "kyriarchy." Schüssler Fiorenza, *But She Said*, 115, 123.

[6] Mary E. Hines, "Community for Liberation: Church," in *Freeing Theology: The Essentials of Theology in Feminist Perspective*, ed. Catherine Mowry LaCugna (New York: HarperCollins, 1993), 161–184; and Mary E. Hunt, "Feminist Catholic Theology and Practice: From Kyriarchy to Discipleship of Equals," in *Toward a New Heaven and a New Earth*, ed. Segovia, 459–472.

4 *Nevertheless, We Persist*

theo-political meaning or valence of the *ekklesia*[7] and articulate the major contributions of what I call ekklesial work to redefine the praxis of US public theology, especially to develop a more just and emancipatory vision of public life and, in the next chapter, to identify and explore practices of public engagement that enable and enact such a vision. Such practices of public engagement not only include marginated women and men in the US body politic but also critically contest and transformatively change that exclusionary body politic as well as other existing unjust political norms and structures of US public life to better reflect and actualize a more inclusive, just, and emancipatory vision and way of life.

Engaging with and expanding the *ekklesia* of wo/men serves as a key vital and viable theological resource of eschatological hope for elaborating a feminist public theology and its practices of political engagement oriented toward realizing a more just possible future vision of our common life. The *ekklesia* articulates, symbolizes, and witnesses to a critical theoretical and lived counterspace to kyriarchal politics, in which a different reality might be conceptualized and constructed to oppose multiple intersectional oppressions.[8] In predominant public theologies, the public emerges from and aims for rhetorical practices of informed rational inquiry and debate that re/create political community through consensus about public policies. By contrast, a feminist public theology and its particular practices go beyond a discursive notion of the public and its associated rhetorical practices for consensus-building to include alternative rhetorical, symbolic, and prophetic practices that seek community building, that is, a public rooted in and reaching for inclusive participation, intersectional solidarity (via active listening, sustained shared interests, and joint socio-political action),[9] and liberative justice.

Based on feminist and womanist theological perspectives, public theology can be construed in terms of its sacramental and eschatological

---

[7]Ronald F. Thiemann, "Faith and the Public Intellectual," in *Walk in the Ways of Wisdom: Essays in Honor of Elisabeth Schüssler Fiorenza*, ed. Shelly Matthews, Cynthia Briggs Kittredge, and Melanie Johnson-DeBaufre (Harrisburg, PA: Trinity Press International, 2003), 88–105; Susan Abraham, "Justice as the Mark of Catholic Feminist Ecclesiology," in *Frontiers in Catholic Feminist Theology: Shoulder to Shoulder*, ed. Susan Abraham and Elena Procario-Foley (Minneapolis: Fortress Press, 2009), 193–213; and Matthew G. Eggemeier, *Against Empire: Ekklesial Resistance and the Politics of Radical Democracy* (Eugene, OR: Cascade Books, 2020), chap. 4.

[8]Young, *Justice and the Politics of Difference*, 38–65.

[9]Ada María Isasi-Díaz, "A New *Mestizaje/Mulatez*: Reconceptualizing Difference," in *A Dream Unfinished: Theological Reflections on America from the Margins*, ed. Eleazar S. Fernandez and Fernando F. Segovia (Maryknoll, NY: Orbis Books, 2001), 203–219, and "Solidarity: Love of Neighbor in the 21st Century," in *Lift Every Voice: Constructing Christian Theologies from the Underside*, ed. Susan Brooks Thistlethwaite and Mary Potter Engel (Maryknoll, NY: Orbis Books, 1998), 30–39.

Defining Feminist Public Theology 5

significance in the public sphere, that is, in terms of its ability to signify and create community, to stand as an albeit incomplete and imperfect sign of a not yet fully realized good society. Public theology from these perspectives has less to do with how multiple religions participate in US public life to add their religious insights to issues of pressing public significance and more to do with how multiple religions contribute to re-making and re-shaping a more just and liberating US public life itself, by actively pursuing the common good and actively hoping in as well as beginning to realize more just alternative future possibilities. Effective public engagement, in this view, has less to do with faith-based views and statements of institutional religious representatives that get press and other media attention to influence current civic debates and to reshape public discourses and policies. Rather, effective public engagement has more to do with fostering a rich range of democratic practices, of theo-political community-building practices by the whole people of God that aim to critically participate in and transform public life itself, to create a more inclusive and just community in solidarity with marginalized groups that also embraces and enhances our common earthly life together. Engaging feminist and womanist theological perspectives with modern Catholic social teaching on the church's public mission sheds new light on a just common life that is imagined by doing ekklesial work and its associated practices for forging and futuring it.

Public Theology and Public Engagement: Creating Community

US public theology participates in and illuminates a rich tradition of Christian theological reflection and practice that addresses the mutual impact and interplay between religion and significant collective issues and realities in US public life,[10] broadly construed as "the *res publica*, the public order that surrounds and includes people of faith."[11] Conceptualized and developed in various ways, public theology is sometimes defined by how religious actors (e.g., institutional or clerical leaders, theologians, laity in religious or other organizations) address various audiences, communities of accountability, or publics of the church, academy, and society about

---

[10]J. Bryan Hehir, "Forum: Public Theology in Contemporary America," *Religion and American Culture* 10, no. 1 (2000): 20–27, and Kristin Heyer, *Prophetic and Public: The Social Witness of U.S. Catholicism* (Washington, DC: Georgetown University Press 2006), 1–25.

[11]Martin E. Marty, *The Public Church: Mainline-Evangelical-Catholic* (New York: Crossroad, 1981), 3.

6   *Nevertheless, We Persist*

contemporary pressing issues and concerns from religious perspectives to influence public discourse and policymaking en route to creating a more just common life.[12] Public theology is alternately characterized by the method to address those audiences as well as shape public policy, either by making religious claims more broadly accessible to a religiously pluralistic society via shared norms and practices of public reason, of rational public discourse,[13] or by relying on religious institutions to shape and equip persons with virtues for participating in political discourse. Public theology is further determined by its goal to integrate theology and ethics into deliberative democracy and its discursive practices (e.g., lobbying elected officials, shaping public debate by sharing universally acceptable reasons, not particularist or confessional reasons) to add religious perspectives to public discourse and debates about shared pressing policy issues and to aim for consensus. In all these ways, public theology consists of one major and multivalent site of theological reflection regarding the roles and purposes of religion in a multifaith, multicultural US democratic society.[14]

In my view, what unifies these projects is highlighted or marked by the term "public" in public theology. Focusing on the term "public" communicates and reconfigures the purpose of public theology. Public theology can be construed as the work of continually imagining, creating, and sustaining a public, a common life. As historian and theologian W. Clark Gilpin observed, public theology is properly considered "public" because of its "convocative capability," or its ability to conjoin disparate groups into a more ultimate public, to build a more just and justice-oriented future vision of common life in which we live, move, and have our being, personally and

---

[12]David Tracy, *The Analogical Imagination: Christian Theology and the Culture of Pluralism* (New York: Crossroad, 1981), 3–46.

[13]J. Leon Hooper, ed., *Bridging the Sacred and the Secular: Selected Writings of John Courtney Murray* (Washington, DC: Georgetown University Press, 1994), and *Religious Liberty: Catholic Struggles with Pluralism* (Louisville, KY: Westminster John Knox Press, 1993). Cf. David Hollenbach, SJ, ed., "Theology and Philosophy in Public: A Symposium on John Courtney Murray's Unfinished Agenda," *Theological Studies* 40 (1979): 700–715; and David Hollenbach, SJ, "Public Theology in America: Some Questions for Catholicism after John Courtney Murray," *Theological Studies* 37 (1976): 290–303.

[14]US public theology is characterized in many typologies: Victor Anderson, "The Search for Public Theology in the United States," in *Preaching as a Theological Task*, ed. Thomas G. Long and Edward Farley (Louisville, KY: Westminster John Knox Press, 1996), 19–31; Gaspar Martinez, *Confronting the Mystery of God: Political, Liberation, and Public Theologies* (New York: Continuum, 2001), 170–171; Martin E. Marty, "Introduction: Eight Approaches toward Understanding Public Religion and Politics in America," in *Religion, Politics, and the American Experience: Reflections on Religion and American Public Life*, ed. Edith L. Blumhofer (Tuscaloosa: University of Alabama Press, 2002), 1–15; and Kristin E. Heyer, "How Does Theology Go Public? Rethinking the Debate between David Tracy and George Lindbeck," *Political Theology* 5, no. 3 (2004): 307–327.

Defining Feminist Public Theology 7

politically.[15] Public theology acts on its convocative imperative to perform community-building work, to remake both ourselves and the world, to theologically envision and enliven US public life in ways that counter both an excessive individualism and a potentially divisive and polarizing identity politics that further fracture and fragment an already fraught US public life.[16] Public engagement in faith-based social movements, for example, takes place for religio-political moral and ethical reasons, that is, to achieve intersectional social, political, economic, and eco-justice, and in doing so enacts and enables both personal and social change, or crafts a more loving, just, and peaceful society. In public theology "we see realized—if only for a moment, or only in imagination—something of the world we seek to make. . . . In living out what is most sacred to ourselves, we choose the path that is most likely to take us all to that new world."[17] If public theology centers on an imperative to convoke or make a public, to create a more inclusive and just community, then what kind of ultimate public is envisioned? What kinds of practices of political engagement shape and realize that vision? The following analysis explicitly engages this oftentimes implicit task of US public theology, namely, its community-creating praxis.

In most public theologies, the public is portrayed as a deliberative democracy, or an open, equal, shared associational space of political inquiry and debate among diverse perspectives in a pluralistic society. Public theology helps cultivate a public within the US socio-political order via civil society, or a shared space of assembly, deliberative inquiry, argument, and action in democratic societies in which all citizens collectively decide their common life via reasoned debate about socially significant issues.[18] The public and engagement in it are construed discursively; public

---

[15]W. Clark Gilpin, *A Preface to Theology* (Chicago: University of Chicago Press, 1996), 160–172, esp. 167–168.

[16]Robert Bellah et al., *Habits of the Heart: Individualism and Commitment in American Life* (Berkeley: University of California Press, 2007); Robert D. Putnam, *Bowling Alone: The Collapse and Revival of American Community* (New York: Simon & Schuster, 2000); Benjamin Valentin, *Mapping Public Theology: Beyond Culture, Identity, and Difference* (Harrisburg, PA: Trinity Press International, 2002), esp. xiii–xiv, 67–80, 101–106; and Robert D. Putnam and David E. Campbell, *American Grace: How Religion Unites and Divides Us* (New York: Simon and Schuster, 2012).

[17]Roger S. Gottlieb, *Joining Hands: Politics and Religion Together for Social Change* (Boulder, CO: Westview Press, 2002), 214.

[18]Hannah Arendt, *The Human Condition*, 2nd ed. (Chicago: University of Chicago Press, 1998); Richard J. Bernstein, "The Meaning of Public Life," in *Religion and American Public Life: Interpretations and Explorations*, ed. Robin Lovin (New York: Paulist Press, 1986), esp. 36–40; William Dean, "Forum: Public Theology in Contemporary America," *Religion and American Culture* 10, no. 1 (2000):1–8; and David O'Brien, *Public Catholicism* (Maryknoll, NY: Orbis Books, 1996), 31–33. Cf. Michael Edwards, *Civil Society*, 3rd ed. (Cambridge, UK: Polity, 2014).

8   *Nevertheless, We Persist*

theologies construct the public as rational discourse or reasoned debate and conversation among diverse plural voices. The public is characterized as well as co-constituted by such shared norms and practices of rational argument, or rhetorical practices of giving and exchanging reasons in a deliberative democracy.[19] Major figures in US public theology identify the public with a discursive realm of deliberative decision-making that is defined primarily through public reason. Theological understandings of the public are grounded in this deliberative model of democracy, in which the church's participation in public/political life takes place via rational argument and debate about socially significant issues. Analyzing selected writings from these figures shows that in a discursive vision of the public and its practices of civic debate, religious claims are introduced and expressed in the US public forum in a widely intelligible way by adhering to shared norms of rational discourse and argument. Appealing to and applying theological perspectives to address major issues and policies through reasoned argument cultivates lively civic debate and begins to build an emerging consensus for the common good.[20]

David Tracy considers the "public realm" a "shared rational space" that is enabled by "a shared concept of reason."[21] Participation in US civic debate depends on and occurs through a communicative practice of persuasive argument, that is, the giving and exchanging of reasons for political positions and policies in a deliberative democracy.[22] Tracy acknowledges that reason is socio-historically located and conditioned but still defends its ability to establish a more comprehensive public realm without fueling competing irreconcilable "particularist interest groups."[23] In a pluralistic public life, reason functions to evaluate not the "origins" but the "effects" or implications of religious claims, symbols, and texts for existential issues and especially possibilities of human life together.[24]

---

[19]Gary Simpson, *Critical Social Theory: Prophetic Reason, Civil Society, and Christian Imagination* (Minneapolis: Fortress Press, 2002), 131–134.

[20]Margaret Farley, "The Church in the Public Forum: Scandal or Prophetic Witness?" *CTSA Proceedings of the Fifty-fifth Annual Convention* 55 (2000): 87–88. Cf. R. Bruce Douglass and David Hollenbach, eds., *Catholicism and Liberalism: Contributions to American Public Philosophy* (Cambridge: Cambridge University Press, 1994), and Mark G. Toulouse, *God in Public: Four Ways American Christianity and Public Life Relate* (Louisville, KY: Westminster John Knox Press, 2006), 135–138, 197–199.

[21]David Tracy, "Theology, Critical Social Theory, and the Public Realm," in *Habermas, Modernity, and Public Theology*, ed. Don S. Browning and Francis Schüssler Fiorenza (New York: Crossroad, 1992), 19; cf. 23, 41.

[22]David Tracy, "Particular Classics, Public Religion, and the American Tradition," in *Religion and American Public Life*, ed. Lovin, esp. 121–122.

[23]Ibid., 118–119; cf. 121–23.

[24]Ibid., 118–120.

Defining Feminist Public Theology 9

Tracy's theological aesthetic shapes his public theology, in that public debate centers on the effects, products, or "classics" of religious traditions.[25] The "classic" highlights the ways in which particular traditions describe and deal with widely shared existential concerns. If religious classics address persistent shared questions about humanity's limits and joys,[26] then all persons can engage in public conversation to exchange and evaluate differing perspectives in different religious traditions by using standards of rational argument, which, for Tracy, include intelligibility, truth, rightness, and reciprocity.[27] A discursive vision of public life enables civic interpretation and debate about the classics to take place and thus forms a community of argument. Moreover, that community of argument plays an integral role in creating consensus about what best supports human dignity and flourishing.

Public theology that advances a discursive vision of public life depends not only on practices of reasoned argument but also on a dialogical notion of political subjectivity, agency, and practice. As Francis Fiorenza contends, religious folxs are prepared to engage in public discourse and its communicative practices because they are socialized in both political and religious life with rhetorical norms and procedures for rational civic debate. The church itself constitutes a community of shared inquiry and debate, or "a community of interpretation," that deliberates morality, justice, and the good life from diverse religious perspectives.[28] The church expresses and embodies a community of inquiry that equips people with certain conversational practices resonant with dialogical practices of public engagement and participation in US democratic debate. Actively deliberating among alternative visions of religious life prepares religious adherents for actively deliberating among alternative visions of public life.

Religious inquiry and debate thus resonate with dialogical practices of democratic debate in US public life. Forming persons with religio-political skills and practices for public life and civic debate is also emphasized by Ronald Thiemann. Public theology for Thiemann involves an "experiment

---

[25]Tracy, *The Analogical Imagination*, 99–154; "Particular Classics" 119–120, 123–125; David Tracy, "Afterword: Theology, Public Discourse, and the American Tradition," in *Religion and TwentiethCentury American Intellectual Life*, ed. Michael J. Lacey (New York: Cambridge University Press, 1989), esp. 196–199.

[26]David Tracy, *Blessed Rage for Order: The New Pluralism in Theology* (Chicago: University of Chicago Press, 1996), 91–118; Tracy, "Afterword," in *Religion and TwentiethCentury American Intellectual Life*, ed. Lacey, 196–197.

[27]Tracy, "Particular Classics," 123, 125; Tracy, "Afterword," 199–200; *The Analogical Imagination*, 66–70.

[28]Francis Schüssler Fiorenza, "The Church as a Community of Interpretation: Political Theology between Discourse Ethics and Hermeneutical Reconstruction," in *Habermas, Modernity, and Public Theology*, ed. Browning and Fiorenza, 66–91, esp. 85.

in constructing a pluralistic society from the many particular communities that constitute our national identity."[29] Thiemann argues not only that democratic debate supports a pluralistic society but also that such debate forms the basis of public life and depends on a virtuous citizenry. Democratic debate requires and upholds such virtues as freedom, equality, mutual respect, and justice, which in turn operate as co-constitutive values that shape common life.[30] Debate depends on and simultaneously shapes a pluralistic political community with such norms and skills; it also inculcates and cultivates such norms and skills in its citizenry in preparation for political engagement. Thus, religious—alongside civic—traditions play important roles in socializing persons with dialogical norms, competencies, and practices for public engagement. Thiemann proposes that by "identify[ing] the particular places where Christian convictions intersect with the practices that characterize contemporary public life,"[31] religious traditions—as historically extended, socially embodied arguments[32]—"school" or inculcate in their members discursive practices and virtues for doing theology that in turn enable their civic virtues and skills for political participation and for a "civic-minded, public-spirited citizenry."[33] In other words, theology that stresses an ongoing revision of a living, historically, and culturally contextualized religious tradition fosters and cultivates certain norms and virtues (e.g., tolerance, risk, and vulnerability) that both characterize public life and continue to influence responsible citizens for public engagement.[34] Simultaneously, religious traditions contain alternate views of the good society that contest and transform prevalent notions of such virtues to instill compassion and care for others, for the poor, for the common good.[35]

Religious traditions parallel and prop up political practices (Fiorenza) as well as virtues (Thiemann) required for public engagement in and for discursive public life. Similarly, according to Monika K. Hellwig, practicing

---

[29]Ronald F. Thiemann, *Religion in Public Life: A Dilemma for Democracy* (Washington, DC: Georgetown University Press, 1996), 172.

[30]Ronald F. Thiemann, "Public Theology: The Moral Dimension of Religion in a Pluralistic Society," *Zeitschrift für Evangelische Ethik* 42 (1998): 176–190; "Public Religion: Bane or Blessing for Democracy?" in *Obligations of Citizenship and Demands of Faith: Religious Accommodation in Pluralist Democracies*, ed. Nancy L. Rosenblum (Princeton, NJ: Princeton University Press, 2000), 73–89.

[31]Ronald F. Thiemann, *Constructing a Public Theology: The Church in a Pluralistic Culture* (Louisville, KY: Westminster John Knox Press, 1991), 21–22.

[32]Alasdair MacIntyre, *After Virtue* (Notre Dame: University of Notre Dame Press, 1981), 207. In Thiemann, *Constructing a Public Theology*, 133–136.

[33]Thiemann, *Constructing a Public Theology*, 43.

[34]Thiemann, *Religion in Public Life*, 85–90, 113–114, 135–141.

[35]Ibid., 86–90; *Constructing a Public Theology*, 43.

Defining Feminist Public Theology

the Christian tradition's cardinal virtues and their correlative humanistic virtues—prudence (the correlation of means and ends), justice (fair and equal standards), fortitude (courage and endurance), and temperance (restraint)—crafts a theological framework to navigate our often polarized public order toward the common good.[36] Empathy and compassion wield moral capital to transcend identity markers, national borders, and politically partisan or religious interests.[37] Empathy and compassion rely on an interdependent rather than individualistic commitment and practice to achieve a major goal in public life: to enjoy and sustain a shared life together in a pluralistic democracy.

Jeffrey Stout proposes a similar perspective about the impact of civic political traditions of conversation on shaping persons with norms and values for public life.[38] Communicative reason—or the giving and exchanging of widely accessible arguments, justifications, and the like in democratic debate—creates the common good, which is grounded in and grows from our discursive rights and mutual responsibilities. Engaging in deliberative debate that follows shared dialogical norms and procedures for rational argument, we participate in a political tradition of practical wisdom that socializes our society and us with a set of democratic norms and virtues. Some of these virtues include imagination, charity, equality, respect and reciprocity, listening, justice, temperance, wisdom, speaking candidly and improvisationally, humility, generosity, hope, courage, luck, and—interestingly—alienation. Both a discursive view of public life and a dialogical understanding of political subjectivity, agency, and practice serve as criteria for and are concurrently produced by participation in public life.

Building on Stout's later work *Blessed Are the Organized*, practicing such political dialogical virtues in grassroots democracy—in which ordinary, politically organized, and responsible people listen to, learn from, respond to, and mutually respect others from diverse and divergent contexts—redresses utilitarian individualism, avoids deeply polarized discourse and divisive body politics, revives as well as sustains a vibrant democracy, and in many ways enables living in and into a renewed public life.[39] Speaking promotes democratic action, especially in the context of

---

[36]Monika K. Hellwig, *Public Dimensions of a Believer's Life: Rediscovering the Cardinal Virtues* (Lanham, MD: Rowman and Littlefield, 2005), 139–143.

[37]Ibid., 88–89, 110–111, 147.

[38]Jeffrey L. Stout, *Democracy and Tradition: Religion, Ethics, and Public Philosophy* (Princeton, NJ: Princeton University Press, 2004).

[39]Jeffrey Stout, *Blessed Are the Organized: Grassroots Democracy in America* (Princeton, NJ: Princeton University Press, 2010), 7, 13, 230–231.

exercising basic citizenship rights (free speech, assembly, etc.), and engaging in an informed, critically reflective exchange about common concerns in various formats with others in face-to-face conversations, small group meetings, and group action.[40] Listening also illustrates "a democratic act" because conversation embodies the work of citizenship—sharing stories about common concerns and responding with empathy as well as with a view toward a more just society.[41] Ultimately, democracy subsists in and is sustained by such discursive relationships of mutual accountability for our socio-political systems as well as the conditions that empower or undermine them.[42] For Stout, hope disengaged from any specific religious tradition is "the virtue one needs when grim facts might tempt one to give up on promoting or protecting important goods. . . . Democratic hope is a virtue that needs grounds . . . grounds for thinking that we have a chance of making a significant difference for the better."[43]

To synthesize some key strands from among these predominant figures, public theology religiously vivifies political dialogue, deliberative debate, and decision-making about pressing issues that impact US common life and that enhance human dignity and rights, justice, and the common good. These figures advance a discursive vision of public life that rests on practices of rational argument and attendant rhetorical norms and virtues to cultivate public conversation; this conversation both presumes and signifies a community, a public, based on shared practices of debate and growing consensus. A discursive vision of public life does not reduce to political procedures for rational discourse; rather, it is founded on and forms morally principled religio-political agents and activities. Participating in both religious and political traditions is constitutively intertwined with becoming a good citizen and engaging in as well as influencing the public or common good. On my reading, public theologians support a discursive vision of public life and its associated practices of deliberative debate to defend the impact and influence of religious discourse, claims, and views in public debate, to legitimate and justify the inclusion of religious views and arguments in US public life, and to enable the insights of particular religions to shape debates as well as the conception of public life. Reasoned debate that reaches for consensus on public policy can be considered an ideal basis for an inclusionary public life. Rather than con-

---

[40]Ibid., xvi, 56–57, 226–227.
[41]Ibid., xvi–xviii.
[42]Ibid., 10, 100, 117, 147.
[43]Ibid., 283.

Defining Feminist Public Theology 13

sider religion a stumbling block to public life,[44] these public theologians encourage religious discourse in a vibrant public life and debate about the good society.

These public theologies often construe the public itself in an idealized way as an equal-access civil society-based arena of communicative practices of reasoned dialogue and debate about socially significant issues that reach for consensus about those issues for the common good. However, public life more often fails to realize such an egalitarian discursive vision of civil society, because it more often blocks than bolsters multiple peoples and discourses. Public life's principles do not align with its practices of imbalanced power, systemic inequities, and othering ideologies. Emerging criticisms of public theology, in my view, focus on its political idealism that insufficiently criticizes the institutionalization of elitist, exceptionalist, and exclusionary ideologies and practices within democracy, and that limits or denies equal access to a discursive public life and its practices of deliberative debate due to race/ethnicity, gender, class, sexuality, and inter/national inequalities. For these reasons, Victor Anderson, Benjamin Valentin, and Harold Recinos shift public theology toward coalitional or solidarity politics among multiple marginalized communities to criticize and contend with such privileged and polarized characteristics of political subjectivity, agency, and action in a society marked by rugged individualism, racism and white supremacy, poverty, and other increasing inequalities, political apathy, globalization, and ecological destruction. Yet these theologians still utilize and underscore a discursive approach to foster such politics.[45] Bryan Massingale aptly illustrates the ongoing influence of a discursive approach to public life and doing public theology: "By 'doing public theology,' I mean (1) addressing issues of public concern, urgency, and import (2) to a religiously pluralistic and diverse audience of fellow members of a civic community (3) in a way that is accessible to people of any or no faith tradition or commitment (4) while rooted in and inspired by one's own faith perspective, commitments, and beliefs."[46]

---

[44]Robin Lovin, "Social Contract or a Public Covenant?" in *Religion and American Public Life*, ed. Lovin, 132–145; Richard Rorty, "Religion as Conversation Stopper," in *Philosophy and Social Hope* (New York: Penguin, 1999), 168–174; William C. Placher, "Revisionist and Postliberal Theologies and the Public Character of Theology," *Thomist* 49 (1985): 392–416.

[45]Victor Anderson, *Pragmatic Theology: Negotiating the Intersections of an American Philosophy of Religion and Public Theology* (Albany: State University of New York Press, 1998); Valentin, *Mapping Public Theology*, 81; and Harold J. Recinos, *Wading through Many Voices: Toward a Theology of Public Conversation* (Lanham, MD: Rowman & Littlefield, 2011).

[46]Bryan N. Massingale, "Doing Public Theology," in "Roundtable on Theology in the Public Sphere in the Twenty–First Century," *Horizons: The Journal of the College Theology Society* 43, no. 2 (2016): 351–356.

14 *Nevertheless, We Persist*

Feminist and womanist theologians point out that public theology is premised on political participation in public life and on equal access to its practices of rational discourse, deliberative debate, and decision-making; thus, it does not address or deal adequately with how US public life operates with and contributes to intersecting social hierarchies of power to exclude multiple marginalized people from political access, representation, voice, as well as agential power to effect change. These theologians expose and challenge underlying existing and entrenched ideologies within a deliberative model of democracy that reflect and reproduce an exclusionary and oppressive politics rather than a fully participatory and just public life. As feminist Rebecca Chopp explains, public life is premised on a "narrative identity" that shapes our "fundamental assumptions" about who constitutes and contributes to US public life. In doing so, it provides "an ideological construct, a means of social and public cohesion" that "fails to fully represent the real" because it trades on exclusionary rather than participatory politics.[47] Thus, political participation and subjectivity are inextricably intertwined with interlocking systemic oppressions that shape a dehumanizing public life and that combine to degrade others as threatening outsiders. Contemporary political life still mainly privileges an idealized political subject, and such idealized bodies invisibilize other bodies, in effect socially and politically marginalizing women and all othered groups from the body politic who do not conform to dominant gendered, racialized, class, sexual, religious, cultural, and other ideologized constructions of political subjectivity and agency.[48] Since exclusionary norms undergird democratic discourse and deliberative practice, US public theology risks not contesting prevailing narratives of public life and political subjectivity and agency that relegate women and all "others" to second-class or non-citizenship in the US body politic as well as reproduce deep political and social antipathies toward "other" groups.[49] As womanist Stephanie Mitchem demonstrates, US public life reifies kyriarchal norms and definitions of being human—elite, white, Euro-American,

---

[47]Rebecca S. Chopp, "Reimagining Public Discourse," in *Black Faith and Public Talk: Critical Essays on James H. Cone's Black Theology and Black Power*, ed. Dwight N. Hopkins (Maryknoll, NY: Orbis Books, 1999), 152.

[48]Rebecca S. Chopp, "A Feminist Perspective: Christianity, Democracy, and Feminist Theology," in *Christianity and Democracy in a Global Context*, ed. John Witte Jr. (Boulder, CO: Westview Press, 1993), 126. Cf. Seyla Benhabib, *The Rights of Others: Aliens, Residents, and Citizens* (Cambridge: Cambridge University Press, 2004).

[49]Elisabeth Schüssler Fiorenza, *Discipleship of Equals: A Critical Feminist Ekklesia-logy of Liberation* (New York: Crossroad, 1993), 332–352, 353–372. Cf. Letty M. Russell, "Encountering the 'Other' in a World of Difference and Danger," *Harvard Theological Review* 99, no. 4 (2006): 457–468.

Defining Feminist Public Theology 15

middle-class, middle-aged, heterosexual, able-bodied identities and experiences—and marginalizes and maligns, dehumanizes and degrades all "othered" peoples. Othering not only disenfranchises peoples from social and public life but also promotes religio-political demonization. US public life thus creates dominative, divisive, agonistic ways of being human in the world, and reproduces oppressive relationships in political life that dehumanize non-dominant, non-white, non-Christian, and immigrant women and men.[50] Consequently, subordinated groups create alternative empowering publics and discourses to critically participate in, resist, and begin to reconstruct alternative possibilities to the dominant public sphere. Feminist theorist Nancy Fraser describes these "subaltern counterpublics" of participatory democracy from diverse communities and groups that "invent and circulate counterdiscourses, which in turn permit them to formulate oppositional interpretations of their identities, interests, and needs."[51] Such counterpublics may serve as community-based organizing sites of social critique and action for subordinated groups not only to gather "bases and training grounds for agitational activities directed toward wider publics," but also to confront and resist "discursive assimilation" into existing unjust norms and structures in US democracy that erode religio-cultural identities. These counterpublics practice "an egalitarian multicultural society [that] makes sense only if we suppose a plurality of public arenas in which groups with diverse values and rhetorics participate."[52]

Lacking political access, voice, representation, and decision-making power in interactive public debate does not mean a lack of public engagement or political efficacy. As feminist political philosopher Iris Marion Young observed, marginalized and disenfranchised groups that lack access to discursive political arenas utilize alternative practices, such as narrative, visual and symbolic media, and protest politics, to reclaim and regain meaningful forms of political participation.[53] Moreover, these practices contribute to "world-making," that is the ability to imagine and at least partly incarnate a more emancipatory future vision of our public life. Effective religious practices of public engagement critically deconstruct an oppressive US public order, and remake or reconstruct a more just and emancipatory alternative yet intra-historical possible future. Faith-based

---

[50]Stephanie Y. Mitchem, *Race, Religion, and Politics: Toward Human Rights in the United States* (Lanham, MD: Rowman and Littlefield, 2019), 24–27, 34–38, 167–172.

[51]Fraser, *Justice Interruptus*, 81.

[52]Ibid., 82, 84. First Nations resist white supremacy, racism, settler colonialism, genocide, and anti-Indigenous sovereignty groups; Mitchem, *Race, Religion, and Politics*, 64–69, 73–75.

[53]Young, *Inclusion and Democracy*, 65, 70–77.

16   *Nevertheless, We Persist*

social justice movements utilize such practices of public engagement to contest and remake public life via an alternative liberative future vision.[54]

Such exclusionary constructions of US public life and political engagement carry grave theo-political implications for public life and for the humanity of persons barred from it. Theologically, any denial of public/political participation or other socio-political disempowerment of persons diminishes the common good, or the totality of conditions that promote full humanity. The common good is interpreted not only on negative terms as freedom from exclusion, domination, and other injustices,[55] but also on positive terms, or what modern Catholic social teaching calls the collective conditions that enable and advance the full humanity or fulfillment and flourishing of all life.[56] For example, voter suppression not only infringes on civil rights (the 2016 US presidential election lacked the full protections of the 1965 Voting Rights Act), but also denies full human equality and dignity, both individually and socially.[57] Human beings, according to Catholic social thought, are created in and for sociality—a relational life with others—in all dimensions of life, and actualize that sociality and relationality by contributing to political life. As womanist theologian M. Shawn Copeland argues, disenfranchised and disempowered persons who are marginalized from public life and political engagement cannot realize their full humanity, either personally or socially. Lack of access, voice, representation, and power as well as political engagement in US public life damages and undermines the common good.[58] The common good resists any individualist, exclusivist, or isolationist group notion of political rights and responsibilities, which are too easily privatized and utilized to sacralize or demonize certain peoples and groups. Also, limiting or denying access and activism to practices of public engagement contradicts Vatican II's theological anthropology or religious understanding of the human person. In its concluding constitution about the church's

---

[54]Gottlieb, *Joining Hands,* 3–23.

[55]Stout, *Blessed Are the Organized,* 39, 41, 139–140, 247–248.

[56]"Pastoral Constitution on the Church in the Modern World: *Gaudium et Spes,* 7 December 1965," in *Vatican Council II: The Basic Sixteen Documents,* ed. Austin Flannery, OP (Northport, NY: Costello, 1996), para. 26, hereafter cited in parentheticals with paragraph numbers. Cf. Donald Kerwin, "Rights, the Common Good, and Sovereignty in Service of the Human Person," in *And You Welcomed Me: Migration and Catholic Social Teaching,* ed. Donald Kerwin and Jill Marie Gerschurtz (Lanham, MD: Rowman and Littlefield, 2009), esp. 101–105.

[57]Dorothy Fadiman, *Stealing America: Vote by Vote* (Menlo Park, CA: Concentric Media, 2008); Kelly Duane de la Vega and Jessica Anthony, "Supreme Court v. the American Voter," *New York Times Op-Doc,* October 7, 2016.

[58]M. Shawn Copeland, "Reconsidering the Idea of the Common Good," in *Catholic Social Thought and the New World Order,* ed. Oliver F. Williams and John E. Houck (South Bend, IN: University of Notre Dame Press, 1993), esp. 309–316, 322–323.

Defining Feminist Public Theology 17

political mission and ministry, *Gaudium et Spes*, Vatican II wrestled with sociocultural, economic, and political barriers to public participation (*Gaudium et Spes* [hereafter *GS*], paras. 4, 27, 73, 75), and proclaimed that public life should "enable all citizens, and not just a few privileged individuals, to exercise their rights effectively as persons" (*GS*, para. 73). Catholic social teaching describes political participation as a concrete practical effect of baptism. Further, this constitution's creation theology purports that human beings are created in and for sociality, in and for interdependent, intersubjective relations in all dimensions of life—personal, emotional, familial, religious, cultural, socio-political, and inter/national. Rather than simply situate a person in an additive way within and at the nexus of multiple communities, including political communities, *Gaudium et Spes* holds that becoming fully human entails and emerges from political agency and public engagement in these communities that co-constitute human identity (*GS*, paras. 24–26, 46, 73–75). Fragmentation in and from public life infringes on full human dignity in all dimensions of life—personal, socio-political, and even religious; a disenfranchised person cannot actualize their God-given dignity or effectively promote wider well-being (*GS*, paras. 73–75). *Gaudium et Spes* places an ultimate public or transcendent public good in an eschatological context of the future kingdom of God that impacts but goes beyond these relationships. That guiding future theo-political vision motivates the church's public mission and ministry to work for this-worldly transformative justice and peace (*GS*, paras. 21, 39, 43, 57).

Moreover, within the field of public theology, analyzing the effectiveness of public engagement is still mainly and politically gauged on discursive terms—gaining media attention; influencing congressional debate, legislation, and votes; shaping and sustaining wider civic conversation; empowering persons for the political process (writing to elected officials)—which risks leaving unchallenged a rationalist and often exclusionary understanding of the public and political subjectivity itself.[59] A participatory democracy that stresses building consensus through interactive rational debate should build on and create an inclusive community. However, as feminist and womanist theologies as well as modern Catholic social teaching have shown, when public engagement is construed as civic discourse, it can alienate, silence, and outright obscure a wide range of persons, rendering them nonpolitical subjects. Moreover, public theology still rests on a modern rationalist view of public life and political subjectivity,

---

[59]Heyer, *Prophetic and Public*, 128, 136, 147–148.

18   *Nevertheless, We Persist*

constituted by autonomous, self-interested individuals, which in effect restricts both public life and political subjectivity as well as praxis in it. According to feminist public theologian Linell Cady, modern public life operates individually, contractually, and juridically, as "the collective sum of autonomous individuals whose values and goals are resolutely private" and "the receptacle that contained individual units. In a very real sense public life in this scenario was the individual writ large, the duplication on the macrocosmic level of its microcosmic atomism."[60] Public theology's modern Enlightenment heritage aligns with, privileges, and is buttressed by a Euro-American model of political subjectivity, of rational humanity, which falsely ontologizes, naturalizes, or normalizes elite gendered, racialized, nativist notions of personhood and marginalizes "others" from public life. Thus, a different anthropology is needed to bolster a different account of public engagement and of political subjectivity; a new approach to public theology and practices of public engagement correlates with a reconstructed sense of both the personal and the political, or political subjectivity and praxis. Exploring the insights of feminist, womanist, and *mujerista* theological anthropologies challenges the normalized rational ordering of public life and persons in it, and reimagines not only new ways of engaging in public life but also reenvisions political personhood— thereby creating a new humanity, personally and politically.

In sum, public theology too narrowly limits a discursive notion of public life and practices of public engagement to rational argument geared toward consensus on public policy, as well as circumscribes rational actors and actions in ways that reinforce predominant kyriarchal ideals of citizenship, thereby excluding, disenfranchising, and dehumanizing a variety of peoples. Public theology thus sidelines and silences other practices of political participation and their potential efficacy in US common life. To articulate and advance a more theo-politically rich understanding of public engagement that better accounts for a plurality of democratic practices, I propose a constructive feminist public theology that (1) redefines public engagement and political subjectivity beyond discursive practices of rational argument and deliberative debate, and, in so doing, (2) opens up an irruptive and illuminative theological space to broaden political action and explore multiple emerging alternate and theologically inspired practices of public engagement that enable both participation in and transformation of US public life. How can women's liberation theologies advance the community-creating work of public theology and its theo-

---

[60]Linell E. Cady, *Religion, Theology and American Public Life* (Albany: State University of New York Press, 1993), 67–68.

Defining Feminist Public Theology

political praxis, in response to such deep criticisms and concerns? Taking the feminist theological category of the *ekklesia* of wo/men as a starting point, I articulate and elaborate in the rest of this and the next chapter a new constructive feminist and womanist theological approach to US public theology, both its view of US public life and its practices of public engagement in and for it. Ekklesial work suggests an innovative index to measure the efficacy of public theology, which shifts from lobbying legislators, gaining media attention, and shaping consensus on public policy to empowering solidarity that seeks social change and liberative justice.

Reclaiming the *Ekklesia* of Wo/men

Feminist New Testament scholar and theologian Elisabeth Schüssler Fiorenza has introduced and elaborated a central theological concept, the *ekklesia* of wo/men, as an alternative to Roman imperial notions of public/political community.[61] Schüssler Fiorenza critically appropriates and reconstructs the *ekklesia* of wo/men from ancient Greco-Roman notions of the *ekklesia* or democratic assembly and congress in which citizens "came together to deliberate and decide the best course of action for pursuing their own well-being and securing the welfare of the polis."[62] *Ekklesia* in its classical Greco-Roman and early Christian contexts referred to "the political decision-making congress or assembly of full citizens" and suggested, at least in principle, a radical democracy in which all citizens enjoy equal rights to full participation.[63] The *ekklesia* of wo/men discloses that classical and contemporary democracy erects substantial roadblocks to political representation and participation, in part due to kyriarchal norms of public life and engagement. *Ekklesia* of wo/men thus functions as a critical theory to analyze democratic egalitarian ideals that conflict with exclusionary kyriarchal practices in political life that largely entitled only Greco-Roman elite, propertied, free-born, educated men to full citizenship,[64] and that still produce a politics of othering in contemporary US public life.

---

[61]Elisabeth Schüssler Fiorenza, *In Memory of Her: A Feminist Theological Reconstruction of Christian Origins* (New York: Crossroad, 1993); *Bread No Stone: The Challenge of Feminist Biblical Interpretation* (Boston: Beacon, 1984); "The Will to Choose or to Reject," in *Feminist Interpretation of the Bible*, ed. Letty M. Russell (Philadelphia: Westminster, 1985), 126–136; *But She Said*, esp. 5–6, 11, 125–132; *Discipleship of Equals* (New York: Crossroad, 1993); *The Power of the Word: Scripture and the Rhetoric of Empire* (Minneapolis: Fortress Press, 2007), 69–109.

[62]Schüssler Fiorenza. *But She Said*, 118.

[63]Ibid., 128; cf. 5, 118.

[64]Schüssler Fiorenza, *But She Said*, 115–122.

Ekklesia when combined with wo/men illuminates and challenges the tensions and outright contradictions between egalitarian principles and actual ideological practices in the church, too. According to early Christian claims about baptism, all people regardless of gender, race, class, or religion become disciples of Jesus by entering voluntarily into the "discipleship of equals," an egalitarian community described in New Testament texts (Gal. 3:26–28).[65] However, early and more contemporary Christian communities adapted to patriarchal socio-political structures and cultures, thereby effacing women's roles, especially leadership.[66] Moreover, womanists Stephanie Mitchem and M. Shawn Copeland elucidate how Christian colonial, slaveholding, Enlightenment-era communities weaponized religious claims, texts, and worldviews to reinforce white imperialist and racist socio-economic structures that spiritually and brutally denied political subjectivity and agency as well as full humanity to Indigenous, Black, Latinx, and non-Christian others.[67] In sum, the *ekklesia* of wo/men signifies discursively "that neither the church nor society are what they claim to be: *ekklesia*, a democratic congress of self-governing citizens" that stresses radical equality and participation.[68]

The *ekklesia* of wo/men critically analyzes kyriarchal religio-political life for marginalizing the majority of peoples from discipleship and citizenship. It also advances a constructive alternative and just future vision of religio-political life. When combined with wo/men, *ekklesia* offers a radically inclusive, egalitarian, and participatory vision of public life. It foregrounds linguistically what has often been backgrounded historically and theologically, namely the active participatory roles of diverse women in religion and society. It celebrates women's right to be the church[69] and to full political participation in transformative ways. As Schüssler Fiorenza articulates, the *ekklesia* of wo/men refers to "a feminist movement of self-identified women and women-identified men" in struggle and in solidarity with marginated women and men to imagine a more emancipatory vision of religio-political life in a kyriarchal world, and to mobilize social justice movements to more fully realize that vision, for women, for

---

[65]Schüssler Fiorenza, *In Memory of Her*, 343–351; *Sharing Her Word* (Boston: Beacon, 1998), 112–121.

[66]Schüssler Fiorenza, *In Memory of Her*, 315–333, and *Discipleship of Equals*. 213–231; cf. Hunt, "Feminist Catholic Theology and Practice," 459–472.

[67]Mitchem, *Race, Religion, and Politics*, 41–61, 63–83, and M. Shawn Copeland, *Enfleshing Freedom: Body, Race, and Being* (Minneapolis: Fortress Press, 2010), 7–38, 107–124.

[68]Schüssler Fiorenza, *But She Said*, 128.

[69]Ibid., 127; Elisabeth Schüssler Fiorenza, "For Women in Men's World," in *The Power of Naming*, ed. Schüssler Fiorenza (Maryknoll, NY: Orbis Books, 1996), 9–10.

Defining Feminist Public Theology 21

all people, and for the earth.[70] To eschew any essentialist or separatist misinterpretations of the *ekklesia* as a religio-political space of, for, and by women only, Schüssler Fiorenza nuances this concept by inserting a strategic slash in wo/men as an effective linguistic strategy to signify and emphasize the integrity, equality, and solidarity of women and men in multiple struggles for a more participatory, just, and liberative vision and practice of religio-political life.[71]

Analyzing and applying Schüssler Fiorenza's conceptual and religious category of the *ekklesia* of wo/men holds much theological promise to formulate, articulate, and thematize a fresh feminist and womanist-informed approach to US public theology, for creating new possibilities for radical democratic community to take shape. What vision of public life, of the socio-political order, does the *ekklesia* of wo/men proffer? Which practices of public engagement and political participation will realize and help implement that vision? The *ekklesia* of wo/men serves, as Schüssler Fiorenza contends, as an alternative counterspace to a predominantly kyriarchal political order, a space that "is at once an historical and an imagined reality, already partially realized but still to be struggled for."[72] Thus, it embraces both an imagined alternative vision of a just, egalitarian, and emancipatory common life, and an activist site of struggle to realize that transformative vision, to embody radical democracy. In other words, the *ekklesia* of wo/men consists of both a guiding theological vision of public life and practices of public engagement (various types of struggle) to begin to bring about that vision. Further theological reflection on eschatology or the end goal of this world as well as the means for reaching that end goal expands on the *ekklesia* of wo/men and its theological vision of political community as well as its practices of political engagement.

The *ekklesia* of wo/men expresses a partially present and a longed-for future reality; it operates as an "imagined community" of solidarity and as "a site of feminist struggles" for alternative radical democratic praxis to usher in social and religio-political transformation to achieve such solidarity. It encompasses both an imagined alternative (ideal future or eschatological) vision of a more just, egalitarian, participatory political life and the contemporary struggles against kyriarchal political life to realize that vision.[73] *As an end*, the *ekklesia* of wo/men provides a theo-

---

[70]Schüssler Fiorenza, "For Women in Men's World," 10.
[71]Schüssler Fiorenza, *Sharing Her Word*, 131–136.
[72]Schüssler Fiorenza, *But She Said*, 130; cf. 5–6.
[73]Cf. Chandra Talpade Mohanty, "Introduction: Cartographies of Struggle," in *Third World Women and the Politics of Feminism*, ed. Chandra Talpade Mohanty, Ann Russo, and Lourdes Torres (Bloomington: Indiana University Press, 1991), 1–47.

22   *Nevertheless, We Persist*

logical vision of eschatological hope for imagining and seeking to create
community, to realize an alternative more egalitarian, participatory, and
just political life. It exemplifies and embodies a creative eschatological
tension between the "already" and the "not yet"—an ideal future political
vision that is already historically present but not yet a fully realized or
actualized religio-political reality.[74] This "already" and "not yet" quality of
the *ekklesia* of wo/men resonates with feminist utopian theory.[75] Yet this
"already" and "not yet" quality—this idealized but not fully actualized
vision—situates the *ekklesia* of wo/men squarely in the context of Christian hope and eschatology because it consists of an imaginative and lived
praxis oriented to an alternative possible future. The *ekklesia* of wo/men
is considered both a historical reality in the present and a future reality
still yet to be fully achieved. Thus, the *ekklesia* of wo/men resonates with
Christian eschatology and can play a vital role in rethinking theologies of
public/political engagement. Because it exemplifies the eschatological tension between the already (an ideal future egalitarian and liberating vision)
and the not yet (a prevailing kyriarchal religio-political life that blocks that
ideal vision), the *ekklesia* of wo/men points to an eschatological telos or
end for public life and thus embodies feminist and womanist theological
options for the future.[76] Its alternative future vision does not provide an
exact blueprint for creating a more just community;[77] rather, it functions
as a kind of theological standard that critically judges our present public
life and that propels and effects socio-political change; it articulates and
advances a future vision that provides a theological basis to criticize and
transform our present socio-political order. In Anglo and Latina feminist
as well as *mujerista* theologies, opting for a more just future epitomizes
prophetic hope. Opting for the future integrates an eschatological vision
of a more just, loving, and peaceful future with continual lived struggles
and movements to actualize that vision.[78]

---

[74]Schüssler Fiorenza, *But She Said*, 5–6, 130.

[75]Elizabeth Castelli, "The *Ekklesia* of Women and/as Utopian Space: Locating the Work of
Elisabeth Schüssler Fiorenza in Feminist Utopian Thought," in *On the Cutting Edge: The Study
of Women in Biblical Worlds*, ed. Jane Schaberg, Alice Bach, and Esther Fuchs (New York:
Continuum, 2004), 36–52.

[76]Letty Russell, *The Future of Partnership* (Philadelphia: Westminster Press, 1979), 51–53;
Liberating Eschatology: Essays in Honor of Letty M. Russell, ed. Margaret A. Farley and Serene
Jones (Louisville, KY: Westminster John Knox, 1999); and Serene Jones, *Feminist Theory and
Christian Theology: Cartographies of Grace* (Minneapolis: Fortress Press, 2000), 1–10, 51–55.

[77]Castelli, "The *Ekklesia* of Women and/as Utopian Space," 45.

[78]Rebecca S. Chopp, "Feminism's Theological Pragmatics: A Social Naturalism of Women's
Experience," *Journal of Religion* 67, no. 2 (April 1987): 239–256; *Saving Work: Feminist Prac-
tices of Theological Education* (Louisville, KY: Westminster John Knox, 1995), 11–12, 78–80;
Marsha Aileen Hewitt, "Dialectic of Hope: The Feminist Liberation Theology of Elisabeth

Defining Feminist Public Theology

Further, *as a means*, the *ekklesia* of wo/men suggests a political realism regarding our inability to fully create and sustain that alternative ideal future; it nevertheless does not lead to despair about socio-political change and transformation of oppressive religio-political realities, but rather propels prophetic struggles[79] of lived religio-political and social movements, and practices for realizing, if only in part, that alternative future.[80] As a means, it stands in an intermediary space between an emancipatory, just future public life and an existing kyriarchal socio-political order, providing all sorts of theological goods (claims, images/symbols, and activities) for promoting political subjectivity, agency, and engagement and for effecting socio-political change. Imagining and actualizing the *ekklesia* of wo/men as "a feminist political alterity," or an alternate more just and liberative reality to kyriarchal politics, allows marginated women and men to enter, disrupt, and transform our existing public life through various practices.[81] Schüssler Fiorenza describes wide-ranging practices: liberation (demystifying patriarchy/kyriarchy), differences (affirming multiple diverse voices/perspectives), equality (egalitarian process), and vision (investigating religious resources that foster such equality).[82] These practices inspire and inculcate imagination, empowerment, transformation, and hope.

Framed in an eschatological way, doing ekklesial work, or imagining and instantiating an alternate more just future public life, takes place "in between" the times, expressed in theological terms as in between this world and the ever-coming fulfillment of the world against the future horizon of long-awaited justice, love, and peace, and in political terms as in between a prevalent kyriarchal socio-political order and a future more just and egalitarian public life. Public theology as ekklesial work occupies a middle space between that ideal vision and the contemporary struggles to bring about that vision. When situated in between a multiply oppressive present and a more just and transformative future vision of

---

Schüssler Fiorenza as a Feminist Critical Theory," in *Toward a New Heaven and a New Earth*, ed. Segovia, 443–458; Ivone Gebara, "Option for the Poor as an Option for Poor Women," in *The Power of Naming*, ed. Schüssler Fiorenza, 142–149; and Ada María Isasi–Díaz, *Mujerista Theology: A Theology for the Twenty–First Century* (Maryknoll, NY: Orbis Books, 1996), 117, 150, 153–158.

[79]Schüssler Fiorenza, "For Women in Men's World," 3–13; and Ada María Isasi–Díaz, *En La Lucha/In the Struggle: Elaborating a Mujerista Theology* (Minneapolis: Fortress Press, 2004), 177–178, 229n8.

[80]Marty, *The Public Church*, 34.

[81]Schüssler Fiorenza, *But She Said*, 118, 130–132, and *Discipleship of Equals*, 348–352, 368–372.

[82]Schüssler Fiorenza, *But She Said*, 131–132. She later redefines liberation as conscientization, aligned with Brazilian educator Paulo Freire; Schüssler Fiorenza, *Wisdom Ways*, 93–98, 151–161.

public life, public theology entails a kind of hope-filled, eschatological praxis. As part of and co-constituted by multiple communities of belonging (origin, affinity, accountability, and solidarity), public theologians do ekklesial work that envisions and seeks to enflesh, if only in part, what we do not yet fully see, hear, or know: a more inclusive, just, liberative, and flourishing community for which we long with one another, with the earth, and with the divine. In this view, doing public theology as ekklesial work expresses eschatological hope in and for that kind of community and at the same time the praxis of being and building it. Ekklesial work thus embraces both intellectual and lived struggles for community building, for human and earthly fulfillment and flourishing.

Engaging and extending the *ekklesia* of wo/men in these feminist and womanist informed ways, I propose that a feminist public theology goes beyond redefining a discursive vision of public life and its rhetorical practices of public debate. It also re-envisions and reshapes public life itself as well as its modes of public engagement. Seeking more than gaining equal access to public debate (although that is involved) and more than adding diverse women's voices to existing kyriarchal politics (although that is also involved), the *ekklesia* of wo/men marks an eschatological counterspace or counterpublic[83] to a kyriarchal status quo with its distinctive vision and practices of liberation to contest and change, to altogether redefine and reconfigure, the body politic and public life—guided by an option for an intra-historical but realistic hope in imagination, empowerment, and transformation.[84] Predominant public theologies offer and foster a discursive vision of public life and public engagement in it via rhetorical practices of reasoned argument to inform political issues from theological perspective that achieve consensus. Feminist and womanist theological critics of public theology show, as discussed previously, that seeking consensus may reinforce an oppressive political status quo in myriad exclusionary and dehumanizing ways. By contrast, a feminist public theology rooted in the *ekklesia* of wo/men links its practices of creating community to transform public life, to struggles for solidarity, social change, and liberation. Moreover, seeking solidarity and social change challenges institutionalized exclusions, inequities, and injustices in public life for the purpose of generating a more inclusive, participatory, and just political community. Consequently, a different political reality is imagined, debated, and already partly but not yet fully constructed through ekklesial work, or visions of

---

[83]Fraser, *Justice Interruptus*, 69–98.
[84]Schüssler Fiorenza, *Wisdom Ways*, 179.

Defining Feminist Public Theology 25

and struggles for liberation. In my view, these visions and struggles admit and affirm multiple voices, encourage envisioning an alternate possible political reality in diverse religio-political ways, and foster solidarity to bring about that alternate emancipatory reality, or what I will articulate and elaborate in the following section as doing ekklesial work.

Ekklesial Work:
Constructive Vision and Critical Principle

In my view, ekklesial work emphasizes and enhances the central convocative task of public theology to create and sustain a more inclusive, egalitarian, and just public life and to engage in practices of public participation for social change and transformation. Ekklesial work can be further elaborated to advance a guiding vision of public life, a critical principle for public engagement, and, as explored in the next chapter, practices to realize that vision. Ekklesial work entails both a critical theological vision of public life and constructive religio-political practices for public engagement, built on rich theological claims and interpretations in modern Catholic social teaching about an eschatological telos of human life as well as the full humanity of all people created in the divine and christic image. Cornerstone Catholic social teachings on the church's public role sharpen a theological, specifically anthropological and eschatological, horizon for public theology's community-building praxis. Feminist and womanist theologies as well as modern Catholic social teaching are jointly attuned to—and when combined can better elucidate—these eschatological and anthropological claims, which I critically revisit and reappropriate from *Gaudium et Spes*, Vatican II's Pastoral Constitution on the Church in the Modern World, and from Rosemary Radford Ruether's critical principle of feminist theology in *Sexism and God-Talk*. Eschatology and the *imago Dei* (by implication the *imago Christi*) offer theological touchstones for a rich vision of public life and associated practices of public engagement that promote the full and equal dignity of all humanity, of all life.

Ekklesial work clarifies and deepens the community-building task of public theology, and thus provides a substantive theological vision of that kind of public life grounded in eschatology and anthropology. As described previously, ekklesial work consists of both and eschatological telos or future goal for public life and the means or practices of sociopolitical engagement for bringing about that goal in the present, rather than postpone it to an otherworldly posthistorical future. Placing public

26 *Nevertheless, We Persist*

theology in an eschatological context encourages public engagement for a kind of this-worldly eschatology.[85] As Vatican II claims, "Far from diminishing our concern to develop this earth, the expectation of a new earth should spur us on, for it is here that the body of a new human family grows, foreshadowing in some way the age which is to come" (*GS*, para. 39). Modern Catholic social teaching on eschatology enriches the ekklesial work or community-building praxis of public theology, to actively hope in shaping and fostering (even if not completely achieving) a more just and emancipatory future common life, a pragmatic hope that in turn lays an explicitly theological basis to critique and transform an unjust present through collective action. Rather than narrowed to select issues, *Gaudium et Spes* envisions a broader social justice agenda to subvert injustice and inequality, whether personal or political (*GS*, paras. 4, 27–29, 73, 75). Rereading the Vatican II pastoral constitution on the relationship of the church and the world provides a more theologically substantive vision and principle for doing public theology as ekklesial work, grounded in eschatology, anthropology, and Christology.

Gaudium et Spes provides a firm theological foundation for doing ekklesial work. The constitution characterizes religio-political engagement as central to love of God and neighbor (*GS*, paras. 24, 27), salvation (*GS*, para. 43), and to realizing the reign of God, or the good society based on love, justice, and peace (*GS*, paras. 39, 45). It identifies the church's central mission—to protect and promote human equality and dignity (*GS*, paras. 73, 76)—and extends that mission to articulate the church's socio-political role as a critical prophetic advocate for human dignity and rights, justice, and the common good, thereby becoming a sacrament or sign of the future reign of God (*GS*, paras. 40–42, 45).[86] It obviates equating certain movements and the reign of God (*GS*, para. 39), as well as explicitly rejects any withdrawal from public life (*GS*, para. 43); instead, it examines the inextricable interconnections of faith and public life. *Gaudium et Spes* addresses the church's mission to realize the common good in public/political life via theological anthropology and Christology. Emphasizing the *imago Dei* offers a theological guideline for

---

[85]Margaret Farley. "Feminism and Hope," in *Full of Hope: Critical Social Perspectives on Theology*, ed. Magdala Thompson (New York: Paulist Press, 2003), esp. 25–27; Rosemary Radford Ruether, "Eschatology and Feminism," in *Lift Every Voice*, ed. Thistlethwaite and Engel 129–142; Rosemary Radford Ruether, *Gaia and God* (San Francisco: Harper San Francisco, 1992), 250–253; Richard Lennan and Nancy Pineda-Madrid, eds., *Hope: Promise, Possibility, and Fulfillment* (New York: Paulist Press, 2013).

[86]These paragraphs function as hermeneutical keys to interpret *Gaudium et Spes* (*GS*): J. Bryan Hehir, "The Social Role of the Church: Leo XIII, Vatican II, and John Paul II," in *Catholic Social Thought and the New World Order*, ed. Williams and Houck, 36–38.

Defining Feminist Public Theology 27

making a just sense of self, which is reciprocally linked to making a just social order via Christology (*GS*, paras. 3, 22, 41).

As Vatican II commentators observe, *Gaudium et Spes* represented the church's initial systematic attempt in conciliar documents to present a theological anthropology,[87] that is, theological reflection about human beings as captured in a set of guiding questions "about humanity's place and role in the universe, about the meaning of the individual and collective endeavor, and finally about the destiny of nature and of humanity" (*GS*, paras. 3, 10). *Gaudium et Spes* elaborates a theological anthropology based on the *imago Dei*, and further interpreted through a communitarian or relational anthropology (*GS*, paras. 12, 23–25). *Gaudium et Spes* outlines basic theological features of a communitarian anthropology, beginning with a theology of creation and of God. In *Gaudium et Spes*, creation in the image of a triune God (*GS*, paras. 12, 19, 24, 29) theologically supports the equal dignity of all human beings as well as points to the multiple communities that co-constitute our identities and interdependent ways of life (*GS*, paras. 5, 23). Humanity is created in and called to communion with God and others (*GS*, paras. 12, 19, 42–43), because human nature is fashioned in the image of a trinitarian God who enjoys perfect co-equal communion among three persons (*GS*, para. 24).[88] Thus, all people enjoy equal dignity based on their creation *in* the image of God and *for* communion with God and with others (cf. *GS*, paras. 12, 19, 29).

Gaudium et Spes accents anthropology to analyze the broader human situation. In *Gaudium et Spes*, a relational anthropology sheds light on both our increasing interdependence (*GS* paras. 5, 23) and resulting complex conflicts (*GS* paras. 10, 25). *Gaudium et Spes* describes persons in terms of this relational and community-based anthropology.[89] A person-in-relation is expressed and embodied in multiple intersecting and mutually co-constituting communities—familial, cultural, social, economic, political, and international.[90] Moreover, *Gaudium et Spes* points out that humanity is created in and for interdependent relationship with the

---

[87]Walter Kasper, "The Theological Anthropology of *Gaudium et Spes*," *Communio* 23 (1996): 129.

[88]John J. Markey, *Creating Communion: The Theology of the Constitutions of the Church* (Hyde Park, NY: New City Press, 2003), 84–99.

[89]Kasper, "The Theological Anthropology of *Gaudium et Spes*," 133–134.

[90]Michael Stogre, "Commentary on the Pastoral Constitution on the Church in the Modern World," in *The Church Renewed: The Documents of Vatican II Reconsidered*, ed. George P. Schner (Lanham, MD: University Press of America, 1986), esp. 25–27; William C. McDonough, "The Church in the Modern World: Rereading *Gaudium et Spes* after Thirty Years," in *Vatican II: The Continuing Agenda*, ed. Anthony J. Cernera (Fairfield, CT: Sacred Heart University Press, 1997), esp. 122, 125–126.

28   *Nevertheless, We Persist*

divine and with others, and is called to better realize that relationality politically by contributing responsibly to the common good (*GS*, paras. 26, 30), supporting social justice (*GS*, para. 29), participating in public life (*GS*, para. 31)—as ultimate expressions of hope in salvation (*GS*, para. 32). In the image of a trinitarian God, all persons, all life, is thus made for egalitarian, mutual relationships. Life-in-community is not only given but also made, shaped, sustained, and continually performed, in public. Because the *imago Dei* is imprinted on all human beings, human life and dignity are connected to community, and thus community is ontologically basic, not "accessory," to human nature (*GS*, para. 25). Individuals and communities are thus intrinsically interrelated. Moreover, the full humanity and dignity of human life consists of communion with God (*GS*, para. 19), within ourselves (*GS*, paras. 24–25), and with others in society (*GS*, paras. 42–43). To both inhabit and build such community, human beings are invited to become artisans or "molders of a new humanity" (*GS*, para. 30).

Living in and for communion is fundamentally distorted and thus only partly realized because many inequalities and injustices result from sin, both structural and personal (*GS*, paras. 13, 37). *Gaudium et Spes* correlates a diminished common good and fragmented public life with a fractured humanity, marked by structural sins (*GS*, paras. 4–6, 8, 10, 13, 37; cf. 24–25) and manifested in institutionalized systemic injustice and inequality along gender, race, class, socio-political, cultural, religious, and inter/national lines (*GS*, paras. 4, 8, 27–29).[91] Our fragmented public life reflects many "imbalances" that distort humanity, personally and collectively (*GS*, paras. 8, 10, 13). Personal sin disrupts relations with God as well as twists relations within ourselves, society, and the earth (*GS*, para. 13). Thus, personal and social divisions interrelate: "The dichotomy affecting the modern world is, in fact, a symptom of the deeper dichotomy that is rooted in humanity itself. . . . [People] feel themselves divided, and the result is a host of discords in social life" (*GS*, para. 10). Structural and personal sins mutually reinforce a fraught public and personal life, and thereby diminish and degrade the equal dignity of all humanity in the *imago Dei*.

Creating community and becoming more fully human amid multiple communities, both personally and politically, remains a this-worldly historical possibility by emulating the prophetic life ministry of Jesus

---

[91]Vatican II failed to contend with or contest the anthropocentric domination of nature (*GS*, paras. 9, 12, 15, 33, 34, 57). Mary Catherine Hilkert, "*Imago Dei*: Does the Symbol Have a Future?" *Santa Clara Lectures* 8, no. 3 (April 2002).

Defining Feminist Public Theology   29

the Christ for the reign of God (*GS*, paras. 17, 26, 37, 39). In *Gaudium et Spes*, social change is inextricably interrelated with personal renewal (*GS*, para. 3), and personal renewal is grounded in Jesus, who represents the paradigmatic model of redeemed human nature (*GS*, paras. 10, 22, 24, 38, 41, 45)[92] and of fulfilled communitarian life (*GS*, para. 32).[93] For example, Jesus became fully human sans sin amid multiple communities (shaped by birth, intellectual life, labor, loving relationships, death, and resurrection). Jesus also continued God's reconciling plan by actively making and transforming a people, that is, by building up the kingdom of God through his life and ministry of preaching, healing, and inclusive table fellowship with multiple marginalized peoples for a more loving, just, and peaceful world (*GS*, paras. 32, 39). Christology in *Gaudium et Spes* proffers "a sharper theological focus on how the gospel points toward the kind of world that Christians should be helping to build."[94] Jesus created a vision and engaged in ministerial practices of and for the kingdom of God, of "a new communion of sisters and brothers" united into "the family of God." According to *Gaudium et Spes*, Jesus offered a vision and praxis of a more "universal communion" and tried to transform society in light of that vision of the kingdom of God (*GS*, para. 38). *Gaudium et Spes* identifies the totality of Jesus' communitarian vision and practice during the entire Christ event—life, ministry, death, and resurrection—with the "work of Jesus Christ" (*GS*, para. 32). The entire Christ event then illustrates what I call the ekklesial work of creating community: "Conformed to the image of the Son who is the firstborn of many brothers and sisters . . . the entire person is inwardly renewed, even to the 'redemption of the body' (Rom. 8:23)" (*GS*, para. 22), and, on my reading, even to the redemption of the body politic.

To be human, then, is to be radically oriented toward others in community, and toward a more just possible future in community. Remaking the personal and the political are mutually interrelated and intertwined via an active imitation of Christ (*GS*, para. 41), including an active praxis of what John Markey has called "creating communion" motivated by Jesus' liberative life, preaching, healing ministry, and table fellowship of

---

[92]*Gaudium et Spes* 22 is commonly considered a Christological key to interpret theological anthropology. Kasper, "The Theological Anthropology of *Gaudium et Spes*," 136–138.

[93]Christology functions as a theological guidepost for interpreting self and society in public theology, but this Christology leads with the ministry of Jesus to build up community, rather than the metaphysical person of Jesus that ontologically unifies divine and human natures.

[94]David Hollenbach, SJ, "Commentary on *Gaudium et Spes*, Pastoral Constitution on the Church in the Modern World," in *Modern Catholic Social Teaching: Commentaries and Interpretations*, ed. Kenneth R. Himes, OFM (Washington, DC: Georgetown University Press, 2005), 271.

30   *Nevertheless, We Persist*

solidarity to be and build up the body of Christ and the reign of God.[95] From this fruitful creation and christic-based anthropology and eschato-praxis, *Gaudium et Spes* invites performing what I call the ekklesial work to create and sustain community in everyday (*GS*, para. 38) and public life by imitating a "craftsman" Christ (*GS*, paras. 32, 43) and by joining in his lifelong praxis as "molders [artisans] of a new humanity" (*GS*, para. 30; cf. 43, 55). According to Mary Catherine Hilkert, *GS* reveals that the "scandal" of the gospel is not the reign of God that Jesus envisioned, preached, and lived, but that "the reign of God is discovered among and entrusted to human persons and communities despite all of our limits. . . . Because Wisdom has pitched her tent among us and sent her Advocate to seal us in the truth, *we have the power to enflesh the communion that is our final destiny—if only in fragmentary ways.*"[96] Enfleshing communion or doing the ekklesial work of creating community is not yet achieved, but is continually envisioned and enacted based on an "incarnational solidarity,"[97] or a christic praxis of solidarity and social justice that emulates Jesus' life and ministry for love, justice, and peace (*GS*, paras. 32–39). Such praxis anticipates and partially creates a more just self and society that ultimately awaits future fulfillment (*GS*, paras. 38–40).[98] Also, by actively imitating Jesus' life and ministry, individuals, groups, and society as a whole can be considered a Christological "harbinger" or a sacrament (*GS*, paras. 42, 45, 92) of justice, love, and peace—while still awaiting an ultimate fulfillment (*GS*, paras. 32, 38–40).

Reengaging with anthropology, Christology, and eschatology in *Gaudium et Spes* provides a vision of humanity as artisans of a more just, loving, and peaceful future, a vision that guides the ekklesial—convocative or community-building—work of public theology. Doing ekklesial work regards Jesus' eschatologically oriented ministry as a theological reference point for a new more just praxis of public life. Making an option for an alternative more just possible future fuels personal and socio-political rebirth through, for example, social justice movements. In addition to this christic-influenced eschatological vision, a critical theological prin-

---

[95]My reading of *Gaudium et Spes* centers especially but not exclusively on community. Community acts as one of "three heuristic keys" to interpret this document, alongside pneumatology and sacramentality; Markey, *Creating Communion*, 85, 94–98.

[96]Hilkert, "*Imago Dei*," 15, 18, my emphasis.

[97]Christine Firer Hinze, "Straining toward Solidarity in a Suffering World: *Gaudium et Spes* after Forty Years," in *Vatican II: Forty Years Later*, ed. William Madges (Maryknoll, NY: Orbis Books, 2006), esp. 170–175.

[98]As Peter Phan states, "Eschatology is anthropology conjugated in the future tense on the basis of Christology." Phan, "Contemporary Context and Issues in Eschatology," *Theological Studies* 55, no. 3 (1994): 516.

Defining Feminist Public Theology

ciple for doing ekklesial work can be resourced from *Gaudium et Spes*'s theological anthropology. *Gaudium et Spes* proposes a critical principle for doing ekklesial work, for creating community, in its claim that "all offenses against life itself . . . all violations of the integrity of the human person . . . all offenses against human dignity . . . all these and the like are criminal: they poison civilization; and, they . . . militate against the honor of the creator" (*GS*, para. 27). Violations of human dignity threaten to unravel the person and the socio-political fabric of public life as well as the common good. Theological claims about the *imago Dei*, about the full and equal dignity of all creation in the image of God, inspire public engagement. *Gaudium et Spes*, therefore, offers important theological vantage points from which to critically challenge political exclusion and inequality (the *imago Dei*) and begin to transformatively change public life in light of a more inclusive and just alternative future (the kingdom of God).

This theological vision and principle, then, cannot be uncritically appropriated from *Gaudium et Spes* to do ekklesial or community-creating and justice-making work in feminist ways. The *imago Dei* and the kingdom of God are both partially present but still longed-for future realities in a personally and structurally sinful world. Theological claims about equal dignity do not necessarily correlate with real material conditions of equality. Claiming equal creation need not subvert social inequalities in race, gender, class, sexual, or human-earthly relations. Because full political subjectivity and agency are actualized within existing broken relations, we always actively attain to and await becoming more fully human in more just and justice-oriented relations, catching only glimpses of the kind of public life that supports such equality and justice. Because realizing our equal creation consists largely of a future reality, creating that kind of public life is then also largely a future reality, already begun and performed in varied praxis but not yet fully realized. While the *imago Dei* should support and protect equal creation, dignity, and rights, it has functioned to justify and reinforce ideological dominating discourses and practices against all so-called others who do not conform to modern Western norms of humanity, including the earth.[99] Moreover, although Vatican II took place during global feminist movements, *Gaudium et Spes* paid

---

[99]The symbol of the *imago Dei* can be critically retrieved to contest rather than support kyriarchal, racist, anthropocentric, and other ideological theologies. Mary Catherine Hilkert, "Cry Beloved Image: Rethinking the Image of God," in *In the Embrace of God: Feminist Approaches to Theological Anthropology*, ed. Ann O'Hara Graff (Maryknoll, NY: Orbis Books, 1995), 190–205.

32 *Nevertheless, We Persist*

remarkably little attention to gender justice in promoting full humanity and the kingdom of God, and instead emphasized global independence movements.[100] A renewed public theology, then, depends on a renewed political anthropology.

Thus, this vision and principle of full humanity can be critically modified to better advocate ekklesial work and its eschatological practices that opt for future intersectional justice. The critical principle of feminist theology proposed by Rosemary Radford Ruether—the "promotion of the full humanity of women"[101]—reinterprets and reframes, in my view, biblical prophetic traditions of equal creation and justice. From a feminist theological perspective, the critical principle of doing public theology as ekklesial work expands to confront any form of oppression that denies and degrades full humanity based on race, gender, class, language, culture, religion (cf. *GS*, para. 29) as well as gender identity, sexuality, ability, imperialism, anthropocentrism, and so on. Elaborating a constructive feminist public theology as ekklesial work with this revised guiding principle ultimately points toward a needed religio-political reconceptualization of human dignity in the *imago Dei*, or a theological notion of political subjectivity and agency in ways that beckon us to live into our full humanity in community, that motivate us to reconstruct a more just social order marked by mutuality, equality, and peace.[102] Moreover, feminist, womanist, and *mujerista* theological anthropologies offer important insights into rethinking subjectivity, both theologically and politically, by critically reappropriating and reconstructing relationality and performativity to expand on what constitutes our being and becoming more fully human in relation to others, eschatologically speaking, that is, what enhances future self and social change and transformation. These theologies better align with and accompany the convocative, community-building goal of public theology as ekklesial work. Creating a more inclusive and just public life in which we actively hope and co-create with one another requires an innovative approach to a relational anthropology that stresses being and becoming more human in, with, and for community, with a future-oriented view of our full humanity and society as an identity and political project which we undertake in the present and most fully realize in an eschatological future horizon that always lies ahead of us.

---

[100]Recent commentaries note human rights, civil rights, antiwar, and postcolonial movements that paralleled the emergence of *Gaudium et Spes*, but pay little attention to feminist movements that preceded and followed Vatican II. Hollenbach, "Commentary on *Gaudium et Spes*," 267–269.

[101]Rosemary Radford Ruether, *Sexism and God-Talk: Toward a Feminist Theology* (Boston: Beacon, 1983), 18–20.

[102]Ibid., 25–26.

Defining Feminist Public Theology

Theological anthropology within women's liberation theologies adopts a materialist approach to critical and constructive theological reflection on the diverse lived experiences and embodied realities of women's social locations and contexts, which are problematized by inequality in terms of gender, race, class, sexuality, ability, religion, culture, nationality, and other features of human identity. In doing so, these theologies avoid, challenge, and undercut any fixed, totalizing, or ontotheological ideal notion of humanity. Thus, these theologies critically analyze and resist any essentialist, reductionist, or ideologically manipulated portrait of humanity that takes shape within Christian theological categories, including but not limited to the divine, creation, Christology, soteriology, eschatology, and so on. To emphasize the concrete and complex multidimensionality of human experience, these theologies characterize the human person as (1) divinely created in and for relationship with God, ourselves, others, and the earth, even unto the cosmos; (2) broken and damaged in those relationships by original sin; (3) actively and perpetually distorting and de-creating those relationships through structural and personal sin; (4) continually healed in those relationships through the divine gift of grace as self-love, love of others, and love of God; (5) creatively, cooperatively, and constantly living into reclaimed and reconciled relationships through grace-filled and empowered personal, liturgical, social, and political praxis; and (6) ultimately open to and reaching for the full potential and flourishing of those relationships, of being and becoming human together, in a perennially not-yet realized eschatological future. Also, these theologies contend with modern kyriarchal paradigms of personhood that negatively portray differences and perpetuate hierarchical dominant-subordinate relational norms of human identity such as racism, hetero/sexism, poverty, neo/colonialism, militarism and imperialism, and globalization.[103] As a result, multiple theological models of the person have emerged in women's liberation theologies, especially a multipolar model that identifies a shared set of anthropological constants but shaped differently in and by different social locations, and a transformative model that supports full subjectivity, participation in, and transformation of self, church, and society through Jesus' ministry for justice and peace.[104]

---

[103]Ada María Isasi-Díaz, *Mujerista Theology: A Theology for the Twenty-First Century* (Maryknoll, NY: Orbis Books, 1996), 79–81.

[104]Mary Ann Hinsdale, "Heeding the Voices: An Historical Overview," in *In the Embrace of God*, ed. Graff, 22–48; Donna Teevan, "Challenge to the Role of Theological Anthropology in Feminist Theologies," *Theological Studies* 64 (2003): 582–597; Michelle A. Gonzalez, *Created in God's Image: An Introduction to Feminist Theological Anthropology* (Maryknoll, NY: Orbis Books, 2007), 109–112.

34 *Nevertheless, We Persist*

Illustrated by Elizabeth A. Johnson, M. Shawn Copeland, and Ada María lsasi-Díaz, respectively, women's liberation theologies in feminist, womanist, and *mujerista* perspectives situate sex and gender among varied "anthropological constants" or intersecting characteristics that co-constitute and condition diverse ways of being human, in order to critically offset Christian theological tendencies toward ideological definitions of humanity couched in an allegedly divinely designed hierarchical dualistic order that dignifies an ideal image of God in some and differentially ranks, degrades, or outright denies it in others. Johnson envisions a complex multifaceted relational matrix of personhood that embraces and entails multiple coinciding features: relationships to our bodies, to sexuality, to other persons, to the earth, to socio-historical, political, and economic institutions and structures, to the process of culture-making, and to the future.[105] Copeland takes the imposed and internalized suffering in Black women's lived realities at the intersections of race, gender, class, and sexuality together with the incarnation of the divine in Jesus the Christ as an embodied sacramental starting point to signify some shared features of human personhood: a divine creation; an incarnate spirit, marked by race, gender, sex, sexuality, and culture; a person made in and for living in just community with God and with others via personal responsibility and freedom; a social being that embraces difference and interdependence; and, a person struggling for the survival, ongoing creation, and future of all life.[106] For Copeland, sacramentality suffuses these aspects of personhood—the person, in particular the body, signifies the *imago Dei* enfleshed, revealed, and at work in transfiguring persons in communion.[107] Isasi-Díaz reflects on the *mestizaje/mulatez*-based social locations of Latina women's lives at the borders of and between different worlds, shaped by racial, cultural, religious, socio-historical, and other forms of violent intermingling resulting from Eurocentric colonialism and US expansion, annexation, and imperialism in the American southwest, the Caribbean, and the Pacific. Isasi-Díaz elaborates on the negative and positive implications of this term to place personhood in the context of extended relations, and thus enact a way of living at and crossing multiple

---

[105]Elizabeth A. Johnson, *She Who Is: The Mystery of God in Feminist Theological Discourse* (New York: Crossroad, 1992), 154–156; "The Maleness of Christ," in *The Power of Naming*, ed. Schüssler Fiorenza, 307–315.

[106]Copeland, *Enfleshing Freedom*, 24, 91–92.

[107]Ibid., 24–25, 125. Solidarity is considered a central social praxis to realizing and fulfilling humanity that involves a Christic mimesis to embrace, oppose, and ultimately cease the social sufferings of others; ibid., 94–95, 99–101, 104–105.

Defining Feminist Public Theology

borders of racial, cultural, religious, and many other differences,[108] in which, as Johnson concurs, "difference itself . . . can function as a creative community-shaping force."[109] Eschatological practices for realizing the kindom of God, or eschato-praxis, flow from a renewed and reconstructed sense of equal creation in the *imago Dei*. As Isasi-Díaz argues:

> Each of us also mediates the kingdom of God. . . . Each and every one of us is an image of God, an *imago Dei*. . . . This is precisely one of the key reasons why we can . . . incarnate [the kingdom] . . . in our midst . . . why we see our struggles in this world as part of the overall work of God's creation. It continues in us and with us.[110]

More recent trends in feminist theological anthropology emphasize intersectionality and performance[111] to situate persons amid multiple social contexts and relations that we actively and perennially process, navigate, and negotiate to create an integrated sense, at least partly, of self-identity-in-community, in public life. Feminist theologians urge a constructivist subjectivity that forefronts women as "bricoleurs," cobbling together identity in relation and in resistance to already given scripted social roles and settings.[112] Human "nature" is not static, fixed, or already biophysically, ontologically, or socio-culturally determined and defined; rather, personhood is continually re/created and re/constructed into a more holistic self-identity by an active agential negotiation of multiple intersectional relations and communities of belonging. As feminist public theologian Linell Cady explains, feminist anthropology in the context of public theology "recognizes that identity is multiple, fluid, and shifting,

---

[108]Isasi-Díaz, *Mujerista Theology*, 64; *En La Lucha/In the Struggle*, 2–3, 33; *La Lucha Continues: Mujerista Theology* (Maryknoll, NY: Orbis Books, 2004), 61, 69–91. Cf. Néstor Medina, *Mestizaje: (Re)Mapping Race, Culture, and Faith in Latina/o Catholicism* (Maryknoll, NY: Orbis Books, 2009).

[109]Johnson, "The Maleness of Christ," 311.

[110]Isasi-Díaz, *La Lucha Continues*, 247.

[111]Judith Butler, *Gender Trouble: Feminism and the Subversion of Identity* (New York: Routledge, 1989); Judith Butler, *Giving an Account of Oneself* (New York: Fordham University Press, 2005). Cf. Laura Taylor, "Redeeming Christ: Imitation or (Re)citation?" in *Frontiers in Catholic Feminist Theology*, ed. Abraham and Procario-Foley, 119–140.

[112]Serene Jones, *Feminist Theory and Christian Theology: Cartographies of Grace* (Minneapolis: Fortress Press, 2000), 22–48. Cf. Tina Allik, "Human Finitude and the Concept of Women's Experience," *Modern Theology* 9, no. 1 (1993): 67–85; Mary Ann Zimmer, "Stepping Stones in Feminist Theory," in *In the Embrace of God*, ed. Graff, 7–21; Mary McClintock Fulkerson, *Changing the Subject: Women's Discourses and Feminist Theology* (Minneapolis: Fortress Press, 1994); Anne-Louise Eriksson, *The Meaning of Gender in Theology: Problems and Possibilities* (Minneapolis: Augsburg Fortress, 1995); and, Elaine L. Graham, *Making the Difference: Gender, Personhood, and Theology* (London: Mowbray, 1995).

36   *Nevertheless, We Persist*

but for all that, it is not fictitious, ephemeral, or limitless. . . . Identity is constituted by the subject's creative, agential negotiation of the intersecting currents and competing loyalties."[113] For Cady, our subjectivity or sense of self is continually reproduced; we perennially reconfigure and "rewrite" identity while negotiating our particular personal and communal given and chosen web of intersectional relations.[114] Personhood, then, is regarded in more recent feminist perspectives as an affective, relational, and performative reality of empathetic engagement across differences.[115] For Michele Saracino, creation and Christology catalyze hybridity. Reinterpreting creation stories shows humanity's inherent hybridity, carrying both divinity and humanity. Reinterpreting the gospels underscores the multistoried identity of Jesus, illustrated by his hypostatic union of divinity and humanity, navigation of diverse identities, and other-oriented and bodily healing ministry.[116]

Highlighting creativity and performativity in a relational subjectivity, Asian American feminist theologian Rita Nakashima Brock examines and expands on an interstitial anthropology, which underscores how Asian American women approach an integrated identity at the interstices, or in between connective spaces, of multiple communities of belonging that co-constitute them. In keeping with a critical strategic transnational analysis, "Asian"[117] in Asian American feminist theologies refers to women's experiences intersected by kyriarchal effective histories of racism, sexism, neo/colonialism, nationalism, imperialism, and globalization. These experiences resist any singular or unitary way of being Asian or being an Asian woman due to diverse cultures, languages, religions, and so on, but nonetheless coalesce strategically in the term "Asian" as an identity political concept that evokes both a common history of oppression and joint coalitional struggles for justice.[118] This multidimensionality of being

---

[113]Linell E. Cady, "Identity, Feminist Theory, and Theology," in *Horizons in Feminist Theology: Identity, Tradition, Norms*, ed. Rebecca S. Chopp and Sheila Greeve Davaney (Minneapolis: Fortress Press, 1997), 24.

[114]Ibid., 24, 25.

[115]Michele Saracino, *Being about Borders: A Christian Anthropology of Difference* (Collegeville, MN: Liturgical Press, 2011), 36, 39, 44–46, 66–67, 126–128, 137–141.

[116]Ibid., 29–34, 49–51.

[117]Gale A. Yee, " 'She Stood in Tears amid the Alien Corn': Ruth, the Perpetual Foreigner and Model Minority," in *Off the Menu: Asian and Asian North American Women's Religion and Theology*, ed. Rita Nakashima Brock et al. (Louisville, KY: Westminster John Knox Press, 2007), 45–52.

[118]Introduction to *Off the Menu*, ed. Brock, xiv–xix; cf. in that same volume, Kwok Pui Lan, "Fishing the Asia Pacific: Transnationalism and Feminist Theology," 4–5, and Nami Kim, "The 'Indigestible' Asian," 23–26, 34–39.

Defining Feminist Public Theology

human—based on race, ethnicity, culture, religion, gender, class, sexuality, state, and other identity markers—requires a process of becoming human at these intersections, at these in-between spaces, at the borders of and within social locations for social change.[119] Interstitiality or being in between attends to *both* multiple communities of belonging that co-constitute our identities and our society *and* emphasizes the active connective sculpting of a meaningful sense of self-unity and community at often clashing and conflicting interstices.[120] Rita Nakashima Brock describes interstitial integrity as the ongoing improvisational performance of self-identity, knowledge, and community at the negative and positive intersections of diverse social and communal ingredients found within us and impinging on us. Interstitiality—meaningful self-identity amid multiple group identities—challenges the binarity or polarity that feeds into racism, sexism, and ethnic/cultural prejudices, including American myths of elect/chosen peoples versus conquered/colonized peoples that then map onto political anthropologies, such as citizen versus slave, patriot versus terrorist.[121] Moreover, interstitiality fosters recognizing and residing at the nexus of multiple worlds that simultaneously inhabit us (as "layers" or "others who live in us" engaged in fluid "constant conversation" among different social locations, cultures, histories, religions, etc.) and which we partly but never totally inhabit but nevertheless reshape.[122] For Brock, interstitiality resonates with being an incarnated spirit, "refusing to split ourselves" and struggling to bring together multiple layered worlds both in one person and into a new more just world.[123] Being human, thus, means being intersected by our personal and social identity markers in a web of kyriarchal power, reintegrating at times deeply dissonant relations within our self-identities, and likewise becoming more interconnected through personal and transnational solidarity in shared struggles for justice.

Living in and cultivating connective, collective meaning of multiple worlds that always already inform and shape us helps achieve some enhanced and transformed sense of personal identity and community.

---

[119]Kwok, "Fishing the Asia Pacific," 5–7, 16–17.

[120]Rita Nakashima Brock, "Interstitial Integrity: Reflections Toward an Asian American Woman's Theology," in *Introduction to Christian Theology: Contemporary North American Perspectives*, ed. Rodger A. Badham (Louisville, KY: Westminster John Knox Press, 1998), 183–196, and "Cooking without Recipes: Interstitial Integrity," in *Off the Menu*, ed. Brock, 125–144. Interstitial integrity is not individually therapeutic but takes place in solidarity for social justice. Brock, "Interstitial Integrity," 191–192.

[121]Brock, "Cooking without Recipes," 126–128, 132–133.

[122]Ibid., 133–137.

[123]Ibid., 139–140.

Embracing interstitiality, or the in-between spaces and social locations where different peoples, cultures, and ideas converge and compete, aids in feminist public theology's praxis of ekklesial work to undo and transcend unjust norms of personhood and public life. In doing so, human beings embody the image of a God of the interstices envisioned by Kwok Pui Lan as a divine matrix of power: "divine interstitial power . . . is energizing and enabling, because it rejoices in creating 'synergistic relations,' readjusts and shifts to find new strength, and discovers hope in the densely woven web of life that sustains us."[124]

In sum, feminist, womanist, and *mujerista* perspectives disentangle public theology from dominant modern rationalist, isolationist, and elitist portraits of human being, rejuvenate political subjectivity and agency in relational, performative, and interstitial ways, and thus theologize about doing public theology as ekklesial work more effectively. Appealing to the notion of interstitiality or in-betweenness in women's liberation theologies illuminates and supports the community-building practice of ekklesial work. Interstitiality (1) foregrounds multiple groups and communities that co-constitute ourselves and society via multiple identity markers and their implicated communities of not/belonging and not/flourishing and (2) highlights the in-between role that theologians increasingly play in interlinking multiple groups into a more just common life. Integrating these insights into the constructive vision and critical principle of public theology, feminist public theology affirms that full humanity unfolds as we continually unpack and understand our relations and their political implications for a more just society. We continually craft identity-in-relation and in public life. As Linell Cady writes:

> We are, of course, not members of only one community or tradition that serves as our exclusive "point of entry" to the cultivation of a global order. . . . Not only is there no overarching coherent order within which each of these associations can be located, but the social units themselves are marked by varying degrees of tension and discord. . . . It makes vividly clear that the creation of public life is a perennial task.[125]

Personhood is both given and made in public; a person is already situated in a set of relations, and a person's subjectivity emerges and is shaped via self-narration of these relations in political ways. Moreover,

---

[124]Kwok, "Fishing the Asia Pacific," 19.
[125]Cady, *Religion, Theology, and American Public Life*, 162.

Defining Feminist Public Theology   39

this relational understanding makes possible shared stories in the public sphere that lead to solidarity. Akin to Catholic social teaching, women's liberation theologies locate public/political life as intrinsic rather than extrinsic to humanity, as one among a variety of communities that require ongoing negotiation and synthesis to achieve full humanity and inspire as well as aspire to a more just common life.[126] Re/membering and re/performing relationality serves as an important way for doing public theology as ekklesial work to address some of the most pressing issues in our common life today that epitomize the loss of such relationality. As Copeland argues, our "body marks" result from and are reinforced by kyriarchy, slavocracy, empire, and globalization to disrupt and devalue our relations by reducing most of humanity to parts consumed for the pleasure and profit of the few.[127] Being situated at and traversing multiple worlds emphasizes that we engage in critical mobility and negotiation in pursuit of an elusive emancipatory eschatological ideal of both redeemed humanity and radical democracy.

Shaped by women's liberation theologies, public theology as ekklesial work refers primarily to a theology that is located or situated at the relational intersections or interstices of multiple groups, a theology that knits, stitches, or weaves multiple groups together into a more comprehensive, inclusive, and just social fabric of public life, and that is differentiated by its forms of community-creating praxis. As Copeland claims, remaking and reconciling—or re/membering—all of our bodies takes place in the body of Christ by ritually and politically becoming the body of Christ, which incorporates and embraces all bodies, and which effects the healing of personal and ecclesial bodies as well as the body politic. Enacting Eucharistic solidarity stands as a symbolic icon of socio-political change and transfiguration from brokenness to wholeness, as a countersign to racialized and other forms of violence against bodies, and as radical Christian theo-political engagement and praxis for healing and justice.[128] Being and building up a reconciled just body in oneself parallels and propels the community-creating work in and for the body politic, to create and sustain a more just common life.

Together, anthropology, Christology, and eschatology, as this chapter has argued, catalyze a guiding constructive vision and critical principle for doing public theology as ekklesial work, for critically engaging in and

---

[126]Ibid., 66–68, 85.

[127]Copeland, *Enfleshing Freedom*, 29–38, 56–57, 65–66.

[128]Ibid., 81–83. Ritually re/membering the body of Christ and all bodies carries theological implications for creation and political implications for re-creating public life; ibid., 51–53.

more justly remaking and transforming US public life. Theological claims about the *imago Dei* and eschatology lay key theological foundations to envision and engage in public life in ways that promote the full dignity and flourishing of all life. The divine image that dignifies all life and the struggles for a this-worldly realization of the love, justice, and peace that characterize an ever-coming more just future serve as theological signposts for engaging in as well as reshaping public life. Doing ekklesial work from a Catholic and feminist theological perspective brings to the foreground an anthropological and eschatological vision of our already but not yet fully dignified and flourishing public life. As a this-worldly eschatology, ekklesial work glimpses and partly realizes justice, love, and peace, theologically signified by Jesus' ministry for the kingdom of God. Doing ekklesial work contributes, in small but significant christic ways, to a theo-political praxis of creating community, while ever expecting a future fulfillment of the personal and the political. Thus, doing ekklesial work amid its multiple practices, outlined in the next chapter, represents a sign or a sacrament of that future communion, but is not entirely equated with it (*GS*, para. 39).

2

Doing Ekklesial Work

Practices

> Practical theology entails . . . the study of practices, contexts, cultures, and communities in dialogue with faith traditions and informed by . . . "a reading of the signs of the times in light of the Gospel"—a move that involves serious engagement and discerning interpretation of contemporary experience and practice; a deep remembering and critical analysis of the tradition; imaginative theological visioning of future practice; and a hopeful and prophetic tending to the ongoing life of the faith community . . . [and] our common life.
> —Claire Wolfteich, *Invitation to Practical Theology: Catholic Voices and Visions*

Practical and public theology while distinct theological fields are not mutually exclusive but critically inform and resonate with one another in creative and productive tension. From the anthropological, Christological, and eschatological vision and critical principle for doing public theology, as elaborated in the previous chapter, ekklesial work opens up theological space to illuminate an expansive range of many practices of socio-political engagement. Doing ekklesial work raises a range of related questions that are addressed and engaged robustly in this chapter: which practices are involved in contesting and redressing the relative power and/or exclusion of multiple persons from US public life, in shaping and sustaining a more just US public/common life, and more so, how do social justice movements exemplify such practices? Looking beyond predominant notions of public life as civic conversation and debate, its rational ordering of political community, and its practices of dialogical argument that seek consensus reveals diverse effective practices of political participation not

42   *Nevertheless, We Persist*

only to engage in but also to reshape public life, to do ekklesial work and its community-creating praxis to revitalize theological notions of religio-political subjectivity and agency, on the one hand, and imagine and enact a more emancipatory alternative form of common life, on the other hand. These faith-based practices of public engagement emerge in interpretive responses to socio-political issues and the ongoing divine presence in the world. Also aligned with the vision and critical principle of ekklesial work, these practices express an eschatological function: to critically re-present our reality and constructively introduce another alternative possible future reality for more dignified and flourishing life. This chapter engages and expands especially on rhetorical, symbolic, and prophetic practices for doing ekklesial work that critically counter and re-envision an oppressive socio-political order and simultaneously make reconstructive space for an alternative and more transformative political community to take shape, especially within faith-based perspectives and social justice movements.

Practices address basic human needs in our vulnerable and broken world, and thus encompass any collective and socially significant action.[1] Moreover, faith-based practices enact identity-expressing and identity-shaping power; they not only establish, mark, and enforce boundaries of religious and other forms of identity but also disrupt, extend, and chart new existential contours for individual and communal identity. In other words, practices evoke and elicit new possible ways of conceptualizing, living, and renewing our common life for a more just, loving, and peaceful world. Making practices the starting point for doing public theology exceeds "invit[ing] theological reflection on the ordinary, concrete activities of actual people—and also on the knowledge of God that shapes, infuses, and arises from these activities."[2] It also surpasses deriving theological meaning or claims that inform and emerge from lived, material, or popular religious practices. Rather, prioritizing practices in doing public theology emphasizes "taking part in God's work of creation and new creation."[3] It signifies that religious claims, images, and community actions not only carry descriptive explanatory power to make meaning of ourselves and of the world but also hold prescriptive and effective emancipatory power to remake us and the world into more humane worlds of meaning and action.[4]

---

[1]Craig Dykstra and Dorothy Bass, "A Theological Understanding of Christian Practices," in *Practicing Theology: Beliefs and Practices in Christian Life*, ed. Miroslav Volf and Dorothy C. Bass (Grand Rapids, MI: Eerdmans, 2002), 18; cf. 21, 22–29.

[2]Ibid., 3.

[3]Ibid., 21; cf. 29.

[4]William E. Paden, *Religious Worlds: The Comparative Study of Religion* (Boston: Beacon

Doing Ekklesial Work 43

Ekklesial work lays theological foundations for a feminist public theology, and also offers a critical theological framework for understanding religious ways of engaging in as well as reimaging and reshaping US public life for greater justice, inspired by anthropological views of full and equal dignity and eschatological views of justice. Feminist and womanist theological perspectives are continually sourced in this chapter to critically theorize and theologize about a variety of alternate praxes of creating community, of doing ekklesial work. More specifically, this chapter illustrates trifold practices of religio-political participation and engagement for doing ekklesial work of creating community, especially rhetorical, symbolic, and prophetic practices (1) that tell and weave personal and communal stories into joint coalitional politics with potentially national impact on the common good, (2) that further "the struggle over democratic identities, spaces, and ideals"[5] through symbols that support solidarity, and (3) that strive through collective action to create a public itself, a more participatory, just, and transformative community. These practices embody, express, and exercise self-defining agency and community-creating ekklesial work, by reclaiming theo-political dignity to shape personal and communal lives as well as to reshape more just alternative religio-political visions and realities in our common life.[6]

Rhetorical Practices

Rhetorical practices encompass and tap into a variety of promising aesthetic forms or genres for proactive political participation in US public life, for example, sermons, speeches, and testimony, literature including auto/biographies, memoirs, poetry, fiction, music, and the arts, including film. These practices envoice, gain recognition for, and urge solidarity with subaltern marginalized peoples, too often denied political subjectivity and agency.[7] Rhetorical practices from subaltern groups embody an important

---

Press, 1994). Darlene M. Juschka, ed., *Feminism in the Study of Religion: A Reader* (London: Continuum, 2001), 18.

[5]Henry A. Giroux, "Reading Hurricane Katrina: Race, Class and the Biopolitics of Disposability," *College Literature* 33, no. 3 (Summer 2006): 190.

[6]Stephanie Mitchem, *Introducing Womanist Theology* (Maryknoll, NY: Orbis Books, 2002), 20–21, 109.

[7]Rebecca S. Chopp, "Theology and the Poetics of Testimony," in *Converging on Culture: Theologians in Dialogue with Cultural Analysis and Criticism*, ed. Delwin Brown, Sheila Greeve Davaney, and Kathryn Tanner (Oxford: Oxford University Press, 2001), 56–70; Rebecca S. Chopp, "Reimagining Public Discourse," in *Black Faith and Public Talk: Critical Essays on James H. Cone's Black Theology and Black Power*, ed. Dwight N. Hopkins (Maryknoll, NY: Orbis Books, 1999), 150–164. Cf. Mary Ann Hinsdale, *Women Shaping Theology* (New York:

intervention in deeply embedded kyriarchal political structures, norms, and practices that justify and perpetuate the exclusion of persons and discourses from US public life. These practices educate about institutionalized injustices, contest commonly held constitutive values of US and geopolitical life that feed and foment these injustices, and pave an alternative path for a politics of recognition, empathy, and solidarity that seeks justice, for individuals, communities, and society.[8] Rhetorical practices function in an irruptive and constructive way: to break open political space for hearing and empathizing with excluded peoples and stories from dominant US politics, and thereby to shed a new critical light on reconfiguring public life. Rhetorical practices, such as narrative, testimony, and other linguistic strategies of individual and collective storytelling, carry personal and political significance for their impact on socio-political change for the public good.[9] Practices of storytelling underscore diverse alternative ways and sites for public engagement, whether "written, published, televised, taped, filmed, staged, cross-indexed, and footnoted."[10] Such practices not only afford alternative ways to regain and proclaim political voice and recognition in public life, but also point toward ways of using voice, broadly construed, to resist and reimagine public life itself, to build and bolster relationships. Rhetorical practices consist of an identity-shaping and a political act, which reclaims religio-political subjectivity amid varied struggles, enables solidarity, and motivates and mobilizes joint action for social change.

Integrating these insights about rhetorical practices, subaltern groups describe their personal and collective experiences, raise religio-political awareness about suffering and injustice, share and exchange stories of struggle to make meaningful sense of their own stories of resistance interlinked with others, prescribe an alternative more just future common life, and mobilize joint political action as well as build solidarity for that more just future. As Mary Ann Hinsdale observes, rhetorical practices entail "naming the pain" of dehumanizing realities and "retrieving dangerous memories" of resistance to those realities to foster joint struggle in solidarity and in eschatological practices of active hope in a more

---

Paulist Press, 2006), 2, 105–106, 108–111.

[8]The public realm functions as "the pre-eminent space of public pedagogy—that is, a space where subjectivities are shaped, public commitments are formed, and choices are made" with respect to "pursuing truly egalitarian models of democracy." Giroux, "Reading Hurricane Katrina," 190, 191.

[9]Ada María Isasi-Díaz, *La Lucha Continues: Mujerista Theology* (Maryknoll, NY: Orbis Books, 2004), 56, 61.

[10]Mitchem, *Introducing Womanist Theology*, 21.

Doing Ekklesial Work   **45**

liberating future.[11] Rhetorical practices thus resonate with prophetic practices, discussed below, namely to disrupt and denounce an unjust status quo as well as announce and seek to enact a more just alternative to it. Further critical theoretical and theological reflections on narrative, especially in moral and political philosophy, feminist critical theory, and feminist, womanist, and *mujerista* theological perspectives, will identify and amplify some key insights and potential implications of rhetorical practices not only for political participation but mainly for doing ekklesial work, the community-creating praxis of public theology, in US public life.

Feminist and womanist theologies treat narrative as a critical experiential starting point, for theo-political reasons. Narrative that encompasses wide-ranging genres of personal and communal stories has played a major transformative role in women's liberation theologies.[12] Theologically, prioritizing lived experiences and material realities to critically reinterpret scripture and tradition[13] has led to groundbreaking work in constructive feminist and womanist biblical studies and theology, elaborating more emancipatory understandings of the divine.[14] Politically, sharing personal and communal stories resists and subverts social injustices and suffering, fosters coalition politics and public engagement, and hopes in eschatological justice that projects and performs an alternative future vision for the broader public good.

As thematized by Rebecca Chopp, narrative and testimony hold much theo-political potential to engage in and reconfigure common life, especially its tacit shared self-understanding or "narrative identity" that presently underwrites US common life, or our common assumptions about who contributes to public life, what can be spoken or said in public discourse, and how that discourse is articulated, regulated, and judged.[15] Through testimony, marginalized peoples remember and retell narratives of suffering and of hope, reclaim and proclaim a voice and place in public life, critically question predominant organizing visions, values, practices, and

---

[11]Hinsdale, *Women Shaping Theology*, esp. 59–64, 94–111; cf. Elizabeth A. Johnson, *Quest for the Living God: Mapping Frontiers in the Theology of God* (New York: Continuum, 2007), 54–56, 65–69.

[12]Jane Kopas, "Something Particular: Women's Self-Narratives as a Resource for Theology," in *Themes in Feminist Theology for the New Millennium (I)*, ed. Francis A. Eigo (Villanova, PA: Villanova University Press, 2002), esp. 3–4, 23–27, 29–30.

[13]Hinsdale, *Women Shaping Theology*, 100–107.

[14]For example, Johnson, *Quest for the Living God*; Delores S. Williams, *Sisters in the Wilderness: The Challenge of Womanist God-Talk* (Maryknoll, NY: Orbis Books, 1993); Karen Baker Fletcher, *Dancing with God: The Trinity from a Womanist Perspective* (St. Louis, MO: Chalice Press, 2007); and Lisa Isherwood, *Introducing Feminist Christologies* (Cleveland, OH: Pilgrim Press, 2002).

[15]Chopp, "Reimagining Public Discourse," 152.

so on, that structure and shape our often oppressive common life, elicit empathy, and foster shared action and/or solidarity against such suffering for the purpose of social change.[16] Testimony enlarges our narrative identity, or our self-understanding of common life, as well as imagines more emancipatory possibilities for it, through gaining public recognition, solidarity, and justice for multiple peoples. Testimonies "have criticized and reshaped who 'we' are, as a social public and as Christianity, by making public the memories of suffering and giving public hearing to new voices, experiences, and expressions of life, while calling into question essentialist and hegemonic definitions of these publics."[17] To accomplish this purpose, which far exceeds public inclusion and intelligibility, testimony presents an ethical summons to end suffering and to imagine a more transformative vision of common life, based on what Chopp calls "an ethos of cultivating compassion" that leads to responsibility to and with others and collective action for transformative social change.[18] Thus, testimony carries and reinforces eschatological significance for doing ekklesial work: "Testimony in public discourse narrates a story, a story that allows the transcendent, the possibility of the new, to break in and open us to change and transformation."[19] Testimony involves the telling and hearing of marginalized peoples' stories of suffering and hope, in order to break open a counterpublic space to empower political actors, to raise broader public awareness about injustice, to enable empathy as well as achieve greater solidarity with suffering peoples, and to express collective and active hope in the possibility of creating a more just future and flourishing common life.[20] These spaces, according to Henry Giroux, revitalize our democracy and our very humanity, because they hold pedagogical potential to educate about confronting multiple forms of oppression and to inspire solidarity and hope in an alternative future: "Their diverse forms, sites, and content offer pedagogical and political possibilities for strengthening the social bonds of democracy, new spaces within which to cultivate the capacities for critical modes of individual and social agency, and crucial opportunities to form alliances."[21]

Womanist theology engages a rich interdisciplinary analysis of Black women's storytelling to source their theological meanings for the well-

---

[16]Ibid., 156–158, 160–161.
[17]Ibid., 154. Cf. Diana Hayes, *And Still We Rise: An Introduction to Black Liberation Theology* (New York: Paulist Press, 1996), 116–134.
[18]Chopp, "Reimagining Public Discourse," 157, 159.
[19]Ibid., 157.
[20]Ibid., 160–163.
[21]Giroux, "Reading Hurricane Katrina," 191.

Doing Ekklesial Work   47

being of Black women, the African American community, and the US common good. Womanist theologian Diana Hayes elaborates on the theological centrality of narratives to create and sustain African American women's and communal identity amid US racist religio-political realities. Narrative, or "the telling and re-telling of a people's story," recounts and remembers the "subversive memory" of individuals and communities "on the underside of history" who suffered, endured, struggled, survived, and thrived to live more fully authentic lives.[22] Simultaneously oriented to past, present, and future, and situated at the nexus of anthropology and eschatology, narrative re/creates a people's shared identity, especially via divine encounters, which in the past influenced and in the present continue to inform their identities in and for the future, "the story of the coming to be of a new people."[23]

Narrative comprises not only personal and communal identity-shaping and future-shaping stories, but also a transformative eschatological and political act. Testimony, according to Hayes, recounts both scriptural and everyday events of divine intervention and at times deliverance from evil, represented, for example, by the Exodus, the life, ministry, death, and resurrection of Jesus, or the story of Hagar—the Egyptian slave and sexual surrogate of Abraham and Sarah who was expelled from their family, experienced divine accompaniment and empowerment, and survived and carved out a better quality of life for herself and her son, Ishmael.[24] Such stories create an alternative counterstory or counternarrative to slavery and its associated legacies of lynching, segregation, incarceration, and ongoing forms of racist discrimination. Such stories edge toward the political, since they support subversive struggles for and active hope in personal and communal self-determination and survival in the face of persistent racism; in other words, counternarratives point toward a more liberative future for marginalized communities and our wider society.[25] Narrative in womanist theology is performed as a religio-political act due to its eschatology; people testify to reclaim and reaffirm personal and communal dignity, as well as witness to engage in activism that anticipates further emancipatory acts of God for the well-being of African American

---

[22]Hayes, *And Still We Rise*, 120–122.

[23]Ibid., 116, 118, 121.

[24]Womanist scholarship about Hagar includes Williams, *Sisters in the Wilderness*; Renita J. Weems, *Just a Sister Away: A Womanist Vision of Women's Relationships in the Bible* (San Diego: Lura Media, 1988); Diana L. Hayes, *Hagar's Daughters: Womanist Ways of Being in the World* (New York: Paulist Press, 1995); and Phyllis Trible and Letty M. Russell, eds., *Hagar, Sarah, and Their Children: Jewish, Christian, and Muslim Perspectives* (Louisville, KY: Westminster John Knox Press, 2006).

[25]Hayes, *And Still We Rise*, 130–132.

48   *Nevertheless, We Persist*

women, the African American community, and the wider society.[26]

Illustrating how narrative enables personally, communally, and politically empowering and liberatory practices for marginalized peoples, womanist theologians focus on emancipated slave autobiographies to restore a sense of self-defined voice and political freedom, of "somebodiness," to African American women. According to M. Shawn Copeland, narrative and other rhetorical practices such as courageous sass and backtalk exemplify some ways in which African American women both resisted prevalent racist, sexist, and slavery-based ideologies that devalued their identities, bodies, and work, and reclaimed their full human dignity despite those ideologies and their effective histories in US public life.[27] Remembering and retelling narratives of resistance to multiple physical and social sufferings inspire contemporary African American women to emulate such strategies for imagining an alternative liberating reality.[28]

Rhetorical practices critically engage with and transform or transfigure the present in light of an alternative liberative future, particularly a Christian eschatological imagination. Women's liberation theologies articulate a rhetorical art or practice of opting for the future. The late Cuban American theologian and ethicist Ada María Isasi-Díaz elaborated *mujerista* theology as a critical reflective liberatory act of giving voice to US Latina women's understandings, experiences, and struggles, both individually and communally, for religio-political subjectivity and agency amid intersectional destructive forces of racism, ethnic prejudice/nationalism, sexism, poverty, colonialism, and xenophobia.[29] Rather than seek religious or political authority to legitimate their voices, histories, and theologies, rhetorical practices reassert and reclaim Latinas' full humanity, personally and politically, to participate in co-creating their own lives and the larger society, as Isasi-Díaz stated, by "speaking our own

---

[26]Testimony and witness embrace both religious doxology and political participation. Rosetta E. Ross distinguishes between testifying as "telling stories of divine intervention (often in a worship service) through speech, while witnessing is attesting to faith in the divine by living in expectation of divine intervention and experiencing God in everyday life." Rosetta E. Ross, *Witnessing and Testifying: Black Women, Religion, and Civil Rights* (Minneapolis: Fortress Press, 2003), 15; cf. 223–235.

[27]M. Shawn Copeland, "Wading through Many Sorrows: Toward a Theology of Suffering in Womanist Perspective," in *A Troubling in My Soul: Womanist Perspectives on Evil and Suffering*, ed. emilie m. townes (Maryknoll, NY: Orbis Books, 1993), esp. 110–111, 121, 122–124.

[28]Ibid., 123–124; cf. emilie m. townes, "Walking on the Rim Bones of Nothingness: Scholarship and Activism," *Journal of the American Academy of Religion* 77, no. 1 (March 2009): 1–15.

[29]Isasi-Díaz, *La Lucha Continues*, 19, 47–68 (esp. 50–51), 177–179. Cf. Isasi-Díaz, *Mujerista Theology: A Theology for the Twenty-First Century* (Maryknoll, NY: Orbis Books, 1996), 60–62, 73–74, and *En La Lucha/In the Struggle: Elaborating a Mujerista Theology* (Minneapolis: Fortress Press, 2004), 23, 176–187.

Doing Ekklesial Work 49

word, naming our own reality, reflecting upon and making explicit our own religious understandings and practices."[30] For Isasi-Díaz, struggle (*la lucha*), voice (*permitanme hablar*), and community (*la comunidad*) serve as the starting points for such practices.[31] *La lucha* emphasizes an active hope in everyday Latinas' struggles "to survive and live fully," which responds to and partners with divine struggles for a more just and flourishing life, signified by the eschatological notion of the kin-dom of God. Latinas via *la lucha* negotiate moral, religious, and socio-historical and political agency through active struggles and resistance to daily oppressive realities and through celebrations of everyday joys amid those realities. Narrative combines personal and communal stories of struggle with scriptural stories of divine struggle for ultimate freedom and justice.[32] *Permitanme hablar* facilitates the importance of speaking to reclaim Latinas' historical and political subjectivity and agency, that is, for claiming public voice in Latinx history and for making or constructing that history.[33] As Isasi-Díaz states, "Our insistence on speaking is not only a matter of making known our past; it is also a matter of participating in making present and future history, of being protagonists, of being agents of our own history."[34] Theologically, Latinas speak out of their history and their everyday lives, or *lo cotidiano*,[35] to oppose dominant racist cultures that demonize differences,[36] and instead, to promote human fulfillment via *mestizaje/mulatez*, or a way of living at and across multiple intersections or borders of racial, cultural, religious, and other differences.[37] "When we use this phrase we are asking for a respectful silence from all those who have power to set up definitions of what it is to be human . . . so others can indeed hear our cries denouncing oppression and injustice . . . [and] understand our vision of a just society."[38]

Eschatologically, this phrase interrelates personal and communal narratives of resistance to suffering with prophetic hope in well-being and justice—a social, political, and religiously rooted praxis that is concretely connected with public theology, with the role of religion in creating and enhancing the public good. Such practices critically denounce an unjust

---

[30]Isasi-Díaz, *En La Lucha*, 187; cf. Isasi-Díaz, *Mujerista Theology*, 135–137, and *La Lucha Continues*, 48–51.

[31]Isasi-Díaz, *Mujerista Theology*, 128, 144–145.

[32]Ibid., 129–131.

[33]Ibid., 132–134.

[34]Ibid., 133; *La Lucha Continues*, 54–55.

[35]Isasi-Díaz, *Mujerista Theology*, 66–71, 78; *La Lucha Continues*, 50–54, 92–106.

[36]Isasi-Díaz, *Mujerista Theology*, 64–65.

[37]Ibid., 64; *En La Lucha*, 2–3, 33; *La Lucha Continues*, 61, 69–91.

[38]Isasi-Díaz, *Mujerista Theology*, 136.

oppressive present and constructively announce or envision, as well as embody and enact in multiple ways, more just future possible worlds.[39] Rhetorical practices, among others, create a new future religious understanding of humanity and of a more just world, which Isasi-Díaz theologically describes as "bring[ing] to birth new women and new men" in the kin-dom of God.[40] *La comunidad* underscores Latinas' participation in struggles as social, historical, and political actors in relation to various communities and vast networks of relationships that condition and co-constitute us to bring about this kin-dom. We belong to and become fully human through a community of relations, of origin, affinity, and solidarity. *La comunidad* is not construed as the kyriarchal family but more broadly understood as far-reaching networks of kin and chosen community relationships, of "we others," which expands beyond the nuclear and extended family into the *familia de Dios*. It emphasizes Latinas' eschatological praxis of mediating a christic-inspired vision of an anti-imperial, this-worldly just society, namely the kin-dom of God.[41]

Engaging in rhetorical practices for the coming kin-dom comprises many public theological genres, including symbolic and prophetic practices, as Isasi-Díaz argued, "not only linear, logical argumentation but also prophetic denunciation, songs and poems of protest and hope, lamentations, and language of consolation. And our theological language is not only a matter of written words but also of liturgical rituals, street demonstrations, and protest actions."[42] In *mujerista* eschatology, the kin-dom is neither completely separated from this world nor entirely postponed to an other-worldly afterlife. Rather, it gives a theological horizon of meaning to *mujerista*'s historical project, or, in my view, to the ekklesial work of public theology, to imagine and begin to realize a this-worldly vision of a more "participatory community" characterized by inclusivity, love, justice, and peace.[43] Latinas' stories of struggle for survival and fullness of life enable us to "recognize those eschatological glimpses [in the present], rejoice in them, and struggle to make those glimpses become our whole horizon."[44] Everyday rhetorical practices take place within this horizon of imagining and enacting the kin-dom of God, energized by its theological ideals of justice and peace.[45]

---

[39]Isasi-Díaz, *En La Lucha*, 52–54, 181, 183.
[40]Isasi–Díaz, *Mujerista Theology*, 64–74, quote at 62.
[41]Isasi-Díaz, *La Lucha Continues*, 243–251.
[42]Isasi-Díaz, *En La Lucha*, 184.
[43]Isasi-Díaz, *Mujerista Theology*, 65–66, 117–118; *En La Lucha*, 4–5, 52–53, 59–60.
[44]Isasi-Díaz, *Mujerista Theology*, 63.
[45]Neomi De Anda, "Latina Feminist and *Mujerista* Theologies as Political Theologies?" in

Doing Ekklesial Work 51

Narrative figures prominently in the works of moral and political philosophers like Hannah Arendt and Paul Ricoeur and feminist critical theorist María Pía Lara, standing as one rhetorical practice of political recognition for marginalized groups to create community by reconfiguring public life for solidarity and justice. Arendt and Ricoeur portray a dialogical understanding of public life as well as persons in it; both public life and persons are discursively mediated and constituted in relations in which we exchange both our stories and selves. In other words, persons participate in as well as emerge from public discourse; not only our society but also our very selves are adjudicated and remade through rhetorical practices. According to Arendt, "Being seen and being heard by others derive their significance from the fact that everybody sees and hears from a different position. This is the meaning of public life."[46] Lacking multiple stories and storytellers portends the altogether end of the public: "The end of the common world has come when it is seen only under one aspect and is permitted to present itself in only one perspective."[47] Thus, narrative or storytelling connects private and public spheres of life, or provides the glue that constitutes and sustains our common life.[48] As Arendt argues, our public words and deeds, or what she named in one place "the web of human relationships," reveal and shape our shared identities. Our self-narratives—which result from making interpretive sense of these multiple communities—are not solely our own stories but serve as shared narratives.[49] Our stories are intertwined with other stories, thereby inviting empathy as well as social change. Similarly for Ricoeur, rhetorical practices like narrative co-constitute the self and society. We re-create and reconstruct our identities by negotiating our socio-political "entanglement" in the stories of others.[50] Making meaningful sense of our embeddedness in a web of multiple relations and stories both empowers an individual to recount a self-narrative (through multiple genres) and places an individual in responsible relations with others.[51] The power of "naming" oneself, according to Ricoeur, is articulated and enacted "in

---

T&T Clark Handbook of Political Theology, ed. Rubén Rosario Rodríguez (London: Bloomsbury, 2019), 271–284.

[46]Hannah Arendt, *The Human Condition*, 2nd ed. (Chicago: University of Chicago Press, 1998), 57.

[47]Ibid., 58.

[48]Ibid., 50–51.

[49]Ibid., 175–181, 183–184.

[50]Paul Ricoeur, *Oneself as Another*, trans. Kathleen Blamey (Chicago: University of Chicago Press, 1995), 107, 161.

[51]Ibid., 114n1, 148–150 regarding multiple genres for self-narratives. Cf. Henry Isaac Venema, *Identifying Selfhood: Imagination, Narrative, and Hermeneutics in the Thought of Paul Ricoeur* (Albany: State University of New York Press, 2000), chap. 4.

52   *Nevertheless, We Persist*

the power to say, in the power to do, in the power to recognize oneself as a character in a narrative, in the power, finally, to respond" to others.[52]

In women's liberation theologies, religio-political subjectivity is claimed, constituted, and crafted, or better incarnated, through narrative.[53] Lara argues that narratives imagine and inspire self-recognition as a political subject, personal and collective participation in public life, and a more just understanding of the public good.[54] Narrative neither simply rehearses the past nor reinforces the present; rather, according to Lara, narrative resembles an experimental laboratory to enact and enable new conceptions of self and society.[55] In particular, women's narratives offer an opportunity to envision and explore new forms of common life. According to Lara, "Women's narratives grasped the potential of a utopian horizon that created a critical space in which they could become authentic subjects."[56] Opting for the future—future talk and praxis—shape political and religious practices of public engagement within narrative. Narrative not only includes diverse peoples and enlarges political community through empathy with the stories of others, but also, as Mary Doak elaborates, a narrative approach to the church's public discourse and practice judges US public life from a Christian eschatology that anticipates the ultimate flourishing of all life. Multiple narratives from multiple groups show how US public life is or is not geared toward personal and social future fulfillment.[57] In the same vein, womanist theology reframes self and social renaming within narrative as "generative powers: the power of voice, the power of making do, the power of memory, the power of holding things together, and the power of generation."[58] Thus, our story is interrelated with and retains responsibilities to others' stories in—and the future of—public life.

Integrating these insights, narrative, or testimony, witness, and storytelling more generally, provides a political platform from which marginalized groups regain political access, representation, and participation, enact political agency, and reshape the contours and constitutive values of US public discourse and life to seek solidarity and justice. In doing so, these

---

[52]Ricoeur, *Oneself as Another*, 22, 54; cf. 111–112, 143–148.

[53]Kopas, "Something Particular," 8, 13.

[54]María Pía Lara, *Moral Textures: Feminist Narratives in the Public Sphere* (Berkeley: University of California Press, 1998), 88, 142, 144.

[55]Ibid., 5–6, 14–17, 35–44, 49.

[56]Ibid., 59; cf. 70. Lara analyzes several women's literary works that effected this goal; ibid., 44–49, 71–78, 89–100.

[57]Mary Doak, *Reclaiming Narrative for Public Theology* (Albany: State University of New York Press, 2004), 19–23, 159–171.

[58]Karen Baker-Fletcher, *A Singing Something: Womanist Reflections on Anna Julia Cooper* (New York: Crossroad, 1994), 188–206. In Mitchem, *Introducing Womanist Theology*, 122.

Doing Ekklesial Work 53

groups leverage their personal and communal stories into a theo-political critical commentary about the means to cease social suffering and to better realize the common good by building solidarity with others' stories.

Symbolic Practices

Often converging with and reinforcing rhetorical practices, religious claims and symbols shape and sustain a worldview as well as imbue religious adherents with a sense of identity and morality or mutual rights and responsibilities in that world. Symbols carry broader socio-political implications for critically reimagining our common life on explicitly religious grounds. Symbols in the religio-cultural and political imagination mediate knowledge of God and the world, as well as provide a meaningful ethical framework to understand, navigate, and act in the world so as to enhance our praxis with respect to divine, human, and earthly responsible and just relations. Christian symbols of God, such as the Trinity in which the three persons of Creator, Liberator, and Sustainer participate in nonhierarchical, nondominating relations, express and embody—in their integrity, equality, and unity—religio-political notions of egalitarian community. Also, the trinitarian God's relation with the world in creating, liberating, and sustaining life educates us with a particular identity and sense of mutual responsibility within the inherent interrelation and interdependence of all life in that community. A trinitarian relational ontology of persons-in-communion articulated by feminist theologian Catherine Mowry LaCugna envisions such an egalitarian view and praxis of religio-political community, of belonging.[59] Nevertheless, such symbols can also channel and collude with dominant ideological worldviews in ways that justify, reinforce, or sacralize unjust oppressive kyriarchal power relations, as well as reinscribe dehumanizing race, gender, class, cultural, religious, and sexual structures and norms.[60] Religious symbols thus provide one potent theological locus for raising critical questions about reimagining the relationship between a Christian imaginary and the vision and values of public life. Religious symbols can fuel a theological criticism of oppression as well as engender a theologically inspired vision of emancipatory transformation.

In historian Martin Marty's view, public theology weaves together a

---

[59]Catherine Mowry LaCugna, *God for Us: The Trinity and Christian Life* (San Francisco: HarperCollins, 1991), and Elizabeth T. Groppe, "Catherine Mowry LaCugna's Contribution to Trinitarian Theology," *Theological Studies* 63 (2002): 730–763.

[60]Johnson, *Quest for the Living God.*

54 *Nevertheless, We Persist*

"communion of communions," because religious adherents strive "to interpret the life of a people in light of a transcendent reference."[61] Particular religious groups possess within their founding events a drive not toward sectarian withdrawal or political apathy but toward collective life with others and with the divine. For example, Christianity rests on fundamentally corporate events, such as creation, fall, and redemption, which join or covenant a divided and estranged people into relationship with one another and God.[62] Appealing to religious symbols helps articulate a common moral framework that combines disparate groups together by exploring religio-political underpinnings for the public good. A covenantal theology specifies mutual responsibilities and expectations, and "makes thematic our debt and obligation to one another, our expectation from one another." [63] Rather than directly correspond with an explicit belief system or code of conduct, religious symbols establish a common moral foundation and fabric for common life. Religious symbols refract this transcendent reference and suffuse public life with a transcendent moral sensibility or shared moral vocabulary about a religio-political anthropology, that is, about the meaning of human being, the mutual ethical obligations of human beings to one another and society, and whether religious symbols highlight those obligations as well as inspire social change to better actualize those obligations. Religious symbols communicate "who a human being is, what the good life for a human being ought to be, and what kinds of relationships among human beings promote the good life."[64] Moreover, rather than support or sacralize a theocratic nation-state, justify a certain socio-political order, or demand confessional conformity to a Christian theological imaginary, reinterpreting religious symbols can criticize US common life and engender a more emancipatory alternative vision of it on theological grounds by redirecting our socio-political moral imaginary toward justice, toward the ever-present but still ever-coming reign of God. For example, the cross in Christianity both criticizes social

---

[61]Martin E. Marty, *The Public Church: Mainline-Evangelical-Catholic* (New York: Crossroad, 1981), 16.

[62]Marty, *The Public Church*, 53.

[63]Daniel J. Elazar, "Recovenanting the American Polity," in *A Nation Under God? Essays on the Future of Religion in American Public Life*, ed, R. Bruce Douglass and Joshua Mitchell (New York: Rowman & Littlefield, 2000), 66. Covenants in a multifaith and multicultural world still unify people around a shared moral vocabulary; ibid., 81–82.

[64]Michael Himes, "Public Theology in Service to a National Conversation," in *Religion, Politics, and the American Experience: Reflections on Religion and American Public Life*, ed. Edith L. Blumhofer (Tuscaloosa: University of Alabama Press, 2002), 138. Cf. Michael J. Himes and Kenneth R. Himes, *Fullness of Faith: The Public Significance of Theology* (New York: Paulist, 1993), 4; W. Clark Gilpin, *A Preface to Theology* (Chicago: University of Chicago Press, 1996), 173–183, esp. 182; cf. 129–131, 147.

Doing Ekklesial Work 55

suffering and portrays an alternative worldview for communal life that compels us to build solidarity with suffering peoples and actively seeks to support their movements to cease suffering.[65]

Symbolic practices according to Michael Himes and Kenneth Himes explore the theo-political significance and implications of central religious symbols to construct a shared normative moral grounding or framework or "moral compass"[66] of mutual rights and responsibilities in public life. These practices reclaim, reinterpret, and reimagine relevant religious symbols for their contemporary critical socio-political efficacy, and thereby craft a shared political space of moral discourse and practice about human dignity and rights as well as the public good. Linell Cady outlines a public theological method for such symbolic practices to shore up and begin to repair relations in our public life, called extensional theology. Religious symbols are revisited to innovate and furnish an alternative moral basis for public life, to reach toward a reshaped more liberative sense of the common good. Extensional theology thematizes a religious, cultural, or political tradition through its organizing symbols—e.g., God-talk—and then draws on or extends that tradition and its symbols for their political implications, to develop and formulate shared moral rights and responsibilities.[67] Theological symbols critically address contemporary socio-political realities and constructively as well as prospectively instantiate a more just future.

Rereading and resourcing a tradition theocentrically, God-talk illuminates the intrinsic worth and interdependent nature of all earthly life, and thus provides a theological basis for articulating and promoting rights to freely participate and flourish in community, especially via the anthropological symbol of the human person made in the image of God and made for community.[68] An inherent *imago Dei*–based human right to relationship and to community theologically articulates and bolsters a

---

[65]Nancy Pineda-Madrid, *Suffering and Salvation in Ciudad Juárez* (Minneapolis: Fortress Press, 2011), esp. chaps. 4–5.

[66]Himes and Himes, *Fullness of Faith*, 4. Religious activists who seek to end rather than engender violence "integrate religiously-inspired principles of justice and respect for all people into the fabric of society." Sharon Erickson Nepstad, "Religion, Violence, and Peacemaking," *Journal for the Scientific Study of Religion* 43, no. 3 (2004): 301. Moral cohesion serves as a primary goal of this praxis. Robin Lovin, "Religion and American Public Life: Three Relationships," in *Religion and American Public Life* (New York: Paulist Press, 1986), 7–28.

[67]Linell E. Cady, *Religion, Theology and American Public Life* (Albany: State University of New York Press, 1993), 51–57, 62–64; Linell E. Cady, "H. Richard Niebuhr and the Task of Public Theology," in *The Legacy of H. Richard Niebuhr*, ed. Ronald Thiemann (Minneapolis: Fortress Press, 1991), 107–129.

[68]Cady, *Religion, Theology and American Public Life*, 99–109; Himes and Himes, *Fullness of Faith*, 55–66, 70.

universal human rights agenda. Creation in the divine image and likeness signifies a religious basis (but does not disregard other bases, religious or secular) for universal human dignity, while various legal, political, and social structures assure and actualize that dignity. Such symbols do not directly correspond with a certain political order, translate into a formal legal code or theory of human rights, or disregard religious and cultural pluralism.[69] Rather, such symbols contribute to a normative account of human nature, which then leverages a faith-based critical social theory to critically assess current social, economic, and political structures and inform political advocacy for broad-based justice, perhaps through ongoing struggles to more fully realize our humanity in social justice movements. In this way, symbolic practices regard religious traditions not as a static, objective, or reified deposit of truths to be protected or proof-texted to legitimate contemporary theo-political attitudes and actions. Rather, iconic interpretation, resistance, and transformation attends to tradition as a historically contextual and dynamic living and organic tradition in need of reinvention in each era with creative fidelity. Moreover, reconstructing theological symbols of God bears socio-political and ecological significance, for their ability to transform our definitions of humanity and of the public, especially to better accommodate the notion that full humanity emerges in recognition of and in accountability to a more diverse and justice-seeking public, which includes our common and cosmic life in and with whom we live, move, and have our being.

Some critics lament theology's absence from or theology's demise in public theology. Public theology is said to undermine or undercut rather than support substantive theological reflection, especially when religious claims and symbols are allegedly instrumentalized, functionalized, or translated into widely accessible and intelligible discourse. Public theologians tend to advance a discursive vision of public life and practices of public engagement that may focus on and follow shared rhetorical practices of rational argument but at the expense of substantive theological claims and symbols.[70] This criticism suggests that theological claims and symbols are leveraged on the basis of publicly shared norms and practices of rational debate and not on the basis of theological warrants. So, when

---

[69]Himes and Himes, *Fullness of Faith*, 61–64. Cf. J. Milburn Thompson, *Justice and Peace: A Christian Primer*, 2nd ed. (Maryknoll, NY: Orbis Books, 2003), 92–102.

[70]William Lindsey, "Public Theology as Civil Discourse: What Are We Talking About?" *Horizons* 19, no. 1 (1992): 44–69; Michael J. Baxter, "The Non-Catholic Character of the 'Public Church,'" *Modern Theology* 11 (April 1995): 243–258; William T. Cavanaugh, "Is Public Theology Really Public? Some Problems with Civil Society," *Annual of the Society of Christian Ethics* 21 (2001): 105–123; and Philip Ziegler, "God and Some Recent Public Theologies," *International Journal of Systematic Theology* 4, no. 2 (2002): 137–155.

Doing Ekklesial Work   57

theology goes public, it may compromise or sacrifice theological integrity for the sake of public intelligibility.

We can think with public theologians to respond to the alleged absence or inadequacy of theology in public theology. As already demonstrated, David Tracy suggests that public theology discusses and disputes the "effects" of religious traditions, for example, the classics produced by religious traditions. These classics contain rather specific (and at times conflicting) theological claims about the meaning, purpose, and flourishing of human life. Similarly, Kathryn Tanner contends that public theology examines and evaluates the socio-politically significant "conclusions" of religious claims and symbols for human dignity and flourishing.[71] Tanner sidesteps social Trinitarian theologies which too easily take immanent Trinitarian relations as a map or model for human social relations without attending to the categorical differences between divine and human relationality or to the deeply fraught nature of human relations.[72] Tanner instead proposes public theology as a communicative process of religio-political discourse, which parallels her understanding of Christian tradition as a task of continued conversation. Focusing on the public/ political "effects" or "conclusions" of religious claims, symbols, and practices for their critical, practical, and transformative implications in and for public life neither assesses their religious bases nor requires a priori agreement with them nor occludes their theological dimensions. Christian communities, understood by Tanner as discursive communities bound together by argument, socialize their members with certain communicative and conversational, or better disputational, virtues, such as humility and open-mindedness (to listen to and entertain all interpretations and claims), mutual accountability (to correct and be corrected by others), responsibility (not only for embracing conflict but also continuing the dialogue with others across different times and places), and courage and hope (for recognition even amid conflict).[73] In this communicative and conversational process of tradition, theology is not erased in doing public theology, especially if we take seriously the term "public" and treat these critical practical effects or conclusions of theological claims, symbols, and practices in terms of their faith-based contributions to a more transformative vision of and way of enacting public life.

---

[71]Kathryn Tanner, "Public Theology and the Character of Public Debate," *Annual of the Society of Christian Ethics* (1996): esp. 87–91, 94–96.

[72]Kathryn Tanner, *Jesus, Humanity, and the Trinity: A Brief Systematic Theology* (Minneapolis: Fortress Press, 2001), 77–83.

[73]Kathryn Tanner, *Theories of Culture: A New Agenda for Theology* (Minneapolis: Fortress Press, 1997), 123–128, 151–155, and 172–175.

Prophetic Practices

In keeping with scriptural studies of prophetic traditions where central defining relations with God rethink and reshape a new, alternative community of freedom and justice, prophetic practices religiously "criticize" or challenge an existing unjust socio-political order and simultaneously "energize" or actualize religious movements for social change that engage in imagined and lived or in other ways performed hope in and for more just alternative future possibilities to emerge.[74] Prophetic practices publicly denounce injustice and announce a more transformative social vision that in multiple ways motivates solidarity and social change. In the history of US social justice movements, prophetic activism utilizes various forms of nonviolent protest politics to promote an alternative future vision of justice, hope, and peace, often combined with rhetorical and symbolic practices that are rooted in religious claims about universal dignity and rights, divine love and justice, and solidarity. Prophetic practices aid marginalized, oppressed, and disenfranchised communities to reclaim their stake in public life as well as to reshape it for greater solidarity and justice. These practices often entail nonviolent grassroots collective action that confronts the prevailing unjust socio-political order and attempts to educate about as well as partly actualize an alternative possibility to that order through strikes, picket lines, boycotts, marches, rallies, sit-ins, street theatre, and other kinds of demonstrations, thereby edging us toward a more inclusive and just life. Multireligious and intergenerational collective action raises public awareness about and fosters justice as well as solidarity with suffering peoples, and begins to reconstruct contemporary public life in more just loving ways.[75]

Prophetic practices both cultivate an alternative possible future vision of our socio-political order, and in so doing begin to prefigure that vision. Prophetic praxis consists of several other features. In keeping with symbolic practices, it taps into theological roots of the equal dignity, sacrality, and interrelatedness of all life by appealing to an equal creation, to divine love and justice, and to an eschatological "vision of hope for a transformed future in which justice will be realized, right relations be-

---

[74]Walter Brueggemann, *The Prophetic Imagination*, 2nd ed. (Minneapolis: Fortress Press, 2001), 1–19. Cf. Rosemary Radford Ruether, *Sexism and God-Talk: Toward a Feminist Theology* (Boston: Beacon Press, 1983), 22–27, 31–33.

[75]Helene Slessarev-Jamir, *Prophetic Activism: Progressive Religious Justice Movements in Contemporary America* (New York: New York University Press, 2011), 1–20, esp. 4–9.

Doing Ekklesial Work 59

tween nations restored, and peace ushered in."[76] It emphasizes communal rather than individualistic or isolationist spiritualities in an effort to envision and exercise political love.[77] It often takes a pluralistic or multifaith approach to such social change. Similar to rhetorical practices, it raises public awareness about and stands in solidarity with or accompanies marginalized peoples; these actions often require relying on and then relinquishing privileges related to race, gender, class, sexuality, citizenship, education, religion, or other forms of privilege to participate with marginalized activists who are ultimately undoing that same privilege.[78] In these ways, prophetic praxis eschews a major risk of world-making: it prevents serving existing exclusionary, conflict-based, and oppressive ideologies. It avoids both reinforcing status quo power relations and ignoring our limits in doing this transformative work.

Prophetic traditions decry injustice and simultaneously point to as well as begin to realize an alternate just liberative common life through collective action and social movements. Prophetic praxis and its varied features are revealed in various US Christian social justice movements: abolition, worker rights, anti-poverty, anti-racism/civil rights, antiwar/pacifism, feminism, LGBTQ+ rights, environmentalism, immigrant rights, prison reform, human rights, among many more. These movements have contested and critically transformed status quo public life, albeit partly, inspiring us to better embrace and enhance our common life together through "increased political rights, greater distributive justice, widespread democratization of power, and a commitment to recognizing and respecting the previously marginalized and oppressed. They call both for individual freedoms and for a more compassionate and rewarding life for the community."[79] These movements demonstrate and engage in world-making, or ways of fusing religion and politics that "remake the world" by criticizing intersectional injustices of US and global public life, and by actualizing (i.e., imagining and partly incarnating) an alternative more just liberative common life.[80] Religion and politics both constitute ways of world-making, of articulating an alternative more just social order. While religion like politics may oppress rather than liberate and may at times sacralize and reinforce a prevailing unjust social order, its emphasis on critical self and social transcendence offers an alternative future vision

---

[76]Ibid., 4.

[77]Ibid., 19–20.

[78]Ibid., 58–64.

[79]Roger S. Gottlieb, *Joining Hands: Politics and Religion Together for Social Change* (Boulder, CO: Westview Press, 2002), 18–19.

[80]Ibid., 3–23, esp. 4–6, 9.

and reality of what we can become, personally and communally, and thus "contains the seeds of radical, dramatic, critical evaluation of and action against an unjust social order."[81] Faith-based social movements critically evaluate and seek to transformatively change society in conjunction with progressive political ideals of reason (to join epistemology and ethics to achieve human fulfillment), freedom (to remake ourselves and our world), and democracy (to enjoy equal rights).[82] Moreover, faith-based social justice movements in and beyond the US utilize prophetic praxis to critically disrupt and reconstruct the status quo in light of a more just and emancipatory alternative intra-historical future, envisioned and enacted in theological terms.

Prophetic practices rest firmly on fertile theological grounds, and often draw on symbolic practices such as a Christological imaginary. Feminist theologian, theatre director, and playwright Victoria Rue elaborates on the threefold religious character of theatre as incarnational, communal, and sacramental. In a christic vein, Rue contends that interpreting and enacting sacred texts requires that "a body moves; words come alive. Word is enfleshed."[83] Moreover, Rue proposes that theatre simultaneously makes our reality and another reality present to us: "Theatre is an enfleshment, an incarnation, a groping, stumbling attempt to approach and understand our world and beyond our world. As plays help us to reimagine those worlds, so the process of making theatre is a laboratory for testing those visions. Theatre as a laboratory . . . becomes a rehearsal for what we would like to see happen in our lives."[84] Moreover, theatre functions as a forum for creating community, which also expresses the eschatological element of theatre, a "rehearsal for building community" within ourselves and with others that carries broader implications for our wider society.[85] Finally, Rue argues that theatre explores "the body as a signpost for the Holy."[86] Creating, inhabiting, and transforming a character builds empathy between the characters—who communicate using various means, whether physical gestures and postures, visual cues, verbal and nonverbal dialogue, and so on—and with the audience about another possible future reality.[87]

---

[81]Ibid., 7–9, quote at 9.

[82]Ibid., 10, 19–20.

[83]Victoria Rue, *Acting Religious: Theatre as Pedagogy in Religious Studies* (Cleveland, OH: Pilgrim Press, 2005), 107.

[84]Ibid., 9.

[85]Ibid., 23, 73.

[86]Ibid., 12.

[87]Ibid., 17–18.

Doing Ekklesial Work   61

Theatre may appear an unlikely ally for creating a counterpublic space, for doing ekklesial work, as it allegedly trends toward the irresponsible sides of humanity. It replaces (or worse, absolves us from) ethical praxis, and reinscribes a prevalent media culture of spectacle that consumes others' stories for escapist entertainment. However, theatre need not put contemporary public life and its pressing issues on display for consumptive spectacle. Rather, it enacts and engages these issues to rethink the contours of contemporary public life in alternative ways. In other words, theatre does not mystify and obfuscate social issues as a kind of escapism, but rather confronts social problems, and functions as an important illuminating medium for invoking a prophetic voice and praxis in public life.

Prophetic theatric praxis further carries theo-political significance, because it resonates with a this-worldly eschatology. Remembering a fundamental relationship with God resists an oppressive socio-political order and simultaneously sparks an imagined and lived alternative to it. This praxis confronts contemporary socio-political issues and mediates the present with more hope-filled future realities, or "enable[s] . . . activists to taste the world for which they work." For example, theatre can invoke and provoke prophetic praxis in public life. Faith-based social justice movements often incorporate theatre or theatrical politics to demonstrate how socially and politically marginalized groups rely on important alternative aesthetic means to reclaim political recognition, to regain political participation and agency, and to empower and effect political change.[88] Mark Taylor proposes a theo-political "Christian theatrics of counterterror" rooted in the dramatic political action of both Christology and US social justice movements. Prophetic practices in the Christian tradition often draw on Christology as a *locus theologicus* to critically engage with and to constructively reshape US public life. Imitating Jesus involves a prophetic Christological praxis or performative witness to Jesus' countercultural life, message, ministry, death, and resurrection for the reign of God.[89] Just as Jesus wielded the cross for the purpose of life rather than for Roman imperial purposes of punishment, repression, and death, so too, Christian social justice movements enact and emulate the way that Jesus "steals the show" or subverts a state-backed culture of oppression at the risk of retribution. Theatre, and the arts more generally, in these movements "unlock[s] an actual world-making power in social

---

[88]Augusto Boal, *Theatre of the Oppressed* (New York: Theatre Communications Group, 1993); Augusto Boal, *The Aesthetics of the Oppressed* (New York: Routledge, 2006).

[89]Mark Lewis Taylor, *The Executed God: The Way of the Cross in Lockdown America* (Minneapolis: Fortress Press, 2001), esp. 70–78, 90–118, 127–133.

and political settings. The world that is tasted aesthetically, acted out, especially when done repeatedly, issues in the enactment of new worlds, of new patterns of social and political interaction."[90] Theatre thus participates in and enacts prophetic practices of ekklesial work, in that it critically dramatizes contemporary issues and also explores faith-based ways for addressing those issues that at the same time envision, rehearse, and usher in alternate more just possible worlds. Beyond the performing arts, Taylor probes the world-making significance of other creative arts, such as painting, literature, music/song, poetry, sculpture, and textiles.[91] The artful practices of marginalized peoples carry a "symbolic force" that envoices and empowers them to resist and flourish via that art and "to weigh in to create the world anew."[92] Politically marginalized and minoritized groups mobilize public support via dramatic symbolic and prophetic acts and are accompanied by elite empowered groups through this artful prophetic praxis that both dramatizes injustice and also attempts to partly actualize an alternative possibility to it via a variety of forms of collective and aesthetic action.

Likewise, theologies of women's liberation engage in prophetic theo-political world-making. Opting for themselves, their communities, and a more just future beyond religious and socio-political kyriarchies serves as a key starting point. As feminist theologian Elisabeth Schüssler Fiorenza claims, women's liberation theologies "imagine the domination and violence-free world intended by God and envision it anew with the help of religious traditions and language."[93] Critically reclaiming and re-creating religious language, symbols, rituals, and art catalyzes a religio-political space for the inbreaking of this alternative world.[94] As womanist theologian Barbara Holmes similarly argues, womanist theology embodies "a politics of creativity" that "requires the artistry of humaneness" and "reclaims the past and projects new realities" beyond the intersectional injustices of racism, sexism, and global economic interests that historically distorted and continued to distort not only Black women's lives but all our lives.[95] Yet making new worlds may also involve "spiritual incongru-

---

[90]Ibid., 117.

[91]Taylor, *The Theological and the Political: On the Weight of the World* (Minneapolis: Fortress Press, 2011), 114, 136.

[92]Ibid., 12–14, 114; cf. chap. 3.

[93]Elisabeth Schüssler Fiorenza, *Transforming Vision: Explorations in Feminist The*logy* (Minneapolis: Fortress Press, 2011), 19.

[94]Ibid., 20. Laurie Cassidy and Maureen H. O'Connell, eds., *She Who Imagines: Feminist Theological Aesthetics* (Collegeville, MN: Liturgical Press, 2012).

[95]Barbara A. Holmes, "'We'll Make Us a World': A Post-Obama Politics of Embodied Creativity," in *Ain't I A Womanist, Too? Third Wave Womanist Religious Thought*, ed. Monica A.

Doing Ekklesial Work   63

ity," or the audacity to reject past religious traditions and socio-political strategies in favor of "creativity in the church and in the public square."[96]

Synthesizing the insights of these introductory chapters, ekklesial work affords a fruitful theological perspective from which to critically analyze and judge as well as to constructively reshape and reimagine public life. Ekklesial work *theologizes* the vision, principle, and practices of public theology more effectively as community building, as world-making work. Redefining public theology as ekklesial work helps enhance its project in at least three ways. Ekklesial work illuminates religio-political dimensions of feminist and womanist theologies, thus highlighting their potential contributions to public theology. Also, it redefines what I see as a central goal or task of public theology—to convoke a public, create a political community—in theological terms, by providing a substantive theological and eschatological vision and principle. Finally, ekklesial work provides a conceptual theological leverage point for gaining a better understanding of critical and constructive practices of religio-political engagement in US public life. Public theology that is configured and focused too narrowly on rational discourse in a deliberative model of democracy may significantly limit or obscure other kinds of public engagement beyond the rational, the rhetorical.[97] By contrast, ekklesial work expands practices of public engagement beyond rhetorical practices and opens up a new theological space to examine and explore multiple kinds of practices for being and building up a just, loving, and peaceful community. In this way, ekklesial work thus theologically supports a rich repertoire of eschatological practices that usher in a longed-for but not yet fully realized future vision of public life for the well-being, belonging, and flourishing of all. Ekklesial work illuminates and advances diverse practices—rhetorical, symbolic, and prophetic—for participating in, countering, and ultimately revisioning public life. These practices disrupt, destabilize, and otherwise intervene in a prevailing oppressive US political status quo to make a liberative eschatological space for the inbreaking of an alternative more just, more flourishing public life for all life to take shape. Rhetorical practices regain and reclaim public voice and space to educate everyday citizens and political leaders alike about systemic injustices and re-articulate as well as re-imagine public life through solidarity with marginalized groups.

Coleman (Minneapolis: Fortress Press, 2013), 188, 189, 191.

[96]Ibid., 195, 196.

[97]Robert Wuthnow, "Rationality and the Limits of Rational Theory: A Sociological Critique," in *Habermas, Modernity, and Public Theology*, ed. Don S. Browning and Francis Schüssler Fiorenza (New York: Crossroad, 1992), 206–225.

64   Nevertheless, We Persist

Symbolic practices reflect on and reinterpret central iconic religio-political symbols for their political significance and implications to relocate or redirect a shared moral imaginary, framework, or groundings for resisting and transforming public life but without coercing any religious conformity to a Christian theological imaginary. Prophetic practices of faith-based protest take nonviolent direct collective action to edge our US public life and political order toward a more emancipatory vision and life. Ekklesial work, thus, democratizes public theology and moreso allows us to engage with social justice movements for insights about and examples of such practices.

Taken together, these practices provide eschatological examples of what it means to undertake ekklesial work, that is, to constructively point to an alternative vision of US public life and to critically engage in public life to realize that vision. These distinct but interrelated rhetorical, symbolic, and prophetic practices of public engagement urge and usher in a more inclusive, participatory, and just public life, and thereby hold theological potential to shed new light on as well as revitalize the convocative, community-creating, or world-making praxis of public theology. What makes public theology and its practices "public" involves more than intelligibly stating or expressing religious claims in the US public sphere to shape public debates and policies; what makes public theology and its practices "public" consists in their ability to create community in a divisive, polarized, and exclusionary world, to point toward a more just socio-political order, and to offer a theological horizon that brings to birth new possibilities for a more inclusive, dignifying, and just common life. In keeping with Catholic social thought and with theological anthropology, these practices urge us eschatologically toward a more just and humane life, collectively and individually. Public theology and its practices align with what feminist theologian Linell Cady calls "a perennial struggle to reform this life in light of the eschatological goal toward which creation, it may be hoped, asymptotically moves."[98] Together, these practices participate in and cultivate an eschatological pull toward a not yet fully realized alternative vision of our humanity and our socio-political order, and in so doing begin to prefigure that order, contributing in hope-filled eschatological ways to being and becoming more fully human in relations of love, justice, and peace. In keeping with feminist and womanist anthropologies, these practices reinforce a relational and performative view of the person and public life—in which we perform the relationships that inhere in our humanity but that are always imperfectly and unjustly realized in our common life. In other words, world-making parallels and

---

[98]Cady, *Religion, Theology, and American Public Life*, 111.

Doing Ekklesial Work 65

influences an eschatological process of self-making, and vice versa.

These practices also advance the praxis of traditioning Christianity.[99] Tradition entails an agential, dynamic, performative act of handing on and in that passing-on process of critically reinventing a heritage. Tradition in recent theologies is defined in terms of both content (Latin: *tradita*) and process (Latin: *traditio*). It comprises both the reception of inherited Christian texts, beliefs, and practices and the active transmission of these reinterpreted and remade texts, beliefs, and practices across different times and places in response to various contexts and crises. These two aspects of tradition, materiality and performance, have been characterized in various ways in the history of Christian thought. At times, tradition is portrayed as an unchanging, uniform consensus about the materials that shape and determine the performance of Christian identities and ways of life. To disrupt this fixed, universalized, and at time totalizing content of tradition—this deposit of faith—associated with Eurocentric neo/colonialism, tradition is construed at other times through local, contextual, diverse, and divergent Christian groups which reinterpret and remake religious traditions as part of challenging inherited oftentimes oppressive ways of life. Besides highlighting either the stability or the particularity of the material content of tradition, tradition is treated at still other times as the praxis of traditioning, of the dynamic performance of receiving and transmitting inherited Christian materials and ways of life in light of different socio-historical situations and issues. Invoking this more postmodern Christian approach to tradition, Kathryn Tanner regards tradition as style or as invention to emphasize the constructive role that agents (individuals or groups) play in recrafting and reworking Christian materials and ways of life in innovative responses to particularly pressing times, places, and concerns.[100] Tradition is not fabricated, thereby undermining the importance of long-standing Christian beliefs and practices. Rather, according to Tanner, framing tradition as style and invention better situates Christianity as always already a cultural product—as a task that is part of our ongoing shared struggle to engage and make meaningful sense of the world within a variety of inherited resources.[101] Tanner characterizes this praxis of traditioning, of re/constructing Christian tradition, as "an argument

---

[99]Terrence W. Tilley, *Inventing Catholic Tradition* (Maryknoll, NY: Orbis Books, 2000); M. Shawn Copeland, "Tradition and the Traditions of African American Catholicism," *Theological Studies* 61 (2000): 632–655; and Orlando Espín and Gary Macy, eds., *Futuring Our Past: Explorations in the Theology of Tradition* (Maryknoll, NY: Orbis Books, 2006).

[100]Tanner, *Theories of Culture*, 87–92, 144–151. Moreover, style and invention reinforce the inherent interactions of different religions and cultures within Christian tradition; in other words, religious and other cultures dynamically and variously interact in the creative re/making of Christian traditions; ibid., 110–119.

[101]Ibid., 151–155.

that is engaged throughout the whole of Christian social practices. . . . In order for such a common project of argument to be viable . . . something like the community of solidarity and hope . . . may be required."[102]

Ekklesial work better evokes, expresses, and embodies the convocative or community-creating task of public theology, because it advances emancipatory religious claims, symbols, and collective actions that engage in critical and creative world-making for religio-political transformation. It decries intersectional injustices and envisions as well as engages in practices to enact more just alternative possible worlds. It constructs more capacious worldviews and ways of being, living, and relating to one another that encourage solidarity, justice, and peace, and that better address the world's pressing issues and needs by critically and constructively leveraging religious claims, symbols, and community actions. With this shared task, it mobilizes Christianity and other religions to reimagine and remake the world for more empowering and enlivening alternative possibilities for public life to emerge, take root, and flourish.

Public theology's practices constitute a way of world-making, of envisioning and enacting worlds, which involves critiquing and deconstructing oppressive worlds, on the one hand, and constructing and creating alternate more liberative worlds, on the other hand. US social justice movements and their attendant theological claims, symbols, and prophetic engagements exemplify, in my view, ekklesial work as a community creating praxis, or praxis of world-making that imagines and incarnates the world otherwise, that offers hope-filled spaces for liberative work and futures, and that edges an alternative possible world into existence. Effective public engagement takes place through a rich array of these practices for social change. The following chapters identify and interpret community-creating practices of ekklesial work in US social justice movements. Each chapter maps and elucidates these distinct yet intersecting practices—from the perspective of ekklesial work and of women—in select social justice movements to rethink and regenerate public theology in our time as well as to show how these movements and practices bring about a more just, more emancipatory, more flourishing vision of public life.

Doing ekklesial work encompasses a variety of ways of forging and performing a more just and justice-seeking public life. Recent studies of public theology recognize its performative praxis via social movements.[103] To engage and effect this performative and practical turn in public the-

---

[102]Ibid., 125.

[103]Katie Day and Sebastian Kim, Introduction to *A Companion to Public Theology*, ed. Sebastian Kim and Katie Day (Leiden: Brill, 2017), 1–21.

Doing Ekklesial Work 67

ology more robustly, each subsequent chapter describes and explores a rich interrelated range of rhetorical, symbolic, and prophetic practices, grounded in and retrieved from selected US Christian and multifaith social justice movements that engage and transform US public life for greater inclusion, equity, and justice. My analysis holds these practices in dynamic tension under the notion of ekklesial work to illustrate and interpret multiple ways that religious resources propel participation in as well as reshape public life for dignity, diversity, equity, and justice. Each subsequent chapter proceeds with a brief but in-depth analysis of prominent figures in select US Christian and multifaith-based social justice movements, highlighting their practices for public engagement and social justice: gaining and leveraging voice in public life, reconstructing religio-political symbols to reshape core norms and values that provide and promote a shared moral framework for public life, and criticizing and refiguring public life through prophetic protest to realize those norms and values. Each chapter offers critical and constructive theological reflection on rhetorical strategies, religious symbols, and prophetic political praxis of historical and emergent US social justice movements that exemplify a praxis of world-making, imagining and incarnating the world otherwise than racism, sexism, poverty, war, ecocide, xenophobic hate crimes, and white nationalist movements that predominate in our day. Also, each chapter explores women's religio-political witness within these movements as theological models for women's audacious ways of doing public/political theology today, that is, of generating alternative possible futures of love and justice that foster the flourishing of all.

3

Poverty, Personalism, and the Catholic Worker

The only answer in this life to the loneliness we are all bound to feel is community.
—Dorothy Day, *The Long Loneliness*

Founded in 1970, the Los Angeles Catholic Worker (LACW)[1] is animated by the practice of the gospel-inspired works of mercy (Matt. 25:31–46) and Catholic social teachings, illustrated by its mission stated on its website "to comfort the afflicted and afflict the comfortable." It operates two donor-funded locations—a community house of hospitality in Boyle Heights, where members and unhoused folxs reside and celebrate an ecumenical liturgy on Wednesday evenings which often follow LA-area faith-based weekly public witness, and a community kitchen that offers meals three times weekly together with a clinic and service center in LA's Skid Row. The LACW embodies what I call a feminist approach to public theology, or ekklesial work, in its rhetorical, symbolic, and prophetic practices of creating community. It publishes the bimonthly *The Catholic Agitator* to educate and engage in outreach and in 2021 inaugurated a "Reckoning with Our Mission Histories" series to process and begin to redress and repair the complex legacies of settler colonialism and promote Indigenous justice in critical response to Los Angeles Archbishop José Gomez's launch of a Jubilee Year marking the 250th anniversary of California Catholic missions. It organizes an annual Good Friday Stations of the Cross that highlights the ongoing multiple crucifixions of local and global peoples. In its protest politics, as stated on its website, the LACW

---

[1]Jeff Dietrich, *Broken and Shared: Food, Dignity, and the Poor on Los Angeles' Skid Row* (Los Angeles: Marymount Institute Press / Tsehai Publishers, 2011), and *The Good Samaritan: Stories from the Los Angeles Catholic Worker on Skid Row* (Los Angeles: Marymount Institute Press / Tsehai Publishers, 2014).

Poverty, Personalism, and the Catholic Worker 69

attempts to take a prophetic stand for and with the poor and unhoused . . . and thus periodically engages in various nonviolent dem-
onstrations/protests and acts of civil disobedience. . . . The LACW's
prophetic stand as a resistance community is also validated in our
regular vigils, demonstrations/protests, and nonviolent direct action
campaigns in opposition to war and militarism, which not only
oppresses the poor in foreign lands but robs our domestic poor of
essential resources as well. We also stand against this nation's harsh
immigration policies, racial injustices, housing crisis, economic inequality, climate emergency, and capital punishment.

During the COVID-19 pandemic, LACW continued its annual protest
vigil and nonviolent direct action at Vandenberg Air Force Base in central
coastal California on August 7, 2021, to mark the 76th anniversary of
the US bombing of Hiroshima and Nagasaki on August 6, 1945, and to
advocate for the abolition of nuclear war and all US war-making efforts.
This vigil aligns not only with international treaties that prohibit nuclear
weapons but also with Catholic bishops' pastoral letters on nuclear
disarmament.[2] During the pandemic, which disproportionately affected
communities of color and vulnerable populations, LACW switched to
serving meals in to-go boxes or containers and almost doubled its usual
food preparation because of increased demand; it also closed its garden
(sometimes called Paradise or Eden), which ordinarily offers opportunities for the unhoused to gather for meals and community; it supplied
Skid Row residents with hand sanitizer to use in the often-unserved but
city-supplied toilets and wash stations.[3]

The founder of the LACW, Catherine Morris, met the co-founder of
the Catholic Worker Movement (CWM), Dorothy Day, when both Morris and Day were arrested and imprisoned as part of the United Farm
Worker (UFW) strikes and protests in 1973 in Fresno, California. Like
Morris, Day resided and protested with the farmworkers, and that solidarity continued into a two-week jail sentence, her last jail sentence for
justice. In this chapter, I examine selective aspects of Day's life and writings, theology, and activism to map and elucidate this movement from my
perspective of a constructive feminist public theology, of ekklesial work,
to create community through a theo-political ethic of love for justice. In

---

[2] Archbishop of Santa Fe John Wester, "Living in the Light of Christ's Peace: A Conversation
Toward Nuclear Disarmament," January 11, 2022.
[3] Alejandra Molina, "On LA's Skid Row, Catholic Worker's 'Hippie Kitchen' Adjusts to CO-
VID-19," *National Catholic Reporter*, April 3, 2020.

70 *Nevertheless, We Persist*

my view, Day integrated rhetorical, symbolic, and prophetic practices of public engagement in founding and forwarding the CWM. Day articulated through the newspaper *The Catholic Worker*, thematized theologically through the symbols of creation and Christology, and enacted prophetically through protest politics the CWM's faith-based program of action for social, economic, and racial justice and peace. The contemporary Revolutionary Love Project amplifies and radicalizes, in my view, Day's and the CWM's religio-politics of the beloved community in our time.

The Catholic Worker

Dorothy Day (1897–1980) was a journalist, a Catholic, and an activist—vocations that emerged and converged in the CWM, a Catholic lay religious and political movement for justice and peace, primarily concerned with anti-poverty activism during the Great Depression but which expanded during the twentieth century into the present to resist all forms of social, racial, and economic injustice, including poverty, hunger, and homelessness, the world debt crisis that creates increasing inequalities between the geopolitical North and South, and war.[4] The CWM was co-founded in 1933 by Day and French Catholic philosopher Peter Maurin to address the plights and to advance the rights of poor, unemployed, and exploited workers from a faith-based perspective as well as to enlighten complacent Catholics about social change. To express, embody, and effect this purpose, the CWM embraced and implemented a "program of action" for social change, which consisted of a newspaper, *The Catholic Worker*, initially distributed for a penny a copy on May Day in Union Square, New York, and now published by the New York Catholic Worker seven times a year at a twenty-five-cent annual subscription rate. The Catholic Worker also operated urban houses of hospitality in New York and across the US that practiced voluntary poverty and the works

---

[4]Select significant studies of the CWM include Kate Hennessy, *Dorothy Day: The World Will Be Saved by Beauty: An Intimate Portrait of My Grandmother* (New York, Scribner, 2017), and *Dorothy Day and the Catholic Worker Movement: The Miracle of Our Continuance* (New York: Fordham University Press, 2016); Patrick Jordan, ed., *Hold Nothing Back: Writings by Dorothy Day* (Collegeville, MN: Liturgical Press, 2016); Jim Forest, *All Is Grace: A Biography of Dorothy Day* (New York: Orbis Books, 2011); Dan McKanan, *The Catholic Worker after Dorothy: Practicing the Works of Mercy in a New Generation* (Collegeville, MN: Liturgical Press, 2008); Claudia Larson, *Dorothy Day: Don't Call Me a Saint* (One Lucky Dog Production, 2006); Anne Klejment and Nancy L. Roberts, eds., *American Catholic Pacifism: The Influence of Dorothy Day and the Catholic Worker Movement* (Westport, CT: Praeger, 1996); and Robert Ellsberg, ed., *Dorothy Day: Selected Writings* (Maryknoll, NY: Orbis Books, 1992).

Poverty, Personalism, and the Catholic Worker 71

of mercy (Matt. 25:31–46) and farming communes. In 2022 according to the Catholic Worker website, the CWM consists of 160 communities and 19 farms nationwide, and 27 communities and 4 farms globally. The CWM's program centralized a personalist politics or took personal responsibility for others' well-being to achieve distributive justice in which all people in their dignity and freedom have "sufficient of this world's goods to enable [them] to lead a good life." This program also inspired a long-term "green revolution" or a vision of a decentralized and pacifist society that decommodified people and goods, restored ownership and management of work, and emphasized a cooperative economy rather than an industrial, corporate, high-tech, or agribusiness economy.[5] The CWM also integrated nonviolent direct action such as the strike, along with other forms of political protest, into its program for social change, to realize personal and political transformation for the greening of the good society, characterized by meaningful labor and just relations among humanity and with the land.[6]

In my view, the CWM's political action for progressive socio-political change integrated a rich array of practices of public engagement for criticizing the then contemporary industrial capitalist socio-political order—practices that involved journalism, theology, and protest politics. And in keeping with my argument that ekklesial work entails a dual critical and constructive role of religion in public life, examining the CWM through these practices illuminates that the CWM articulated and attempted to incarnate an alternative vision of the socio-political order—modeled on making the theological notion of the body of Christ an actual visible socio-political reality.

Writing figures prominently in Day's own life and in founding the CWM for the purpose of gaining public recognition and rights for marginalized peoples and for building solidarity with the poor. Regarding her own life, Day was raised in a Protestant middle-class background and a newspaper family in Brooklyn Heights, New York; the family moved frequently for her father's career, which included major cities such as San Francisco and Chicago. After two years of college at the University of Illinois at Urbana where she discerned "a call, a vocation, a direction to my life,"[7] she moved to New York in 1916 and worked in Greenwich Village as

---

[5]Dorothy Day, *The Long Loneliness* (New York: Harper Collins, 1980 [1952]), 56, 85, 172–173, 185–187, 193, 195, 220–221, 224, 234.

[6]"Aims and Means of the Catholic Worker," in *American Catholic Social Teaching*, vol. 2, ed. Thomas J. Massaro and Thomas A. Shannon (Collegeville, MN: Liturgical Press, 2002), 95–96. Reprinted in the 86th anniversary issue of *The Catholic Worker*, May 2019.

[7]Day, *Long Loneliness*, 38.

a reporter for several socialist and radical papers, and befriended many writers seeking social change by rousing the public conscience about and challenging multiple social injustices. After returning from a European tour and a failed marriage, she moved to Chicago in 1922 and worked for similar newspapers, then for the City News Bureau. Aligned with many themes in Pope Leo XIII's encyclical *Rerum Novarum* issued in 1891, Day turned to journalism to educate about the unsafe and insecure living and working conditions of poor workers; to protest the injustices of a growing economic disparity between an industrial capitalist elite and an increasingly poor and exploited working class; and to foster social well-being, that is, to abate loneliness, both her own and others, who were alienated and ostracized from US socio-political and economic life.[8] Journalism facilitated Day's main criticisms of US public life: to indict industrial and corporate capitalist greed, and to challenge a growing socio-political apathy, especially among Catholics.[9] As a reporter, Day covered and thus empowered various demonstrations for workers' rights as well as participated in solidarity with such demonstrations; thus, journalism overlapped with Day's other practices of critically engaging in public life, namely protest politics.

Day articulated three main reasons that justified her conversion to Catholicism: gratitude, community, and solidarity. Day's solidarity with poor workers as a journalist and as a workers' rights activist also inspired the CWM. According to her autobiography, Day not only entered the Catholic Church in gratitude for co-creating her daughter Tamar with God and with her partner atheist, anarchist, and biologist Forster Batterham, and to give Tamar a sense of belonging to a community, but also joined the Church to better advocate and ally with the poor, to realize the theological notion of human dignity and of the mystical body of Christ that "we are the members one of another."[10] Day explained: "My very experience as a radical, my whole make-up, led me to want to associate myself with others, with the masses, in loving and praising God. Without even looking into the claims of the Catholic Church, I was willing to admit that for me she was the one true Church . . . . She claimed and held the allegiance of the masses of people in all the cities where I had lived."[11] After her conversion to Catholicism in 1927 which traumatically ended her relationship with

---

[8] Ibid., 51.
[9] Ibid., 39–42, 45–46, 65–66, 72.
[10] Ibid., 132–136, 139–141, quote at 147.
[11] Ibid., 139.

Poverty, Personalism, and the Catholic Worker 73

Forster,[12] Day was hired in 1932 to report on a major "demonstration of the unemployed"—the Hunger March—on Washington, DC, for two Catholic magazines, *Commonweal* and *America*. Reflecting on her article, Day expressed increasing frustration with the inconsistent private and public morality among most Catholics and questioned Catholic leaders' apathetic lack of prophetic activism.[13] Although Day practiced a traditionalist Catholicism marked by attending daily mass, praying the rosary, and reading the Bible as well as spiritual and contemporary literature, Day articulated a revolutionary Christology that emulated the Sermon on the Mount and Christ's public acts of upending unjust religio-political norms and practices. At the crossroads of Catholic and radical leanings, Day visited the National Shrine of the Immaculate Conception before she departed DC to pray for an emerging vocation.[14] From my feminist perspective of public theology as ekklesial work, she wrestled with these questions, seeking a way to engage in world-making, to resist the unjust status quo and to create more just communities and possibilities through rhetorical, symbolic, and prophetic activism. Upon returning from DC, she coincidentally met and collaborated with Maurin to co-found the CWM.

With regard to the CWM, journalism continued to facilitate Day's criticism of US socio-economic structures of poverty, war, and racism and to galvanize protest politics. Day relied on journalism, especially the newspaper, to rouse public engagement around poverty, worker rights, and later anti-racist and anti-war activism. The newspaper's name, *The Catholic Worker*, illustrated the CWM's aims and purposes: to point out the glaring inconsistencies between personal and social morality among most US Catholics and build solidarity with exploited workers, especially but not only Catholics.[15] In 1933, the newspaper distributed about 2,500 copies, for a penny a copy; by 1936, the circulation increased to 150,000,[16] and in 2022 the newspaper costs twenty-five cents for an annual subscription with seven issues a year, with widely varying estimates of its circulation.

Beyond journalism, Day entertained a variety of other rhetorical genres during her life and career, such as the screenplay for a Hollywood film production of her 1924 novel *The Eleventh Virgin* about a time in Day's life when she was entangled in several bad relationships. Day did not find these genres socially and politically relevant—though the Hollywood

---

[12]Ibid., 136–137, 140, 148, 151.
[13]Ibid., 149–150, 165; cf. 144, 162–166, 210.
[14]Ibid., 141–142, 165–166.
[15]Ibid., 139, 173–175, 210.
[16]Ibid., 182.

74   *Nevertheless, We Persist*

purchase of the film rights on the novel enabled Day to buy a beach cottage on Raritan Bay, Staten Island, and build a close network of friends, "liberal, radical, bohemian, engaging in literature controversies."[17] About twenty years after co-founding the CWM, Day turned to the genre of autobiography to give an account of herself, to recount her experiences of being "haunted" by God and the "things which had brought me to God." Autobiography allowed Day to utilize the events of her life to explore major Christian theological claims about anthropology, Christology, and ecclesiology as well as eschatology that bolster the CWM—that all human beings are made in the image and likeness of God, and that all human beings are oriented to community with the transcendent and one another.[18] Such theological claims directly contested and confronted the loneliness that Day regarded as a common existential human condition. Yet Day expressed an ambivalence about writing an autobiography, because it amounted to a self-indulgent luxury: "I am a journalist, not a biographer, not a book writer. The sustained effort of writing, of putting pen to paper so may hours a day when there are human beings around who need me, when there is sickness, and hunger, and sorrow, is a harrowingly painful job."[19] In my view, journalism functions for Day as a rhetorical genre aptly suited to public engagement—to criticize the predominant socio-political order; to critically engage in public discourse about anti-poverty, anti-war, and anti-racist resistance; and to instigate political action that embodies and envisions alternative more just futures.

In addition to rhetorical practices, mainly but not only of journalism, Day relied on symbolic practices, especially to recount her conversion memoir and to give a religious rationale for the CWM's program of action and its prophetic protest politics, grounded in gospel imperatives. Day's attitudes toward religion and God evolved through various episodes in her life which she experienced and described as "natural contemplation."[20] As a child in Berkeley, California, she both revered the holiness of the Bible and feared an impersonal force, an angry wrathful God, connected to the 1906 San Francisco earthquake.[21] Wheeling her younger brother through Chicago's South Side profoundly impressed on Day the poor's resilience, which ignited her interest in the labor movement and its class-conscious literature. She also encountered God in nature,

---

[17]Ibid., 114.
[18]Ibid., 10, 12, 94.
[19]Ibid., 11.
[20]Ibid., 19.
[21]Ibid., 20–21.

Poverty, Personalism, and the Catholic Worker 75

which revealed to Day the sacramental reality of God or universal divine presence of a good Creator in creation: "How I love the park in winter! So solitary and so awful in the truest meaning of the word. God is there. Of course, [God] is everywhere but under the trees and looking over the wide expanse of lake [God] communicates [Godself] to me and fills me with a deep, quiet peace."[22] Later, as a student activist in the labor movement at the University of Illinois, Day portrayed God as a provider of abundant life, while religion reinforced poverty and supported systemic social inequities as divinely ordained and justified.[23] Borrowing Marxist criticisms of religion as a drug or prop to cope with existential and social challenges, Day observed an increasing asymmetry between religion and radical movements—a meek God promotes passive workers, while Day envisioned a God of action, inspiring and empowering religious people as social change activists.

> Where were all the saints to try to change the social order, and not just minister to the slaves but do away with the slavery?. . . . Jesus said, "Blessed are the meek," but I could not be meek at the thought of injustice. I wanted a Lord who would scourge the money-changers out of the temple, and I wanted to help all those who raised their hand against oppression. For me Christ no longer walked the streets of this world. He was two thousand years dead and new prophets had risen up in His place. I was in love now with the masses. . . . The poor and the oppressed were going to rise up, they were collectively the new Messiah.[24]

For Day, institutional religion espoused an escapist and other-worldly attitude. Day observed how religious people ignored, dismissed, or disregarded global injustices, whereas the gospels commanded social justice.[25]

Jail served as an important crucible to further develop and deepen Day's encounters with God. When arrested and imprisoned with forty women after a 1917 suffragist rally in Washington, DC, and during the anti-immigrant and anti-socialist Palmer Red Raids in 1922 in Chicago, Day experienced a God of comfort and consolation, imaged as a supportive hand, by reading the Psalms, and, more significantly, committed to solidarity with prisoners, with human suffering.[26] Throughout her jobs

---

[22]Ibid., 33–34.
[23]Ibid., 38.
[24]Ibid., 45, 46.
[25]Ibid., 39, 41–43.
[26]Ibid., 81, 104.

76   *Nevertheless, We Persist*

as a journalist and a nurse during the flu pandemic and World War I in New York, Day attended mass regularly, engaged in worship and prayer, and engaged existential questions about humanity, suffering, and love.[27] In Chicago and then in New Orleans, Day was introduced to Catholic spirituality and literature mainly through Catholic women and families, pairing daily mass and devotions (rosaries, novenas) with New Testament study.[28] Through the relationship with her partner Forster and the birth of their child, Day discovered and basked in "natural happiness," which shaped her love of creation and the Creator, as well as affected her view of humanity as co-creators in the image and likeness of God.[29]

Moreover, Day provided a theological rationale for the CWM ministry in the houses of hospitality—to provide food, clothing, and shelter for poor, unemployed, unhoused, and hungry people—by expanding on central Christian claims regarding salvation and incarnation. Day referred to these claims not only to justify the houses on theological grounds, but also, in my view, to better articulate from a Christian theological perspective some shared principles—such as dignity, sacrifice, solidarity, and justice—for reshaping and sustaining US common life.

The houses of hospitality started with the inaugural houses that developed into communities for women (Maryhouse) and men (St. Joseph House) in New York and continue to flourish nationally and globally. Day forged a theological connection between human salvation, on the one hand, and the effective transfiguration of society to meet fundamental human needs for and rights to food, clothing, health and well-being, secure housing, meaningful and just work, liberation from imprisonment and all sorts of captivity, love and relationship, on the other hand, by theologically tapping into the works of mercy (Matt. 25:31–46).[30] Given that love of God and love of neighbor figure centrally in the Christian scriptures, and given that love of God is demonstrated through performing the works of mercy, loving God for Day is expressed in loving others, in showing love for others through performing these works.[31] Performing the works of mercy at the houses of hospitality—in which others personify the historical Jesus or other Christs (Matt. 25:40)—depends on a theological understanding of the incarnation of God in the life, ministry, death, and resurrection of Jesus. Regarding the person of Jesus, the doctrinal

---

[27]Ibid., 84–85, 93.

[28]Ibid., 105–109.

[29]Ibid., 134–135, 140.

[30]Ibid., 181, 220, 244. Day, "The Scandal of the Works of Mercy," in *Dorothy Day: Selected Writings*, ed. Ellsberg, 98–99.

[31]Day, *Long Loneliness*, 171, 246–247.

Poverty, Personalism, and the Catholic Worker 77

metaphysical union of divine and human natures in the person of Jesus Christ underscores, according to Day, both the christomorphic ability of all people to reflect and represent Christ, and the dignity and worth of all humanity, especially the poor, based on that ability—"they [the poor] are Christ."[32] Regarding Jesus' ministry, Day stressed that oppressed peoples represented Christ today, because Day emulated the purpose and praxis of Jesus' life and ministry.

> The great mystery of the Incarnation . . . was a mystery that we as Catholics accepted, but there were also the facts of Christ's life, that He was born in a stable, that He did not come to be a temporal King, that He worked with His hands, spent the first years of His life in exile, and the rest of His early manhood in a crude carpenter shop in Nazareth. He fulfilled his religious duties in the synagogue and the temple. He trod the roads in His public life and the first men He called were fishermen, small owners of boats and nets. He was familiar with the migrant worker and the proletariat, and some of His parables dealt with them. He spoke of the living wage. . . . He died between two thieves because He would not be made an earthly King. He lived in an occupied country for thirty years without starting an underground movement. . . . He directed His sublime words to the poorest of the poor, to the people who thronged the towns and followed after John the Baptist, who hung around, sick and poverty-stricken, at the doors of rich men. He had set us an example and the poor and destitute were the ones we wished to reach.[33]

Day paradoxically contested and embraced poverty. Catholic Workers practiced the works of mercy in the houses of hospitality "at a personal sacrifice," that is, through voluntary poverty.[34] Voluntary poverty, as Day explained, encompasses self-sacrifice and solidarity with the poor, that is, an ethics of sharing material goods and an engaged praxis of the preferential option for the poor. First, voluntary poverty, for Day, acts as a "liberating force" that strips us of all luxury goods and other marks of privilege; it disconnects us from a grasping and acquisitive lifestyle, so that the necessities of life are available to all people.[35] Thus, voluntary poverty prioritizes and performs an ethics of giving to realize distribu-

---

[32]Day, *Long Loneliness*, 171. Day, "Room for Christ," in *Dorothy Day: Selected Writings*, ed. Ellsberg, 97.

[33]Day, *Long Loneliness*, 204–205.

[34]Ibid., 244–245.

[35]Ibid., 179, 195, 215.

78 *Nevertheless, We Persist*

tive justice. Second, voluntary poverty entails a firsthand experience and praxis of material poverty itself. As Day observed,

> Going around and seeing such sights is not enough. To help the organizers, to give what you have for relief, to pledge yourself to voluntary poverty for life so that you can share with your brothers is not enough. One must live with them, share with them their sufferings, too. Give up one's privacy, and mental and spiritual comforts as well as physical. . . . Going to the people is the purest and best act in Christian tradition and revolutionary tradition and is the beginning of world brotherhood.[36]

Voluntary poverty is embodied in the CWM in theo-political ways. According to Day, voluntary poverty through the practice of the works of mercy enabled an imitation of Christ,[37] slowly conforming to a revolutionary Christ who was profoundly shaped by and actively resisted poverty and other forms of injustice in his own person and ministry under Roman imperial conquest and occupation. It also mediated love of God by loving others, especially an encounter with Christ in and with oppressed peoples; giving hospitality to the poor and alleviating in some way their "long-continuing crucifixion" is equated with giving hospitality to Christ. As Day explained, "The mystery of the poor is this: That they are Jesus, and what you do for them you do for Him. . . . The mystery of poverty is that by sharing in it, by making ourselves poor in giving to others, we increase our knowledge of and belief in love."[38] Thus, the CWM both challenged and accepted poverty. According to Day, seeing, knowing, helping, and standing in solidarity with others could not occur "without first stripping ourselves." Stripping reforms or transforms human nature through voluntary poverty, from a grasping, acquisitive, self-preservationist nature to a compassionate, caring nature. At the same time, Day protested the structural "precarity" of poverty, or economic insecurity about work, wages, and the future.[39]

To summarize my understanding of Day's symbolic practices, Day's theological reflections on major Christian claims about salvation and

---

[36]Ibid., 214, 216.

[37]Ibid., 246–247, 256.

[38]Dorothy Day, "They Knew Him in the Breaking of the Bread," in *Dorothy Day: Selected Writings*, ed. Ellsberg, 81; and, "The Mystery of the Poor," in *Dorothy Day: Selected Writings*, ed. Ellsberg, 330.

[39]Dorothy Day, "Poverty and Precarity" and "Little by Little," in *Dorothy Day: Selected Writings*, ed. Ellsberg, 109, 110.

Poverty, Personalism, and the Catholic Worker   79

Christology formed a moral basis for the houses of hospitality. Moreover, Day's theological claims emphasized certain moral groundings to enhance the quality of our common life (such as dignity, sacrifice, solidarity, and justice), rather than to advance a personal salvific experience for privileged peoples living among and serving poor peoples. These moral groundings, principles, and responsibilities—extrapolated from Christian claims about realizing the image of God in humanity through creativity and emulating the person, life, and ministry of Jesus—resisted the objectification of poor workers as tools for industrial capitalist profit or as vehicles for mediating the divine presence. Rather, these moral groundings contributed to a Christian theological imaginary that dignified all life.

Besides rhetorical and theological practices, prophetic practices constituted a significant part of Day's public engagement. Day's protest politics started as a suffragist when she picketed the White House in 1917. She initiated a ten-day hunger strike for political prisoners' rights during her thirty-day jail sentence, identifying with the imprisoned, protesting brutality and injustice, as well as "casting our seeds . . . [with] the promise of the harvest to come."[40] She continued that protest politics during World War I and the global flu pandemic, when she adopted a pacifist view as a nurse in 1918 at King's County Hospital. Day's pacifist views expanded and further informed her protests, arrests, and jail sentences between 1955 and 1961 when many US cities conducted civil defense drills during the Cold War. These annual drills signified and strengthened the psychology of war and its fear and alienation of enemies, while Day together with the CWM and other activists engaged in acts of civil disobedience and organized protests in public streets and parks to show and stress community and love. In the 1959 protest, Day carried a placard with Catholic social teaching and papal statements: "Why should the resources of human genius and the riches of the people turn more often to preparing arms . . . than to increasing the welfare of all classes of citizens and particularly of the poor? Pope John XXIII." Returning to Rome during Vatican II, Day lobbied the conciliar bishops to oppose war. "In 1963, Day was one of fifty 'Mothers for Peace' who went to Rome to thank Pope John for his encyclical *Pacem in Terris* . . . at one of his last public audiences [he] blessed the pilgrims, asking them to continue their labors."[41] In 1965, she participated in a ten-day fast with twenty global women in Rome organized by the Ark, a French pacifist community, near the close of the council discussions about conscience, war, and peace. These

---

[40]Forest, *All Is Grace*, 43.

[41]Jim Forest, "Servant of God Dorothy Day," The Catholic Worker Movement website, 2013.

80   *Nevertheless, We Persist*

women followed a daily regimen of mass, meditation, readings, lectures, and discussions about nonviolence, as well as wellness visits. Ultimately, the bishops condemned nuclear war, while Day offered her fast for the victims of global famine, in solidarity with "the hunger of the world."[42] During the Vietnam War, Day objected to the war and conscription by supporting the burning of draft cards. When Catholic Worker Roger LaPorte immolated himself in the front of the United Nations to protest the war, similar to Buddhist monks and nuns in Vietnam, Day interpreted Roger's death as a Christological act of global solidarity with the poor and victims of war, laying down his life so that others might live.[43] In 1973, Day accompanied UFW leaders César Chávez and Dolores Huerta, farmworkers, and over 100 priests, nuns, and lay people during strikes and protests in the San Joaquin Valley, California. She was arrested and imprisoned for twelve days in solidarity with the UFW, particularly with farmworker women who signed her prison uniform, which affirmed the dignity, justice, and community-based power of workers' nonviolent direct action for social change.[44]

Throughout her protest politics, Day together with the CWM and other activists were jailed for civil disobedience, but jail, as Day reflected during the anti–civil defense drills, facilitated the gospel imperative to identify in solidarity with the poor.

> We were frankly hoping for jail. Perhaps jail, we thought, would put another compulsion on us, of being more truly poor. Then we would not be running a house of hospitality . . . but would be truly one with them. We would be truly among the least of God's children, sharing with them in their misery.[45]

During these protests, which involved pacifist groups, civil disobedience, jail, and fasting, Day proclaimed the dignity and freedom of all humanity, made in the image and likeness of God.[46]

Similar to biblical prophetic traditions, Day drew on religious traditions that could facilitate critical dissent from an oppressive socio-political order as well as propel collective action (demonstrations, marches, rallies, and the like) against that order. The CWM engaged in varied protest politics

---

[42]Dorothy Day, "Prayer for Peace," in *Dorothy Day: Selected Writings*, ed. Ellsberg, 333.

[43]Dorothy Day, "A Brief Flame," in *Dorothy Day: Selected Writings*, ed. Ellsberg, 165–168.

[44]Dorothy Day, "Migrant Worker" and "A Brief Sojourn in Jail," in *Dorothy Day: Selected Writings*, ed. Ellsberg, 247–248, 253–258.

[45]Dorothy Day, "Visiting the Prisoner," in *Dorothy Day: Selected Writings*, ed. Ellsberg, 279.

[46]Day, "Prayer for Peace," 335.

Poverty, Personalism, and the Catholic Worker 81

to improve the living and working conditions of poor workers, and to advocate for socio-political change, beginning with but not limited to workers' rights. Day provided this protest politics with a theologically based vision of community to cure loneliness that, for Day, fundamentally and existentially characterized the human condition and especially plagued US socio-economic and political life.[47] Paralleling my feminist theological perspective of public theology as creating community, as ekklesial work, Day along with Maurin argued that "God is our creator, God made us in [their] image and likeness. . . . We become co-creators by our responsible acts, whether in bringing forth children, or producing food, furniture or clothing. The joy of creativeness should be ours."[48] Taking collective action through protest politics, in my view, better enabled Day and the CWM to express and begin to constructively create community and embody a good society modeled on Christian claims about the body of Christ.

The CWM farms can be construed as a prophetic practice of the human capacity for creating community. As Day observed, these farms were constituted by a "a community of families with a combination of private and communal property," who performed manual sustainable labor that supported themselves as well as the houses of hospitality, not only with food but also with retreats—"an oasis in the desert"—that involved masses, classes, farm labor, and in other ways material and spiritual sustenance.[49] However, in my understanding, Day strived to build an alternative social order, to create community politically, based on the theological notion of the mystical body of Christ (the interconnection and interdependence of all life in the reality of God) and engaged in prophetic protest politics to begin to realize that social order: "The vision is this. We are working for 'a new heaven and a new earth wherein justice dwelleth.' We are trying to say with action, 'Thy will be done on earth as it is in heaven.' We are working for a Christian social order."[50]

Christology informed and influenced a theo-symbolic rationale both for Day's protest politics and for Day's vision of the good society which these protest politics aimed to realize through the nonviolent "weapons of the works of mercy for immediate means to show our love and to alleviate suffering."[51] Day's theological vision of the *imago Dei* and of the good society, based on theological notions of the body of Christ and

---

[47]Day, *Long Loneliness*, 243, 286.
[48]Ibid., 227.
[49]Ibid., 224, 234, 250–251, 263.
[50]Dorothy Day, "Aims and Purposes," in *Dorothy Day: Selected Writings*, ed. Ellsberg, 91.
[51]Day, *Long Loneliness*, 181.

82   *Nevertheless, We Persist*

the kingdom of God, reconfigures a more emancipatory public life. Day argued that the first act of Jesus' public ministry involved overturning the moneylenders' tables in the Jerusalem temple, and not turning water into wine at the wedding feast at Cana in Galilee.[52] Built on a Christological basis of active public engagement, the CWM mounted a protest politics in collaborative solidarity with the perspectives, platforms, and organized protests of workers. The CWM participated in a variety of political actions, such as boycotts, strikes, and marches, as well as reported on these actions against unjust labor practices in multiple industries.[53] Through these actions, the CWM relied on the strike and the weapons of journalism to raise awareness about and eliminate the increasing inequalities of industrial corporate capitalism.

Through this protest politics, the CWM imagined and attempted to actualize an alternative social order, and Christology served as a theological cornerstone of Day's vision for a new this-worldly social order. Day together with Maurin imagined a good society, "a new society within the shell of the old" that emphasizes and recognizes our "common humanity" and enables "a society in which it is easier for [people] to be good."[54] Day's vision of a good society was shaped by social and civic life in the aftermath of the 1906 San Francisco earthquake, a vision rooted in distributive justice to lead an abundant life.[55] In addition to this formative early childhood experience, Day described her vision of the good society in theological terms of the mystical body of Christ, in which "we are all members one of another"; the image of the body of Christ (1 Cor. 12:12–27) underscores the interconnection and interdependence of all people in one another and in God. As Maurin affirmed about the CWM, "We are not an organization, we are an organism."[56] On this theological basis, Day articulated "a Christian social order" in which "a new heaven and a new earth" could become a possible intra-historical reality. Day strived for a this-worldly rather than otherworldly eschatological vision and reality of the good society, of the body of Christ. She characterized the CWM's small-scale work "to change the world. . . . We can work for the oasis, the little cell of joy and peace in a harried world. We can throw our pebble in the pond and be confident that its ever-widening circle will reach around the world."[57] She portrayed the CWM as a utopia, not in

---

[52]Ibid., 165–166.
[53]Ibid., 180–181, 205–213.
[54]Ibid., 170, 181.
[55]Ibid., 21–22, 39, 56.
[56]Ibid., 147, 182.
[57]Dorothy Day, "Love Is the Measure," in *Dorothy Day: Selected Writings*, ed. Ellsberg, 98.

Poverty, Personalism, and the Catholic Worker 83

the sense of no-place but in the sense of a this-worldly good place or good society that the CWM envisioned and partly actualized: "We were like workers for a utopia already living in their utopia." Such future-casting theo-politics contrasts with a Marxist criticism of religion as an opiate, a drug, and a prop for the weak, in which religion promotes an other-worldly eschatology or a postponed realization of the good life, of the kingdom of God, to a heavenly hereafter.[58]

Throughout the CWM's political protests which confronted the intersectional injustices of labor and immigration, war, racism, and violence, the CWM aimed to create an alternative Christologically based vision of an interdependent community by fostering a personalist theo-politics. Day articulated a theology of personalism which emphasized the personal worth and dignity of workers as persons, not objects, not the masses, not tools for making corporate profits.[59] A personalist theo-politics respects the dignity and worth of all people, is geared toward supporting personal relationships, and highlights taking personal responsibility for oneself, others, and society. Personalism does not promote a privatist, self-centered, egoistic, individualist approach to life; rather it prioritizes relationships. It also stresses the mutual cooperation and obligation of individuals and communities, rather than the city, state, or federal government, to initiate and sustain social change, which parallels the Catholic principle of subsidiarity.[60] An extended example from the CWM's anti-war activism shows, in my view, an inextricable interconnection between protest politics and a personalist interdependent society rooted in the body of Christ, which Day sought to co-create through action, through political praxis.

From its outset, the CWM and its revolutionary Christology espoused a protest politics that interconnected resistance to capitalism and poverty with anti-war attitudes and activism,[61] because both poverty and war undermine human rights to live and thrive. The CWM professed an unpopular pacifist approach to World War II, the Cold War, and the Vietnam War; for example, during WWII, the US houses of hospitality declined by half, and the newspaper's circulation was reduced. Day justified the CWM's anti-poverty and anti-war activism by fusing the gospel imperative for a new vision of a peaceful social order through the Sermon on the Mount with a critical analysis of a war-based economy: "Our whole modern economy is based on preparations for war and that is one of

---

[58]Day, *Long Loneliness*, 38–39, 43, quote at 247.
[59]Ibid., 220–221.
[60]Ibid., 179, 195, and "Aims and Means," 95–96.
[61]Day, *Long Loneliness*, 264.

the great modern arguments for poverty. If the comfort one has gained has resulted in the deaths of thousands in Korea and in other parts of the world, then that comfort will have to be atoned for. The argument now is that there is no civilian population, that all are involved in the war (misnamed 'defense') effort."[62] Day bolstered the CWM's pacifism through theological claims about the message and ministry of Christ, illustrated in the Sermon on the Mount (Matt. 5) and in the crucifixion. Jesus' message and ministry served as a theological basis for Day's vision of a pacifist society. Moreover, Jesus' death supported nonviolent practices of socio-political change. Day rejected any violent means toward social change on the basis of the cross; she rejected Communist, fascist, and Americanist views "that only by use of force, only by killing our enemies, not by loving them and giving ourselves up to death, giving ourselves up to the cross, will we conquer."[63] The CWM continues this Christological rationale for nonviolent peaceful protest: "Jesus taught us to take suffering upon ourselves rather than inflict it upon others. . . . Refusal to pay taxes for war, to register for conscription, to comply with any unjust legislation; participation in nonviolent strikes and boycotts, protests, or vigils; withdrawal of support from dominant systems, corporate funding or usurious practices are all excellent means to establish peace."[64] The cross of Christ, which exemplifies self-sacrifice for others, stresses conquest through suffering rather than through war. Based on a traditional theological interpretation of the cross, the CWM utilized nonviolent direct action as a means of protest which reflected the kind of pacifist society that Day sought.

The CWM's pacifism extended to Cold War protests, or resistance to the stockpiling of weapons of mass destruction, including nuclear weapons, in the US and the Soviet Union in the aftermath of WWII. Between 1955 and 1961, New York conducted civil defense drills in preparation for possible attacks. In contrast to these drills, which mandated that all citizens leave public spaces and enter shelters, Day participated in public acts of civil disobedience by organizing annual public protests or community gatherings in City Hall Park. These protests criticized war and an ever more military-based economy; as Day explained, "We were setting our faces against the world, against things as they are, the terrible injustice of our capitalist industrial system which lives by war and preparing for war; setting our faces against race hatreds and all nationalist strivings.

---

[62]Ibid., 263–264, and Day, "Little by Little," 111.
[63]Dorothy Day, "Use of Force," in *Dorothy Day: Selected Writings*, ed. Ellsberg, 78.
[64]Day, "Aims and Means," 96.

Poverty, Personalism, and the Catholic Worker 85

But especially we wanted to act against war and preparation for war ... against the entire military state."[65] Also, these protests attempted to publicize and realize the CWM's vision of community; the air raid drills promoted isolation, fear, and alienation, while the park protests demonstrated a communal gathering in solidarity, which grew to thousands by the time the drills ended in 1961.

Through practices of writing, theology, and public protests, Day and the CWM articulated and attempted to make real their fundamental theological commitments to basic human dignity of all people, grounded in theological claims about the body of Christ. Poverty and war diminished that dignity and freedom; reporting, rethinking theological claims and symbols, and taking collective action through protest politics not only constituted critical public engagement, but also partly constructed and enacted an alternative vision of a good society based on theological claims to build and enhance community, exemplified by the life, ministry, death, and resurrection of Jesus.

Women, Public Theology, and a Praxical Christology

When Pope Francis visited the US and addressed a joint session of the US Congress in Fall 2015, he praised Day's "social activism, her passion for justice and for the cause of the oppressed, [which] were inspired by the Gospel, her faith, and the example of the saints."[66] The CWM's program of action advocated for and allied with the poor and the oppressed, flowed from a gospel praxis-based Christology sourced in the Sermon on the Mount and the works of mercy, and utilized multiple rhetorical, symbolic, and prophetic practices of public engagement—illustrated by Day's journalism, theology, and protest politics—all to actively co-create a new vision of a just and peaceful social order based on the theological notions of equal human dignity in the image of God and in the body of Christ. The CWM aims to be and build up the body of Christ in US public life by performing Christological acts of solidarity, by emulating Christ's life, ministry, death, and resurrection through multiple forms of public engagement. Day's prophetic praxis of protest politics particularly combined critical dissent with collective action to visibilize and actualize the mystical body of Christ, a new socio-political order that advanced and enhanced the interrelational interdependence of all life.

---

[65]Day, "Visiting the Prisoner," 280.

[66]Stephanie Kirchgaessner, "Pope Francis's Message to Congress," *The Guardian*, September 24, 2015.

Christological symbols can be leveraged to legitimate and sustain patriarchal/kyriarchal worldviews and norms, or they can be reconstructed to promote alternative liberating worldviews; to rethink gender, race, class, sexual, and interreligious norms; and, ultimately, to edge us toward more egalitarian and just relations. Within public theology, Christology serves as a particularly problematic theological symbol in dominant Christian theologies with respect to its implications for who and what constitutes the church's religious and public actors and activities. A feminist public theology of ekklesial work, of creating community through multiple religio-political practices, cannot easily follow predominant Catholic Christologies, in which Jesus embodies the image of God and models discipleship as well as redeemed humanity in community. As the following analysis will show, the symbol of Christ functions in major magisterial writings—from Pope John Paul II to Pope Benedict XVI—in a fixed physicalist way that reduces the incarnation to Jesus' male or masculinized body, and consequently justifies patriarchal/kyriarchal constructions of gender norms, roles, and relations in both religious and political life. Catholic magisterial theologies religiously justify and reinforce kyriarchal norms, roles, and relations for men and women in the church and in society, in ways that reduce women and men to biophysically based and ontologically fixed or determined attributes that dictate and differentiate gender and other roles, religiously and politically.

Women's prophetic witness and praxis in contemporary US faith-based social movements like the Catholic Worker begin to birth a new world that supports and safeguards civil and human rights for all people of all genders, races/ethnicities, classes, orientations, abilities, and religions. Although US Catholic women, increasingly women religious, demonstrate the *de facto* face of public Catholicism, they lack *de jure* theological legitimacy to do public theology, to act as the public church. In other words, although Vatican II identifies political participation for all Catholics as a practical effect of the sacrament of baptism (*GS*, para. 43),[67] in the US Catholic context, women's religio-political witness is situated in a highly contested site of who counts as authoritative agents and what counts as authoritative practices of public Catholicism. In this context, women are disregarded as public theologians for anthropological, Christological, and soteriological reasons. Women are barred from imitating and resignifying Christ in ecclesial leadership positions and thus are excluded from public ministry, from doing public theology.

---

[67]"Pastoral Constitution on the Church in the Modern World: *Gaudium et Spes*, 7 December 1965," in *Vatican Council II: The Basic Sixteen Documents*, ed. Austin Flannery, OP (Northport, NY: Costello, 1996). Cited in parentheticals with paragraph numbers.

Poverty, Personalism, and the Catholic Worker

In the 1995 "Letter to Women," written for the United Nations conference on women in Beijing,[68] the late Pope John Paul II advocated for "real" gender equality, especially with regard to women's social, economic, and political rights (paras. 4, 6). Equal creation in the image of God (paras. 7–8) grounds a theological basis for gender equality. However, claiming equal creation in the *imago Dei* need not subvert social inequalities in race, gender, class, sexual, and human-earthly relations. This papal letter elaborated a "different but equal" theological anthropology that, in fact, leads to a "different and unequal" status for women. The letter emphasized gender complementarity, or defined women primarily in relation to men on the physical, psychological, and ontological grounds of women's capacity for self-gift. Women's capacity for self-gift, to give help to men (paras. 7, 10), in the letter is attributed to women's reproductive and maternal ability. Moreover, as the late Pope argued, women's biological and social capacity to give and nurture life shapes and structures women's ways of knowing and being human, such that all women express an "affective, cultural and spiritual motherhood" (para. 9) in service (para. 12).

When applied to public theology, the late Pope elaborated a biologically determinist view of women's political subjectivity, agency, and engagement, which reduces women to their maternal body and elides or negates the plurality of their embodied experiences of race, gender, class, sexuality, and ability shaped by varied social, cultural, and historical contexts. In the letter, women's bio-physical maternal nature or "genius" (paras. 9, 11, 12) fits all women—regardless of parental status or context, social location, etc.—for rendering an altruistic "service of love" (para. 10) to others and society in pursuit of producing a "civilization of love" (para. 4). Parallel to romantic or cultural feminism, which bases women's political action on highly idealized kyriarchal norms of heteronormative motherhood,[69] the late Pope proposed that women participate in public life, because they actualize their maternal genius to improve the public good.

Nearly a decade later in the 2004 "Letter to Bishops,"[70] written by the late Pope Benedict XVI, then Cardinal Joseph Ratzinger and the head of the Congregation for the Doctrine of the Faith, reasserted an anthropology of heteronormative gender complementarity on the theological grounds of creation, Christology, and soteriology. Although appealing to the Trinity

---

[68]Pope John Paul II, "Letter to Women," June 29, 1995. Cited in parentheticals with paragraph numbers.

[69]Rosemarie Putnam Tong, *Feminist Thought: A More Comprehensive Introduction*, 4th ed. (Boulder, CO: Westview Press, 2013).

[70]"Letter to the Bishops of the Catholic Church on the Collaboration of Men and Women in the Church and in the World," May 31, 2004. Cited in parentheticals with paragraph numbers.

as a model of egalitarian human relations (paras. 6, 7) and advocating for women's equal access to social, economic, and political life (paras. 13, 14), the letter utilized a creation-based account of physical, psychological, and ontological complementarity between men and women (paras. 5, 6, 8). Against the biblical backdrop of Genesis 2, women's identities in the letter are structured according to their bodily (in this case, bio-physical) heteronormative nature and status (para. 13). Consequently, women are intrinsically endowed with certain gendered "values" and "traits" (paras. 14, 16)—such as "listening, welcoming, humility"—which orient them by their nature in a submissive, subservient way to and "for the other" (paras. 6, 14), to serve the common good by actualizing their nature and associated traits. Arguably cultivated by all baptized members of the church, women signify these traits ontologically or naturally, which corresponds theologically with a soteriological marital metaphor between Christ and the church (para. 16).

Moreover, this letter theologically legitimates heteronormative gender relations through its interpretation of a divinely ordained marital metaphor within a soteriological economy. In Catholic theology, salvation in Christ is portrayed in the scriptures via spousal symbolism between Christ and the church (Eph. 5:22–33), in which Christ the Bridegroom and head of the church saves the bride and body of the church. In addition to reinforcing all sorts of hierarchical gendered and other dualisms, the letter applies this soteriological spousal symbolism as a literalized theological norm to justify and prescribe "the very nature" of divine-human relations in salvation (paras. 9–10) as well as gender roles and relations between clergy and laity (paras. 11–12). These sexed and gendered soteriological symbols carry deep implications for heteronormative binary sex and gender roles and relations; this nuptial ecclesiology and Christology undergird an "iconic complementarity" for gender roles in the church and in society. When situated within this literalized soteriological spousal imagery, women cannot function as Christ, the church's head, and thereby cannot be ordained or participate in decision-making roles. Only men definitively represent Christ's active offer of salvation as the Bridegroom to the church, who receives and responds to the offer as the Bride. Summarizing the institutional church's scriptural, historical, theological, and pastoral arguments on the non-ordination of Catholic women,[71] women cannot serve as Christic icons in ordained ministry because they are not male;

---

[71]Deborah Halter, *The Papal No: The Vatican's Refusal to Ordain Women* (New York: Crossroad, 2004).

Poverty, Personalism, and the Catholic Worker 89

they do not resignify the masculinized head of the church derived from the male-sexed body of Jesus in the incarnation. Thus, this soteriological symbolism asserts a patriarchal/kyriarchal Christology and anthropology in which most women, like the church, are defined in submissive and responsive relations to elite, ordained men who resignify Christ. When framed within this literalized imagery, women together with non-ordained men are actively "listening and receiving the Word of God" (para. 15); in effect, women are alienated from imitating or emulating Christ, boxed into modeling dominant anthropologies and their associated ideologies, portrayed as passive recipients rather than active agents of the church's mission and message in ecclesial and, by implication, public life. Thus, women are excluded from resignifying Christ in ordained ministry, and invisibilized in the church's public ministry.

In sum, both letters utilize theological symbols such as creation in the divine image to justify gender equality in the church and society. Nonetheless, both letters ultimately undermine that equality with a bio-physicalist anthropology and static symbol of the *imago Christi*, which in turn alienates women from leadership roles in the church's ordained and public ministry. Imitating Christ in dominant magisterial theologies is connected to religious constructions of biologically based and hetero-normative gender norms and roles. Unable to stand *in persona Christi*, women's capacity to engage in public life emerges from and is closely linked with their biological maternal genius. In both letters, dominant theological constructions of anthropology and Christology prove problematic for women, theologically and politically. Theologically, women's political agency and activism in both letters is situated within kyriarchal images and norms of motherhood, such that women embody service to the common good via their biological nature and its associated traits, rather than through their political praxis. Politically, both letters advance highly romanticized, hyperpatriarchal feminine roles for women as mothers that restrict women's ability to stand *in persona Christi*, whether in ecclesial ministry or public life. Excluded from sacramental ministry on anthropological and Christological grounds that they are not men and, therefore, cannot resignify the church's salvific mission, women are also barred from public ministry, from being the public church or doing public theology in ways that actualize the church's mission to advocate for human rights and the common good.

Christology, in conjunction with an anthropology of complementarity, blocks women from leading church positions (both in ecclesiastical and ecclesial ministry) and limits women's religio-political agency and activ-

90 *Nevertheless, We Persist*

ism, effectively shaping a primarily clericalist face and voice of the public church. A static or fixed incarnate identity of divine and human natures in the historical male person of Jesus proves problematic for women, both theologically and politically. As Elizabeth Johnson argues, the myopic focus on Jesus' maleness within dominant Christologies carries an "effective history" that questions women's theomorphic, Christomorphic, and salvific capacities, thereby relegating women to second-class citizens in the body of Christ and, by implication, in the body politic. Women cannot be construed as representatives of the public church, of the body of Christ in public, under a static physicalist incarnationalism that stresses the necessity of Jesus' maleness to know and image God, imitate Christ, and be saved.[72] Nevertheless, Christology still matters and can be critically appropriated for feminist theological reflection on the church's public engagement, for elaborating a feminist public theology of ekklesial work. Rather than judged theologically bankrupt for its apparent lack of emancipatory religio-political implications, Christology can be reconstructed in a feminist perspective to eschew essentialism or biological determinism found within patriarchal theologies, as well as to edge toward a more just theology of political participation, so that women are viewed as active agents of public theology.

Christology in *Gaudium et Spes* associated with Jesus' life-ministry for the coming kingdom of God and with becoming "artisans of a new humanity" holds untapped transformative theo-political potential for women to reclaim being the public church and doing public theology. Such an alternative theological symbolic for the public church may be advanced through a feminist reinterpretation of *Gaudium et Spes*, as elaborated in the preceding chapter. Although Vatican II paralleled US feminist movements, *Gaudium et Spes* attends primarily to human rights, civil rights, anti-war, and post-colonial movements rather than to gender justice in its pursuit of a more just public life.[73] The links between Christology and the Wisdom tradition are implicitly embedded in *Gaudium et Spes*. Passages that serve as the interpretive key to the entire constitution (*GS*, paras. 10, 22)[74] demonstrate, but do not yet forge, explicit links between

---

[72]Elizabeth A. Johnson, "The Maleness of Christ," in *The Power of Naming: A Concilium Reader in Feminist Liberation Theology,* ed. Elisabeth Schüssler Fiorenza (Maryknoll, NY: Orbis Books, 1996), 307–315, esp. 307–308, and *She Who Is: Mystery of God in Feminist Theological Discourse* (New York: Crossroad, 1992), 151–153.

[73]Anne E. Patrick, "Toward Renewing the 'Life and Culture of Fallen Man': *Gaudium et Spes* as Catalyst for Catholic Feminist Theology," in *Feminist Ethics and the Catholic Moral Tradition,* ed. Charles E. Curran, Margaret A. Farley, and Richard A. McCormick, S.J. (New York: Paulist, 1996), 483–510.

[74]Walter Kasper, "The Theological Anthropology of *Gaudium et Spes*," *Communio* 23 (1996):

Poverty, Personalism, and the Catholic Worker 91

its Christology and the Wisdom tradition. These passages refer to Jesus as "the image of the invisible God, the firstborn of all creation," from Colossians 1:15, which belongs within the Wisdom literature of Jewish scriptures. Applying an insight from Mary Catherine Hilkert, I propose to critically retrieve and recuperate a performative Christology in *Gaudium et Spes* through the Wisdom tradition.[75]

Feminist theologians and biblical scholars have critically engaged the Wisdom tradition to challenge exclusively enshrined elite masculinist and racialized symbols and language for God as well as restrictions on the imitation as well as sacramental signification of Jesus the Christ, the incarnate but often West-centric whitewashed male image of God.[76] Appearing in the biblical and apocryphal texts of Proverbs, Sirach, the Wisdom of Solomon, and others, the Wisdom tradition describes a female personification of the divine (Prov. 1:20–33, 8:22–26) who participates in creating, redeeming, and sustaining everyday life (Prov. 3:18–19, 4:13, 8:27–31), especially by acting as prophetic street preacher (Prov. 8:1–6) and banquet host of justice and peace (Prov. 9:1–6). Early Christian communities borrowed from the Wisdom tradition to explain Jesus' divine identity and soteriological significance. What Jesus did in his prophetic life-ministry disclosed who Jesus was, namely, his identity as the earthly representative of divine Wisdom and the redeemer. Jesus the Christ proclaimed by early Christian communities as incarnate Wisdom, Sophia, has less to do with the metaphysical makeup of Jesus' human and divine natures codified in the Christological councils, and more to do with his deeds, his performative praxis of empowering right relations. Portraying Jesus as Wisdom contests and counteracts prevalent ideological symbols and language for the reality of God and the imitation of Jesus, thereby opening up theological space for women to regain their theomorphic ability to identify with and image God in Jesus, in both sacred and political ways. Furthermore, a feminist critical appropriation of the Wisdom

---

129–140, esp. 137.

[75]Mary Catherine Hilkert, "*Imago Dei*: Does the Symbol Have a Future?" *The Santa Clara Lectures* 8, no. 3 (April 2002). Proverbs is bookended by parallel portraits of Wisdom (Prov. 1–9) and the capable wife (Prov. 31). Both figures are contrasted with the strange woman (Prov. 2:16–19, 5:3–6, 7:5–27). Biblical scholars caution against how Wisdom traditions reinscribe patriarchal gender stereotypes. Claudia Camp, *Wisdom and the Feminine in the Book of Proverbs* (Decatur, GA: Almond Press, 1985), and *Wise, Strange, and Holy: The Strange Woman and the Making of the Bible* (Sheffield, UK: Sheffield Academic Press, 2000).

[76]Johnson, *She Who Is*, 86–100, and "Redeeming the Name of Christ: Christology," in *Freeing Theology: The Essentials of Theology in Feminist Perspective*, ed. Catherine Mowry LaCugna (New York: HarperCollins, 1993), 115–137, esp. 120–127; Elisabeth Schüssler Fiorenza, *In Memory of Her: A Feminist Theological Reconstruction of Christian Origins* (New York: Crossroad, 1983), and *Jesus: Miriam's Child, Sophia's Prophet* (New York: Continuum, 1994).

tradition highlights the salvific significance of Jesus' life-ministry for bringing about the kingdom of God. Focusing on Wisdom's empowering and vivifying deeds of creation, liberation, and sustainability shown in Jesus' liberative preaching, healing, and inclusive eating practices (*GS*, para. 32) as well as in similar deeds of his followers enables women and men to reclaim their Christomorphic capacity to emulate Jesus in their liberative praxis, not in their bodies.

This reading of *Gaudium et Spes* from feminist theological perspectives on the Wisdom tradition reveals its often overlooked Wisdom Christology that restores theological significance and visibility to women's religio-political action for the common good. Vatican II's Constitution on the Church in the Modern World associates the church's faith-based public engagement with realizing the already-present but always ever-coming eschatological reign of God, that is, the good society of love, justice, and peace. This constitution identifies the church's public role as a critical advocate for a broad social justice agenda that seeks to subvert injustice and inequality along gender, race, class, socio-political, religious, and inter/national lines. To enact this agenda and to fulfill the church's sacramental religio-political significance, this constitution calls for emulating the prophetic life-ministry of Jesus. Living out a political kind of discipleship based on Jesus' prophetic lifework for the kingdom of God serves as a theological touchstone for women to reclaim their baptismal and religio-political rights to faith-based activism for justice in the US public sphere. In a critical feminist retrieval of Wisdom Christology in *Gaudium et Spes*, women imitate Christ by actively participating in a liberating ministry for creating community, and by engaging in a political and praxical kind of discipleship based on living out major principles and patterns of Jesus' prophetic lifework for the kingdom of God. From a feminist perspective, women's religio-political participation has more to do with their active agency for justice, with becoming Christic "artisans of a new humanity" than with their maternal nature. Feminist Wisdom Christology, thus, shifts the theological emphasis from the person to the ministry of Jesus, and in so doing enables and empowers women to reclaim their right to be the public church, to identify with and imitate Jesus' mission—to resignify Jesus—by actively continuing his life-ministry through their political praxis. Conformity to Christ (Gal. 3:26-28; 2 Cor. 3:18; cf. *GS*, para. 22) consists of imitating Jesus' ministry, not his maleness or any feature of his historical identity. As Johnson concludes, "Being christomorphic is not a sex distinctive gift. The image of Christ does not lie in sexual similarity to the human man Jesus but in coherence with the narrative

Poverty, Personalism, and the Catholic Worker   93

shape of his compassionate liberating life in the world, through the power of the Spirit."[77] Being Christomorphic involves political and performative—not biological—solidarity with Jesus. Expanding on Hilkert's insight, enfleshing communion or what I call ekklesial work—to build just and life-giving, transforming, and sustaining community with others, including the earth—is performed, individually and collectively.

Womanist theologies "as an opportunity to state the meanings of God in the real time of Black women's lives"[78] complexify a feminist Christological focus on Jesus' liberating ministry to further entail a ministry of mutual accompaniment and struggle with suffering peoples[79] in sustaining the search for solidarity, through which we continually re/create ourselves and our world in and for inclusive just relationships, for equal, mutual, solidaristic relations. Womanist theology prioritizes Black women's lived realities of the troubling intersections among racism, hetero/sexism, and poverty, and engages in critical and constructive theological praxis to advocate for the full humanity of Black women and the Black community,[80] confronted by the dehumanizing legacies of slavery, Jim Crow segregation, the new Jim Crow of hyperracialized incarceration, state-sanctioned violence and police brutality, and the repeated resurgent rise of US white nationalist populist movements that emerge from and legitimate racist ideologies of white supremacy and privilege. Elucidating and enacting key principles from Alice Walker's innovative definition of the term, womanists' strong self-love and love of the community, regardless, prompt audacious, sociopolitically courageous, Spirit-inspired struggle for the agency, survival, and wholeness of an entire people as they "confront, racism, sexism, classism, and heterosexism not only as they impinge upon the Black community, but also as they are nurtured within that community . . . , remain in solidarity with their oppressed sisters around the world . . . [and] recognize the importance of wholeness," personally and communally.[81]

Delores Williams's trailblazing work in womanist God-talk drew on multidisciplinary sources[82] to firmly found womanist theology both on

---

[77]Johnson, "The Maleness of Christ," 313, and "Redeeming the Name of Christ," 129.

[78]Stephanie Y. Mitchem, *Introducing Womanist Theology* (Maryknoll, NY: Orbis Books, 2002), 60.

[79]Jacquelyn Grant, "'Come to My Help, Lord, for I'm in Trouble': Womanist Jesus as the Mutual Struggle for Liberation," in *Reconstructing the Christ Symbol: Essays in Feminist Christology*, ed. Maryanne Stevens (New York: Paulist Press, 1993), 66–69; Kelly Brown Douglas, *The Black Christ* (Maryknoll, NY: Orbis Books, 1994), 108–110.

[80]Grant, "'Come to My Help, Lord, for I'm in Trouble,'" 54–66.

[81]Douglas, *The Black Christ*, 98–99, 102, 104.

[82]Mitchem, *Introducing Womanist Theology*, 55–64, 87–91.

94 *Nevertheless, We Persist*

Black women's intersectional[83] experiences of religion with race, gender, sexuality, and class, and on Black women's experiences of varied "struggle for survival and for the development of a positive, productive quality of life" that depends on divine accompaniment and divinely empowered human actions for seeking well-being and freedom amid the death-dealing religio-political cultures of demonarchy.[84] In the same theological vein, M. Shawn Copeland explores the postmodern theological turn to the subject—to the marginalized subject, not the Enlightenment's nationally, culturally, and racially privileged subject of individuality, autonomy, and rationality[85]—with implications for a social Trinitarian theology rooted in Christology. Copeland prioritizes the embodied subjectivity of poor women of color to challenge how "we have all betrayed the very meaning of humanity—our own, the humanity of exploited, despised women of color, and the humanity of our God."[86] Exemplified by the subjugated body of Jesus under Roman imperial rule and colonial culture, all our bodies are regulated, negatively marked, and thereby fragmented from ourselves, one another, and the earth, and ultimately from God by contemporary forms of imperialism, such as racism, hetero/sexism, xenophobic backlash against immigrants and refugees, war, poverty, and so on.[87] Situating subjectivity in an incarnational frame of the inclusive solidaristic ministry of Jesus in relation to God and others in the quest for God's reign of love and justice,[88] being human for Copeland can oppose such de-creation and instead can interpret body marks positively, in ways that "ground intelligence, discovery, beauty, and joy; enable apprehension and response to sensible experiences; and shape culture, society, and religion. . . . The body's marks complexify through creolization, *mestizaje*, and hybridity."[89] Copeland thus proposes a Christology and social Trinitarian theology in which "we all may recognize, love, and realize our bodyselves as Jesus' own flesh, as the body of Christ,"[90] especially in solidaristic relations. As Copeland argues, "If personhood is now understood to flow from formative living in community, rather than individualism, from the embrace of

---

[83]Kimberlé Crenshaw, "Demarginalizing the Intersection of Race and Sex: A Black Feminist Critique of Antidiscrimination Doctrine, Feminist Theory and Antiracist Politics," *University of Chicago Legal Forum* (1989): 139–167.

[84]Delores S. Williams, *Sisters in the Wilderness: The Challenge of Womanist God-talk* (Maryknoll, NY: Orbis Books, 1993), xii, 6–7, 33.

[85]M. Shawn Copeland, *Enfleshing Freedom: Body, Race, and Being* (Minneapolis: Fortress Press, 2010), 9–12.

[86]Ibid., 88, 90.

[87]Ibid., 55–61, 65–78.

[88]Ibid., 61–65, 80–81.

[89]Ibid., 56.

[90]Ibid., 78.

Poverty, Personalism, and the Catholic Worker 95

difference and interdependence rather than their exclusion, then we can realize our personhood only in solidarity with the exploited, despised, poor 'other.' "[91] As Copeland shows, perichoretic mutual love relations of the divine persons within God and between God and humanity in the body of Christ "reminds us of our inalienable relation to one another in God, and steadies our efforts on that absolute future that only God can give."[92] Realizing more just communal relations, albeit partially and imperfectly, is grounded in Christological solidarity. Moreover, this solidarity in light of Trinitarian theology stresses the full realization of personhood through the present communal praxis of social justice-oriented relations as an eschatological foretaste of our already but not yet fully realized future participation in Trinitarian relations. By constructing such a praxis-based rather than physicalist Christology from the resources of Vatican II and feminist as well as womanist theology, doing public theology widens to incorporate any person or group (organization, social movement, and the like) which serves as a Christological "harbinger" (*GS*, para. 92) or sacrament of the already begun but not yet fully realized relationship in the Trinity, in the family of God.

More importantly for the Catholic Worker's aim to birth a new future, birthing a new world resists *both* Catholic magisterial anthropologies, which essentialize and politicize women's bio-physical abilities to give birth, *and* traditionalist political ideologies, which domesticize and thereby disqualify women as reasoning and judging citizens in the public sphere and instead portray their interests as aligned solely with the nonpolitical or private sphere, that is, with the reproduction of future citizens. Rather than concede to patriarchal/kyriarchal theologies and politics, birthing metaphors can be reclaimed for their religio-political salience. Birthing metaphors need not be trapped in and need not entrap women in a reductive view of reproductivity.[93] For example, feminist biblical interpretations of the family structure in the kingdom of God broaden maternity beyond biology into a larger social-political notion of generativity. As long noted by feminist and *mujerista* theologians as well as biblical scholars, the kin-dom or family of God is defined in the Gospels and early Christian literature not by blood kinship and patriarchal structures of family relations, but by discipleship. Situated within a

---

[91]Ibid., 89; cf. 92–95, 99–101.
[92]Ibid., 102–103, quote at 103; cf. 104.
[93]Susan A. Ross, *Extravagant Affections: A Feminist Sacramental Theology* (New York: Continuum, 1998), and Christine E. Gudorf, "The Power to Create: Sacraments and Men's Need to Birth," *Horizons* 14, no. 2 (1987): 296–309.

96   *Nevertheless, We Persist*

rich theological horizon of generativity that is not reduced to maternity, the new family of God includes women and men who act as hearers and doers of the eschatological message and ministry of Jesus for justice (Matt. 12:46–50; Mark 3:31–35; Luke 8:19–21). By elaborating a participatory and praxical Christology through the theological resources of feminist Wisdom Christology and gospel-based views of the family of God, a feminist public theology stresses generativity as a major feature of the church's public engagement. Rather than limited to clerical or other institutional church representatives who speak in public about pressing political concerns from a religious perspective, a feminist approach to public theology emphasizes the kind of society that is generated—i.e., imagined, created, and sustained—through the church's—i.e., the whole church's—political agency and action. Also, biblical texts describe all creation groaning (in travail, in childbirth) for fulfillment, that is, for a just and peaceful society (Rom. 8:18–23). Together with creation and the cosmos, all are called to play a part in actively creating, generating, or birthing a new society, signifying in their praxis the metaphorical birth pangs of the reign of God. From this feminist theological perspective of ekklesial work, creativity broadens, deepens, and democratizes the agents and the activities of public theology. Women are enabled to reclaim their right to do public theology through religio-political prophetic praxis of actively co-creating communities of justice and peace. Creating and witnessing to a more just common life—which we as artisans according to *Gaudium et Spes* co-create with God and with one another—takes place among men and women, clergy and laity, scholars and activists, single leaders and social movements, that induce in and through their praxis the birth pangs of being in and becoming the reign of God, of ushering in religio-political conditions that nurture justice, love, and peace.

Revolutionary Love Project

As illustrated by the Catholic Worker Movement (CWM) and its leading light, Dorothy Day, women's public or religio-political engagement taps a shared human capacity for creativity. From feminist and womanist Christological perspectives, women's approaches to public theology stress a solidarity-based praxis of political Christologically based love to embody and build community, which together open up new horizons for public theo-political imagination and activism, especially now in more intercultural and interreligious ways. Doing public theology rooted in

Poverty, Personalism, and the Catholic Worker 97

troubling, disruptive, and liberative political love and in interreligious engagement particularly but not only takes place in contemporary social justice movements like the Revolutionary Love Project (RLP).

Describing and analyzing the RLP led by Valarie Kaur yields fresh insights into women's religio-political roles and praxis of what I call creating community or ekklesial work in US public life. RLP redefines and expands the public sphere of religion and politics in multiracial, multicultural, and multifaith ways. In an unexpected parallel with the CWM, RLP reclaims and elaborates on love as a theo-political ethic of justice based on its trifold notion and praxis of love as seeing no strangers, tending personal and socio-political wounds, and birthing a new future. RLP's praxis provides potent insights into a feminist public theology of love and justice, with broader implications for the role and purpose of religion in US public life. Kaur invokes religio-political imagery between death and new life to accentuate that we live in liminal times between an oppressive present and an alternative more just future, in spaces between seemingly perennially polarized and potentially interconnected groups. Based on insights from feminist theological anthropology in an earlier chapter, these interstitial times and spaces offer opportunities for new movements to arise and build solidarity. In these ways, RLP exemplifies women's faith-based public engagement for prophetic world-making, that is, the fusion of religion and politics to denounce and criticize an unjust US public life, on the one hand, and to announce and actualize—imagine and partly incarnate, or envision and enflesh—an alternative more just liberative world, on the other hand.

Valarie Kaur stands out among contemporary religious leaders in the US public square involved in prophetic work.[94] Kaur is a Sikh activist, award-winning documentary filmmaker, and civil rights lawyer who partnered with communities of color and other marginalized communities (Sikh, Muslim, Black, Latinx, LGBTQ+, and Indigenous peoples) since the 9/11 terrorist attacks and since the November 2016 US presidential election to oppose the rise in Islamophobic and white nationalist hate crimes as well as other forms of patriarchal/kyriarchal authoritarianism. Emerging from such solidarity work, Kaur launched RLP, a project of the nonprofit organization Community Fathers, and housed virtually at its ever-expanding website. RLP sponsored a multi-city nationwide Together Tour in 2016 to emphasize love as a public ethic that opposes anti-Sikh, anti-Muslim,

---

[94]Valarie Kaur, *See No Stranger: A Memoir and Manifesto of Revolutionary Love* (New York: OneWorld, 2020).

98   *Nevertheless, We Persist*

and anti-Asian racism, nationalism, and hate. After the election, Kaur collaborated with many movement leaders to host a Watch Night Service at the historic Metropolitan AME Church in Washington, DC, on New Year's Eve, as well as coordinated a fast, multifaith prayer gathering, and march on Inauguration Day 2017. In 2017, RLP sponsored one hundred film screenings, workshops, and keynotes for college students as well as lobbied congressional leaders to oppose the US Muslim travel ban, along with other discriminatory immigration and refugee policies, such as racial profiling and surveillance, special registries, detention, family separation, deportation, and border walls. RLP stood on the front lines after mass shootings of Sikhs in the gurdwara in Oak Creek, Wisconsin; African American Christians in Mother Emanuel AME Church in Charleston, South Carolina; Jews at the Tree of Life Synagogue in Pittsburgh, Pennsylvania; and Muslims at mosques in Christchurch, New Zealand.

RLP's activities have spanned a book, reading guides about racial justice and solidarity for book clubs, media (e.g., podcasts, meditations, film, and TV episodes), an annual conference for more than three hundred grassroots multifaith leaders, and a retreat for Sikh women leaders, In addition RLP has sponsored nonviolent direct action campaigns, such as keynotes, anti-racism workshops, sermons in multifaith communities, get-out-the-vote rallies, and letters of love and solidarity to immigrants seeking asylum at the US border, especially women and children. For example, RLP co-sponsored a solidarity rally with the Poor People's Campaign on June 23, 2018, two hundred dialogues about practicing revolutionary love, and two thousand #VoteTogether gatherings during the US congressional midterm elections in Fall 2018. Also, Kaur with thirty-two diverse women leaders organized the third annual Women's March on January 19, 2019.[95] All these activities expose and oppose intersectional injustices of racism, poverty, militarism, sexism, and ecological devastation that manifest in the rollback of voting rights, women's rights, immigrant rights, just health care, and climate change policies. Most importantly, these mass mobilized actions embody love as a public ethic that fosters and births a new future for race, gender, economic, sexual, immigrant, and eco-justice.

Kaur delivered a highly acclaimed TED Talk that elaborated a feminist love ethic during the 2017 TEDWomen gathering. Kaur described this process of birthing a new world as a kind of midwifery. This one million-

---

[95]Women's March, or the most recent inter/national collective and coalitional protest for women's rights as human rights, initially consisted of over 670 marches, and totaled nearly 5 million marchers worldwide in solidarity with the over 1 million marchers on Washington, DC, on January 21, 2017. Mischa Hedges, *Women's March* (TrimTab Media, 2017).

Poverty, Personalism, and the Catholic Worker 99

plus-viewed talk[96] also informed Kaur's address to the 2018 Parliament of the World's Religions (PWR), in which she reiterated this ethic's three main practices of love of others, opponents, and ourselves to over eight thousand attendees, whom she described as "midwives . . . tasked with birthing a new future for all of us . . . [who] labor for justice with and through love together . . . [who] can begin to deliver the world we dream," a world that is multiracial, multicultural, multifaith, and rooted in revolutionary love seeking justice.[97] Since its inception, RLP has joined with about 550 organizations annually on Valentine's Day, both personally and virtually, to reclaim love as a public ethic. RLP allied with the Poor People's Campaign and Women's March leaders, among other US social justice movements, to sponsor "The Day of Revolutionary Love, The Day of Rising" in February 2018 to coincide with its annual V-Day actions to end gender-based violence. Reaching 14+ million people, this coalitional mass action countered the startling global rise of gender-based violence, xenophobic hate crimes, and white supremacist and nationalist movements. RLP partnered with more than fifty organizations for its V-Day activities in February 2019, including NETWORK, CLUE, and other interfaith groups, to articulate its three practices in a Declaration of Revolutionary Love.

Both Kaur's talks examine this three-pronged feminist love ethic and its public practices, which she described at the PWR as "a human birthright, a kind of labor that all of us are capable of," to advance and enhance a more just world for all. Love means to trouble, to disrupt an oppressive status quo, and ultimately to liberate. Kaur stated in her TED Talk, "Revolutionary love is the choice to enter into labor for others who do not look like us, for our opponents who hurt us, and for ourselves. . . . Love must be practiced in all three directions to be revolutionary."

First, love for others entails a practice, Kaur states, of seeing no stranger. Love for others as a rhetorical practice involves listening to others' stories in humility and in wonder, and enables us to see no stranger, to challenge the stereotypes that distort our vision of "black as criminal, of brown as illegal, of queer and trans as immoral, of Indigenous peoples as savage, and of women and girls as property," and ultimately to stand in solidarity with others, to labor with others through vigils, marches, and other forms of political participation. In my view, seeing no stranger, which Kaur claims is "a part of me I do not yet know," evokes a new theological

---

[96]Valarie Kaur, "Three Lessons of Revolutionary Love in a Time of Rage," TEDWomen 17, November 2017.

[97]Valarie Kaur, "Parliament of the World's Religions," YouTube video, February 14, 2019.

anthropology, or religious understanding of the human person as inherently interrelated in and with communities of origin and of solidarity, including the earth community. As the Declaration proclaims, "we vow to see one another as brothers, sisters, and siblings. Our humanity binds us together, and we vow to fight for a world where all of us can flourish."

Second, love for opponents necessitates a practice, Kaur explains, of symbolically and pragmatically tending the wound—that is, to seek structural and policy change toward reparative justice and healing, toward transformative reconciliation. Tending the wound in others, even enemies, entails moral and pragmatic practices; it reveals oppressive systems and structures that normalize and radicalize harm as well as erode the capability to love. As stated in the Declaration, "We vow to fight not with violence and vitriol, but by challenging the cultures and institutions that promote hate." Beyond resisting and replacing bad actors and policies, birthing a new just world begins by tending personal and socio-political wounds, by challenging and remaking those systemic structures of injustice that collide and collude in us and in our world to de-create, to undo all of our belonging and flourishing.

Third, love for ourselves is characterized by Kaur as a feminist intervention in this religio-political ethic of love, and illustrated by a prophetic practice of breathe and push. Love for others and oppressors requires self-love, as Kaur says to "love our own flesh" and "make our own flourishing matter" especially amid a rising politics of fear in anti-immigrant, anti-worker, anti-Asian, anti-Black, anti-Latinx, and anti-LGBTQIA+ hate. Self-love takes place in community to fully embrace ourselves and push through hostile times together. Self-love in community is emphasized in the Declaration: "We will protect our capacity for joy. We will rise and dance. We will honor our ancestors whose bodies, breath, and blood call us to a life of courage." Also, practicing self-love inspired Kaur to release in 2019 a meditation app with four tracks that integrate self-care (breathing together) and community care (pushing together for change).

Kaur offered encouragement to persevere and persist in the "labor for justice" in these bleak times, and reiterated this future-birthing, world-making imagery in ways that resonate with Christian notions of death and resurrection. Merging similar ideas from both talks, which Kaur initially developed for the Watch Night address, Kaur states:

> What if this darkness in the world is not the darkness of the tomb, but what if it is the darkness of the womb? What if our future, our America is not dead but is a country, a nation still waiting to be

Poverty, Personalism, and the Catholic Worker   **101**

born? What if a new world is waiting to be born?. . . What if the story of America is one long labor?. . . What if this is our nation's, our time of great transition? The midwife tells us to breathe and then to push. Because if we don't push we will die. If we don't breathe we will die. If we don't push now, our nation will die.[98]

Although Kaur outlined this feminist love ethic by drawing on Sikh theology and the writings of Black feminist bell hooks and others, RLP illuminates what I propose and outline as ekklesial work or community creating practice, expressed in women's ways of doing public theology.

Dorothy Day's Christology aligns with what Valarie Kaur describes as love of others, as tending our socio-political wounds. Day situated the historical Jesus' life and death in the imperial, colonial, oppressed context of his ministry in Roman-ruled Palestine in order to follow that Christological-model of solidarity through the direct practice of love for justice via the works of mercy in the houses of hospitality, to criticize contemporary social structures of injustice through journalism, and to constructively advocate for change through prophetic protest politics and activism. In our time, Black Catholic womanist theologian M. Shawn Copeland articulates a political Christology in which the body of the crucified Jesus inflicted by Roman imperial indignities and injustices refracts the wounds similarly inflicted on marginalized peoples by contemporary empires. Opposition and otherness based on dominant and subordinate relations along race, gender, class, religious, sexual, and many other identity marks of our differences in turn justify assault, conquest, occupation, detention, torture, incarceration, sexual shame and abuse, even execution. Prophetic social movements like the Catholic Worker and RLP identify and tend these wounds to effect social change and justice.

Moreover, Day's Christology enabled and enacted new ways of seeing the *imago Dei* and the *imago Christi* in all as other Christs, thereby seeing with new eyes no stranger but in all Jesus the Christ, and ultimately to seeing beyond Jesus, to take what she has seen and heard and to prophetically proclaim and enact justice. Seeing no stranger creates new visions of life-giving communities that as Copeland states "re-order us, re-member us, restore us, and make us one" not only in the body of Christ but also, as Kaur expresses, in the US body politic.[99]

---

[98]Valarie Kaur, "Video: Valarie Kaur Delivers Rousing Speech in Church," SikhNet, January 20, 2017.

[99]Copeland, *Enfleshing Freedom*, 82–83, 128.

102   *Nevertheless, We Persist*

Finally, self-love and communal solidarity coincide, as demonstrated by Kaur's questions in the PWR address: "How are you breathing today?. . . Who are you breathing with? . . . with the ones you love . . . with the earth, sea, and sky . . . with some of the ancestors at your back?. . . Can you breathe in order to remember all that is beautiful and good and worth fighting for?" In deeply distressing times, CWM retreats allowed Day and activists to regroup, reorganize, and remobilize their ongoing witness together; their self-love empowered them to envision and realize new more loving and justice-seeking ways of life.

RLP offers compelling personal and political ways for doing the community building, the world-making, of a feminist public theology of ekklesial work, that is, to imagine and incarnate, to envision and enflesh, a more just world for the flourishing of all. RLP amplifies and expands on Day's and the CWM's radical love in community. Kaur states, "Close your eyes. Can you feel it? What does it feel like in your body to live in that future?. . . .If we can inhabit this vision in our minds and bodies, then we can birth it."[100] Building on its trifold public ethic of love (others, opponents, ourselves), which links personal and socio-political change, RLP led the way in such world-making via the People's Inauguration in January 2021, modeled on RLP virtual gatherings held between March and June 2020 during the COVID-19 pandemic. Starting on January 21, 2021, and continuing for the ensuing ten days, this teaching series featured approximately seventy-five visionaries, faith and social movement leaders, activists, and artists. The People's Inauguration encouraged 115 million online attendees to individually and collectively take oaths to recommit to one another, to core moral values, and to themselves—to "be inaugurated into that long labor of healing and reimagining and rebuilding this country," as Kaur stated in the kickoff event, to envision and co-create an inclusive common good for all of we, the people in US public life.

During the People's Inauguration, prophetic practices supported and enacted rhetorical and symbolic practices of RLP to imagine and point to new possibilities for an anti-racist, equitable, and sustainable beloved community that offers new ways of seeing each other and catalyzes new shifts toward a more expansive cultural consciousness of who belongs in we, the people. RLP's vision of a multifaith, multiracial democracy takes such revolutions of conscience and culture, love, and what Kaur called "this labor of birthing the America that we dream," or what I call ekklesial work to reimagine, rebuild, re-create community in US public life.

---

[100]Valarie Kaur, "Rainbow Wave! What's Next after the Midterms," November 7, 2018.

Poverty, Personalism, and the Catholic Worker 103

In the People's Inauguration opening event, rhetorical practices such as prayer, poetry, storytelling, and taking the people's oath alongside the US presidential oath opened up space, as Japanese American and Korean American poet and professor of creative writing at Fresno State University Brynn Saito stated, to "tend to history's wounds" and "sing this country into its new beginning," by inhabiting and futuring a more liberative way of being. As Kaur explained, taking the people's oath proclaimed accountability to one another and that future. An opening prayer, blessing, and land acknowledgment by Allie Young of the Diné (Navajo) Nation urged all to "remember the dark truths of the country—that is how we begin healing together." This blessing framed and accompanied the rhetorical practice of oath-taking to mark an important collective shift toward birthing a new nation, in which all learned from and with Indigenous eco-knowledge of caretaking. As Young's prayer reiterated, we walk with beauty before and behind us, on this earth, in our bodies, around and above us: "It all ends in beauty."

Kaur modified the US presidential oath of office into the people's oath to commit to making a more perfect union. The oath centralized identity and dignity in community, kinship and affinity with multiple communities, and shared goals to oppose oppression and violence in order to achieve and realize community.

> I, (insert name), do solemnly vow that I will faithfully execute my role in healing, reimagining, and rebuilding our country, and will to the best of my ability, preserve, protect, and defend dignity, justice, and joy for myself and for all around me, and that I will do so with love.

As Brynn Saito's poem stated, "Every oath tells a new story." Different oaths highlighted diverse US positionalities. The oath offered both powerful and empowered witness to national unity in diversity. Ai-Jen Poo, director of the National Domestic Workers Alliance, reflected on community organizing—"everyday people and everyday acts of courage could change the course of history"—to pass Domestic Workers' Bills of Rights. Ai-Jen modified the oath to "expand" dignity, justice, and joy "for those who have been unseen, unheard, and undervalued." Afro-Indigenous activist Amber Starks reflected on oath-taking as an identity-shaping and political activity in "kinship and relationship to my community and the natural world. . . . My inheritance is justice and my birthright is Black liberation and Indigenous sovereignty." Starks rooted the oath in "healing and building up of our peoples . . . with my ancestors behind me, my relatives beside me, and my descendants in front of me." Eric Parrie, a white teacher at predominantly Black GW Carver High School in New Orleans' Ninth Ward, took the oath in recognition of students, "the authors of their own stories . . . they showed me that dreaming and love are what Toni Morrison called first order human business." Parrie centralized a relational self, by situating himself in community with his family of origin and by "honor[ing] the courage and limitless potential of my Carver High family." Transgender Latinx activist and founder of TransLatin@ Now Coalition Bamby Salcedo reflected on intersectional injustices and intergenerational traumas in her life, which she overcame in community with transcestors. Salcedo focused her oath on "healing intergenerational wounds" and her "fight for Black liberation, Indigenous sovereignty, and lives of transpeople with my creator and my movement siblings beside me."

Moreover, RLP's website for the People's Inauguration provided multiple templates for taking the oath, for families, artists, educators, writers, community organizations, and religious communities, including Sikh, Jewish, Muslim, Hindu, and Christian communities. Each template religiously contextualized and ritualized the oath. For Sikhs, the oath aligned with core religious principles and sacred texts about the flourishing of all, connecting with the Divine by rejecting fear and hate, and not only remembering but also dwelling in creation's oneness. Gathering and centering rituals involved breath and meditative chanting in the spirit of *Chardi Kala* ("ever rising spirits, even in darkness, ever rising joy even in suffering"), followed by the oath, and concluded with rituals for community sharing of *langar*, food, and conviviality. For Jews, scriptural traditions about covenants resonated with communal and divine relationships of identity-in-accountability for the repair and renewal of diverse relationships among the Divine, one another, and the "civil covenant" that unites America. This template offered several ritual options—for Shabbat candle-lighting ceremonies to extend covenant-making and keeping with God and the community to include rebuilding the civil covenant; for communal and congregational covenants during religious and political holidays; and for scripture study sessions about national and political identity. For Muslims, the oath built on prayer, one of Islam's five pillars, and invited Muslims to incorporate supplementary prayers into their prescribed daily prayer practice, followed by taking the oath in a religious frame: "in the name of God, the Most Gracious, the Most Merciful." For Hindus, the oath reverberated with rituals of intention, in this case for receiving and acting upon Divine grace for compassionate

Poverty, Personalism, and the Catholic Worker 105

service to others. The template provided a religiously ritualized recitation of the oath as a formal meditative prayer (*bhakti sankalpa*), as a part of daily worship and ceremonial offerings to the Deity, or as a part of spiritual practice (*sadhana*) such as meditation, devotional reading of sacred texts or singing, performing yoga, or offering sanctified food to loved ones and to those facing food insecurity. For Christians, the oath embodied a religio-political recommitment to the common good versus divisive culture wars, and emerged from an ethics of love of God, neighbor, and self, especially the oppressed. The template suggested rituals for congregations, families, and small groups to engage in religio-political reflection and conversation about what to release from the past few years and what kind of society to build in the future. The template seated members in a circle around a central candle, recommended prayer (guided mediation on scripture readings about parables of love of others/neighbors), and urged poetry, prayer, or art to creatively envision their view of the future—in preparation to take the oath.

Symbolic practices associated with the People's Inauguration mainly involved the oath as articulating a new story of an America awaiting rebirth, reclaiming love or the beloved community rooted in justice and justice-seeking practices, and utilizing breath as a ritual for what participants felt or carried, wanted to release or let go, and aimed to claim or commit to via the oath. Rather than place one hand on sacred texts and scriptures, oath takers rested hands on their hearts. Rather than recite the US constitutional oath, oath takers professed their own lived experiences and hopes. Rather than swear the oath in front of US Supreme Court justices, oath takers swore their oaths in coalition with the broader community to witness this act. Together, these oaths facilitated a transition from resistance to reimagining and rebuilding the US for all, and underscored that love is cultivated and performed in community. These oaths and oath-taking practices integrally interconnected personal/communal experiences and political activism. The symbols involved in these oaths—hand, heart, community gathering and witness, breath, including the 150+ partner organizations that organized nationwide events—offered an opportunity to rethink underlying norms of US political subjectivity and community.

Prophetic practices continued beyond this initial oath-taking ritual, including virtual gatherings during the subsequent ten days for teach-ins anchored in RLP core concepts and practices, further reinforced by multiple practices that more than forty thousand people used to reclaim love as a socio-political ethic of justice. Each day tapped into one practice of what Kaur named the "revolutionary love compass"—seeing no stranger entails a love of others (wonder, grieve, fight); tending wounds encompasses love of opponents (rage, listen, reimagine); and love of ourselves (breathe, push, transition) is sustained by joy. Each day Kaur addressed and elaborated on each practice with interfaith leaders, public theologians, and spiritual activists from Indigenous, Sikh, Christian, Jewish, Muslim, and Buddhist traditions alongside influential educators, political commentators, podcast hosts, and intersectional justice and healing activists.

In the first part of the revolutionary love compass, wonder sets a foundational cornerstone or "building block" for love of others. Wonder enables an attitude and a practice of humble openness to an interconnected, interdependent web of relations, or what Kaur interpreted through familial symbols as an expansive "circle of care." Wonder is mobilized as a socially transformative and anti-racism practice to contest and reject any normalized hierarchical systems, structures, and values of othering. Indigenous religious traditions about all life's oneness are cultivated through creation stories of kinship broken by colonialism and extractivism, through songs and ceremonies that reinforce or restore balance amid violence and trauma, and through ecological wisdom about the earthly cycle of life amid death. Sikh values of *ik onkar* or the world's interconnectedness challenge individualist, egocentric ways of thinking and living, and *vismaad* or ecstatic wonder serves as a religious basis for healing a divisive, polarized world.

Grief and fight complete this part of the compass. Grief is channeled into fighting for justice. Shared grieving is expressed in interpersonal interactions, in private rituals, in public vigils, in political marches and demonstrations to protest immigration bans or to proclaim Black Lives Matter. Shared grieving enables being present with and witnessing another's loss, injustice, and violence, and thus creates as well as deepens new relationships through agential nonviolent power to affect change. Shared grieving often occurs through rhetorical practices of storytelling to counter dominant narratives that cause, perpetuate, suppress, and invisibilize or erase suffering. From Kaur's perspective, grieving—about the rise in Islamophobic hate crimes, about the murder of George Floyd, the multiracial uprising for racial justice and for Black Lives, about the COVID-19 pandemic and its associated injustices—also takes place in and creates community. Public grief propels us toward relational and political solidarity, ultimately to act as allies and accomplices, to stand up and show up with and for others to organize, struggle, and fight for a regained sense of belonging. Faith leaders and activists expounded on

Poverty, Personalism, and the Catholic Worker

religious traditions of expressing grief and practicing presence through political solidarity. Reverend Traci Blackmon, United Church of Christ, organized vigils of Black lament and civil disobedience in Ferguson, MO, called for police repentance for Michael Brown's murder, and rooted these actions in the Black community's intergenerational suffering and resilience. For Najeeba Sayeed, professor of Muslim and Interreligious Studies, grief consists of an intertwined spiritual and social act, that activates a shared connection to the Divine, and that opposes all systemic and structural violence. Mourners transform into movement allies or accomplices, and Kaur spotlighted several frontline groups in gender justice movements. Ai-Jen Poo, National Domestic Workers Alliance, centered and amplified women of color voices as "the real futurists in our society" to redesign a care economy with universal family care, dignified jobs, and family-sustaining wages. Translatina activist Isa Noyola at Mijente empowers Latinx people about issues of race, economics, climate justice, and gender justice. Noyola shared that memorials for victims of transphobic violence re-grounded her in community, to resist relentless violence against the trans community and to draw from the wellspring of spiritual ancestral resources to persist.

In the second part of the revolutionary love compass, rage serves as the starting point of love of opponents, called tending the wound in ourselves, others, and society. Anger and love—of self, of others, and of the future—are intimately interlinked. Rage unites personal and divine rage at injustice with witnessing prophetic rage in oppressed communities. Religious traditions model how to process and harness such rage in safe and creative ways for transformative social change—through Indigenous and Hindu traditions of the fierce mother goddess, in Christian portraits of Jesus' violent overthrow of Roman imperial colonialism in the Jerusalem temple, or Buddhist meditation to access and release rage. Religion also galvanizes social change, channeling divine energies toward an alternative socio-political order. Rev. Dr. Jacqueline J. Lewis, Middle Church, expressed "beautiful, hard, public anger" at a time of COVID-19 illness and death, anti-Black racist state and police violence, and poverty in communities of color. Evoking lyrics from the Black national anthem "Lift Every Voice and Sing," Lewis reflected on ancestral anger, grief, and rage in the Black community, released in multiple religious traditions through embodied song and dance. Lewis contrasted Black healing rage with the white nationalist insurrection at the US Capitol: "White rage is still sacred, a sacrament, holy, blessed. Black rage frightens the hell out of people. . . . How do we create spaces for lament? . . . . That is such an important growing edge for faith communities . . . to say actually from the pulpits or from the bema, this anger is holy. And to have it is to become whole." Rabbi Sharon Brous, IKAR, shared Jewish traditions for rebuilding the world, after being "exiled, excommunicated, nearly exterminated, when the world nearly ends, and then you're able to begin again. How do we lay a world to rest? How do we birth a new world into being?" Jewish traditions of public grief and lament, of truth-telling, and of repairing the world offer, according to Brous, a blueprint for focusing biblical traditions of lament, of divine and prophetic rage into creative social change.

Love of others/opponents is enriched by listening to understand, not legitimate, them and their wounds, by discerning our ability to safely enter such listening based on our own wounds, and by the resulting possibilities for future social change. Kaur attended to moral and strategic motives for and impact of such listening. Listening as a learning process orients us to opponents in a learning posture and opens up bridge-building spaces, beyond polarized politics. Sr. Simone Campbell, NETWORK, reflected on the radical ramifications of listening as holy curiosity during Nuns on the Bus tours. Radical acceptance and compassion are centered in this listening practice that questions all assumptions about ourselves and others. These listening practices stem from and are sustained by a religiously infused radical acceptance of others' humanity; when joined with fighting for a vision, and not against others, these practices draw us to "the sacred place where we have to take off our shoes . . . change our world. . . . That's what we hunger for. . . . Hearing that deeper story is the way to radical acceptance and finding a way forward together. That is that passionate flame that can make a difference."

Rounding out love of others/opponents, tending wounds in ourselves via rage and in others via listening generate the practice of boldly reimagining the world and creating the beloved community. Kaur reconstructed the beloved community from Civil Rights Movement activism, and further nuanced it as an anti-racist, equitable, and sustainable community. Art, ritual, and learning from social justice movements and contemporary communities of color figured prominently in this resistant and reimaginative practice. Faith-based movements for social justice have resisted injustice and opened up creative spaces to reimagine an alternative more just world via various practices, or engaged in that labor of what I call ekklesial work.

Our greatest social reformers did more than resist oppressors. They held up a vision of the world as they dreamt it. Nanak sang it, Mu-

Poverty, Personalism, and the Catholic Worker 109

hammad led it, Jesus taught it, Buddha envisioned it, King dreamt it, Dorothy Day labored for it, Mandela lived it, Gandhi died for it. . . . They all called for us not only to unseat bad actors, but to reimagine institutions of power, the institutions that order our world. . . . To undo the injustice, we have to imagine new institutions and step in to lead them.

For example, Kaur relayed how a predominantly Latinx Catholic Church in East Haven, Connecticut, mobilized its faith-based people power and shared its community testimonies to take on and reform local police culture based on the community's demands to end biased and brutal policing. Sherrilyn Ifill, of the NAACP Legal Defense and Education Fund, described resisting systemic injustice and violence and reimagining systemic change as "deep democracy work." Ifill relied on voice, representation, and power "to transform the material conditions of their communities" to critically interrogate the features of the good society, of the beloved community, noting the need for an intersectional "iterative loop of thinking, of intellectual work, of heart work, of spiritual work." Public theologian Lisa Sharon Harper, Freedom Road, described the origins of the Black Church as the space for envisioning an alternative future, for remembering and reclaiming humanity, for embodying ways to create the beloved community, based on faith leaders' spiritual and justice work. Radical connection stemmed, for Harper, from religiously motivated politics of neighbor love and of soulforce (spiritual strength) which sustained and invigorated social justice movements: "To heal the depth of the woundedness that has been caused on this earth between people, between genders, between us and the rest of creation, and between us and God, there needs to be a depth of spiritual soulforce." Public theologian Brian D. McLaren, Center for Action and Contemplation, advanced Jesus' notion of the kingdom of God as "a different realm, a different economy, a different system where everyone belongs, everyone matters. . . . We're all insiders in this group, in this larger beloved community." McLaren introduced different religious rituals of celebratory meals—Jewish Passover, Muslim feasts after fasts, Sikh *langar*, Christian Eucharist—to offer glimpses of radical dignity, connectedness, compassion, justice, and humility, to reimagine and enable community in America through multidimensional roles: caregivers, visionaries, builders, disruptors, frontline responders, storytellers, guides, and so on. Similarly, Latina feminist theologian María Pilar Aquino urges Christian theologians to inhabit and adapt to various roles of supportive solidarity with social justice movements that fashion alternative just futures: listeners, organizers, ruckus-raisers as well as "activists, advocates, educators, unifiers, socializers, envisioners, peacebuilders, reconcilers, liturgical celebrants, policy developers, and coalition builders, and also consider functions such as dissenter, agitator, rebel, subversive, and revolutionary."[101]

In the third part of the revolutionary love compass, Kaur envisaged loving ourselves, practiced through breathe, push, and transition and interpreted as well as intensified by midwifery wisdom: "Perhaps breathing and pushing can give us the wisdom, the bravery to create . . . new possibilities, new worlds." Self-love as breathing in community grounds and grows capacities for other parts of the compass. Breathing takes place in and reinstantiates community. In Kaur's view, self-love reframed as community care (with co-conspirators) serves as an originary site "to find longevity in the labor" and also to engage in a political intervention. Drawing on Black feminists bell hooks and Audre Lorde, Kaur attested that "the kind of labor, the kind of care that we pour out into the world, we must also be able to pour that into ourselves. We are worthy of it. We are beloved." Breathing thus evokes a life-giving political act for Kaur and provokes world-making: "Think about all the forces of injustice in this country that make it so difficult, literally and figuratively, for us to live viable lives." In community with co-conspirators, breathing as love of ourselves, others, and the future enables a more just, more livable world that supports all of our wellness and "all of our creative labors. The labor of making a living, the labor of building a movement, the labor of birthing a nation."

Breathing practices prepare for push practices, for transformative healing, forgiveness, reconciliation, and justice, at the levels of personal and social liberation "to birth new possibilities in ourselves and others," especially to transition our lives and worlds in the US which has perpetrated and perpetuated racist, patriarchal, colonialist, militarist, imperialist, and capitalist harms and trauma. As Kaur claimed, the "labor to birth the America we dream . . . requires us to tell the truth about our past in order to do the healing in the present to make a new future possible." African American Zen Buddhist Rev. angel Kyodo williams focused on liberation of self and society through pause and push practices. Sitting meditation forges the way forward to push practices for transformative social change; it helps restructure, reframe, and regain access to our identities, to who we want to be and become amid systemic and structural

---

[101]María Pilar Aquino, "Presidential Address: Theology Renewing Life: Prophetic Interventions and Enduring Commitments," *CTSA Proceedings* 75 (2021): 71.

Poverty, Personalism, and the Catholic Worker 111

violence and injustice, and then "to contemplate what it would mean to actually envision and structure and begin to put some elbow grease into the push for an actual new America." The push then entails tapping into and actualizing communal resistance and resilience to confront oppression and its effective intergenerational legacies.

Breathe and push culminate in transition, by rooting ourselves and our communities in prophetic wisdom and courage to confront an agonistic unjust world and to birth "new life, new worlds, new forms of liberation," as Kaur asserted, in this case a new nation that fosters a multiracial, multicultural, multifaith democracy for a sustainable future. Indigenous women and women of color lead the way to spark and effect these transitions due to their long-term impact by and resistance against colonialism, genocide, slavery, and multiple harms of white supremacy, capitalism, and environmental racism. Rev. Dr. Otis Moss III, Trinity United Church of Christ, referred to Black feminist Maya Angelou and Black theologian James Cone to critically evaluate the roles of faith, courage, and imagination in creating alternative possible futures, in which "the algorithm of difference, of caste, and race is . . . rewritten by an algorithm of revolutionary love."

The revolutionary love compass and its mutually interlocking parts of loving others, opponents, and ourselves is grounded in and grows from joy. Kaur expanded on joy as a Sikh spiritual practice as well as a practice of moral and political resistance. Rather than evade the struggle for justice amid racism, poverty, violence against women and people of color, ecocide, lack of health care, a war economy, and religious nationalism in an escapist way, joy amid hate and terror for Kaur "gives us the energy for that long labor for justice. Joy makes the labor an end in itself. . . . Even the hardest days can still contain joy. . . . Choosing to let in joy is a revolutionary act." Joy claims small achievements amid so much entrenched systemic injustice. Rev. Dr. William J. Barber II, Poor People's Campaign, highlighted biblical traditions that portray the kingdom of God as justice, peace, and joy counter to imperial Roman violent colonial rule: "Prophetic imagination . . . is prophetic joy." Having survived the COVID-19 pandemic in communities of color disproportionately affected by it, Barber committed to joy, to use his breath to "resuscitate love and justice." Rev. Dr. Liz Theoharis, Poor People's Campaign, analogized between the joy of the forty-five state chapters collaborating with 140 million poor and low wealth people in the US and the "jubilee, a biblical concept of freedom . . .and organizing society around the needs of those who are, in many traditions, called the least of these but who are most of us. And that comes, that era of change and justice is rung in. . . . We hear the sound . . . of change and of justice." Ultimately, as Kaur asserted, "Joy is our birthright. Joy returns us to everything that is good and beautiful and worth fighting for," and thus sustains the longevity of labor for justice.

Joy anticipates and makes possible that hoped-for loving, just, liberating, healing, and flourishing future. RLP enacts and builds that anticipated future beloved community—of seeing each other as interrelated and belonging together—in my view, through rhetorical, symbolic, and prophetic practices of solidarity. In April 2021, RLP organized a virtual Solidarity Vigil to end anti-Asian hate with more than thirty faith and movement leaders and artists, giving testimony and witness through music, poetry, and prayer to collective grief at racialized traumas and to solidarity for renewed action with Sikh as well as Asian American communities affected by mass shootings in Indianapolis and Atlanta. Ten thousand people and 145 organizations attended to claim their interrelated positionalities and to opt for a more just future together—i.e., to affirm and prefigure a multiracial, multicultural, multifaith beloved community in US democracy and society—rooted in identity-shaping and sustaining power of spirituality and culture for a people to persevere and persist, and centered on anti-racist praxis to see "our well-being, our flourishing, and indeed our liberation . . . tied together" and to activate a shared "capacity to see it all, to mourn it all, . . . to stand against it all, to fight against it all. We all are brothers and sisters."

4

Racism, Nonviolent Collective Action, and the Civil Rights Movement

Witness and testimony are means of embodying and practicing particular virtues. Witness and testimony carry religious values and practices into the public square, and identify and pass on values that help form other individuals [and society].
—Rosetta Ross, *Witnessing and Testifying*

We know that the way things are is not the way things have to be. Or, to riff on James Baldwin, we made this world, that means we also have the power to re-make it. That is our hope.
—Rev. Dr. William J. Barber II

Racism as the original sin of America has produced and reproduced a racially polarized and agonistic nation. US racist realities and their accompanying institutionalized and normalized discourses and structures about people of color disenfranchise, degrade, and consistently dispose of Black lives, because they differ from kyriarchal privileged race, gender, class, sexual, and other norms or identity markers of citizenship and of personhood. At Independence Hall in Philadelphia, former US President Barack H. Obama delivered a speech "A More Perfect Union" on March 18, 2008, that addressed the US history of racism. In this first-term presidential campaign speech, Obama responded to the growing controversy about his former pastor Rev. Jeremiah Wright's sermons, in which Wright invoked the biblical prophetic tradition of the jeremiad[1] and called for

---

[1]Angela D. Sims, F. Douglas Powe Jr., and Johnny Bernard Hill, *Religio-Political Narratives in the United States: From Martin Luther King Jr. to Jeremiah Wright* (New York: Palgrave Macmillan, 2014).

divine retributive justice for America's original sin of racism, for its broken covenant with African American citizens. Obama noted that the political and racial fault lines that divide America were exposed by various responses to Wright's sermons. Rather than disavow Wright and submit to a postracial or colorblind politics in America,[2] Obama resignified the site of his speech at the birthplace of US democracy to articulate the nation's original sin of racial injustice and persistent racial inequalities and tensions in America which undercut and deny its founding and foundational political ideals. Liberty, equality, and justice are enshrined in America's ethos, but have yet to be fully instantiated in political history and reality; the US has witnessed civil war, social justice movements, and amendments to redress these damaging political incongruities between American political ideals and everyday African American realities and experiences. Although Obama distanced himself from Wright and consequently jeopardized Black social movements and prophetic religiosity[3] (because Wright appeared to "commit the supreme sin of anti-Americanism"),[4] Obama situated himself squarely within the Black Church tradition, which confirmed and sustained his own spiritual commitments and faith-based community organizing for social justice.[5]

As Obama observed, the original sin of racism and its effective history of slavery, segregation, racialized violence, incarceration, and police and judicial discrimination cannot be resolved in election cycles, but in his view the longed-for yet ever-receding horizon of full racial equality and justice requires US public engagement and renewal through storytelling. While recounting his own multi-storied identity, Obama noted in this speech that listening to each other's stories deepens solidarity around common needs and goals: "We cannot solve the challenges of our time unless we solve them together—unless we perfect our union by understanding that we may have different stories, but we hold common hopes." Thus, Obama urged a national conversation about race to confront and resolve entrenched and engrained post–civil rights era racial inequalities regarding

---

[2]Barack H. Obama, *The Audacity of Hope: Thoughts on Reclaiming the American Dream* (New York: Three Rivers Press, 2006), chap. 7.

[3]Black scholars critically appraised Obama's two-term presidency, which supported Wall Street bailouts, increased warfare, and rising immigrant deportation rates as well as incarceration rates. Cornel West, "The State of Black America in the Age of Obama Has Been One of Desperation, Confusion, and Capitulation," *Salon*, October 5, 2014; Marvin A. McMickle, ed., *Audacity of Faith: Christian Leaders Reflect on the Election of Barack Obama* (Valley Forge, PA: Judson Press, 2009); and Cornel West, *Black Prophetic Fire* (Boston: Beacon Press, 2014).

[4]Rosemary Radford Ruether, "Damning America: Right and Left," *Religion Dispatches*, May 27, 2009.

[5]Obama, *The Audacity of Hope*, chap. 6.

inequitable education, growing wealth and income gaps, lack of public and social services and spaces in urban neighborhoods, and the increased criminalization and incarceration of people of color. This conversation would enable all of "we the people" to deliberate and reach consensus about other overarching national issues such as terrorism, education, the economy, health care, and climate change, which differentially impact but crosscut racial lines. From Obama's perspective, this conversation on race could potentially hurdle what he termed the US "racial stalemate" if we build a coalition-based politics of solidarity across race, class, and gender lines around similar issues facing all Americans.

As a rhetorical practice of ekklesial work, of community-building political praxis, stories serve as a means of mutual recognition in political life, of building interpersonal and political solidarity, and thereby attest to as well as constitute our being and becoming more fully human in interrelationship with others. Telling our own and hearing others' stories alter existing dominant and dominating singular stories of ourselves, others, and our world, moving beyond them toward more complex and deeper relations of solidarity in a multi-storied world.[6] Stories, then, help to shape our identity in relation, build coalitional politics across our different stories, and renew and revitalize US public life to achieve greater solidarity, especially in relation to realizing an anti-racist and more inclusive just future vision of the world.

Yet conversations about race at times fail to confront and resist, and thus perpetuate, the sociostructural legacy of US slavery and its effective history of systemic racism and racialized structures of inequality, injustice, and discrimination in post–Jim Crow, post–civil rights era America, especially in health care, education, law enforcement, mass incarceration, housing, and economics.[7] White habitus erects seemingly insurmountable roadblocks to such conversations and social change. According to sociologist Eduardo Bonilla-Silva, white habitus consists of socialized semantic strategies and styles that elite whites utilize to misrecognize or ignore racialized social structures of inequality and injustice, including the socio-structural legacy of US slavery and its effective racist history. Most whites operate in what Bonilla-Silva terms "a world of racism without racists," that is, they agree with racial equality "but are quietly oblivious to injustice around them. . . . We are not racists, but we accept a system that

---

[6]Michele Saracino, *Being about Borders: A Christian Anthropology of Difference* (Collegeville, MN: Liturgical Press, 2011).

[7]Michelle Alexander, *The New Jim Crow: Mass Incarceration in the Age of Colorblindness* (New York: New Press, 2012).

116   *Nevertheless, We Persist*

acts in racist ways."[8] Undoing US systemic racist structures and undoing white supremacist norms of being human and subsequently of political rights, agency, and action entail not only being schooled in the effective history of Black oppression and struggles, but also walking the talk, that is, practicing a political solidarity with Black-led social justice movements.

Freedom Movements in the Obama Era

Since the summer of 2014, US public protests about racial injustice and inequality have escalated in response to ever-increasing events of state-sanctioned police violence and brutality against Black men and women. Eric Garner died in July 2014 after a New York City police officer applied an illegal chokehold during Garner's arrest. Michael Brown was fatally shot by Ferguson, Missouri, police in early August 2014. Both Garner and Brown were unarmed, and grand juries in both cases decided not to indict the officers in these police killings of Black men, igniting both nationwide conversations and nonviolent protests. In my view, ekklesial work and its rhetorical, symbolic, and prophetic practices of public engagement were prominently demonstrated and displayed in the aftermath of Ferguson, practices that both denounced racism and its dehumanizing, death-dealing forms, and proclaimed Black religio-political subjectivity, agency, and community.

Public engagement at times mediated by religious groups surfaced in salient ways. The protests began in Ferguson in August 2014, calling for both reform of police tactics and accountability for police brutality. In August, October, and again in November, interfaith clergy (coordinated with approximately 170 actions around the country) marched alongside and accompanied protesters, to decry the criminalization of Black men and women and to testify to the truth from different religious perspectives that Black Lives Matter. Religious leaders proclaimed this truth about the equal dignity of Black lives

> in the face of racism—that fundamental lie that runs through American history. In the Jim Crow era, the false claim that some people matter more than others was proclaimed from every drinking fountain, voting, booth, and restaurant counter. . . . [Now] we are

---

[8]Eduardo Bonilla-Silva, *Racism without Racists: Colorblind Racism and the Persistence of Racial Inequality in America*, 4th ed. (New York: Rowman and Littlefield, 2014), 73–78; cf. 151–152, 171–172 on white habitus, and cf. chap. 4 for analysis of elite white discursive styles.

Racism, Nonviolent Collective Action, and the Civil Rights Movement **117**

swimming in a sea of deception and spin. That peaceful protesters are criminals, that tanks are needed on suburban streets, that jaywalking is a capital offense. It is vital in this context to lay hold of a truth that cannot be undone.[9]

In the wake of the grand jury decisions that exonerated police officers in the killings of these Black men, #BlackLivesMatter protests took place across the United States. During the first two weeks of Advent in 2014, churches participated in faith-based protests in response to these grand jury decisions which so sharply demonstrated intransigent US racist systems and structures. On November 30 in St. Louis, some churches offered Lay It on the Table services, a public forum in which congregants spoke and listened to one another about their deepest fears and hopes in these horrific times. After "'laying down their lives' on the sacramental table, the congregations celebrated the sacrament at this table." The Eucharist, or the re-membering of the church as the body of Christ, paved the way for the re-membering or the revitalization of the US body politic suffering from racism: "Perhaps conversations started during [these] services . . . will make their way into homes, and workplaces, and educational institutions, and civic forums, until people can envision change in the structures that constitute our lives together."[10]

On December 7, Father Michael Pfleger of Saint Sabina Catholic Church on Chicago's South Side urged his parishioners to pursue acts of nonviolent civil disobedience, marching in and thereby disrupting status quo daily traffic. Before exiting the church, Father Pfleger said during morning services, "It is no coincidence to me that Michael Brown lifted his hands up because he understood what we know, when your hands are up, it's reaching to the strength and the power of who it is that holds us." Led by the youth group at Saint Sabina, the congregants repeatedly chanted "Black lives matter" and "Hands up, don't shoot," performed a die-in in the street, and sang "Amazing Grace" while walking back to the church. Characterizing the protests that occurred around Chicago and briefly halted the city's ordinary daily life often oblivious to its systemic racism, Pfleger argued against religio-political complacency: "The church, the synagogue, the mosque are supposed to be the conscience of a society. . . . If we do not speak out, and if we remain silent, if we do not

---

[9]Shannon Craigo-Snell, "What the Ferguson Protests Mean for Religious Progressive Activism," *Religion Dispatches*. November 26, 2014.

[10]Rick Nutt, "Ferguson Congregations 'Lay It on the Table,' Taking a Step toward Honest Dialogue," *Sightings*, December 4, 2014.

118   *Nevertheless, We Persist*

show our outrage with this, then I think the church is going to become irrelevant."[11] Pfleger echoed and highlighted Martin Luther King Jr.'s argument in letters and sermons for US Christian churches to practice a Good Samaritan–based ethics and politics of "dangerous unselfishness" and to engage in struggles for African American rights as well as human rights, or otherwise run the theo-political risk of further scarring the body of Christ and becoming an irrelevant social club.[12] Thus, in addition to this moral and socio-political role of religion in US public life, Pfleger in keeping with King articulated a Christological and ecclesiological rationale for faith-based anti-racist nonviolent public engagement.

Within a week, nationwide marches coincided on December 13. In Washington, DC, nearly 10,000 people occupied Pennsylvania Avenue, and in New York protesters packed Washington Square, with similar chants and cries for justice despite these grand jury decisions. Speaking at the Washington rally, Garner's mother Gwen Carr stressed the march's racial and religious diversity, calling it "a history-making moment. We need to stand like this at all times." Sybrina Fulton, the mother of Trayvon Martin who was shot and killed by a neighborhood watch volunteer in Florida in 2012, urged the protesters to continue this work for justice: "This is not something new that started. . . . Don't just come to the rally and go home. . . . It cannot stop here."[13]

Black churches simultaneously staged their own in-church protests, which resonated throughout the US public square. On Black Lives Matter Sunday, December 14, organized by many historically Black churches to occur the day after nationwide nonviolent protests and demonstrations, church members wore black or T-shirts with the slogans "Black Lives Matter" and "I Can't Breathe" to Advent services. On New Year's Eve 2014 in New York, protesters marched from Union Square to Times Square, carrying placards that read "we can't breathe," recalling Garner's death and calling for justice amid highly militarized police tactics. On the same night in Boston, Massachusetts, protesters carried similar placards and staged a die-in, in which protesters recalled Brown's death. In both nonviolent protests, some participants, perhaps still in vigil, lit candles,

---

[11]Stephanie K. Baer, "Chicago Pastors Lead Protests over Deaths by Police in Ferguson, NYC," *Chicago Tribune*, December 7, 2014; Mike Krauser, "Pfleger Wants Churches to Lead Protests of Ferguson, NYC Police Killing Cases," *CBS Chicago*, December 4, 2014.

[12]Martin Luther King Jr., "Letter from a Birmingham Jail (1963)" and "I See the Promised Land (1968)," in *I Have a Dream: Writings and Speeches That Changed the World*, ed. James M. Washington (New York: Harper Collins, 1992), 95–98, 200–201.

[13]Matt Hansen, "Marches against Police Killings Draw Thousands in Washington, New York," *Los Angeles Times*, December 13, 2014.

Racism, Nonviolent Collective Action, and the Civil Rights Movement 119

not only in prolonged Advent-like anticipation of a new year but also in hope for justice for these victims, their families, and the nation.

Finally, protesters marked Martin Luther King Day in January 2015 with nationwide calls to action that included a sit-in near Ebenezer Baptist Church in Atlanta and die-ins in New York's Union Square as well as in Boston Common. At a thousand-strong gathering in Harlem, a #Black-LivesMatter march broadcasted King's speeches as they walked through the Upper East Side.[14] Together with protests at Chicago's Magnificent Mile and the White House, these prophetic actions "demanded that the traditional holiday rituals of speechmaking, community service, and prayer breakfasts give way to denunciations of injustice and inequality," calling for police reforms, educational funding for high-need schools, and an increased minimum wage. In Atlanta, "the protesters argued that the holiday had become corrupted by corporate involvement, diluting Dr. King's ideas about economics as well as race. With signs, slogans, and shouts, they inserted themselves into the annual parade. . . . Several times, the group sat and lay en masse in the middle of the street, raising fists toward the air." Near Ebenezer Baptist Church, protesters carried a cardboard coffin to the stage during a service and chanted "Black people are dying."[15]

In the midst of these nonviolent collective direct actions, more than thirty African American leaders in US theological schools reflected on the religio-political implications of Christian God-talk for prophetic protest. Beneath a picture of a protest marcher carrying a placard that read "God Can't Breathe," these leaders recounted in the rhetorical style of Black Church preaching the events which galvanized their theological call.

From a manger in Bethlehem, a Bantustan in Soweto, a bus in Montgomery, a freedom Summer in Mississippi, a bridge in Selma, a street in Ferguson, a doorway and shots fired in Detroit, a Moral Monday in Raleigh, an assault in an elevator in Atlantic City, an office building in Colorado Springs, a market in Paris, a wall in Palestine, a pilgrimage to the shrine of Rincon and a restoration of ties between Cuba and the United States on December 17th, the kidnapping and assault of young school-aged girls and the reported killing of 2,000 women, children, and men in Nigeria, a new generation of dream defenders, a transgender teen's suicide note, to our

---

[14]Michael Paulson, "Martin Luther King's Birthday Marked by Protests over Deaths of Black Men," *New York Times*, January 19, 2015.

[15]Ibid.

abuse of the environment—God sends a sign—a Kairos moment. The racial climate in the United States, and the respect for our common humanity everywhere, is clearly in decline.[16]

Appealing to foundational principles in the US Constitution regarding a divine equal creation and a common commitment to liberty and justice for all, these leaders called on Congress to model humanity in politics and on local leaders as well as ordinary citizens to reject practices that contradict these constitutional claims, instead embracing King's "beloved community" grounded in the protection of human rights. These leaders particularly counseled "churches and every house of faith to challenge their members and communities to live out an inclusive commitment to love God, self, the neighbor, the enemy, and creation across any and all boundaries that would dehumanize, alienate, and separate."

This snapshot of mainly but not only faith-based anti-racist political actors and activism between 2014 and 2015 embodies and exemplifies rhetorical, symbolic, and prophetic practices of ekklesial work, of community-building praxis, across racial and multiple lines that divide rather than unite us. Protesters in church and street rallies and vigils interpreted "hands up, don't shoot" and "I can't breathe" as both chants of political protest and religious symbols of prayer. Eucharistic celebrations re-membered the church as the broken and restored body of Christ, offering a powerful religio-political symbol to dramatize political fracture and fragmentation as well as begin in grassroots ways to reconcile all bodies in the US body politic. Demonstrators performed prophetic die-ins and ritual memorials, particularly during MLK Day celebrations.

In all these ways, faith-based anti-racist activism both challenged racism and its multiple dehumanizing as well as death-dealing forms in American life and recovered the role of religion in reshaping US public life, rooted in part in faith-based notions of equality and solidarity. As Judith Butler puts it, "On the streets, we see a complex set of solidarities . . . that seek to show what a concrete and living sense of bodies that matter can be."[17] The protests in the aftermath of Ferguson in 2014–2015, during the Civil Rights Movement, and in the renewed Poor People's Campaign can be portrayed from the perspective of ekklesial work as public assemblies that presage and signify in their interracial and interreligious character

---

[16]"An Open Letter to Presidents and Deans of Theological Schools in the United States," January 17, 2015.

[17]George Yancy and Judith Butler, "What's Wrong with 'All Lives Matter'?" *New York Times*, January 12, 2015.

Racism, Nonviolent Collective Action, and the Civil Rights Movement **121**

the inclusive, just, and egalitarian US public life that these protests seek to incarnate and forge.

#BlackLivesMatter protests, sparked by the police killings of young Black men and women, parallel civil rights era prophetic acts of protest which were similarly mobilized and galvanized by the police brutality and mob attacks against Southern Christian Leadership Conference (SCLC) and Student Nonviolent Coordinating Committee (SNCC) protesters as well as their allies, particularly for voting rights. March 7, 2015, marked the 50th anniversary of Bloody Sunday, the first of three marches for Black voting rights from Selma to Montgomery, Alabama, during which the police pushed back, assaulted, tear-gassed, trampled, and brutally beat the marchers at the Edmund Pettus Bridge. After Bloody Sunday aroused nationwide demonstrations of solidarity, President Lyndon Johnson prioritized and signed the Voting Rights Act of 1965, citing the social suffering of Blacks and their white allies, which served the pedagogical purpose of educating the nation about the illegality and immorality of US racism.[18]

President Obama's speech at the 50th anniversary of Bloody Sunday in Selma commemorated and appraised the effects and efficacy of past and present anti-racist activism.[19] In this speech, Obama recounted US progress regarding anti-racist social change without espousing a white habitus-based gradualist approach. He situated the march within America's creed which professes equality, liberty, and justice as divinely endowed rights for shaping and transforming national unity, without reverting to white habitus-based conversational styles, which invoke these same values to scuttle affirmative action, ignore educational inequalities, and so on. This creed functions as "a call to action, a roadmap for citizenship, and an insistence on the capacity of free men and women to shape our own destiny." Against this constitutional and religious backdrop, Obama framed the march within a multigenerational perspective that spanned slavery and the Civil War to legalized segregation and the Civil Rights Movement. This African American civil rights march blazed a legal and social trail for other marginalized groups, such as women, Latinx and Asian Americans, Americans with disabilities, and LGBTQT Americans, to advocate for their equal rights in public policy and everyday practices. In making America's creed not only an ideational but an incarnate reality, the American experiment or project is still "not yet finished" but inspires and requires each generation to respond to the "imperative of citizenship" to "remake this

---

[18]Andrew Beck Grace, "A Call from Selma," *New York Times Op-Docs*, March 6, 2015.

[19]National Archives, "Remarks by the President at the 50th Anniversary of the Selma to Montgomery Marches," March 7, 2015.

122   *Nevertheless, We Persist*

nation to more closely align with our highest ideals." Referring to relentless police killings of Black men and women, Obama claimed prophetic social justice struggles persist to create an anti-racist America.

> We know the march is not yet over, the race is not yet won. . . . Fifty years from Bloody Sunday, our march is not yet finished. But we are getting closer. Two hundred and thirty-nine years after this nation's founding, our union is not yet perfect. But we are getting closer. . . . When the torch we've been passed feels too heavy, we will remember these early travelers, and draw strength from their example, and hold firmly the words of the prophet Isaiah: "Those who hope in the Lord will renew their strength."

In Obama's view, anti-racist activists involved in the American project will thus continue to draw life-giving water from the wellsprings of multiple social justice movements and from multiple religious traditions in order to bolster their religio-political agency and foster their religio-political practices of public engagement for an anti-racist inclusive and just public life.

Yet Black lives, both personally and politically, are still dismissed, disregarded, and considered disposable in American politics. In Ferguson's wake, Obama created the Task Force on 21st Century Policing, which in part hosted listening sessions and roundtable discussions on equity and accountability in police practices.[20] The Department of Justice also issued an investigative report that confirmed the Ferguson Police Department's systemic racist practices.[21] The police lynchings of Sandra Bland in Texas and Kindra Chapman in Alabama[22] and other Black women demonstrated such pernicious racist policing. At the same time, the US Supreme Court dismantled parts of the Voting Rights Acts and allowed voter redistricting and other tactics, which effectively undermined Black political power and voter equality in primarily southern states.[23] That same summer, a young white supremacist killed nine African Americans, including State Senator and Rev. Clementa Pinckney, during a midweek Bible study meeting on June 17, 2015, at the historic Mother Emanuel AME Church in Charleston, South Carolina. Elected officials like then Governor Nikki Haley,

---

[20]Charles M. Blow, "Beyond 'Black Lives Matter,' " *New York Times*, February 9, 2015.

[21]Ta-Nehisi Coates, "The Gangsters of Ferguson," *Atlantic*, March 3, 2015.

[22]Charles M. Blow, "Sandra and Kindra: Suicides or Something Sinister?" *New York Times*, July 20, 2015.

[23]Adam Liptak, "Supreme Court Invalidates Key Part of Voting Rights Act," *New York Times*, June 25, 2013; Editorial Board, "Race, Politics, and Drawing Maps: The Supreme Court Hears an Alabama Case on the Voting Rights Act," *New York Times*, November 13, 2014.

Racism, Nonviolent Collective Action, and the Civil Rights Movement 123

faith leaders like Rev. Jacqui Lewis, and growing public opinion united to confront racism and other forms of institutionalized violence against Black and marginalized communities, symbolized by the Confederate flag at the South Carolina state capitol. That flag was erected in resistance to civil rights and racial equality in the 1960s. In the past, arguments from southern tradition and ancestral heritage kept that flag and other Confederate emblems on public display. Acknowledging the flag's role in perpetuating a racist worldview and systemic oppression that must be dismantled, these elected officials and faith leaders testified to our ability as a collective community and a nation to confront and challenge another form of white habitus or what E. J. Dionne calls a "politics of evasion."[24]

Reframed by a feminist perspective on public theology as ekklesial or community-creating work in rhetorical, symbolic, and prophetic ways, achieving racial justice includes but goes beyond improving public dialogue and changing public symbols of American civil religion. Many Black churches burned as a result of arson after the Charleston shootings; thus, prophetic action that enables mourning and lament as well as motivates social change, or what Rev. Jacqui Lewis called prophetic grief, is also needed in the face of a politics of fear and public terror. Obama's eulogy at Pinckney's funeral shows that faith-based anti-racist activism will continue to enter into these tragedies, to deconstruct what passes for status quo discourse about our shared common life, and to introduce new symbols, religious and political, as well as present alternative creative protests (blending religious rituals with political action) that urge ever more inclusive and just ways of being and living in community. To paraphrase Obama's eulogy, which included collective national grief and communal singing of "Amazing Grace," the US does not only need more critical and courageous talk but also concrete theological and political cooperation with divine grace for individual and collective salvation, and more importantly for prophetic social change and transformation toward a just society.[25] Exemplified by Obama's eulogy, these rhetorical, symbolic, and prophetic practices of ekklesial or community-creating work have been continually present and enacted religiously and politically in the history of the Black Church and in civil rights–era organizations and beyond that oppose anti-Black racism, embody Black dignity and full humanity, and advocate for more expansive human rights and freedoms.[26]

---

[24]E. J. Dionne Jr., "Charleston and the Politics of Evasion," *Commonweal*, June 22, 2015.

[25]Adam Chandler, "A Eulogy in Charleston," *Atlantic*, June 26, 2015; "President Obama Delivers Eulogy—Full Video (C-SPAN)," June 26, 2015.

[26]Salient Black Church studies include Alton B. Pollard III and Carol B. Duncan, eds., *The*

124   *Nevertheless, We Persist*

This chapter illuminates how rhetorical, symbolic, and prophetic practices of ekklesial or community-creating work are engaged and foregrounded in faith-based anti-racist social justice movements, especially the Civil Rights Movement and the Poor People's Campaign. Drawing on some salient leaders and moments, this chapter examines underlying religious claims, symbols, and prophetic practices in both movements to imagine and actualize an alternative just vision of public life, to transform religious and political spaces into counterpublics and counterspaces that edge toward a more just and emancipatory society for the well-being and flourishing of all.

The Civil Rights Movement

In sermons, speeches, letters, and other writings, Nobel Peace Prize winner Rev. Dr. Martin Luther King Jr. (1929–1968) critically denounced the brutal realities of racial oppression and racial, political, and economic injustice under US legalized segregation as well as constructively announced an alternative religio-political vision of US common life that encompassed both racial justice and wider human rights, well-being, and flourishing.[27] Freedom movements are always labeled untimely. In his 1963 "Letter from a Birmingham Jail," King recounted major racist episodes and experiences against the African American community with an increasingly breathless rhythm to reject gradualist theories of inevitable progress and to defend the Movement's aim to reclaim and regain African Americans' God-given civil and human rights.[28]

To educate the American public and the wider global public about the racist realities of segregated social institutions, systems, and structures, and to catalyze radical social and political change, King and Movement

---

Black Church Studies Reader (New York: Palgrave Macmillan, 2016); Juan M. Floyd-Thomas, *Liberating Black Church History: Making It Plain* (Nashville, TN: Abingdon Press, 2014); David J. Endres, ed., *Black Catholic Studies Reader: History and Theology* (Washington, DC: Catholic University of America Press, 2021); Henry Louis Gates, Jr., *The Black Church: This Is Our Story, This Is Our Song* (New York: Penguin, 2021), and the similarly titled documentary film (McGee Media, Inkwell Media, in association with Get Lifted, 2021).

[27] Martin Luther King Jr., *The Autobiography of Martin Luther King, Jr.*, ed. Clayborne Carson (New York: Warner, 1998); James M. Washington, ed., *A Testament of Hope: The Essential Writings and Speeches of Martin Luther King Jr.* (1986; New York: HarperCollins, 1991); Clayborne Carson and Kris Shepard, eds., *A Call to Conscience: The Landmark Speeches of Dr. Martin Luther King, Jr.* (New York: Warner, 2001); and Lewis V. Baldwin et al., *The Legacy of Martin Luther King, Jr.: The Boundaries of Law, Politics, and Religion* (Notre Dame: University of Notre Dame Press, 2002).

[28] King, "Letter from the Birmingham Jail (1963)," in *I Have a Dream*, 88–89, 92.

Racism, Nonviolent Collective Action, and the Civil Rights Movement **125**

activists utilized nonviolent direct collective action and civil disobedience to instigate "creative tension" and "dramatize the issue" or radically expose racism and its attendant systemic "evils of our society" on the local and national public stage.[29] Movement activists engaged in prophetic protests—mass meetings, marches, sit-ins, pray-ins, strikes, boycotts, freedom rides, and other kinds of demonstrations—at personal and collective risk of jail, beatings, and even death. King interpreted and infused these practices with biblical prophetic traditions and US political traditions of creative extremism and maladjustment to injustice.[30] According to Black Catholic theologian Jamie Phelps, "Authentic Black spirituality leads to prophetic action on behalf of justice, a justice that requires liberation from sin and its effects. . . . A person imbued with the life-force at the center of Black spirituality—with the Spirit of God—is willing to struggle for this liberation."[31] King located Black power in such struggles to achieve socio-economic and political change, especially in the ways that Movement activists creatively wielded "levers of power . . . [as] ideological, economic, and political forces." The Movement mobilized and regained ideological power through nonviolent collective action to redefine democracy; economic power through boycotts, strikes, unions to reclaim Black power within racial capitalist societies; and political power through voting and community-based organizations to sway elections and lobby for more just policies.[32] Moreover, the state's systemic, physical, and violent retaliation against such protests—manifested in the traumatic beatings of the Freedom Riders in 1961, in the police dogs and fire hoses used against demonstrators in Birmingham in 1963, and the violent police pushback against voting rights marchers from Selma to Montgomery in 1965—served the pedagogical purpose of raising public awareness about US racism and inspiring solidarity against the state-sponsored means of enacting and enforcing it. These events aroused the public conscience as well as garnered widespread political and presidential support for African

---

[29]King, "Letter," in *I Have a Dream*, 86. King defended the SCLC's nonviolent direct actions in response to the rise of more militant groups within the Movement; King, "Nonviolence: The Only Road to Freedom (1966)," in *I Have a Dream*, 131.

[30]King, "Letter," in *I Have a Dream*, 94, and "The Power of Nonviolence (1958)," in *I Have a Dream*, 33.

[31]In Diana L. Hayes, "A Great Cloud of Witnesses: Martin Luther King Jr.'s Roots in the African American Religious and Spiritual Traditions," in *Revives My Soul Again: The Spirituality of Martin Luther King Jr.*, ed. Lewis V. Baldwin and Victor Anderson (Minneapolis: Fortress Press, 2018), 56.

[32]King, "Black Power Defined (1967)," in *I Have a Dream*, 154, 155–159, and "Where Do We Go From Here? (1967)," in *I Have a Dream*, 172.

126   *Nevertheless, We Persist*

American citizenship rights and human rights,[33] enshrined in the 1964 Civil Rights Act and 1965 Voting Rights Act.

These rhetorical and prophetic practices embody what feminist critical theorist Judith Butler terms "modes of address" or "a way of speaking . . . a general way of approaching another . . . with gesture, signs, and movement, but also through media and technology."[34] As a counter-address or counter-narrative to predominant US racist worldviews, realities, and ways of life which marginalize and criminalize people of color as threats to the US body politic, rhetorical practices in the Movement recognize and reclaim full humanity of Black Americans, a theological anthropology derived from both African religious traditions and from Christianity,[35] and thereby reassert Black religio-political subjectivity as well as redefine American identity. Akin to later social justice movements for women's liberation, LGBTQ+ rights, and #Black Lives Matter, these practices "foreground those lives that are not mattering now, to mark that exclusion, and militate against it."[36]

With regard to symbolic practices, King and the Movement found firm religious footing in the Black Social Gospel tradition, which rejects a distorted white supremacist Christianity and recovers a central liberating strand within Christianity—God sides with the marginalized and oppressed, and the church plays significant religio-political roles to upend injustices as well as defend civil and human rights. In its tradition of the jeremiad, liberationist Christianity provides both a prophetic criticism of unjust US political and public life, as well as deepens and fulfills US democratic principles of equality, freedom, and peacemaking.[37] Theological anthropology, or divine creation in the *imago Dei*, establishes the dignity, equality, and freedom of all, and US democratic institutions and traditions actualize as well as protect those rights. Standing squarely within the Black Church and the Black Social Gospel tradition (in addition to the liberal Social Gospel and Gandhian nonviolence), King modified a traditional Christology of redemptive suffering to theologically articulate the reasons for and the risks entailed in the Movement's nonviolent

---

[33]King, "The Social Organization of Nonviolence (1959)," in *I Have a Dream*, 53.

[34]Yancy and Butler, "What's Wrong with 'All Lives Matter.' "

[35]Hayes, "A Great Cloud of Witnesses," 44–45.

[36]Yancy and Butler, "What's Wrong with 'All Lives Matter.' "

[37]Hayes, "A Great Cloud of Witnesses," 49–56. Cf. Clayborne Carson, "Martin Luther King Jr. and the African American Social Gospel," in *African American Religious Thought: An Anthology*, ed. Cornel West and Eddie S. Glaude Jr. (Louisville, KY: Westminster John Knox Press, 2003); Gary Dorrien, *Breaking White Supremacy: Martin Luther King Jr. and the Black Social Gospel* (New Haven, CT: Yale University Press, 2018).

Racism, Nonviolent Collective Action, and the Civil Rights Movement **127**

protests against multiple injustices in US political and public life.[38] King drew on the cross to provide a religious justification for boycotts, sit-ins, marches, and other protests and for their goal of achieving an egalitarian society.[39] In his writings on nonviolent methods of civil disobedience and social change, King stated that the Movement identified with and emulated the "sacrificial spirit " of early Christian martyrs[40] to "put an end to suffering by willingly suffering themselves."[41] However, King revised and recast this theology of redemptive suffering to avoid any uncritical acceptance of African American suffering from racist retaliatory violence as in itself Christic. To do so, King highlighted the cross as a possible outcome of nonviolent direct action: "Stand[ing] up and protest[ing] against injustice . . . will mean suffering, . . . going to jail, . . . fill[ing] up the jail houses, . . . even . . . death."[42] As the late Black theologian James Cone argues, the cross symbolized divine agency in reconciling broken relationships as well as "an inherent part of the Christian life in the struggle for freedom."[43] Nonviolent direct collective action, then, does not reinscribe racism, negate the agency of Movement activists by reducing them to victims, or eschew the physical and psychological pain of activists or the culpability of state and local perpetrators of these horrific acts. On the contrary, nonviolent direct action highlights and resists the evils of racism, reinforces the agency of activists who regularly participated in preparatory workshops for such protests, and underscores the responsibility of racist systems for perpetrating and perpetuating such violence. As feminist and womanist theological criticisms of redemptive suffering have argued, enduring personal or social suffering is not Christic in itself, but carries Christic implications when such suffering results from taking prophetic action in solidarity.[44]

---

[38]Roger Gottlieb, *Joining Hands: Politics and Religion Together for Social Change* (Cambridge, MA: Westview Perseus Press, 2002), 101–128, and Brian E. Brandt, "The Theology of the Cross and the Ethic of Redemptive Suffering in the Life and Work of Martin Luther King, Jr." (PhD diss., Loyola University of Chicago, 2002).

[39]Joanne Marie Tyrell, *Power in the Blood? The Cross in the African American Experience* (Maryknoll, NY: Orbis Books, 1998), 77–83, 96; and Charles Marsh, *The Beloved Community: How Faith Shapes Social Justice, from the Civil Rights Movement to Today* (New York: Basic Books, 2005), 45.

[40]King, "Letter," in *I Have a Dream*, 97.

[41]King, "Nonviolence," in *I Have a Dream*, 134; cf. 129–130. Redemptive suffering did not fulfill its putative moral purpose; it mobilized collective socio-political and economic pressure to empower African Americans, rather than spark a moral metanoia in US society and politics. Gottlieb, *Joining Hands*, 116–117, 119, 121, 124.

[42]King, "Facing the Challenge of a New Age (1957)," in *I Have a Dream*, 26.

[43]James H. Cone, *Martin, Malcolm, and America: A Dream or a Nightmare* (Maryknoll, NY: Orbis Books, 1991), 127–128.

[44]Elizabeth Johnson, M. Shawn Copeland, and Ada María Isasi-Díaz are analyzed in Rosemary

128   *Nevertheless, We Persist*

In addition to Christology, King and the Movement relied on religious symbols of a universal loving creator and justice-oriented God to appeal to transcendent theological claims and to mobilize prophetic action in opposition to US racist public life. Rhetorically in his speeches, letters, and sermons, King centrally situated the Movement in the context of Christian claims and symbols, US constitutional and democratic principles, and international decolonial movements to proclaim that "the universe is on the side of justice." The Movement thus participated in divinely aligned global political freedom movements, justified by a divine will for love and justice and by democratic principles of equal dignity and freedom. In King's theological view, Movement activists engaged in nonviolent direct action for racial justice to imitate divine love that equalizes and dignifies all life created by God, to disobey unjust laws that contravene divine laws, and to become "co-workers with God" for justice, or co-create with God the beloved community of equality, justice, and peace.[45]

Contending with racism and re-membering relationality through symbols of divine love and justice serve as theological starting points to confront and contest ever-growing polarities and inequalities in US society not only around race but also gender, class, sexuality, religion, and national identity. Black theologians have identified Trinitarian theology as a religio-political symbol that can aid and actualize the social repair of US public life. Reframing Black identity by the "God . . . who calls us into relationship with the divine, reconciles us to the divine, and then helps to sustain us in that relationship"[46] provides a theological way to dignify Black identities, Moreover, understanding God as inherently relational through the doctrine of perichoresis, or the way in which the Trinitarian persons engage in a divine dance of "mak[ing] space for one another in community," creates a model of "a dynamic and relational community [which] will change how we dialogue publicly."[47] A perichoretic God constituted by a divine dance of mutual co-equal relationship acts as an analogy to emulate, not an exact blueprint to directly imitate in our own negotiated and improvised dances of public conversation and public life. Black theologians—as well as feminist and womanist theologians[48]—are

---

P. Carbine, "Contextualizing the Cross for the Sake of Subjectivity," in *Cross-Examinations: Readings on the Meaning of the Cross Today*, ed. Marit A. Trelstad (Minneapolis: Fortress Press, 2006), 91–107, 287–290.

[45]King, "New Age," in *I Have a Dream*, 22–23, "Letter," in *I Have a Dream*, 89–90, 92, and "Where Do We Go From Here? (1967)," in *I Have a Dream*, 176.

[46]Sims, Powe, and Hill, *Religio-Political Narratives in the United States*, 89.

[47]Ibid., 90–91.

[48]Karen Baker-Fletcher, *Dancing with God: The Trinity from a Womanist Perspective* (St. Louis: Chalice Press, 2006); Catherine Mowry LaCugna, *God for Us: The Trinity and Christian*

Racism, Nonviolent Collective Action, and the Civil Rights Movement 129

keenly aware of the fraught finite nature of human relations. Thus, they appeal to Trinitarian theology to testify to a transcendent truth about human beings as made in the image of a relational God, and thereby expose from a religio-political view how US political culture and common life damage and distort that relationality.

Beyond confronting a racist status quo by reenacting and resisting it on a public stage in a Christic and other theological ways, major demonstrations within the Movement, such as the 1963 March on Washington for Jobs and Freedom, served as prophetic practices because they incarnated, at least fleetingly, a more interrelated and interconnected society as well as a more fully participatory democracy—a theo-political instance of what King envisioned as the beloved community. The beloved community offers a rich expansive symbolic view as well as prophetic practice of ekklesial work, in my view, of King's egalitarian and emancipatory political vision. In King's theological terms, the Movement aimed to eliminate segregation through faith-based prophetic witness, that is, nonviolent direct action, and to establish the beloved community, a racially integrated and reconciled society anchored in the theological moorings of divine justice, agape or altruistic love, and shared power, or what King called the art and power of alliance politics, that is, the social force of multiple groups in solidarity to effect social change through coalitional or collective nonviolent action.[49]

Studying the origins and multiple legacies of this term, Charles Marsh chronicles the emergence of the beloved community during the 1955 Montgomery bus boycott.[50] King continually reminded Movement activists that nonviolent direct action accomplishes the political goal of civil disobedience to repeal unjust segregation laws that diminish human dignity, and the religious goal of converting an oppressive society: it "is merely a means to awaken a sense of shame in the oppressor and challenge his false sense of superiority. But the end is reconciliation, the end is redemption, the end is the creation of the beloved community."[51] One year after the bus boycott, King addressed the Institute on Nonviolence and Social Change, and appealed to both religion and politics to mediate in an interstitial way, as I have argued, between two worlds, an unjust present and a more just future. King criticized the sinful, evil, and antidemocratic nature of segregation on Christological and constitutional

---

Life (New York: HarperCollins, 1993).

[49]King, "Social Organization," in *I Have a Dream*, 52–53; cf. King, "Black Power Defined," in *I Have a Dream*, 159, 161–162, 165.

[50]Marsh, *The Beloved Community*, 11–50.

[51]King, "New Age," in *I Have a Dream*, 22, and "Nonviolence," in *I Have a Dream*, 130.

130

grounds; American apartheid dehumanizes as well as breaks the body of Christ, and contradicts the equal dignity of all citizens enshrined in its democratic institutions.[52] Aiding "the birth of a new age" and a new multiracial and multicultural America, the Movement envisioned and ushered in a world that globalized the beloved community into "a new world of geographic togetherness," characterized by dignity, justice, and peace.[53]

The Movement further developed, elaborated, and enacted the religio-political symbol of the beloved community through subsequent nonviolent direct actions and prophetic praxis. During the March on Washington in 1963, which centered racial and economic inequalities faced by poor Blacks and whites, King intertwined religious and constitutional principles of human dignity and equality and thereby reconceptualized and reimagined US public life to endorse and embrace African American citizenship rights: "Now is the time to make real the promises of democracy. ... Now is the time to make justice a reality for all God's children." In his renowned "I Have a Dream" speech, King leveraged religio-political creeds of justice and freedom from biblical prophetic traditions and from African American spirituals to radicalize US constitutional citizenship rights and thus realize African American political dignity, equality, and freedom.[54] King creatively and strategically synthesized rhetorical tropes and tools of American civil religion, biblical prophetic traditions, and Black Church preaching to reinterpret and reconstrue US identity for racial justice and equality.[55]

Moreover, in his last sermon during the Memphis sanitation workers strike in 1968, part of the SCLC-initiated Poor People's Campaign, King reinterpreted the Exodus story as a theo-political paradigm for overcoming contemporary racist and economic inequalities that similarly plagued Blacks and whites. In that sermon, he closed with a radical mystical-political and eschatological vision of the kingdom of God, of the beloved community, stylizing himself as another Moses on the mountaintop in sight of the promised land of African American civil rights and universal human dignity and rights.[56]

Prophetic religion and practices remade and more fully realized political and economic rights and freedoms in the Movement. King avoided politi-

---

[52]King, "New Age," in *I Have a Dream*, 24.

[53]Ibid., 15–16, 19, 27.

[54]King, "I Have a Dream (1963)," in *I Have a Dream*, 103–106.

[55]Nichole R. Phillips, "A 'Spirituality of Improvisation': Martin Luther King Jr.'s 'I Have a Dream' in Rearticulating American National Identity," in *Revives My Soul Again,* ed. Baldwin and Anderson, 185–205.

[56]King, "I See the Promised Land (1968)," in *I Have a Dream*, 194–196, 203.

cal theories of gradual inevitable progress to instantiate this symbolic and prophetic vision of the good society, the beloved community. Likewise, he eschewed an otherworldly eschatology that encouraged a complacent church with an irrelevant ministry.[57] In coining this symbol, the beloved community, King advocated for African American rights and equality in a world embedded and entrenched in its originating sin of racism. He opted for and promoted a realized eschatology that enjoined leaders, scholars, and activists to collaborate and cooperate as co-workers with God in local and global freedom movements in order to introduce and actualize the beloved community, a this-worldly just society modeled on divine love and justice.[58]

In his 1967 sermon against the Vietnam War at Riverside Church and presidential address to the SCLC, King emphasized divine love present in all world religions as a transcendent moral basis for anti-war activism and for a more inclusive and expansive view of the beloved community. God's universal love as a creator and a liberator theologically supports and compels a global pacifist scope of the beloved community. In the sermon, King argued economic and political reasons for the Movement's anti-war activism—war increases poverty and endangers democracy, replacing freedom with violence—that stemmed from this theological imaginary. Theological symbols and claims about God as the universal creator and about love of the *imago Dei* in all life prompted and propelled a new social order that rejects "the god of hate," a gospel of militarism and materialism, and "the altar of retaliation" and instead embraces the beloved community. Taken together, in this sermon and speech, King theo-politically reshaped and recast the Movement in terms of civil rights and human rights, as a global movement for broader systemic and structural change, which paralleled the Movement's resistance to "the triple evils" or intersectional oppressions of racism, poverty, and militarism.[59] King's complex religio-political worldview and activism demonstrates that, as Stephanie Mitchem has argued, "human rights expand the capabilities of religion to address Black oppression."[60]

Ultimately, the beloved community in the Movement carried eccle-

---

[57]King, "Letter," in *I Have a Dream*, 92, 97, and "Promised Land," in *I Have a Dream*, 197–198.

[58]King, "Letter," in *I Have a Dream*, 92, and "Promised Land," in *I Have a Dream*, 194–195; cf. Richard Wills, *Martin Luther King, Jr. and the Image of God* (New York: Oxford University Press, 2009), 139–164.

[59]King, "A Time to Break Silence (1967)," in *I Have a Dream*, 140, 147, 150, and "Where Do We Go from Here? (1967)," in *I Have a Dream*, 176–177.

[60]Stephanie Y. Mitchem, *Race, Religion, and Politics: Toward Human Rights in the United States* (Lanham, MD: Rowman and Littlefield, 2019), 100.

132   *Nevertheless, We Persist*

siological implications for US public life, as a theological symbol of and prophetic praxis for the kingdom of God, and as a political vision of American democratic life. It both captured and constructed King's and activists' ever more encompassing vision of redemptive social change in and of a racist society: an eschatological hope in divine justice that undergirds rather than undoes human efforts to realize that justice, at least partly, through moral, spiritual, and political forces of transformative love. The beloved community, as utilized by King, pointed out and disputed the anti-democratic, sinful nature of American society; also, the beloved community was partly instantiated by prophetic resistance via the "powerful weapons [of] the voices, the feet, and the bodies" of Movement activists in marches, sit-ins, and other nonviolent direct actions.[61] In other words, these demonstrations not only confronted and countered a racist status quo but also embodied a religio-political praxis of world-making, of ekklesial work, to reconstruct a more just alternative common life. For example, the March on Washington participated in a politics of national memory, because it resignified sacred sites and spaces of American political religion, especially its iconic texts and figures on the National Mall. The March "strategically appropriated Lincoln's memory and monument as political weapons" for racial justice, reinterpreting those same sites and spaces, texts and figures, and monuments within a Black religio-political imaginary and hermeneutics.[62] This iconic moment in the Movement combined rhetorical, symbolic, and prophetic practices of what I call ekklesial work, of community-creating praxis. The March transformed whitewashed (architecturally and socio-politically) public spaces and refigured the National Mall into an alternative reimagined religio-political space that briefly but boldly enacted racial equality, justice, solidarity, and freedom.

In my view, a feminist public theology that amplifies ekklesial or community-creating work problematizes and decenters a one-sided story of clericalist leaders in the Black Freedom Movement, particularly the Civil Rights Movement, by elaborating on key women leaders and their often eclipsed or erased anti-racist, human rights, and community building work in the Movement. Ella Baker (1903–1986) conceptualized and struggled through religio-political practices for a more inclusive, just, humane, and participatory democratic world with well-known leaders

---

[61]King, "Social Organization," in *I Have a Dream*, 53.

[62]Melissa V. Harris-Lacewell, "African Americans, Religion, and the American Presidency," in *Religion, Race, and the American Presidency*, ed. Gastón Espinosa (Lanham, MD: Rowman and Littlefield, 2008), 206–208, and quoting historian Scott Sandage on 212.

Racism, Nonviolent Collective Action, and the Civil Rights Movement   133

but mostly with grassroots groups and organizers in the Black Freedom Movement for full and equal human and citizenship rights between the 1930s and 1960s.[63] "Radical change for Ella Baker was about a persistent and protracted process of discourse, debate, consensus, reflection, and struggle. . . . Baker's theory of social change and political organizing was inscribed in her practice. Her ideas were written in her work: a coherent body of lived text." Baker's lifework consisted of anti-racist left-leaning democratic politics and practices that combined intellectual, interracial, and international activism from Harlem to Mississippi, and beyond to Vietnam, Puerto Rico, and South Africa.[64] Reexamining and revisiting Baker's life, social and religious influences, community work, and religio-political claims and engagement hold much transformative promise and potential to further develop and advance a feminist approach to public theology as ekklesial work, especially what I propose as its interrelated rhetorical, symbolic, and prophetic practices.

Upon graduation from Shaw University, Baker participated in the Great Migration of African Americans to the northern US in the 1930s, seeking greater socio-economic opportunities. Baker resided in Harlem, which she considered "a hotbed of radical thinking" and which informed and influenced her political vision of democratic politics for the common good as well as her organizing practice of grassroots collective action.[65] Baker's many activities included reporting about Black women's racialized and sexualized labor,[66] labor organizing and consumer education in churches, unions, schools, and community groups, and directing a national cooperative to empower Black people through participatory rather than racialized capitalist democracy. In addition to her activism, Baker flourished as a teacher at the New York Public Library. Baker sponsored educational programs such as the Young People's Forum that focused on wide-ranging social, political, cultural, economic, and international issues, including anti-lynching advocacy.[67] Through these events, Baker developed a "popular democratic pedagogy, which emphasized the importance of tapping oppressed communities for their own knowledge, strength, and

---

[63]Joanne Grant, *Fundi: The Story of Ella Baker* (New York: First Run/Icarus Films, 1981); Joanne Grant, *Ella Baker: Freedom Bound* (New York: Wiley and Sons, 1998); Barbara Ransby, *Ella Baker and the Black Freedom Movement: A Radical Democratic Vision* (Chapel Hill: University of North Carolina Press, 2003); Rosetta E. Ross, *Witnessing and Testifying: Black Women, Religion, and Civil Rights* (Minneapolis: Fortress Press, 2003); and Kathy Janich, "This Week in Street Art: Black Women Celebrated on Charmaine Minniefield Murals," *ArtsATL*, May 23, 2019.

[64]Ransby, *Ella Baker*, 1, 6.

[65]Ibid., 66–67; Ross, *Witnessing and Testifying*, 38–39.

[66]Ross, *Witnessing and Testifying*, 40–41.

[67]Ransby, *Ella Baker*, 69–70; Ross, *Witnessing and Testifying*, 39–40.

leadership in constructing models of social change."[68] Social change education together with cooperative economics and radical democratic politics could chart a course toward, culminate in, and foster community-driven transformative social change. Moreover, Harlem established and functioned as "a vibrant Black public sphere"; the library together with community organizations and international activism constituted, for Baker, "democratic public spaces where community members, either formally educated or self-taught, gathered, debated, and collaborated. In all these venues, women were central participants."[69] Similar to Dorothy Day, Baker "valued the localized process of intensive small group discussions and planning that a 'cell' structure composed"[70] to inhabit and create vibrant transformative worldviews.

In the 1940s, Baker worked initially as NAACP field secretary and then later was appointed its national director of branches. She traveled half of each year (while resisting segregation laws)[71] and sustained an active schedule that sometimes involved crisscrossing a state in a two-week time frame. Between September and November 1941, she gave sixty-three speeches in seven cities, with "speeches at up to five churches on a given Sunday afternoon."[72] Although Baker bypassed career paths in teaching and in medical missionary work, she "liv[ed] a missionary's existence: traveling from one town to another preaching the 'Gospel' of racial justice and at times attempting as she herself put it to 'pass a miracle.' "[73] Contrary to the NAACP's aim for nationally significant and powerful legal changes, Baker focused on movement building for radical change by cultivating and nurturing relationships with local organizers, by empowering local branches and leaders in their contexts and campaigns, and by increasing local members' participation. In Baker's view, "People have to be made to understand that they cannot look for salvation anywhere but to themselves."[74] Between 1944 and 1946, Baker launched regional leadership conferences throughout the northeastern, southeastern, and midwestern US. These conferences rejected hierarchical leadership and engaged in "the mechanics of movement building," featuring such topics as "protest, political pressure, education and propaganda, legal action, and

---

[68]Ransby, *Ella Baker*, 362.
[69]Ibid., 72, 73; cf. 79.
[70]Ibid., 96.
[71]Ibid., 124–128.
[72]Ibid., 117–118, 291.
[73]Ibid., 130.
[74]Ross, *Witnessing and Testifying*, 42.

Racism, Nonviolent Collective Action, and the Civil Rights Movement 135

cooperation and collaboration with other groups." Ministers played key invited roles, and meetings took place in both local YMCAs and churches.[75]

In both NAACP positions, Baker lobbied for a more inclusive, democratic, and egalitarian organizations as well as for more militant mass action campaigns, in solidarity with the labor movement and with gender inclusion and equity movements.[76] In 1946, she resigned the NAACP director position due to her social, economic, and political concerns with its deeply entrenched race, class, and gender politics, which coalesced in its elitist bureaucratic nature, its class and gender biases, and its predominantly legalistic goals. These characteristics were contrary to the multidimensional approach that Baker promoted to effect more transformative social change and justice.[77] She criticized the NAACP's restrictive politics of respectability, which identified middle-class upwardly mobile Blacks as ideal candidates for campaigns to win African American citizenship rights; by contrast Baker continued to defy predominant race and gender norms by dialoguing and organizing in decentralized ways with majority low-wealth and working-class Blacks, and by modeling "an alternative image of womanhood."[78]

> To young women, Black and white, Baker embodied the possibility of escaping the restrictions that defined conventional femininity. Authoritative yet unassuming, self-confident and assertive, forcing others to take her seriously simply by presuming that they would, Baker was a revelation.... Ella Baker was the comforting, nurturing, rock-solid mother to the movement.... She was a militant activist, an insurgent intellectual, and a revolutionary, descriptors that are usually associated with men rather than women and with youth rather than the middle-aged. Baker's complex, carefully crafted persona enabled her to cross gender and generational boundaries within the movement.[79]

The Montgomery Bus Boycott in 1955–1956—initiated by Rosa Parks with allied veteran organizers in the Women's Political Council and the Montgomery NAACP[80]—reignited the Black Freedom Movement with

---

[75]Ransby, *Ella Baker*, 140–142.
[76]Ibid., 106, 110, 132, 135–136.
[77]Ross, *Witnessing and Testifying*, 43–44.
[78]Ransby, *Ella Baker*, 120, 128, 137–139, 142, 256.
[79]Ibid., 258.
[80]Rosa Parks was prominently involved for nearly six decades in civil rights activism in

136   *Nevertheless, We Persist*

mass nonviolent protests and actions. In its aftermath, in 1957 Baker co-created with Bayard Rustin the SCLC, a southwide organization headed by Martin Luther King Jr. and centered at Ebenezer Baptist Church in Atlanta. It was a coalition of church-based leaders and committed to faith-based grassroots nonviolent campaigns. Baker served as the interim director.[81] Baker played a pivotal role as a strategic liaison among a broad coalition of groups that constituted the SCLC, negotiating class and gender tensions that predated its founding and prefigured its subsequent problems: between leaders and activists, between national spokespersons and community-based participants, between planning mass actions and empowering local communities, and so on.[82] Baker together with Rustin mapped and implemented the SCLC's first national campaign's guiding principles and logistics, the Prayer Pilgrimage for Freedom at the Lincoln Memorial in May 1957, to commemorate the third anniversary of racially integrated education, to reduce rivalry among civil rights organizations, and to situate the movement solidly on religious grounds, claims, and practices.[83] Indeed, "the church provided Blacks with the technical skills to enter the political arena: literacy, fundraising, public speaking, management, and organization. In addition, the church provided its members with a powerful moral language within which to frame political issues."[84] President Eisenhower met with civil rights leaders thereafter, and signed the Civil Rights Act into law in August 1957.

Building on this political policy success, the SCLC kicked off a voter registration project in over twenty cities in 1958, and King eventually invited Baker to lead it, given her well-honed social networking and political organizing skills.[85] Beyond voter registration and local campaigns in affiliated groups, this SCLC project also featured hearings to "draw national attention to ... the undemocratic racial exclusion that dominated the political process. ... Organizing people to testify at hearings was a way to embolden local leaders and prospective activists."[86] The hearings underscored and resisted racist politics, on the one hand, and reclaimed and recovered grassroots political agency and action as a site

---

Montgomery and later in Detroit, particularly regarding desegregation, voter rights and registration, housing and employment discrimination, and criminal and sexual justice. *Rosa Parks: My Story* (New York: Puffin Books, 1992, 1999); Jeanne Theoharis, *The Rebellious Life of Mrs. Rosa Parks* (Boston: Beacon Press, 2015).

[81]Ransby, *Ella Baker*, 174–175.
[82]Ibid., 172, 192.
[83]Ibid., 176–177.
[84]Ibid., 192.
[85]Ibid., 178–183.
[86]Ibid., 183.

Racism, Nonviolent Collective Action, and the Civil Rights Movement **137**

of shared pursuit, of common ground activism across civil rights groups, on the other hand. Baker continually urged the SCLC to go beyond its rallies with charismatic leaders and "develop programs for mass action . . . target women for activist campaigns" and "called for the formation of youth and action teams to help ignite the work" beyond the limited results of this project.[87]

When students mobilized various desegregation sit-in demonstrations throughout the South through college organizations and groups, Baker identified with their creative risk-taking actions and expansive emancipatory agenda to end all kinds of discrimination and violence. Baker organized and facilitated a transformative Easter weekend meeting of these interracial and interregional students at Shaw University in April 1960.[88] From that meeting emerged the SNCC, an independent student-led group unaffiliated but coalitioned with leading civil rights groups such as the NAACP, SCLC, and others in order to build nonviolently an alternative more loving and just world, the beloved community.[89] Baker ultimately resigned from the SCLC interim or acting director position to guide, advise, and coordinate support for SNCC as its "generating force"[90] until 1966.

Baker gained the respect of interracial radical youth in this self-determined student movement and refused to continue to contend and wrestle with the SCLC's patriarchal theo-politics of respectability and messianic cult of personality, which centralized "good citizen" preacher leaders or saviors while it marginalized women and grassroots groups.[91] "Baker criticized unchecked egos, objected to undemocratic structures, protested unilateral decision making, condemned elitism, and refused to nod in loyal deference to everything 'the leader' had to say."[92] Moreover, Baker preferred and promoted democratic decentralized or localized leadership in collective decision-making and movements which contrasted sharply with the southern Black clerical leadership embodied by King and other SCLC leaders.[93] For Baker, "revolution was an ongoing process intimately bound up with one's vision of the future and with how one interacted with others on a daily basis" to enable and enact that future into reality.[94] Thus, SNCC opened up new horizons for group-based leadership and lo-

---

[87]Ransby, *Ella Baker*, 187, and Ross, *Witnessing and Testifying*, 44–45.
[88]Ransby, *Ella Baker*, 239–242, 245.
[89]Ibid., 247; Ross, *Witnessing and Testifying*, 226.
[90]Ransby, *Ella Baker*, 271.
[91]Ibid., 175–176, 184–185, 188.
[92]Ibid., 4.
[93]Ibid., 192–193.
[94]Ibid., 251.

138 *Nevertheless, We Persist*

cal activism that pressed beyond then current constraints of an educated professional middle-class clergy to prioritize primarily marginalized Blacks and especially Black women in the movement.[95]

As the 1960s progressed, SNCC broadened and then critically evaluated its desegregation agenda of restaurants, transportation, theatres, and so on, to confront systemic and structural issues of economic and political justice. Nonviolent campaigns, demonstrations, arrests, and at times vigilante mobs and violent police actions, especially against the SNCC-sponsored Freedom Rides to integrate interstate buses, gained nationwide attention and some political success for the resurgent movement.[96] Baker urged SNCC activists to stand in solidarity with, to learn from and with working-class and poor Black community organizers and activists across Alabama, Mississippi, and Louisiana.[97] With Baker's intellectual, spiritual, and political example, longtime grassroots networks, and financial as well as other support, SNCC coordinated with, empowered, and emboldened local communities through Freedom Schools to determine their political agenda and to organize new or revitalize local campaigns for race, class, and gender equality, particularly but not only by gaining social and political capital through voter registration.[98]

In Freedom Summer 1964, local activists together with SNCC and interracial student volunteers engaged in a voter education and registration campaign in Mississippi.[99] This long-running campaign that culminated in Freedom Summer witnessed an immediate and sustained counter-campaign of public terror, with violent retaliatory confrontations at protests. For example, tenant farmer-turned-civil rights leader Fannie Lou Hamer attended SNCC meetings at her home Baptist Church in Ruleville in 1962 and afterward volunteered with other grassroots activists to promote voter registration in Indianola. Police stopped the bus and arrested all activists on the return trip; Hamer supported the group with songs, such as "This Little Light of Mine," "Freedom's Coming and It Won't Be Long," and "Down by the Riverside." Hamer was also fired and continually harassed for months afterward. She only intensified her commitment to work as a SNCC field secretary, intimately interlinking her religious worldview with democracy and freedom through protest, music (gospel and freedom songs), and prayer. In 1963, while returning from a voter

---

[95]Ibid., 279–280, 291–295, 297–298; Ross, *Witnessing and Testifying*, 45.
[96]Ransby, *Ella Baker*, 265–267.
[97]Ibid., 261–262, 301–306.
[98]Ibid., 269–270, 273–274, 299–300, 326–329, 365.
[99]Ibid., 320–325.

Racism, Nonviolent Collective Action, and the Civil Rights Movement **139**

registration workshop in Georgia, Hamer and five other activists were arrested, jailed, and severely beaten. Throughout this traumatic experience, Hamer and the activists sang, prayed biblical verses, and relied on religious arguments to rebuke the jailers.[100] Retaliatory racialized violence led to a dozen murders during that three-year campaign and firebombings at nearly forty churches during Freedom Summer.[101]

Nevertheless, the Mississippi voter registration project helped create in April 1964 the Mississippi Freedom Democratic Party. Founded by Fannie Lou Hamer, the MFDP was organized at a rally in response to racist exclusion and rejection by the state's Democratic Party. The MFDP convention selected its sixty-eight freedom delegates to attend the Democratic National Convention (DNC) in Atlantic City, New Jersey, in August 1964. As the director of the MFDP's Washington office, Baker not only spoke in Mississippi churches and meeting halls but also lobbied Congress along with northern left-wing allied labor and civil rights organizations to shed light on and gain support for the MFDP at the DNC.[102] Together with the vice chair of the MFDP delegates Fannie Lou Hamer, Baker spent three weeks soliciting donors and supporters at rallies, press conferences, and church meetings in Washington, DC, Maryland, and Pennsylvania.[103] Introduced by SNCC to interpreting the signs of the times in light of Christian scriptures, Hamer characterized the events of 1964 religio-politically in terms of eschatological hope: "Faith is the substance of things hoped for and the evidence of things not seen. . . . In 1964 the faith that we had hoped for started to be translated into action."[104] At the same time, SNCC volunteers embedded in and canvassed communities across Mississippi "spreading the gospel about the MFDP and documenting instances of Black voter intimidation and outright obstruction."[105] When denied entry into the DNC and when initially endorsed but then disavowed by civil

---

[100]Ross, *Witnessing and Testifying*, 90–91, 94–96, 99–101, 103–106. Grounded in that same religious worldview, Hamer fully recognized both the promises and pitfalls of the Black Church tradition; she affirmed how Black churches sustained African Americans amid a racialized and violent society, and at the same time criticized Black churches for "selling out to the white power structure." Ibid., 111–112. Recent biographies of Hamer include Keisha N. Blain, *Until I Am Free: Fannie Lou Hamer's Enduring Message to America* (Boston: Beacon Press, 2021), and Kate Clifford Larson, *Walk with Me: A Biography of Fannie Lou Hamer* (New York: Oxford University Press, 2021), as well as the documentary film by Joy Davenport, *Fannie Lou Hamer's America* (Women Make Movies, 2022).

[101]Ransby, *Ella Baker*, 311–313.

[102]Ibid., 330–332, 335.

[103]Ibid., 337.

[104]Ross, *Witnessing and Testifying*, 112–113, 233. Hamer offered her own socio-political interpretations of Christian scriptures—a constructive public theology—to inspire civil rights activism, and to interlink that activism to Christian emancipatory and eschatological goals.

[105]Ransby, *Ella Baker*, 334.

140

rights leaders as a result of multiple political and economic pressures, the MFDP delegates with Hamer, Baker, and other high-profile MFDP women leaders held rallies and vigils outside the New Jersey convention hall to critically question and contest Mississippi's all-white delegates as well as demand equal political representation and rights. Despite a church-based meeting with impassioned speakers, the MFDP refused the backdoor-brokered compromise to seat two delegates at the DNC, based on their own "political pilgrimage" and the ongoing racist misrepresentation of Mississippi. Despite Fannie Lou Hamer's nationally televised speech about the MFDP's agenda, the MFDP was not seated but still contributed to strategic political change. Thereafter, the DNC delegates were required to reflect equitable representation in terms of race, gender, and so on. Hamer served as a Mississippi delegate to the DNC in 1968 and again in 1972.[106]

In the mid-1960s, Baker's activism continually evolved into a multi-dimensional freedom platform that was significantly shaped by global political events: urban Black uprisings in Harlem, Watts, and elsewhere, anti-Vietnam War protests, the assassination of Malcolm X, the Bloody Sunday police action against Selma civil rights marchers, and the assassination of Martin Luther King Jr.[107] Baker guided and defended SNCC while she was alienated from it and when it collapsed by the late 1960s. It embraced and employed a more revolutionary vision and method of Black power rather than a nonviolent inclusive interracial beloved community, which led many whites to leave or be expelled by SNCC.[108] By the late 1960s and early 1970s, Baker urged communities to mobilize and struggle against the interlocking systems of racism, capitalism, colonialism, and imperialism. In 1971 at rallies to free Angela Davis who had been wrongfully arrested and imprisoned, Baker identified with Davis's radical intellectual and activist views and provided a compelling perspective about Davis's imprisonment as a symbolic shutdown of Black insurgent visions and actions. Speaking at both churches and universities, Baker argued, "We have rights only as long as we are willing to struggle for them."[109] Later, at a New York rally for Puerto Rican independence in 1974, she similarly inspired activists "to make the fight for freedom every day in the year, every year until [we] win it."

Baker's practices of what I call doing ekklesial or community-creating work can be elaborated through the trifold lens of rhetorical, symbolic,

---

[106]Ransby, *Ella Baker*, 337–338, 341; Ross, *Witnessing and Testifying*, 108–109.
[107]Ransby, *Ella Baker*, 344–345, 350.
[108]Ibid., 344, 346, 348.
[109]Ibid., 353.

Racism, Nonviolent Collective Action, and the Civil Rights Movement 141

and prophetic practices, which envisioned and aimed to realize a more just and humane world. According to historian Barbara Ransby, Baker's rhetorical practices embodied "a conscious reflection of her egalitarian and democratic politics . . . [which] conveyed a message about who she was and what kind of political vision she wanted to project to her listeners."[110] That multidimensional vision consisted of respect, dignity, equality, freedom based on mutual recognition and responsibility, community building and empowerment, and universal well-being and flourishing. Baker addressed an overflowing church crowd on January 1964 Freedom Day, as they mourned the assassination of NAACP field secretary and civil rights worker Medgar Evers. In this speech, Baker renewed the liberatory struggle for a comprehensive "freedom of the human spirit, a larger freedom that encompasses all of [humanity]," at the intersections of race, class, and politics, but also economics, job and food security, education, health care, and so on.[111] Similarly, in the 1964 MFDP keynote address, Baker eulogized three murdered Mississippi civil rights workers as well as politically galvanized the party with that same underlying vision of freedom, rooted in undoing race, gender, and sexual privileges and politics: "Until the killing of Black men, Black mothers' sons, is as important to the rest of the country as the killing of white mothers' sons, we who believe in freedom cannot rest."[112]

Baker's speeches pointed to and co-created with communities of struggle the possibility of a more expansive vision and practice of divinely created and gifted freedom; she testified and witnessed to a new world that imagined and enacted freedom from dehumanization and degradation as well as freedom for self-realization in community.[113] Grounded in her early Harlem years and further developed during her Movement community-organizing efforts, Baker emphasized freedom as individual free exercise; collective organizing for dignity and equality; racial, gender, sexual, and bodyrights, and so on.[114] Fannie Lou Hamer similarly elaborated on the radical Christological implications and impact of freedom on the role of religion in public life: "We can't separate Christ from freedom and freedom from Christ. The first words of Jesus' public ministry were in Luke 4:18, where freedom is the central theme."[115] While less explicitly theological but always framed by religious contexts and settings, Baker's

---

[110]Ibid., 361.
[111]Ibid., 318–320.
[112]Ibid., 335.
[113]Ross, *Witnessing and Testifying*, 49.
[114]Ibid., 40–41.
[115]Ibid., 225.

142 *Nevertheless, We Persist*

worldview articulated in her speeches illustrated a radical democratic humanist tradition, which consisted of democratic practices to centralize, empower, envoice, and enfranchise socially, economically, and politically marginalized peoples; egalitarian structures for the purpose of inclusive participatory democracy; a critical race, class, and gender analysis of injustice; and interracial and interclass community-based organizing and struggle.[116] In religious terms, Baker's rhetorical practices "stressed a theological positive humanism emphasizing what people can achieve cooperatively by their own organized initiatives on the basis of capacities given to them by God."[117] Thus, founder of the SNCC Freedom Singers and founder-artistic director of the African American women's a capella group Sweet Honey in the Rock Bernice Johnson Reagon fittingly eulogized Baker at her funeral by singing one of Baker's favorite movement songs, "Guide My Feet": "Guide my feet while I run this race . . . for I do not want to run this race alone . . . for I do not want to run this race in vain."[118]

Baker's rhetorical practices fused with and concurrently influenced her symbolic practices to reconstruct religious beliefs about human freedom and dignity that in turn reshaped radical democratic practices in US public life. Baker's religiosity not only was sustained by lifelong ties to the Baptist Church in North Carolina and New York, but also was expressed pragmatically in "what you do" for others and thus how you "share your lives with people."[119] Baker emulated her grandfather's pastoral work and her mother's mission work in community ministries to meet material human needs regardless of social class hierarchies, and translated those community ministries into her own positive humanist view of full human dignity and rights.[120] Womanist theologian Rosetta Ross demonstrates how Baker combined Christian beliefs in divinely endowed human dignity, self-worth, and potential for self-expression and self-realization with radical democratic, participatory, and egalitarian practices to envision an alternative more just social order, or to put it simply in Baker's words to advocate for "the cause of humanity." Democracy and egalitarianism enabled witnessing to and more fully incarnating Baker's bedrock faith

---

[116]Ransby, *Ella Baker*, 364–365, 368–370; Ross, *Witnessing and Testifying*, 46–47.

[117]Ross, *Witnessing and Testifying*, 49, 233.

[118]Ransby, *Ella Baker*, 12. Bernice Johnson Reagon's artistry and scholarship is in part represented by Smithsonian Folkways Recordings, *Voices of the Civil Rights Movement: Black American Freedom Songs 1960–1966*, compiled by Bernice Johnson Reagon, and Reagon, "Music in the Civil Rights Movement," PBS American Experience, 2006.

[119]Ross, *Witnessing and Testifying*, 34–35.

[120]Ibid., 32–37, 43.

Racism, Nonviolent Collective Action, and the Civil Rights Movement **143**

in human freedom and dignity, or "the basic right of people to realize as fully as possible the capacities with which they have been endowed by their Creator."[121] In addition to Baker's theological anthropology of mutually appreciating and realizing full humanity through empowered personal agency and communal organizing, Fannie Lou Hamer also referred to and interpreted Freedom Summer in explicitly Christological and eschatological terms, embodying a more just, inclusive, and diverse society: "The 1964 summer project was the beginning of a New Kingdom right here on earth. . . . They started something that no one could ever stop. . . . They did something in Mississippi that gave us the hope that we prayed for so many years. . . . Christ was a revolutionary person, out there where it was happening."[122]

Analyzed by Ross, women's community work against racism and other systemic injustices encompasses wide-ranging activities for the survival and enhanced quality of life of Black and other oppressed communities: "'arguing, obstructing, organizing, teaching, lecturing, demonstrating, suing, writing letters,' and other activities, often concluding as organized actions and programs," such as advocacy, protest, and other forms of political agitation.[123] Baker's lived text and body of work as a community organizer and social justice practitioner illuminate these and other prophetic practices of women in the Black Freedom Movement. Baker served both religious and religiously affiliated institutions, but she also played central roles in education and outreach programs of "para-religious organizations that attend to poverty, homelessness, education, political participation, and other community interests."[124] Moreover, from this feminist and womanist theological perspective of public theology as ekklesial work, as creating community, Baker's prophetic practices integrated with and infused everyday activities. "In the ordinary processes of living and moving on down the freedom road, practices for social change and liberation emerge." Those practices "pass on particular virtues that attend to surviving and thriving as persons, . . . to work in partnership with God for community survival and positive quality of life, . . . to attend to the needs of the least, . . . to participate in community-building and community-sustaining practices."[125] According to Ransby, Baker's practices recall and reveal "a crazy quilt," which provides "a warm and

---

[121]Ibid., 46–48, 50.
[122]Ibid., 114–115.
[123]Ibid., 10, 235.
[124]Ibid., 11.
[125]Ross, *Witnessing and Testifying*, 11–12.

complex work of art, a reminder of the process, a way of working and living, a way of looking at that which may seem of little value and finding its enormous transformative power."[126]

The Poor People's Campaign

US public life prevented and still prevents marginalized peoples from rightful political recognition and meaningful public participation, as a result of originary and growing inequalities around race, gender, and class as well as political inequalities related to representation, voting, and other forms of political access and agency. The 1968 Poor People's Campaign (PPC) challenged intersectional injustices of militarism, racism, and poverty. Nearly fifty years later, the revived Poor People's Campaign elevated the testimonies, theological claims and symbols, marches, rallies, and other protests of poor and low-wealth Americans as well as their allies nationwide about the devastating intersections of systemic racism, poverty, militarist war economics, and environmental crises in their lives. Combining rhetorical, symbolic, and prophetic practices, the PPC amplifies both the voices of community leaders and activists as they recount their stories and explicitly interpret social sufferings from the perspectives of race, gender, class, geography, and so on, and also the witness of marginalized peoples to illuminate and illustrate both exclusionary and future emancipatory politics via theological symbols and prophetic actions.

Charting a mediatory course between leaders and activists, between national spokespersons and community-based participants, between planning mass actions and empowering local communities, and between a civil rights agenda and a human rights agenda, the contemporary PPC rejuvenated this similarly named 1968 civil rights–era faith-based social movement and campaign for economic justice against the triple evils of racism, poverty, and militarism that damage, diminish, and endanger US democracy and human rights.[127] In terms of the current movement's purpose and methods of community organizing and engagement, the PPC

---

[126]Ransby, *Ella Baker*, 374.

[127]Anna Diamond, "Remember Resurrection City and the Poor People's Campaign of 1968," *Smithsonian Magazine*, May 2018; Rev. Dr. William J. Barber II with Jonathan Wilson-Hartgrove, *The Third Reconstruction: How a Moral Movement Is Overcoming the Politics of Division and Fear* (Boston: Beacon Press, 2016); Harmeet Kaur, "A Social Justice Movement Inspired by MLK Is Waging a New War on Poverty," CNN, January 20, 2019; Rev. Dr. William J Barber II, *We Are Called to Be a Movement* (New York: Workman Publishing, 2020); Rev. Dr. Liz Theoharis, ed., *We Cry Justice: Reading the Bible with the Poor People's Campaign* (Minneapolis: Broadleaf Books, 2021).

Racism, Nonviolent Collective Action, and the Civil Rights Movement **145**

co-founded by Rev. Dr. William J. Barber II and Rev. Dr. Liz Theoharis coordinated nationwide marches in forty state capitals and Washington, DC, in late spring and early summer 2018 to hear and heed the voices and concerns of 140+ million poor and low-wealth people about five major intersectional injustices of racism, poverty, war economics, ecological degradation, and the distorted narrative of religious nationalism.[128] Akin to the 1968 campaign which allied Black, Latinx, Indigenous, white, and all poor people in demonstrating at different federal agencies from its Resurrection City near the Lincoln Memorial, these marches mobilized a multiracial, multicultural, multireligious community into a nonviolent moral fusion movement that articulates and advocates for a new transformative vision of US public life. The renewed PPC aims to empower grassroots people through testimony at local listening sessions as well as congressional hearings (initiated by Sen. Elizabeth Warren and Rep. Elijah Cummings in June 2018), highlighting the presence, voices, and views of inpacted people;[129] through launching state committees and voter registration efforts; and through lobbying in rallies, marches, sit-ins, and the like to introduce and implement more just public policy. The PPC's religious bases and alliances reveal a diverse multi-partner coalition that entails and enacts a racial and religious fusion movement via alliance and solidarity politics, and that is grounded in a moral center of analysis, imagination, and socio-political action to shift the predominant narratives in America and co-create a more just society through empowering people to influence elections as well as policies. While prioritizing interfaith activism to revolutionize US society and public life, the PPC emphasizes and emulates in its religio-political practices the example of a brown first-century Palestinian Jew named Jesus who proclaims jubilee at the outset of his public ministry in the Gospel of Luke, also invoked by SNCC activists and Fannie Lou Hamer to theologically and Christologically contextualize and construct their religio-political engagement.

The PPC exemplifies and deepens what I call a feminist- and womanist-informed approach to public theology as ekklesial or community-creating work, particularly the PPC's world-making in rhetorical, symbolic, and prophetic practices. Rev. Barber addressed the Vatican Pontifical Acad-

---

[128]In a March 18, 2021, email, PPC statistics showed "women and people of color are disproportionately impacted by the poverty wages allowed under [US] current minimum wage laws: 45% of women (74.2 million), 59.7% of Black people (23.7 million), 64.1% of Latinx people (38 million), 40.8% of Asian people (8 million), and 58.9% of Native and Indigenous People (2.14 million)."

[129]Some of the PPC's rhetorical practices of storytelling for social change are shared on the PPC website, "We Cry Power: Stories from the Moral Revolution."

emy for the Social Sciences in October 2021 on the Role of Moral Fusion Coalitions in the Struggle to End Poverty. In an October 8 email, Barber advocated that "the church must have a prophetic moral outcry and must help foster another way of seeing the world. . . . [It] must push a penetrating moral imagination." The PPC's world-making or religio-political envisioning and enacting of a more just society blends religious and political principles and practices for social justice outlined on the PPC website: to create the "yet to be United States." It uses "moral analysis based on our deepest religious and constitutional values that demand justice for all. Moral revival is necessary to save the heart and soul of our democracy." Moreover, it stresses equal protection under the law via the 14th Amendment; it disrupts false narratives of religious nationalism and white supremacy; and it affirms a common line of theological reasoning in the biblical prophetic traditions that "our deepest religious and constitutional values insist that the primary moral issues of our day must be how our society treats the poor, those on the margins, women, LGBTQIA2S+ folks, workers, immigrants, the disabled and the sick."

The PPC's rhetorical and prophetic practices, articulated in the PPC Demands on the website, are rooted in symbolic practices that reinterpret a theology of love, that express "love [for] this democracy enough to go to jail in nonviolent civil disobedience for it, to organize in the streets for it, to sue in courts for it, to register to vote for it." Building on the civil rights era which produced the historical and current movement, the PPC stresses nonviolent moral direct action to build people power; its nonpartisan grassroots groups proclaim the full humanity of oppressed peoples and their allies; and its campaigns address intersectional injustices of systemic racism, poverty, mass incarceration of poor communities of color, the war economy/militarism, and ecological devastation. The PPC's forty-five state coordinating committees together with movement leadership and religious leaders, scholars, advocates, and allied organizations elaborate its policy priorities in a biblically based Jubilee Platform, released in June 2020 on the website and framed as a "reconstruction and restoration agenda . . . [to]repair and transform lives" of low-wealth Americans. This platform as articulated on the PPC website includes comprehensive, free, and just COVID-19 relief, universal health care and housing, living wages, updated poverty measures, federal jobs programs in poor and low-income communities, voting, labor, civil rights, equitable wages and education, just immigration reform, Indigenous peoples' rights, fair taxation, reprioritizing the US federal budget, and establishing a presidential advisory council. In a July 1, 2021, movement email, Rev. Barber reclaimed the theo-political meanings of Jubilee—"Until the poor are lifted, workers

Racism, Nonviolent Collective Action, and the Civil Rights Movement 147

are paid, the sick are healed and insured, voting is not suppressed, police killing is stopped, land, air, and water are not poisoned, war is not pushed, promoted, and promulgated, humanity is respected, children are protected, and civil rights and labor rights and human rights are never neglected—until these things are actualized, their absence must embolden and intensify our dissent and agitation."

Taking a snapshot of its activism in 2020 and 2022, below, further demonstrates how the PPC interweaves shared practices of ekklesial or community-creating work—rhetorical, symbolic, and prophetic practices of witness and protest—to enact its religious and political vision. Prior to the June 20, 2020, gathering, a Mass Poor People's Assembly and Moral March on Washington, PPC state-coordinating committees held town hall meetings and other events to mobilize, organize, register and educate, engage, and empower people to vote (M.O.R.E. events), while the national PPC sponsored monthly digital mass meetings. Explained in March 24, 2020, and June 1, 2020, movement emails, this assembly and march took place as a digital and social media "forum where poor and low-wealth people can share their truths" and "shake the very conscience of this nation." In the first week of June, Cultural Days of Action provided PPC members and allies with toolkits containing banners, songs, signs, and other posts for digital and social media to amplify the coming event; faith leaders convened in a Prophetic Council and in an interfaith service of mourning; and Student Fellows met in a digital town hall to discuss COVID-19 and its impact on campus closings, police and community violence, and economic crises. Recounted in a June 2020 email, that week culminated in a Day of Fasting and Focus, with a moment of silence in honor of George Floyd's death and a litany in the biblical prophetic and jubilee traditions to support the national uprisings and "fast from oppression . . . to loose the chains of bondage . . . to let the oppressed go free, to meet the needs of everyone, to forgive debts, raise wages, and promote the general welfare." The week prior to the June 20 assembly and march, Rev. Dr. Liz Theoharis with activists from the 1968 PPC addressed an online town hall, which also included poetry, music, and other rhetorical forms, to highlight intersectional injustices; that same day, the PPC together with LGBTQ+ and affirming organizations organized a town hall and Pride celebration, emphasizing LGBTQ+ leaders and resistance.

Headlined by clergy, activists, and mostly poor and low-wealth people, viewed by more than 2.5 million people, covered by major media news outlets, and followed by PPC state-based campaigns, June 20, 2020, itself served, according to June 19 and June 24 emails, as "an international stage for the stories and solutions of poor and dispossessed people. They along with 300 mobilizing partners including unions, religious denominations, and social justice organizations will lay out a transformative vision for the nation." Chronicled in a July 19 movement email, the PPC leaders and two hundred activists held a virtual congressional briefing which centralized the testimonies from PPC organizers and outlined the Jubilee Platform's moral policy agenda to disrupt the narrative of religious nationalism, address interlocking injustices, and transform the nation. At the same time, in July 23 and August 11 movement family emails, the PPC kicked off its 100 Days to the Election Call to Action, which included M.O.R.E. events, a voter registration and education campaign prior to the 2020 US presidential election specifically led by poor and low-wealth people, approximately one-third of the electorate. In late August 2020 and mid-October 2020, faith and community organizations during this campaign took a Prophetic Pledge for community trainings to increase voter turnout, and the national PPC with the NAACP Legal Defense Fund, Forward Justice, and other co-sponsoring organizations offered teach-ins about voter registration and protection as well as its Jubilee Platform. Interpreted in a January 14, 2021, movement email, the insurrectionist attack on the US Capitol on January 6, 2021, can be viewed as a violent white supremacist and religious nationalist backlash to empowered voices and votes of poor and low-wealth people united with Black, Latinx, and white voters that prioritize anti-racist and social justice political platforms.

During the 2020 PPC campaign, Rev. Barber's press conferences, letter to Congress about a new reconstruction agenda, and sermons situated the campaign in the midst of national uprisings against systemic racism after the vigilante and police murders of Ahmaud Arbery, Breonna Taylor, George Floyd, and Tony McDade; the COVID-19 pandemic and its exacerbated inequalities at the intersections of race, gender, and class; and major theological events—Pentecost Sunday, Trinity Sunday, and the Feast of Corpus Christi. An interfaith service of mourning with leading Christian, Jewish, Sikh, and Muslim religious activists together with another interfaith service of action for racial justice at St. John's Episcopal Church in Washington, DC, overlooking Black Lives Matter plaza convoked a new body of Christ and a new America that engaged in public mourning, that lamented and also resisted the loss of Indigenous and Black lives as well as potentially of the nation itself, which has historically and continually violated the rights and lives of immigrants and Black, Indigenous, and people of color. Within such a deeply meaningful time at the nexus of theology, Christology, and pneumatology, Rev. Barber characterized the PPC protests in a sermon at Washington National Cathedral on June 14 as a Eucharistic procession, as the body of Christ in the streets involved in the democratic work of the people, as a kind of theo-political liturgy that glimpsed the kin-dom of God or a coming religio-political liberation. A June 4, 2020, movement email stated: "Now when you see people in the streets, that's democracy trying to breathe. . . . We must dedicate ourselves to breathing life into our Constitution and its promises. . . . The very life of our democracy it as stake. Not a democracy that is, but the democracy that could be."

That theo-political interpretation of the PPC campaign as the birth pangs of a new nation and a restored democracy shaped the Prophecy against Pandemics events of Independence Day on July 4 and 5 and the PPC state committees' participation in the Strike for Black Lives on July 20, 2020. According to a July 10 email, nearly 170 interfaith leaders preached sermons against systemic racism and heralded a third reconstruction, built on the First Reconstruction which is associated with the late nineteenth-century 13th, 14th, and 15th Amendments to the US Constitution which abolished slavery, created birthright citizenship, and enfranchised African Americans, and on the Second Reconstruction, which is identified with civil rights–era legislation such as the 1964 Civil Rights Act and the 1965 Voting Rights Act. Translating these rhetorical, symbolic, and prophetic practices into public policy, the PPC together with the US Congressional Progressive Caucus and the Majority Leader's Task Force on Poverty and Opportunity nearly a year later in May 2021 announced a resolution, called "Third Reconstruction—Fully Addressing Poverty and Low Wages from the Bottom Up." This resolution was followed by a coordinated nationwide campaign of PPC state committee actions, explained in movement emails from May 20 and June 6–7, 2021, to rally and hold press conferences at as well as lobby congressional representatives about this resolution against death-dealing politics and for *imago Dei* supporting policies.

In April 19 and June 2, 2021, movement emails, the PPC announced its plans for an online virtual National Poor People's and Low-Wage Workers' Assembly at the Raleigh, North Carolina, state legislature on June 21, 2021, as a national launching pad for year-long events in advance of an in-person Moral March on Washington and to the polls on June 18, 2022. Featuring poor and low-wage workers, forty-five PPC state coordinating committees, religious leaders, economists, and voting rights activists who were backed by nearly two hundred partner organizations, the 2022 event "created a national stage for the voices and leadership of people directly impacted by poverty, racism, and their interlocking injustices . . . [in order] to build a campaign to realize a Third Reconstruction." Particularly stressing rhetorical and prophetic practices as a counter-narrative and counter-witness to prevalent political and economic policies, the June 2022 gathering—as promised in January 13 and March 22 movement emails—"put a face and voice" on systemic interlocking injustices and aimed to "shift the moral narrative" away from "constitutionally inconsistent, morally indefensible, politically insensitive, and economically insane" politics.

Starting a season of nonviolent moral direct action to Save Our Democracy leading toward the June 2022 gathering and ultimately toward ushering in a more just future, the PPC national leaders and state committees in coalition with dozens of partner labor, activist, and religious organizations engaged in a series of Moral Monday events during July and August 2021. These events, outlined in July 10 and 12 movement emails, publicly lobbied the US senators (through call-ins, rallies, and civil disobedience), at their Washington and home offices, to pass voting rights and economic justice policies. Framed theologically as a resurrection of nonviolent moral direct action rather than an insurrection of immoral violence, A Moral March for Democracy also took place in late July 2021 from Georgetown to Austin, Texas, sponsored by the Texas PPC committee and its coalition of interfaith, religious, and activist partners. These nonviolent direct actions climaxed in two Washington, DC, events in August 2021, as described in an August 2 movement email: the National Moral Monday march from Union Plaza to Capitol Hill to resist nationwide voter suppression bills as well as foster economic and immigrant justice policies, and the Make Good Trouble Rally on the anniversary of the March on Washington at the Lincoln Memorial. Continuing to employ symbolic practices, Rev. Barber remarked at length about this rally in religio-political terms in a September 2 movement email.

> And if I could borrow from Dr. King. . . . If our demands for full justice are wrong, then the Constitution is wrong. If our demands are wrong, then the promise of equal protection under the law is wrong. If our demands are wrong, then we might as well tear up the Declaration of Independence and its promise of life, liberty, and the pursuit of happiness for all people. If our demands are wrong, then the Bible is wrong in Isaiah 10 when [the prophet] declares "Woe unto you who legislate evil and rob the poor of their rights." If our demands are wrong, then someone ought to have the courage to say Jesus was wrong when he said the nations will be judged by the question [of Matthew 25].

Racism, Nonviolent Collective Action, and the Civil Rights Movement **151**

The PPC's rhetorical, symbolic, and prophetic practices elaborated a consistent and compelling religio-political critique and reconstruction of US democracy, and gained widespread grassroots traction nationwide. Consequently, the PPC witnessed retaliatory arrests and acts for its nonviolent direct action. As stated in a June 24 movement email, Rev. Barber together with Rev. Jesse Jackson and Rev. Jennifer Butler were arrested for voting rights advocacy during a march from the Supreme Court to the Senate office building in June 2021. Rev. Dr. Liz Theoharis along with nearly one hundred nonviolent PPC protesters and allies from thirty-five states were arrested at the Women's Moral March on Washington in July 2021, as recounted in a July 22 movement email. That same month, Barber together with Jackson and more than thirty-five protesters were arrested at a sit-in at Sen. Kyrsten Sinema's home office in Phoenix, Arizona, as testified in July 27 and July 30 movement emails. When Rev. Barber (and also Rev. Jackson) attended the trial of Ahmaud Arbery's murderers in November 2021, the defense attorney asked the judge to ban the "intimidating" presence of Black pastors, thereby making what the judge considered a racist "reprehensible" argument that criminalized Blackness itself. Barber responded with a theological counterclaim, affirming the *imago Dei* in all people: "Abolitionists who insisted on the full humanity of Black people were seen as intimidating and disruptive to the social order."[130] This failed court ban on the symbolic presence of Black pastors and of theological claims about full humanity and dignity from US public life echoes and compares with Barber's arrest for his rhetorical practices, namely an allegedly disturbing loud preaching voice during a call-response chant protest at the North Carolina state legislature in May 2017.[131] The court ultimately convicted and thereby attempted to silence Barber's rhetorical practices and Black religious speech during prophetic protests in the US public square! Nevertheless, as movement emails on October 15, 2021, and January 14, 2022, demonstrated, the National Civil Rights Museum honored the PPC co-chairs Rev. Barber and Rev. Theoharis with the Freedom Award, alongside former First Lady Michelle Obama, and the Martin Luther King Jr. Center in Atlanta presented Barber with the Beloved Community Award for Civic Leadership.

Another season of direct action in advance of the June 2022 gathering was inaugurated by the PPC in December 2021. During a Moral Monday

---

[130]Rev. William J. Barber II, "My Skin Color Should Not Prevent Me from Attending the Trial of Ahmaud Arbery's Accused Killers," *Washington Post*, November 17, 2021.

[131]Jessica Corbett, "Barber Blasts NC Supreme Court for Refusing to Review Free Speech Case," *Common Dreams*, May 10, 2022.

152 *Nevertheless, We Persist*

rally at Capitol Square as recounted in the December 24 movement email, PPC leaders and impacted people from over thirty states addressed the assembled gathering before they marched down Pennsylvania Avenue; Rev. Dr. Liz Theoharis and seventy people were arrested. Chronicled in a January 14, 2022, movement email, a two-day national launch event in mid-January 2022 involved speeches from economists, organization and faith leaders, and Sen. Elizabeth Warren and Rep. Barbara Lee, followed by a vigil of storytelling from people from thirty-five states about the importance of voting rights to fulfill democracy's promises. From February through June, the PPC engaged in a nationwide M.O.R.E tour with ten stops using similar rhetorical and symbolic practices (speeches, storytelling, and song). In a March 14, 2022, movement email, the PPC riffed on the gospel song "This Joy That I Have," and movement activists sang "This vote we have . . . this power we have . . . God gave it to me. The world didn't give it to me. And the world can't take it away." This multi-month campaign mobilized PPC state committees for the June 2022 gathering, echoed in February 14 and 25, 2022, movement emails. The tour began with two virtual regional events in southern states facing ongoing economic and political violence such as poverty, voter suppression, and lack of health care and living wages (Alabama, Florida, Georgia, and Mississippi on February 14, and Texas, Oklahoma, Louisiana, Arkansas, and Kansas on February 28). Subsequent in-person tour events, consisting of church rallies and marches, took place in midwestern cities (Cleveland, Ohio; Madison, Wisconsin) and the movement's home base in Raleigh, North Carolina, in March; in eastern cities (New York, Philadelphia) in April; and in western (Los Angeles) as well as southern cities (Memphis, the site of King's assassination amid the 1968 PPC) in May. In a mid-April movement email, the PPC released A Poor People's Pandemic Report on its website, which incorporated both data and stories to motivate the movement against intersecting injustices exposed and escalated by COVID-19.

Symbolic practices anchored and permeated the national tour's rhetorical and prophetic practices, including theological claims about crucifixion and resurrection. Framed by King's assassination in Memphis amid the 1968 PPC, the renewed PPC brings resurrected life to the movement, to poor and low-wealth peoples, and to US democracy. In that same vein, about midway through the tour on the 55th anniversary of King's "Beyond Vietnam" speech, the PPC hosted both in-person and virtual readings of the speech on April 4, 2022. A March 30 movement email remembered King's call for a "radical revolution of values" and the PPC's "moral fusion campaign" in coalition and in solidarity with poor and low-wealth

Racism, Nonviolent Collective Action, and the Civil Rights Movement   **153**

people, state leaders, faith communities, labor organizations, and so on. In addition to practices of storytelling and marching for the resurrection of poor people and of US democracy amid death-dealing policies, the PPC also utilized further prophetic practices as a call to action in the immediate weeks ahead of the June 2022 march, by instituting a Digital Drum Majors for Justice social media campaign. Weekly digital drumbeat emails together with a national mobilization tour in several PPC state committees constructed an interracial, intergenerational, and interregional beloved community on the national stage at the June 2022 assembly and march.

After the June 2022 gathering, the PPC issued a Movement Declaration to Reconstruct American Democracy and announced its next nationwide M.O.R.E campaign in advance of the congressional midterm elections in 2022 when 469 seats in Congress were up for election. The seven steps of this 125-day campaign entailed legislative advocacy, voter mobilization, nonviolent direction action, and a call for a White House summit on poverty with delegates of impacted people, religious leaders, and economists. Significantly, this campaign continued to invoke and intertwine trifold rhetorical, symbolic, and prophetic practices of ekklesial or community creating work. In a June 30, 2022, movement email, the PPC stated: "We vote for our people and for our lives. We vote to summon a Third Reconstruction that can birth us out of an impoverished democracy and usher in a new world." Particularly phrased in anthropological and eschatological terms, this Third Reconstruction according to a July 1, 2022, movement email "center[s] those who are most impacted by the interlocking injustices in our laws, policies, systems, and structures, in order to ensure we can all thrive and realize the nation we have yet to be."

In these salient moments of the Black Freedom Movement, rhetorical practices in varied forms contested prevalent understandings of political action and actors as well as public life itself. Subaltern peoples' voices, stories, and religio-political witness in symbolic and prophetic practices functioned as an important counter-hegemonic form of political participation which debunked ideologies of dominance, exclusion, and disposability in the US public realm. Moreover, this witness through religious symbols and prophetic action challenged and changed dominant and dominating notions of political participation and personhood, thereby modeling in those moments a counterpublic realm that would end suffering and edge toward a fuller realization of our common humanity and the common good. The Civil Rights Movement and the PPC created political spaces and places to tell and hear subaltern narratives, to religiously claim and perform both theological full humanity and political subjectivity, and to advocate along with their allies for social, economic, and political policies that enable social and political empathy and recognition as well as rebuild relationships of and for deeper solidarity, values that are also centralized in the major figures and practices of Latinx justice movements.

5

Ethno-nationalism, Community Organizing, and United Farm Workers

We are people of action. . . . We are the people that make world history. The history of the world has always been made by mass movements of the people.

—Dolores Huerta in *Dolores*

The freedom of association means that people can come together in organization to fight for solutions to the problems they confront in their communities. The great social justice changes in our country have happened when people came together, organized, and took direct action. It is this right that sustains and nurtures our democracy today.

—Dolores Huerta, Presidential Medal of Freedom Speech

Poetry and/as Public Theology

Since 2014, Pope Francis initiated the World Meeting of Popular Movements, for regional and international leaders of grassroots organizations and multifaith leaders to interface and dialogue, to address systemic and structural exclusion and inequity, as well as to promote freedom, equality, justice, and dignity in intersectional coalitions. Participating in and advancing this initiative, the US regional meeting in 2017 featured social movements that underscore and stand in solidarity with immigrant rights, workers' rights, criminal justice reform, eco-justice, and racial healing. The fourth global meeting in October 2021 focused on how social movements and grassroots organizations are affected by and yet still advancing their

155

struggles during the COVID-19 pandemic. Francis's address portrayed social and grassroots movement leaders as "social poets," because these movements resist systemic injustices and reclaim as well as proclaim hope. Analogizing between poetry and social justice work, Francis stated, "Poetry means creativity, and you create hope . . . forge the dignity of each person, of families, and of society as a whole." The "poetic capacity . . . to dream together," according to Francis, helps "transcend the narrow limits imposed on us and propose new possible worlds." The Pope charged social movement leaders and activists that "the future of humanity is in great measure in your own hands, through your ability to organize and carry out creative alternatives."[1]

Centered in feminist and womanist theologies, women engage in such poetic work due to their experiences of intersectional injustices at the nexus of race and ethnicity, class, age, religion, sexuality, ability, citizenship and geopolitical status, and so on—or what I articulate as ekkesial or community-creating and eschatologically oriented work as artisans of a new humanity. Latina and *mujerista* theologies emphasize and explore women's everyday praxis (*lo cotidiano*) as part and parcel of the struggle (*la lucha*) in social movements for personal and communal liberation that realizes "justice, equality, human rights, true democracy and greater equality of life for all."[2] Parallel to and compatible with the US Anglo feminist slogan "the personal is political," Latina women's daily lives and struggles in community and in social movements are positioned in US public life for women to reclaim and regain a religio-political subjectivity as well as to elaborate an alternative possible world. Women's rightful claim to subjectivity—to "search for one's own identity" as socio-political actors in struggles and movements for religious and social change and transformation—signifies a religio-political subjectivity that María Pilar Aquino expresses as egalitarian, based on equal creation in the image of God; multidimensional (including the body and sexuality), based on social identities and relations within the destiny of history; and, historically realist but yet freely, creatively, sacramentally, and hopefully oriented toward the future, toward concrete praxis, movements, and struggles for resistance, solidarity, and justice.[3] Aquino further theologizes about social movements from the

---

[1] Benedict Mayaki, SJ, "Pope to Popular Movements: You Create Hope and Forge Dignity," *Vatican News*, October 16, 2021.

[2] María Pilar Aquino, "Latina Feminist Theology: Central Features," in *A Reader in Latina Feminist Theology: Religion and Justice*, ed. María Pilar Aquino, Daisy L. Machado, and Jeanette Rodriguez (Austin: University of Texas Press, 2002), 134.

[3] María Pilar Aquino, *Our Cry for Life: Feminist Theology from Latin America* (Maryknoll, NY: Orbis Books, 1993), 18–25, 81–108, quote at 92; cf. Aquino, "Latina Feminist Theology: Central Features," 149–150.

Ethno-nationalism, Community Organizing, and United Farm Workers 157

perspective of "subversive and liberating faith-based utopias" or eschatological hope as a central task of prophetic theology.[4] Prophetic theological praxis constitutes, for Aquino, a "life-giving discursive praxis that provides the reasons for hope and motivation for faith-based engagement,"[5] rooted in the divine trinitarian life as a community of interdependent, indivisible relations and embodied in the resurrection of Jesus as a vindication of his life and ministry to historically realize the anti-imperial decolonial reign of God.[6] Thus, social movements and women's religio-political subjectivity and action within them participate in what I name rhetorical, symbolic, and prophetic practices that accompany and collaborate with the divine presence to challenge unjust present relationships and to creatively envision as well as build an alternative more just future world.

As Aquino argues, "The global justice movement brings to the world its subversive capacity to prefigure alternative possible futures. . . . Today, any theology seeking to contribute to the historical forces seeking the renewal of life would need to engage the dynamics of the social movements for change."[7] Theologically reflecting on, responding to, and resourcing social movements to shed light on their dynamics or praxis, both historically and currently, would also emphasize and engage with community organizations. The late *mujerista* theologian Ada María Isasi-Díaz analyzed the centrality, vitality, and transformative possibilities of community organizations within Latina women's lived struggles and social movements. What Isasi-Díaz argued about community organizations can comparably apply to understand ekklesial work and its multiple rhetorical, symbolic, and prophetic practices of resistance to an oppressive world and its imaginative activism of an alternative just world. Community organizations and social movements

> provide spaces for us to gather our political will and power to help us question the present structures, . . . enable us to participate in the creation of a different kind of society, . . . make it possible for us to analyze our reality and to explore alternatives, [otherwise] we will not be able to participate politically, socially, or economically at all levels of society; we will not be able to be agents of our own history, to make our *proyecto histórico* a reality.[8]

---

[4]María Pilar Aquino, "Presidential Address: Theology Renewing Life: Prophetic Interventions and Enduring Commitments," *CTSA Proceedings* 75 (2021): 62–79, quote at 63; cf. 77.

[5]Ibid., 70.

[6]Ibid., 69, 76–77.

[7]Ibid., 65.

[8]Ada María Isasi-Díaz, *En La Lucha/In the Struggle: Elaborating a Mujerista Theology* (Minneapolis: Fortress Press, 2004), 59.

158 *Nevertheless, We Persist*

Using an interpretive lens shaped by a feminist and womanist approach to public theology as ekklesial work, this chapter examines and explores how Latinx social movements, illustrated by the United Farm Workers (UFW) and the New Sanctuary Movement (NSM), use and apply rhetorical, symbolic, and prophetic practices of public engagement to critically reimagine and to constructively remake political community and belonging in pursuit of a more just public life. This chapter interprets how both movements and their practices of religio-political engagement challenge and reconceptualize as well as remake political community, and thereby imagine and begin to enact an alternative, radical democratic life. These movements marshal religious resources to raise collective consciousness about social injustice and simultaneously envision and embody alternative publics that urge a more just vision and practice of our shared life together. As this chapter demonstrates, both movements engage in ekklesial work primarily but not only through prophetic praxis, relying on religious claims, symbols, and resources about anthropology, Christology, and eschatology to challenge—both rhetorically and symbolically—an unjust political status quo as well as to reimagine and remold it for more just possibilities. Both movements illustrate prophetic praxis in their respective attempts to build community through various modes of public engagement, mainly but not only through community organizing and nonviolent direct collective action. Moreover, building on the notion of the beloved community in the Civil Rights Movement, the UFW and the NSM appealed to this religious rhetoric and symbol to inspire, motivate, and justify a prophetic vision and praxis that ultimately transformed political and religious spaces themselves into alternative models and praxis of more just political community.

United Farm Workers Movement

Cesar Chavez described and deeply appreciated Dolores Huerta as "physically and spiritually fearless."[9] When former President Barack Obama awarded Dolores Huerta the Presidential Medal of Freedom in 2012, he corrected the misconstrued Latinx social movement history and credited Huerta with coining the UFW slogan "Sí se puede," which Obama integrated into his presidential campaign. Contrary to rising reactionary curricula and revisionist history that in effect eclipse or erase the struggles

---

[9]Barbara L. Baer, "Stopping Traffic: One Woman's Cause," in *A Dolores Huerta Reader*, ed. Mario T. García (Albuquerque: University of New Mexico Press, 2008), 100.

Ethno-nationalism, Community Organizing, and United Farm Workers   159

of Indigenous, Black, and people of color across America, famed murals in Los Angeles and in Sacramento rightfully recognize Dolores Huerta as cofounder and collaborative leader with Cesar Chavez of the UFW union, as a Chicanx and Latinx icon of farmworker rights and civil rights, and as a relentless community organizer and activist for human dignity and rights that expand across intersectional social justice movements for immigrant rights, feminism, LGBTQ+ rights,[10] peace, and environmentalism from the mid-twentieth century to the present. As Angela Davis explains in the documentary film *Dolores*, Dolores Huerta lived these intersectional struggles via her lifework in the UFW from 1962 to 2002 and beyond as she evolved to coalition with other movements and catalyzed along with those movements a broader socio-cultural revolution. "Dolores Huerta played an integral role in the UFW as cofounder; vice-president; key negotiator with growers; advisor to Chavez ; lobbyist in Washington, DC, and Sacramento; and boycott organizer."[11] Huerta perennially problematized and navigated racialized, ethnocentric, gendered, sexualized, and class-based criticisms from powerful political figures, from agribusiness growers, from farmworkers in the union, and from labor activists within rival unions like the Teamsters, which mainly stemmed from white supremacist middle-class norms, and from Latinx patriarchal religious, cultural, and familial norms.[12] In my view, the UFW and particularly Huerta mapped out innovative ways of religio-political engagement—rhetorical, symbolic, and prophetic—that both mobilized for and at the same time modeled an anti-racist, anti-patriarchal world, which posed significant threats to then prevalent and still predominant ideologies. This chapter draws and expands on a key but not yet fully explored point about the UFW and Huerta's integral role in its agenda and advocacy: "Effective political and community action requires the intertwining of individual subjectivities and collective goals. Claiming public space can involve fragile alliances and enduring symbols, rooted in material realities and ethereal visions."[13] Some select episodes of UFW activism exemplify what I call its ekklesial

---

[10]Many farmworkers in the UFW identified in the LGBTQ+ community. Cesar's oldest son Fernando has a lesbian *comadre* (godmother), and she owned a bar called People's which served as a UFW sanctuary. Huerta testified at hearings in San Francisco to oppose anti-LGBTQ+ discrimination, joined some of the first Pride marches in Hollywood and San Francisco, lobbied for marriage equality in California, and one of her daughters, Juanita, identifies as bisexual and is active in the LGBTQ+ rights movement. "'Our Fight Is Your Fight': Civil Rights Leaders Dolores Huerta and Julian Bond Speak Out Loud and Clear for GLBT Equality," in *A Dolores Huerta Reader*, 322–323.

[11]Stacey K. Sowards, *¡Sí, Ella Puede!: The Rhetorical Legacy of Dolores Huerta and the United Farm Workers* (Austin: University of Texas Press, 2019), 2.

[12]Ibid., 4–5, 46–49.

[13]Ibid., 114.

160 *Nevertheless, We Persist*

work or its theological toolkit of world-making praxis, that is, its infusion of religion into different modes of socio-political action—rhetorical, symbolic, and prophetic practices—to create a new community, to envision and begin to enact an alternative more just world. In this ekklesial praxis for creating community in religio-political ways, "political spirituality and spiritual *mestizaje* came to define the UFW."[14]

Major events in Cesar Chavez's life and the UFW's campaigns[15] reveal compelling insights about the socio-economic structures of agribusiness that profoundly shape and affect US farmworker life, labor, realities, and religio-political struggles for just and equitable wages, living and working conditions, health care, education, job security, and, for undocumented migrant and seasonal farmworkers, citizenship.[16] Chavez was born in 1927 and raised in San Luis Valley near Yuma, Arizona. After the family farm foreclosed in 1937 during the Great Depression, the family entered migrant farm labor between Oxnard and San Jose, California. Since American apartheid or legalized segregation prior to the civil rights era affected and applied to all non-white folxs, Chavez experienced and questioned the intertwined injustices of racism, poverty, and ethno-nationalism. Spanish language profoundly marked his outsider status;[17] he completed elementary school, but left high school for field work to support his family. Seasonal rhythms of migrant labor were controlled by crop planting and harvests as well as by corrupt labor contractors, which together created destabilizing and dehumanizing living and working conditions.[18] He also critically confronted and resisted the traumatic realities of ethno-racial segregation that permeated all social, economic, and political structures, even the local theatre.[19] At the end of WWII, he enlisted in the US Navy and in the late 1940s married Helen Fabela; they both engaged in farm labor throughout the San Joaquin Valley, raising their eight children within this seemingly interminable life and labor cycle.

---

[14]Luis D. León, *The Political Spirituality of Cesar Chavez* (Oakland: University of California Press, 2015), 130.

[15]Significant scholarly studies about the lifework of Cesar Chavez and the UFW include but are not limited to John C. Hammerback and Richard J. Jensen, *The Rhetorical Career of Cesar Chavez* (College Station: Texas A&M University Press, 1998); Frederick John Dalton, *The Moral Vision of Cesar Chavez* (Maryknoll, NY: Orbis Books, 2003); Jacques E. Levy, *Cesar Chavez: Autobiography of La Causa* (Minneapolis: University of Minnesota Press, 2007); Mario T. García, ed., *The Gospel of Cesar Chavez: My Faith in Action* (Lanham, MD: Sheed and Ward, 2007); José-Antonio Orosco, *Cesar Chavez and the Common Sense of Nonviolence* (Albuquerque: University of New Mexico Press, 2008); and León, *Political Spirituality.*

[16]Dalton, *Moral Vision*, 2, 6–7.

[17]Levy, *Cesar Chavez*, 24.

[18]Dalton, *Moral Vision*, 12, and Levy, *Cesar Chavez*, 35–36, 45–49, 52–54, 63, 66–67, 76–77.

[19]Dalton, *Moral Vision*, 13, and Levy, *Cesar Chavez*, 84–85.

Ethno-nationalism, Community Organizing, and United Farm Workers   161

By the 1950s, Chavez read widely in Gandhian traditions of nonviolence as well as met Fr. Donald McDonnell and engaged with Catholic social teaching.[20] At the same time, he met Fred Ross, who recruited him for the Community Service Organization (CSO). By 1962, Chavez established more than twenty CSO chapters throughout California, which addressed a wide range of racial and economic justice issues in primarily Latinx communities. Yet Chavez quit the CSO,[21] moved to Delano, California, and co-founded the National Farm Workers Association (NFWA) with Dolores Huerta to mobilize, organize, unionize, and politicize farmworkers. Symbolized by the Aztec eagle with colors signifying suffering, struggle, and hope on the union flag, the NFWA, later called the UFW (United Farm Workers), served as a social movement and a community organization.[22]

In 1965, the NFWA stood in solidarity with Filipino Americans in the Agricultural Workers Organizing Committee strike against grape growers on Mexican Independence Day;[23] later, the two groups merged to form the UFWOC (United Farm Workers Organizing Committee) and established their headquarters at Forty Acres in Delano. During the five-year grape strike, which culminated in successful union contracts, the UFWOC garnered federal government, nationwide consumer, and interfaith support through the 340-mile pilgrimage from Delano to Sacramento in Lent 1966[24] and through other nonviolent prophetic actions, such as strikes, pickets, and boycotts of grapes and lettuce in the late 1960s and early 1970s. UFW women generated a creative religio-political approach in these campaigns; they strategically planned prayer vigils or "liturgies of protest,"[25] based on constitutional rights to religious freedom and assembly, when strikes and picket lines were limited or banned by court orders. Adapting the altars, prayers, and masses celebrated on the picket lines, some vigils lasted two months, and others at courthouses and jails when Chavez was imprisoned took place for twenty days. These vigils consisted of celebrating mass, followed by holding a union meeting and singing spirituals.[26] Chavez also incorporated fasting into the UFW's interrelated repertoire of nonviolent direct action, engaging in a twenty-five-day fast for nonviolence in 1968; US Senator Robert F. Kennedy and

---

[20]Dalton, *Moral Vision*, 48–49, and Levy, *Cesar Chavez*, 89, 91. León complicates the narrative about Chavez's study of Gandhi in *Political Spirituality*, 100–103.

[21]Levy, *Cesar Chavez*, 145–148.

[22]Dalton, *Moral Vision*, 114–115, and Levy, *Cesar Chavez*, 173–176.

[23]Levy, *Cesar Chavez*, 182–183.

[24]Ibid., 206–209.

[25]León, *Political Spirituality*, 129.

[26]Dalton, *Moral Vision*, 42; Levy, *Cesar Chavez*, 225–227, 427, 429–433.

162   *Nevertheless, We Persist*

eight thousand farmworkers and allies celebrated a mass when Chavez broke the fast. Chavez embarked on a second twenty-four-day fast that similarly concluded with a mass of about five thousand farmworkers and supporters including Joan Baez and Joseph Kennedy in 1972 for workers' rights to organize and to demonstrate for justice (during which Dolores Huerta coined the UFW slogan "Sí se puede").[27] Chavez's third thirty-six-day fast for life (continued and completed for Chavez by Rev. Jesse Jackson) also ended with a mass of approximately seven thousand people and allies including Ethel Kennedy in 1988 to reject pesticides.[28]

By the early 1970s, the UFW was chartered by the AFL-CIO, and moved its headquarters to Keene, California, named La Paz (Our Lady of Peace). When UFW contracts with growers expired in 1973, another grape strike and boycott was initiated.[29] That strike and boycott led to multiple contracts with major growers as well as the 1975 Agricultural Labor Relations Act and Board in California, which was initially chaired by UFW ally then Bishop (now retired Cardinal) Roger Mahony and ensured farmworker rights to unions, collective bargaining, and other labor negotiations. By the late 1970s, the UFW reached its peak membership and successfully launched a lettuce strike and boycott, followed by a dairy and grape strike and boycott in the early 1980s.

By the mid-1980s, Chavez and the UFW opposed resurging government anti-union attitudes and policies by starting the successful Wrath of Grapes campaign to ban pesticides. Agribusiness growers were deeply embedded in local, state, and federal governments as well as in police, legal, financial, utility, and other systems. Any farmworker strike then confronted this entire monopoly over migrant workers,[30] justified by an American dream ideology that inextricably tied together individualistic freedom and unregulated free market capitalism.[31] At the same time, the US Catholic bishops issued an episcopal letter titled *Economic Justice for All* in 1986, that specifically elaborated on the injustices of farmworker labor and that supported farmworker rights to unionize and transform agribusiness systems.[32] Catholic social teaching and UFW activism coexisted in a critically co-constitutive relationship. For example, the UFW inaugurated its newspaper *El Malcriado* by situating and framing the union's history, vision, and goals within Pope Leo XIII's encyclical in the

---

[27]Levy, *Cesar Chavez*, 463–464.

[28]Dalton, *Moral Vision*, 131–137; León, *Political Spirituality*, 138–145.

[29]Dalton, *Moral Vision*, 17.

[30]Ibid., 19–21, 67–68.

[31]Dalton, *Moral Vision*, 23–24. Cf. "Bush Campaign Fundraising Dinner," St. Francis Hotel, San Francisco, CA, September 14, 1988.

[32]Dalton, *Moral Vision*, 59–60.

Ethno-nationalism, Community Organizing, and United Farm Workers   163

late-nineteenth-century *Rerum Novarum*, On the Condition of Labor. In September 1965, *El Malcriado* similarly engaged with *Rerum Novarum*, and in the next issue the UFW declared its participation in what would evolve into a five-year grape strike and boycott.[33] In 1966 the bishops of California and in 1968 the US bishops issued statements that similarly outlined and applied key principles of Catholic social teaching—human dignity and rights; the common good; social, racial, and economic justice, the option for the poor, and solidarity; peace; sustainability and eco-justice—to affirm farmworkers' rights in their struggle for just work.[34] Further illustrating this critical and creative interrelationship between the UFW and the institutional Catholic Church, the UFW *both* relied on religious mediators during strikes and boycotts, e.g., Fr. Eugene Boyle together with an Episcopal priest and a Jewish rabbi bridged the UFW-Teamster rivalry,[35] *and* also targeted anti-union Catholic growers as well as opposed the majority of anti-union priests and bishops who would not religio-politically accompany the farmworkers in the struggle, "to sacrifice with the people for social change, for justice."[36] Eventually, the US bishops established a mediatorial committee to assist grower-worker-labor leader negotiations, and the union contracts at the end of the grape strike were signed in Archdiocese of Los Angeles offices in 1970.[37] The US bishops also endorsed subsequent UFW boycotts, and famously accompanied arrested clergy, laity, labor leaders like Chavez, and worker activists in jail in early 1970s. Fr. Eugene Boyle described their release as a resurrection[38] of the workers and the church. To commit to and show their solidarity, the US bishops arranged for Chavez to meet Pope Paul VI in 1974, as part of the UFW's effective efforts to internationalize the second major boycott.[39]

Cesar Chavez died in 1993, and was buried at La Paz. His funeral was the largest public funeral for a US labor leader and community organizer. In 1994, Chavez posthumously received the Presidential Medal of Freedom. Then the newly elected UFW president Arturo Rodriguez repeated the 1966 pilgrimage to inaugurate a revitalized era of UFW campaigns.

Akin to notions of radical democracy which inform my view of ekklesial or community-creating work in US public life, the UFW "worked . . . to establish a deeply democratic society in which ordinary people have the

---

[33]Ibid., 49–51.
[34]Ibid., 46, 51–52.
[35]Levy, *Cesar Chavez*, 260.
[36]Dalton, *Moral Vision*, 52–53, 54–55.
[37]Ibid., 57; Levy, *Cesar Chavez*, 303–305.
[38]Dalton, *Moral Vision*, 58.
[39]León, *Political Spirituality*, 64–66; Levy, *Cesar Chavez*, 522–526.

ability to influence the decision-making processes that affect their lives in the political, as well as economic and social, spheres,"[40] primarily through struggle for recognition and empowerment of marginalized groups. The UFW's approach to power *en la lucha* for *La Causa* informed and influenced its vision and creative practices of religio-political engagement in opposition to systemic structural injustices of agribusiness and US society. Power emerged from *la lucha*, the community's struggle to organize farmworkers for social, economic, and political change (to unionize, to vote) and ultimately for recognition of their humanity.[41] The UFW's vision and innovative practices of public engagement reclaimed and regained the community's power and also reaffirmed and reasserted farmworker dignity and humanity in the *imago Dei*, not in their productivity or profitability, in the *imago Christi's* sacred work to feed the world, and in the everyday lived struggles for a realized eschatology, for a more just, loving, and peaceful future.

> Recognition of the human is recognition of the divine, for humanity is made in the image and likeness of God. For Christians, Jesus is the model of what it means to be a human person fully alive in the love and service of God and neighbor. The work of loving and serving God and others in and through Jesus Christ is the work of the kingdom of God. Cesar understood that to provide water to thirsty farm workers and food to their children through better working conditions and just wages is to labor for the sake of the kingdom.[42]

That realized eschaton in the UFW is motivated by religious claims about humanity's creation in God's image and about nonviolent means of social change and transformation that recognize and respect personhood in seeking justice.[43]

Cesar Chavez's religious vision of faith-based social change, of Catholic theo-political praxis for what I call ekklesial work or creating community, was anchored in and characterized by several features: human dignity, service, and nonviolence. Migrant labor disempowered and degraded farmworkers' dignity, and ultimately not only disabled but also crucified workers: "Every time I see lettuce, that's the first thing I think of, some

---

[40]Orosco, *Chavez and Nonviolence*, 4–5.

[41]Dalton, *Moral Vision*, 25–26. León locates the UFW in the struggle of multiple of movements for "decolonial rehumanization," in *Political Spirituality*, 90.

[42]Dalton, *Moral Vision*, 28; cf. 9–10.

[43]Ibid., 27.

Ethno-nationalism, Community Organizing, and United Farm Workers   165

human being had to thin it. And it's just like being nailed to a cross."[44] Agribusiness racially segregated and economically exploited workers, and thus denied workers' basic human and democratic rights to community, to form associations especially across diverse ethno-racial lines.[45] By contrast, the UFW affirmed farmworkers' dignity and inclusive community, embodying an alternative just society and world in inclusive and nonviolent ways. Thus, "The UFW sought to institutionalize in its practices and policies its commitment to racial, national, cultural, religious, class and gender inclusiveness."[46] For example, illustrating his rhetorical practices, Chavez's Good Friday letter in 1969 emphasized that the farmworkers' struggle reclaimed and advocated God-given dignity and rights: "This struggle itself gives meaning to our life."[47]

Cesar Chavez and UFW volunteers connected this struggle Christologically to sacrificial service of voluntary poverty for justice. As Chavez's statement after the first fast explained, "Only by giving our lives do we find life. I am convinced that the truest act of courage, the strongest act ... is to sacrifice ourselves for others in a totally nonviolent struggle for justice."[48] In this same vein, Chavez and the UFW appealed to different forms of religiously inspired political action, what I am calling symbolic practices, to lobby for migrant farmworker rights, such as pilgrimages, prayer vigils, masses, and fasting. Its flag and its slogans among "the signs and symbols of the UFW witness to the character of the union community and the virtues the union leadership sought to instill in its members" and in US society more broadly.[49]

For example, former UFW organizer Marshall Ganz observes that narrative or storytelling assists US social movements in shaping their political identity and in crafting their particular forms of socio-political agency and action. Cesar Chavez and other UFW leaders situated their new organization in a founding story that blended guiding principles of American civic participation, Roman Catholic social thought, and Mexican and Mexican American activism. These three constitutive political, religious, and cultural themes were manifested in the pilgrimage or

---

[44]Dalton, *Moral Vision*, 64; Levy, *Cesar Chavez*, 74.

[45]Dalton, *Moral Vision*, 65–69.

[46]Ibid., 71.

[47]Ibid., 78–79.

[48]Dalton, *Moral Vision*, 82, 100–101, 105. This statement ended with two further sentences: "To be a man is to suffer for others. God help us to be men!" Levy, *Cesar Chavez*, 286. As the UFW evolved, Chavez contended with and contested internalized structural and cultural violence in Latinx communities, specifically related to race and gender norms to better realize a radical democratic view and praxis. Orosco, *Chavez and Nonviolence*, 71–96.

[49]Dalton, *Moral Vision*, 95.

166   *Nevertheless, We Persist*

march on Sacramento in Spring 1966. Resembling other forms of civic participation like boycotts, picket lines, and acts of civil disobedience, the march featured strikers carrying protest placards and engaging in a Lenten pilgrimage under the symbol of the cross and Guadalupe. From Ganz's perspective, a new story of farmworker activism developed during the march: "The march was storytelling in action, words, and symbols. It enacted an individual and collective journey from slavery to freedom. By choosing to take part, individuals could link their identity with those of others who shared *la causa*, entering upon the stage of history."[50] In other words, narrative empowers marginalized groups to engage in prophetic practices (i.e., the strike, the march) and in symbolic meaning-making as well as future-orienting practices which together reclaim the political subjectivity of subaltern groups and likewise aim to build a broad diverse public that opposes injustice.

Moreover, the UFW's march in Spring 1966 joined the Mexican American icon of national identity, Guadalupe,[51] Catholic devotional practices of pilgrimage, and modern nonviolent forms of political demonstration and protest, including speeches and singing. Chavez fused pilgrimage and protest in his commentary about the march as "a meeting of cultures and traditions; the centuries-old religious tradition of Spanish culture conjoins with the very contemporary cultur[e] . . . of 'demonstration,' springing from the spontaneity of the poor . . . bearing visibly their need and demand for equality and freedom."[52] Together with "The Plan of Delano," the pilgrimage effectively witnessed to, dramatized, and educated about systemic injustices of farmworker life and labor as well as the UFW's vision and struggle for worker rights and broader social justice. Synthesizing rhetorical and symbolic practices, "The Plan" states: "The Pilgrimage we make symbolizes the long historical road we have traveled in this valley alone, and the long road we have yet to travel, with much penance, in order to bring about the Revolution we need."[53] The six propositions that constitute "The Plan" elaborate the UFW's struggle for God-given rights and justice, the adverse and inhumane working and

---

[50]Marshall Louis Ganz, "Why Stories Matter," *Sojourners Magazine*, March 2009; "Resources and Resourcefulness: Strategic Capacity in the Unionization of California Agriculture, 1959–1966," *American Journal of Sociology* 105, no. 4 (2000): 1003–1063; Theda Skocpol, Marshall Ganz, and Ziad Munson, "A Nation of Organizers: The Institutional Origins of Civic Voluntarism in the United States," *American Political Science Review* 94, no. 3 (2000): 527–546.

[51]Guadalupe is widely invoked in Latinx identity and cultural struggles. Nichole M. Flores, *The Aesthetics of Solidarity: Our Lady of Guadalupe and American Democracy* (Washington, DC: Georgetown University Press, 2021), 19–45, 123–151.

[52]Dalton, *Moral Vision*, 85–86.

[53]Ibid., 88.

Ethno-nationalism, Community Organizing, and United Farm Workers   **167**

living conditions of farmworkers, the main principles of Catholic social teaching regarding the rights of workers, the role of suffering in seeking justice, and the UFW's future vision of a more unified, dignified, and egalitarian world.[54] Also integrating with prophetic practices to criticize an unjust society and galvanize more transformative and just spaces for social change, the pilgrimage, the strike, the picket line, the boycott, and fasting all helped build solidarity with *La Causa*[55] among workers and consumers interreligiously and internationally. Using such nonviolent mass actions for social change empowered farm worker activists, appealed to and leveraged moral, religious, and political arguments against systemic injustice, and gained supporters in coalitional solidarity with farmworkers for social justice.[56]

Combined with prophetic practices such as strikes, picket lines, boycotts, and other demonstrations, the UFW's theo-political or symbolic practices effectively but nonviolently put religious, social, economic, and political pressure on California agribusiness as well as state and federal governments to recognize and reinforce farmworker rights. Strikes nonviolently rejected agribusiness, but the UFW experienced violent retaliation from growers, police, and even local and state governments, resulting in two activists' deaths.[57] At times, growers' retaliatory violence to UFW strikes escalated violence on both sides, especially in the UFW strikes against the rival Teamsters union contracts in the early 1970s. Chavez paused the pickets to protect human life and enable the UFW to regroup and remobilize, grounded in its creative and transformative view of human life.[58]

Chavez's three fasts at pivotal points in UFW campaigns in the 1960s, 1970s, and 1980s evoked spiritual practices of suffering and solidarity for justice, but also rhetorical and prophetic nonviolent practices to communicate and end farmworker suffering. Rhetorically, as Chavez stated, "Fasting is probably the most powerful communicative tool . . . not through the written or expressed way. Fasting communicates through the soul. . . . It is the most potent way to communicate that I've ever seen."[59] Prophetically, in a telegram during Chavez's first fast, Martin Luther King Jr. considered the fast a "constructive power of nonviolent action."[60] Celebrating mass

---

[54]Ibid., 88–89.
[55]Levy, *Cesar Chavez*, 272–273, 275, 277, 280–281.
[56]Dalton, *Moral Vision*, 119, 138, 140, 142, and Levy, *Cesar Chavez*, 5–6.
[57]Dalton, *Moral Vision*, 123, and Levy, *Cesar Chavez*, 504–510.
[58]Dalton, *Moral Vision*, 126–127.
[59]Ibid., 137, and Levy, *Cesar Chavez*, 465.
[60]León, *Political Spirituality*, 109.

168   *Nevertheless, We Persist*

and holding a union meeting and rally following the daily mass showed the prophetic practice of Chavez's fasts, which wielded, as he explained, "our bodies and our spirits and the justice of our cause as our weapons,"[61] as a means of nonviolent participation and alliance-building across worldwide struggles for justice. The attendance of farmworkers and allies at masses to conclude each fast provided a compelling praxis of solidarity politics in prophetic practices: "Solidarity with the poor through voluntary poverty and simplicity of lifestyle witnesses to the injustice of impoverishment, with the hope of transforming injustice into justice."[62] Finally, the UFW regularly sponsored boycotts, which functioned to reclaim and renew workers' economic power,[63] and which at times coincided with Chavez's symbolic practices of fasting. Chavez's third fast took place during the grape boycott of 1984–1993 that highlighted the dangers of pesticides to worker, public, and ecological health.[64] In this way, prophetic practices like the boycotts generated power,[65] showed and sustained the UFW's inter/national and intersectional impact and influence through nonviolent direct action, and expanded and evolved the UFW's central organizing issues beyond farmworker justice to interlink labor, food, and eco-justice.

The UFW "performed a Chicano version of the American jeremiad— denouncing the sins of the people while affirming the shared religious aspirations and highest principles that constitute the national mythology. As an American prophet he [Chavez] walked in the path of a religiously inflected political left."[66] In sum, the UFW utilized diverse prophetic practices of nonviolent direct action to wrestle with and upend a dehumanizing, decreative, and violent death-dealing system,[67] by exposing multiple farmworker injustices. Prophetic practices also served a pedagogical purpose as a "classroom for the farmworkers"[68] and for the wider society about human rights struggles through nonviolent action; they also served as collaboratively witnessing to an alternative more humane and just world.[69] Prophetic protests elaborated both critical and creative purposes, both deconstructive and reconstructive goals, that is, to nonviolently imagine and inhabit an alternative more just system, society, and world.[70]

---

[61]Dalton, *Moral Vision*, 134, and Levy, *Cesar Chavez*, 286.
[62]Dalton, *Moral Vision*, 116.
[63]Dalton, *Moral Vision*, 138–139, and Levy, *Cesar Chavez*, 201.
[64]Dalton, *Moral Vision*, 141.
[65]Levy, *Cesar Chavez*, 271.
[66]León, *Political Spirituality*, 21.
[67]Dalton, *Moral Vision*, 119–120.
[68]Ibid., 127.
[69]Ibid., 142.
[70]Ibid., 120.

Ethno-nationalism, Community Organizing, and United Farm Workers   **169**

Dolores Huerta, cofounder and coleader of the UFW, [71] was born in 1930 in Dawson, New Mexico, and raised in Stockton, California, by her single mother and savvy small business owner, who operated a restaurant and a hotel catering primarily to farmworkers. Huerta's mother encouraged gender equality among her children, contrary to Latinx patriarchal norms, and urged Dolores to explore interests in music and dance activities, including the church choir.[72] Huerta embraced and articulated a dream of diversity, inclusivity, acceptance, and justice; she formed that social vision in high school when she critically faced and evaluated the incongruities between race and class in segregated schools, on the one hand, and her family's integrated communities, on the other hand.[73] After graduating from college and obtaining a teacher credential, Huerta refused to conform to Latinx, religious, and patriarchal/kyriarchal gender norms of career, marriage, and motherhood.[74] Her evolving social conscience and activism exceeded these norms that regulated her roles as teacher, wife, and mother; consequently, she divorced, resigned from teaching, and in 1955 met Fred Ross and started community organizing in Stockton through house meetings to address voter registration, education, health care, equitable racial and ethnic representation on police forces, and public services.[75]

In the late 1950s, Huerta served as an elected official in the Agricultural Workers Organizing Committee (AWOC), linked with the AFL-CIO, and as a charter member of the Agricultural Workers Association, unifying Black, white, and Latinx farmworkers. Fred Ross introduced Dolores to Cesar Chavez through the CSO, when Dolores worked in Stockton, and Chavez operated in Oxnard.[76] Shortly after her second marriage ended, Chavez invited Dolores in 1962 to inaugurate a union for farmworkers with him, although he observed that "we will not see a national union in our lifetime, because the growers are too rich, they're too powerful, and they're too racist."[77] Dolores applied and expanded her well-honed community-organizing and legislative lobbying skills to improve the

---

[71]Significant scholarly works about Huerta include García, ed., *A Dolores Huerta Reader*; Sowards, *¡Sí, Ella Puede!*; and Peter Bratt, *Dolores* (Five Stick Films, 2017).

[72]"Dolores Huerta—A Life of Sacrifice for Farm Workers," in *A Dolores Huerta Reader*, 279–281, and "Dolores Huerta on Spirituality: Interview with Mario T. García," in *A Dolores Huerta Reader*, 333.

[73]Richard Griswold del Castillo and Richard A. García, "Coleadership: The Strength of Dolores Huerta," in *A Dolores Huerta Reader*, 27–29.

[74]Sowards, *¡Sí, Ella Puede!*, 39.

[75]Margaret Rose, "Traditional and Nontraditional Patterns of Female Activism in the United Farm Workers of America, 1962–1980," in *A Dolores Huerta Reader*, 56–57.

[76]James Rainey, "The Eternal Soldadera," in *A Dolores Huerta Reader*, 151.

[77]Bratt, *Dolores*.

170   *Nevertheless, We Persist*

working conditions and rights of farmworkers. As Huerta stated, "I like to organize and help people. I like social change. I feel humble because I've been very fortunate in my life. God has put me in this position and provided the opportunities and skills to get things done."[78] She organized the grape boycott in New York, and as a result of a second boycott in the San Francisco Bay area, she lobbied for the 1975 Agricultural Labor Relations Act (ALRA) to recognize and reinforce farmworker labor negotiations in California.[79] The UFW's successes include workplace regulations (rest breaks), sanitation and safety regulations (drinking water, toilets, anti-pesticide laws), and worker benefits (seniority, security, health care and disability insurance, unemployment and pension plans, a credit union). However, the regulations of the ALRA Act and Board were not well enforced (which ignited a mass weeklong UFW picket on its Sacramento headquarters),[80] and did not safeguard workers' rights, especially undocumented workers' rights to workplace complaints, voting, and citizenship. During and beyond the 1980s, many UFW successes were eroded by anti-union government policies and by the UFW's long legal battles with growers, declining membership, and internal strife.

Huerta took a leave from the UFW in the early 1990s to serve on the board of the Feminist Majority, ensuring women's reproductive and body rights as well as empowering Latinas to run for political office.[81] After Chavez died in 1993, the UFW executive board did not vote for Huerta to succeed Chavez as union president. Although the workers and the membership supported her, she avoided a protracted internal fight. Instead, Huerta retired as UFW vice-president in the late 1990s and officially left the UFW in 2002 to subsequently create the Dolores Huerta Foundation, which centralizes community organizing around intersectional struggles and justice. As Huerta explained, "Struggle gives you energy. *La lucha de energía.*"[82]

With regard to rhetorical practices, Huerta's "ability to address the plight of the farmworkers and the goals of the movement . . . effectively transmitted her message to her audiences. She converted them into believing in *La Causa*. The farmworkers' struggle was not just a physical one

---

[78]Griswold del Castillo and García, "Coleadership," 31; cf. Ruth Carranza, "From the Fields into the History Books," in *A Dolores Huerta Reader*, 126.

[79]Rose, "Female Activism," 59.

[80]Judith Coburn, "Dolores Huerta: La Pasionaria of the Farmworkers," in *A Dolores Huerta Reader*, 105–113.

[81]Julie Felner, "Woman of the Year: Dolores Huerta, For a Lifetime of Labor Championing the Rights of Farmworkers," in *A Dolores Huerta Reader*, 139; cf. Frances Ortega, "An Interview with Dolores Huerta," in *A Dolores Huerta Reader*, 299.

[82]Ortega, "Interview," 301.

Ethno-nationalism, Community Organizing, and United Farm Workers   **171**

but a discursive one as well."[83] Huerta's "rhetorical practices reveal much about underrepresented and marginalized lives, motivations for social justice activism, and individual actions from community organizing to broader social movements."[84] More specifically, these practices to raise public awareness across multiple audiences about farmworker justice exemplify how marginalized women "negotiate intersectional identities of gender, race, ethnicity, language and class" as well as religion (often overlooked in Huerta scholarship) through personal experience, argument structure, audience address and participation, and a holistic perspective.[85] These practices were shaped and informed by Huerta's subjectivity and positionality.[86] These practices encompass speeches, interviews, and testimonies and correspond with Huerta's roles as a lobbyist, negotiator, and speaker, in which her "private identity lays the groundwork for a public persona. In the case of Huerta, her public persona involves two components: her womanhood/motherhood and her optimistic, social justice orientation."[87] For example, "She also brought her children to picket lines, protests, boycotts, and bargaining sessions. In essence, she constructed and expanded her public persona through her work and family simultaneously."[88] Together with symbolic and prophetic practices, Huerta's rhetorical practices, or what I collectively call ekklesial or community-creating work, fostered an imagined and concrete lived space to advance and enhance social justice.

As CSO political director and UFW vice president, she lobbied for wide-ranging legislation in Sacramento and in Washington, DC. Huerta incorporated farmworker testimonies[89] and embodied presence (sit-ins or camp-outs at elected officials' offices) into these lobbying efforts. "All that a person has is his or her story. . . . And when you're trying to deny them their story, you're taking away their power."[90] Farmworker stories displayed the exploitative and dehumanizing labor and living conditions that the UFW sought to legally redress. Moreover, these stories revealed the systemic and structural injustices of agribusiness, which suppressed farmworker rights and overall aided and abetted a political, social, and economic "climate of fear."[91] In testimony before the US Senate Subcom-

---

[83]Mario T. García, "Introduction: *La Pasionaria Chicana*," in *A Dolores Huerta Reader*, xxvii.
[84]Sowards, *¡Sí, Ella Puede!*, 1.
[85]Ibid., 8.
[86]Ibid., 32–35.
[87]Ibid., 6.
[88]Ibid., 13.
[89]"Testimony of Dolores Huerta," in *A Dolores Huerta Reader*, 191.
[90]Bratt, *Dolores*.
[91]Coburn, "La Pasionaria," 110–111, 113.

172 *Nevertheless, We Persist*

mittee on Migratory Labor in 1969, Huerta criticized racism, militarism, poverty, and agribusiness, mirrored in the US Department of Defense's purchase of produce for US troops in the Vietnam War during the boycott. As Huerta argued, "Many farm workers are members of minority groups. They are Filipino and Mexican-Americans and Black Americans. These same farmworkers are on the front lines of battle in Vietnam. It is a cruel and ironic slap in the face to these men who have left the fields to fulfill their military obligation to find increasing amounts of non-union grapes in their mess kits."[92] Farmworker voices and her witness to them offered a counternarrative and a counterpublic that reclaimed power and recognition for farmworkers and that incarnated in those hearings themselves a more humane, more liberative and just future.

In the UFW's early years, she and Chavez held house meetings throughout the San Joaquin Valley, quickly gained a 1,000-strong membership, and created through dues a life insurance plan, a credit union, and a cooperative store. They also engaged in immigrant rights work (while at the same time reporting many undocumented workers as strikebreakers during UFW strikes), and mapped out a five-year plan for a regional and nationwide strike. In 1965, when Filipino workers in the AWOC AFL-CIO started a strike against grape growers, the NFWA joined them on September 16, Mexican Independence Day,[93] advancing their plans beyond a membership drive into strikes, pickets, and boycotts. During the pilgrimage from Delano to Sacramento, Huerta negotiated the contracts between the farmworkers union and Schenley Industries, and incorporated a delegation of farmworkers to highlight their stories. After the successful nationwide and international boycott of grapes in the late 1960s, Huerta again negotiated the contracts and agreements with growers, including increased wages, safety regulations, medical plans, and insurance.

The UFW embedded volunteers in major midwest and eastern US cities and in Canada and Europe to manage its strikes and boycotts. Huerta organized and lobbied for the New York grape boycott in 1968 and another grape and lettuce boycott in 1973. By leading these boycotts, Huerta proposed and built coalitions with other social justice leaders and groups in the feminist movement, in the civil rights and Black freedom struggle, and in the Puerto Rican Independence Movement. She played pivotal roles in interfacing with multiple audiences, "mobilizing labor unions, political activists, community organizations, religious supporters, women's clubs, peace groups, student protesters, and concerned

---

[92]"Statement of Dolores Huerta, Vice President, United Farm Workers Organizing Committee, AFL–CIO, to US Senate Subcommittee on Migratory Labor," in *A Dolores Huerta Reader*, 217.

[93]García, "*La Pasionaria Chicana*," xvii.

Ethno-nationalism, Community Organizing, and United Farm Workers   **173**

consumers."[94] Huerta continually focused on farmworkers' lives and stories at community meetings or rallies in other movements, in order to reassert their self-dignity and recognition as well as to reconfigure a more solidarity-based and just world. At one feminist rally, Huerta utilized her well-known call-and-response chant or *gritos*, in which she linked the boycott to interlocking struggles against violence, racism, and sexism, and for a more just egalitarian and emancipatory world: "Down with violence! Abajo! Down with racism! Abajo! Down with sexism! Abajo! Sí se puede, sí se puede, everybody!"[95] The *gritos*, among other practices, opened up and created the possibilities for Huerta to organize, coalition, and build a site of solidarity with multiple groups for farmworker rights as human rights. Often these *gritos* concluded with Huerta's invitation to further activism: "Can all of us . . . can we build this world of brotherhood and sisterhood, peace, and justice? Can we do it? Sí se puede!"[96] With this rhetorical practice, Huerta convoked a new community of solidarity seeking a just world, together.

In 1966 Robert F. Kennedy held Senate Subcommittee on Migratory Labor hearings throughout California to show federal government support for farmworker constitutional, civil, and labor rights, including human rights to hope for the future.[97] In turn, the UFW lobbied for Kennedy's presidential campaign. Kennedy's assassination both politically symbolized "the death of the future"[98] and also religiously reinvigorated the UFW's nonviolent approach to social change. Struggling for human dignity and rights could not devolve into violence. As Huerta argued, "Hatred and racism are extensions of violence, and if we become that which we are trying to end, then you know we are becoming like the oppressor then and we are trying to set up a different system."[99] Nonviolence functioned as a pragmatic tactic to build nationwide solidarity with farmworkers but fundamentally emerged from Huerta's Christian commitments to nonviolence as a "spiritual force" that supports human dignity and rights.[100] The rhetorical power of nonviolence and its religious roots in human dignity influenced the UFW to promote environmental justice as a farmworker and public health issue. The UFW anti-pesticide campaign showed that agribusiness represents a toxic system that re/produces not

---

[94]Rose, "Female Activism," 59.

[95]Bratt, *Dolores*. Other examples of *gritos* are analyzed in Sowards, *¡Sí, Ella Puede!*, 116–117.

[96]"Speech Given by Dolores Huerta, UCLA," in *A Dolores Huerta Reader*, 257.

[97]Levy, *Cesar Chavez*, 204–205.

[98]Bratt, *Dolores*.

[99]Ibid.

[100]García, "*La Pasionaria Chicana*," xxiv; cf. Vincent Harding, "Interview with Dolores Huerta: Early Family Influences," in *A Dolores Huerta Reader*, 183.

174   *Nevertheless, We Persist*

only poverty but also poisons both workers (through disease) and consumers (through food).

With regard to symbolic practices, Huerta personified "a symbol of openness"[101] and effectively functioned as a "potent symbol"[102] of multiple social justice movements for farmworker and immigrant rights (as a vocal advocate for residency and citizenship during testimonies against "a captive labor supply" in 1960[103] and during the immigrant rights marches of 2006), civil and human rights, women's rights, peace, and environmental justice. Despite the institutional Catholic Church's support for the UFW since the late 1960s and early 1970s,[104] Huerta resisted a lot of religious patriarchal/kyriarchal pushback for her activism. Many Catholic priests argued from traditionalist perspectives (that ignored the history of women's varied roles and contributions in labor)[105] that women did not belong in the political/public sphere or that women mismanaged labor/union organizing and negotiations.[106] Nevertheless, Huerta turned to Catholicism to connect with different publics of the UFW, the workers, and more widespread audiences,[107] and moreover, she theologized or reinterpreted religious symbols about human dignity, social justice, and the power of nonviolence[108] to inspire and justify the UFW's and her own religio-political engagement and action. For example, "Before the union's first walkout . . . she led a final unity meeting for nearly 100 workers. Huerta held out a cross and had the mostly Catholic workers place their hands on it. They had to swear they would stick together."[109] Huerta religio-politically lived her Catholic commitments to social justice, emulating the "incarnational side of faith" or the life and ministry of Jesus through prayer and struggle for justice.[110]

Huerta's Catholic theological imaginary and praxis are anchored in prayer, fasting for justice, devotions to Guadalupe, attending mass and taking communion, practicing nonviolence, and criticizing the institutional church about women's rights, reproductive health care, and LGBTQ+

---

[101]Griswold del Castillo and Garcia, "Coleadership," 37.

[102]Rainey, "The Eternal Soldadera," 142.

[103]"Testimony of Dolores Huerta." Cf. Levy, *Cesar Chavez*, 129–130, 132–137.

[104]"Dolores Huerta on Spirituality," 339.

[105]Rose, "Female Activism," 54.

[106]Sowards, *¡Sí, Ella Puede!*, 31, 136, 149; Rose, "Female Activism," 57; and "Dolores Huerta on Spirituality," 335.

[107]Sowards, *¡Sí, Ella Puede!*, 14.

[108]Margaret Rose, "Cesar Chavez and Dolores Huerta: Partners in 'La Causa,'" in *A Dolores Huerta Reader*, 49.

[109]Rainey, "The Eternal Soldadera," 146.

[110]García, "*La Pasionaria Chicana*," xxvii–xxviii, and "Dolores Huerta on Spirituality," 341.

Ethno-nationalism, Community Organizing, and United Farm Workers   175

rights.[111] Huerta relied on her religious faith and values to re-center and re-commit to union work, what I call her ekklesial or community-creating work and eschatological hope for a more just future. She continually prayed for divine signs to justify her decision-making and activism, when she prayed prior to successfully lobby for fifteen bills in Sacramento in the early 1960s, which lifted citizenship requirements for public assistance as well as benefits,[112] and when she risked and sacrificed her family, friends, network, and job in Sacramento to relocate to Delano and undertake as well as centralize union work there.[113] In dialogue with a Catholic sacramental worldview, she portrayed her union work as a "baptism of fire,"[114] a kind of Pentecost experience of spiritual inspiration and motivation.[115]

To garner nationwide support, the UFW designed a 340-mile march from Delano to Sacramento during Lent 1966. The pilgrimage revisioned and resignified religio-political symbols for workers rights and social change such as the cross, Guadalupe, and the flags of Mexico, the Philippines, the United States, as well as the UFW flag emblazoned with the Aztec eagle. The pilgrimage ended on the steps of the capitol in Sacramento with an interfaith gathering on Easter Sunday. The gathering of ten thousand persons on the capitol steps reflected a highly diverse and interfaith group, including Christians, Muslims, Jews, Hindus, Buddhists, and humanists. This interreligious solidarity perhaps parallels and extends the religious hybridity of Chavez's own religious practice, which appealed to and blended Catholicism, Pentecostalism, Judaism, and Hindu-influenced nonviolence and yoga.[116] Huerta's Easter Sunday speech invoked and reinterpreted theological themes of resurrection in broad religio-political ways.

> The workers are on the rise. There will be strikes all over the state and throughout the country because Delano has shown what can be done and the workers know that they are no longer alone. . . . The social and economic revolution of farmworkers is well underway and will not be stopped until we receive equality. The farmworkers are moving . . . to achieve justice.[117]

---

[111]"Dolores Huerta on Spirituality" and " 'Our Fight Is Your Fight.' "

[112]Baer, "Stopping Traffic," 100; cf. Felner, "Woman of the Year," 137; María Luisa Torres, "Labor Leader Dolores Huerta Credits Family and Faith," in *A Dolores Huerta Reader*, 157.

[113]Barbara L. Baer and Glenna Matthews, "The Women of the Boycott," in *A Dolores Huerta Reader*, 82; cf. Rose, "Cesar Chavez and Dolores Huerta," 47, and Sowards, *¡Sí, Ella Puede!*, 109.

[114]Sowards, *¡Sí, Ella Puede!*, 123.

[115]Griswold del Castillo and Garcia, "Coleadership," 34.

[116]Levy, *Cesar Chavez*, 92–93, and León, *Political Spirituality*, 1, 59, 64.

[117]Sowards, *¡Sí, Ella Puede!*, 106.

176   *Nevertheless, We Persist*

Fusing rhetorical and symbolic practices, Huerta's speech demonstrated not only a politics of resistance but also and more importantly a theo-politics of hope in a new politics of relationship, "a kind of utopian narrative . . . [that] enables new imaginaries, potentialities, and possibilities for social activism" and for society.[118]

Huerta also theologized about the UFW's fasting and pilgrimage in religio-political ways during the second boycott in the 1970s, to create community between the farmworkers and global consumers.

> You have a responsibility to farmworkers, because the farmworkers feed you. A farmworker puts food on your table every single day. And so you have a responsibility, so we ask you just do a very simple thing. Fast! Don't eat lettuce. Don't eat grapes. Don't drink wine. That's a very simple thing for people to do. . . . Picketing is just walking, just like a *peregrinacion* . . . you're walking for justice.[119]

Prophetic practices pervade Huerta's lifework: "For Huerta, every moment is an organizing opportunity, every person a potential activist, every minute a chance to change the world."[120] Similar to the UFW women's vigils as liturgies of protest, Huerta interpreted this lifelong struggle for justice as a liturgical or public service praxis,[121] based on a priest's advice: "Don't worry, as long as you're doing what you're doing, that's as good as going to Mass."[122]

With regard to prophetic practices of the strike, the picket line, and the boycott along with many other demonstrations, the UFW was significantly influenced by Gandhian and Kingian nonviolence and also by Catholic traditions of nonviolence, such as liberation theology and its theo-praxis of solidarity or preferential option that the poor make for themselves, their communities, and the future. UFW board members and volunteers practiced solidarity to advocate for and with farmworkers through voluntary poverty as a sacrifice[123]—to give their lives (and in Huerta's case, her children and her extended family network) in service to others for future meaningful lives. Huerta learned this vocation of service as a

---

[118]Ibid., 111–113.

[119]Ibid., 115–116.

[120]Felner, "Woman of the Year," 134.

[121]Cf. Cláudio Carvalhaes, "Worship, Liturgy, and Public Witness," in *A Companion to Public Theology*, ed. Sebastian Kim and Katie Day (Leiden: Brill, 2017), 466–486, and Catherine Pickstock, "Liturgy and Public Theology," in *T & T Clark Handbook of Public Theology*, ed. Christoph Hübenthal and Christiane Alpers (London: Bloomsbury, 2022).

[122]"Dolores Huerta on Spirituality," 343.

[123]García, "*La Pasionaria Chicana*," xxv.

Ethno-nationalism, Community Organizing, and United Farm Workers 177

divinely gifted grace from her mother.[124] Dolores Huerta regularly gave eighteen-hour days, earned a minimal salary, and relied on donated food, clothing, housing, and so on—all at a sacrifice for the cause, *La Causa*, of the union and worker justice.[125] Beyond strikes, boycotts, rallies, lobbying, and negotiations, Huerta endured jailtime for more than twenty arrests and hospitalization (which coincided with the feast of Our Lady of Sorrows) after a police beating.[126] As Huerta states, "And we've all learned that we're not afraid to struggle, that we're not afraid to sacrifice, because you can't make change if you're not willing to give something up."[127]

These prophetic practices tied together with Huerta's hope-filled future vision of another possible world with equitable worker protections and rights.[128] Labor union activist and leader Eliseo Medina introduced Huerta and her vision at a UFW meeting: "I too have a dream that I learned from Dolores Huerta—that farmworkers can share in the wealth that they help to produce."[129] According to Huerta, "The only thing you have to know is how to have power. . . . The power is in your person. And when you come together with other people, and you take direct action, then you can make things happen. Then you can make the changes. . . . Who's got the power? We have the power. What kind of power? People power. Who's got the power? We have the power. What kind of power? People power. Okay, so we gotta use our power."[130] Power in the UFW is mobilized and embodied personally and collectively in various prophetic practices of nonviolent direct action to enact that vision, that dream of economic, social, and political justice—the march, the strike, the picket line, the boycott, and jail.[131] Fasting and prayer, while symbolic practices, also served religio-political prophetic purposes. Fasting and prayer were fused with and flourished alongside the UFW's prophetic practices, such as the strike and boycott. Fasting created community in the UFW—farmworkers accompanied Chavez during each fast by living at Delano—but also between the UFW and broader US society—Huerta asked many groups in coalition with the UFW during the second boy-

---

[124]Julia Bencomo Lobaco, "Dolores Huerta: The Vision and Voice of Her Life's Work," in *A Dolores Huerta Reader*, 304.

[125]Griswold del Castillo and Garcia, "Coleadership," 31; cf. Coburn, "La Pasionaria"; Rose, "Female Activism"; Felner, "Woman of the Year"; Rainey, "The Eternal Soldadera."

[126]Scott Forter, "UFW Official Operated on After S.F. Beating," in *A Dolores Huerta Reader*, 119–121.

[127]Bratt, *Dolores*.

[128]"Dolores Huerta—A Life of Sacrifice," 282.

[129]Bratt, *Dolores*.

[130]Sowards, *¡Sí, Ella Puede!*, 125.

[131]Bratt, *Dolores*.

178   *Nevertheless, We Persist*

cott to fast economically from grapes and from lettuce.[132] Huerta also connected picketing to prayer as a personal and collective embodied act of petition to transform the social conscience for justice.[133] The social and economic pressure of these prophetic practices gained farmworker recognition and labor rights as well as galvanized a broader social and economic revolution for equality.

Dolores Huerta led and legitimated the presence, power, and leadership of women in these wide-ranging activities, and advocated for women's equal participation and contribution in the UFW committees and the executive board.[134] In the 1970s, the more than two hundred contracts previously negotiated in California, Arizona, New Mexico, and Texas expired, and the growers signed contracts with the Teamsters rather than the UFW. The UFW initiated a second strike and another nationwide boycott, which also incorporated nonviolent direct actions of civil disobedience in defiance of the Teamster-backed bans on strikes and picket lines. Women played major roles not only by adding prayer vigils to the UFW's theo-political praxis, but by enduring jailtime for their activities, particularly in Fresno, "rang[ing] from minors to great-grandmothers. There were field workers and nuns, lay religious women and union officials. . . . All the women shared their experiences—the farmworkers told city women like Dorothy Day, editor of the *Catholic Worker*, about their struggle, and learned from her about women's movements in the cities and in the church."[135] Teamster-induced and police violence also led to the deaths of UFW activists.

Huerta critically analyzed these interlocking injustices that historically and still disempowered and disenfranchised women and people of color.

I remember when I first read the Constitution of the United States in grammar school I always felt so proud of being an American. I thought God we have all these rights, you know. In a democracy you make your demands and then somebody will listen to you. Justice will prevail. But I found out that when you do this in an economic situation it does not quite work like that. Once we started making those kind of demands we had the same response that the Black movement has had. Our people were killed. The system doesn't re-

---

[132]Harding, "Interview with Dolores Huerta," 184–185; "Speech Given By Dolores Huerta, UCLA," 245.

[133]"Speech Given By Dolores Huerta, UCLA," 246–247.

[134]Sowards, *¡Sí, Ella Puede!*, 45, and Rose, "Female Activism."

[135]Baer and Matthews, "The Women of the Boycott," 87, and Levy, *Cesar Chavez*, 500–503.

Ethno-nationalism, Community Organizing, and United Farm Workers   *179*

ally want brown people or black people to have an organization and to have any power. I found out that no matter what I did, I could never be an American. Never.[136]

Huerta personally experienced the violence against the UFW when she was severely beaten at and hospitalized after a 1988 protest against a fundraiser in San Francisco for then Vice President Bush's campaign. She faced both bodily and emotional trauma after this protest and police brutality, another kind of solidarity with farmworkers.

As argued previously, doing ekklesial or community-creating work requires an interstitial positionality; a public theologian stands between an unjust present and a more egalitarian and emancipatory future, between multiple groups seeking solidarity and justice, what Asian American feminist theologians call interstitiality or what Latina feminist theorists and theologians name a *mestiza* identity.[137] "Social movement activists like Dolores Huerta seek to understand the interstices where collaborative work is possible so that effective coalition building can work to reduce such social injustice at all levels."[138]

Farmworker rights and immigrant rights movements coalesced at the intersections of the UFW and the Sanctuary Movement, personified particularly in the ministry of Fr. Luis Olivares (d. 1993), a major UFW supporter and a significant Sanctuary Movement leader in Los Angeles. When Fr. Olivares pastored Soledad Church in the 1970s, and then later La Placita Church (Our Lady Queen of Angels) in the 1980s, he opened both churches to UFW advocacy for union meetings and campaigns as well as fed, housed, and supplied other spiritual and material resources for the UFW volunteers and farmworkers. As a close friend and ally of both Huerta and Chavez, Fr. Olivares among other priests participated in UFW demonstrations as well as celebrated mass at UFW rallies and conventions. Extending these UFW ministries, Fr. Olivares declared La Placita a sanctuary parish in 1985, housing Central American refugees and undocumented immigrants. Further demonstrating the links between the UFW and immigrant rights movements, Huerta not only spoke at the mass when La Placita entered the Sanctuary Movement, but also recalled that Fr. Olivares linked *La Causa* to sanctuary: "He really brought home to all the Latinos . . . how important the struggle was in Central America.

---

[136]Bratt, *Dolores*.
[137]Griswold del Castillo and Garcia, "Coleadership," 25, 27.
[138]Sowards, *¡Sí, Ella Puede!*, 152.

180   *Nevertheless, We Persist*

How we were directly linked to it. Because it was also our struggle, it was our cause."[139]

The New Sanctuary Movement

US immigration illuminates an increasingly reductionist economic and legal approach to personhood and citizenship. US immigration reform activists contest an exclusionary anti-democratic trend in US public life based on ethnic, religious, national, and other identity-marking criteria. Speaking of immigrants as "undocumented workers" reduces persons to their labor and often boxes persons into singular racial/ethnic, national, and geopolitical identities; it defines "others" via predominant notions of personhood tied to legal citizenship, guarded by hypermilitarized border walls and economically driven xenophobic nationalism, which only further demonstrates a rising US nativist approach to political subjectivity. The rhetorical, symbolic, and prophetic praxis associated with the beloved community in the Civil Rights Movement further motivated immigrant rights movements. Faith-based immigrant advocacy groups serve as a religio-political leverage point both to challenge dominant notions of political subjectivity and public life and to perform an eschatological ideal of the beloved community—which justifies religious dissent from an exclusionary public life and performs a religiously based inclusive and just alternative.

The NSM—inspired by multifaith religious groups that sheltered and supported Central American civil war refugees in the 1980s[140]—coalesced in fall 2006 and began in spring 2007, after an initial meeting of representatives from eighteen cities, twelve religious traditions, and seven interdenominational organizations in Washington, DC.[141] Between the

---

[139]"Dolores Huerta on Fr. Luis Olivares: Interview with Mario T. García," in *A Dolores Huerta Reader*, 318; "Dolores Huerta on Spirituality," 337. Cf. Mario T. García, *Father Luis Olivares, A Biography: Faith, Politics, and the Origins of the Sanctuary Movement in Los Angeles* (Chapel Hill: University of North Carolina Press, 2018).

[140]Maria Cristina Garcia, "'Dangerous Times Call for Risky Responses': Latino Immigration and Sanctuary, 1981–2001," in *Latino Religions and Civic Activism in the United States*, ed. Gaston Espinosa, Virgilio Elizondo, and Jesse Miranda (New York: Oxford University Press, 2005), 159–173; Jennifer Ridgley; "Cities of Refuge: Immigration Enforcement, Police, and the Insurgent Genealogies of Citizenship in US Sanctuary Cities," *Urban Geography* 29, no. 1 (2008): 53–77.

[141]Louis Sahagun, "L.A. Church in Forefront of Sanctuary Movement," *Los Angeles Times*, March 23, 2007; Sahagun, "Churches Unite to Provide Immigrant Sanctuary," *Los Angeles Times*, March 28, 2007; Ysmael D. Fonseca, "The Catholic Church's Obligation to Serve the Stranger in Defiance of State Immigration Law," *Notre Dame Journal of Law, Ethics, and Public Policy* 23, no. 1 (2009): 291–316.

Ethno-nationalism, Community Organizing, and United Farm Workers **181**

1980s and the 1990s, nearly three thousand US churches, synagogues, Quaker meetings, and varied religious groups declared their communities public sanctuaries for nearly one million refugees seeking political asylum from war-torn Central American countries.[142] These communities drew on different sacred texts, Greco-Roman and European law, and abolitionist movements to form the Sanctuary Movement (SM), which practiced civil disobedience against unjust immigration laws and later morphed into a civil initiative to uphold asylum laws.[143] The US government infiltrated the SM in 1985, indicted sixteen and eventually convicted eight sanctuary workers on seventy-one counts of conspiracy to transport and harbor—conceal or shelter—these immigrants.[144] Liberation theologians justified the SM on theological, ethical, and practical grounds: to encounter the divine by supporting political and war refugees; to shelter refugees who fled wars funded by US Cold War foreign policies; and to model a utopia or alternative just form of public life that directs us toward and deepens solidarity, hospitality, and inalienable democratic rights of all.[145] The SM aimed to build solidarity with refugees and thereby denounce US war and immigration policies that denied them asylum as well as deported them at risk of further persecution.[146]

Whereas the SM provided asylum for refugees, the NSM focuses on Latin American economic migrants seeking to improve their families' lives. Current US anti-immigrant attitudes and policies are fed and spread by nativist and nationalist opponents of economic migration.[147] Defined

---

[142]Gary MacEoin, "A Brief History of the Sanctuary Movement," in *Sanctuary: A Resource Guide for Understanding and Participating in the Central American Refugees' Struggle*, ed. Gary MacEoin (San Francisco: Harper & Row, 1985), 14–29; Ignatius Bau, *This Ground Is Holy: Church Sanctuary and Central American Refugees* (New York: Paulist Press, 1985); Susan Bibler Coutin, *The Culture of Protest: Religious Activism and the US. Sanctuary Movement* (Boulder, CO: Westview Press 1993); Hilary Cunningham, *God and Caesar at the Rio Grande: Sanctuary and the Politics of Religion* (Minneapolis: University of Minnesota Press, 1995); Pamela Begaj, "An Analysis of Historical and Legal Sanctuary and a Cohesive Approach to the Current Movement," *John Marshall Law Review* 42, no. 1 (2008): 135–163.

[143]Bau, *This Ground Is Holy*, 124–161; Renny Golden, "Sanctuary and Women," *Journal of Feminist Studies in Religion* 2, no. 1 (Spring 1986): esp. 133–134; cf. Begaj, "An Analysis of Historical and Legal Sanctuary," 137–141.

[144]Bau, *This Ground Is Holy*, 83–87.

[145]Jon Sobrino, "Sanctuary: A Theological Analysis," trans. Walter Petry Jr., *Cross Currents* 38, no. 2 (Summer 1988): 164–172; Miguel De La Torre, *Trails of Hope and Terror: Testimonies on Immigration* (Maryknoll, NY: Orbis Books, 2009), 11–13.

[146]Golden, "Sanctuary and Women," 131–132, 143, 146, and Hilary Cunningham, "Sanctuary and Sovereignty: Church and State along the US–Mexico Border," *Journal of Church and State* 40, no. 2 (1998): esp. 377.

[147]Contrary to the US Constitution, nativism and ethno-nationalism oppose birthright citizenship or alternative paths to citizenship, and instead favor and foment US restrictive immigration policies. Nativists highlight race, ethnicity, religion, and other inherited attributes to define US identity. Ethno-nationalists ground American identity in assimilation to white supremacist

182   *Nevertheless, We Persist*

mainly by socio-economic, political, and legal constructs of US citizenship, immigrants are all too easily criminally caricatured and labeled as terrorists, drug dealers, or *reconquistas*[148] threatening US national security and stability by draining jobs and social services. Such stereotypes dehumanize immigrants and also absolve the US government from any responsibility for multiple immigrant rights abuses during border crossings, work/workplace raids, arrests, detentions, and deportations.[149] Militarizing border fences in the 1990s symbolically secured and assured US national borders and sovereignty. However, immigrant crossings shifted from major cities to more treacherous desert and mountain regions of Southern California, Arizona, New Mexico, and Texas, thereby leading to a US-caused tragic human rights crisis of more than three to four thousand and rising immigrant deaths.[150] Recurring populist scapegoating of economic immigrants for US social and economic woes during the Great Depression and post–World War II years[151] reflects resurging racist and nationalist xenophobic fears of race, culture, language, and other differences that lead to dehumanizing policies: "closing the border becomes a strategy to minimize the 'browning' of America."[152]

The NSM raises public awareness about immigration reform through prayer vigils, educational events and literature, and hospitality to immigrant families, particularly but not only women, by giving sanctuary

---

norms of religion (Christianity), language (English), European heritage (Protestant work ethic), the rule of law (law and order), etc. Donald Kerwin, "Toward a Catholic Vision of Nationality," *Notre Dame Journal of Law, Ethics, and Public Policy* 23, no. 1 (2009): esp. 197–201. The US government implemented similar policies after the 9/11 terrorist attacks; see Pierrette Hondagneu-Sotelo, *God's Heart Has No Borders: How Religious Activists Are Working for Immigrant Rights* (Berkeley: University of California Press, 2008), 9–13, and Fonseca, "The Catholic Church's Obligation," 300–304.

[148]Motivated by manifest destiny and its divinely mandated US territorial expansion, the Mexican–American War concluded with the 1848 Treaty of Guadalupe-Hidalgo in which the US annexed nearly half of Mexico and created the nearly nineteen-hundred-mile southwesterly US border from California to Texas. De La Torre, *Trails of Hope and Terror*, 9–11.

[149]Coutin, *The Culture of Protest*, 93–96, 99–102; Miguel De La Torre, "For Immigrants," in *To Do Justice: A Guide for Progressive Christians*, ed. Rebecca Todd Peters and Elizabeth Hinson-Hasty (Louisville, KY: Westminster John Knox Press, 2008), esp. 77–80; De La Torre, *Trails of Hope and Terror*, 60–70, 90–91, 109–114; Robert Gittelson, "The Centrists against the Ideologues: What Are the Falsehoods That Divide Americans on the Issue of Comprehensive Immigration Reforms?" *Notre Dame Journal of Law, Ethics, and Public Policy* 23, no. 1 (2009): 113–131; Daniel G. Groody, "Crossing the Divide: Foundations of a Theology of Migration and Refugees," *Theological Studies* 70, no. 3 (2009): esp. 642–644, 656–657; and Kristin E. Heyer, "Strangers in Our Midst: Day Laborers and Just Immigration Reform," *Political Theology* 9, no. 4 (2008): esp. 426–432.

[150]Hondagneu-Sotelo, *God's Heart Has No Borders*, 138–141; De La Torre, *Trails of Hope and Terror*, 14–15.

[151]De La Torre, *Trails of Hope and Terror*, 42–43.

[152]Ibid., 114; cf. 116–119.

Ethno-nationalism, Community Organizing, and United Farm Workers   183

in participating US religious groups. The NSM keeps immigrant families together by advocating (at least in high-profile cases) for women with US-born and therefore citizen children who signify the urgency of US immigration reform.[153] Both the SM and NSM gained and galvanized public attention around major cases of women and children, given the intersectionality of gender, race, and class in the exploitation of women's sexual, familial, economic, and other labor.[154] Sanctuary workers Stacey Merkt and a Roman Catholic sister, along with a newspaper reporter, were arrested in 1984 for transporting Salvadoran Brenda Sanchez-Galan and her two-year-old child Bessie Guadalupe from Casa Oscar Romero in San Benito, Texas, to a Lutheran church in San Antonio, Texas.[155] Similarly, the NSM was sparked by three major events related to immigrant advocacy for women and families: rallies in major US cities during 2006 to contest US House of Representatives bill HR 4437, which criminalized providing basic humanitarian or legal services to undocumented immigrants;[156] the sanctuary of Elvira Arellano in Chicago in 2006–2007 to avoid deportation and family separation from her US-born son Saul;[157] and family fragmentation during US immigration workplace raids in 2006–2007.[158] Arellano created *La Familia Latina Unida*, an organization that lobbied US senators and representatives at federal and state levels to sponsor a bill protecting her and similar parents from such family separation. She was arrested and later deported after attending a Catholic mass and speaking at an immigrant rights rally at Our Lady Queen of Angels in Los Angeles on August 19, 2007.[159] Women such as Elvira Arellano aimed to expose

---

[153]Alexia Salvatierra, "Sacred Refuge," *Sojourners* 36, no. 9 (2007): 12–20; Sasha Abramsky, "Gimme Shelter," *The Nation* 286, no. 7 (February 25, 2008): 24–25; Mason Funk and Leanna Creel, *Sanctuary's Daughter* (Los Angeles: Channel Road Films, in-process).

[154]Gemma Tulud Cruz, "Between Identity and Security: Theological Implications of Migration in the Context of Globalization," *Theological Studies* 69, no. 2 (June 2008): 357–375.

[155]Bau, *This Ground Is Holy*, 76–79; Golden, "Sanctuary and Women," 143.

[156]Roger Cardinal Mahony, "A Nation That Should Know Better," *Los Angeles Times*, June 1, 2005; "The Gospel vs. H.R. 4437," *New York Times*, March 3, 2006; "Called by God to Help," *New York Times*, March 22, 2006.

[157]Louis Sahagun, "A Mother's Plight Revives the Sanctuary Movement," *Los Angeles Times*, June 2, 2007.

[158]Yvonne Abraham and Brian R. Ballou, "350 Are Held in Immigration Raid," *Boston Globe*, March 7, 2007; Louis Sahagun, "L.A. Church in Forefront of Sanctuary Movement," *Los Angeles Times*, March 23, 2007. De La Torre, *Trails of Hope and Terror*, 84–89, and the testimonies by a teacher and a Roman Catholic sister involved in providing sanctuary during the raids, in both schools and churches, 95–98, 139–142. Cf. Kristin Heyer, *Kinship across Borders: A Christian Ethic of Immigration* (Washington, DC: Georgetown University Press, 2012), esp. chap. 3; Kerwin, "Rights, the Common Good. and Sovereignty," 112.

[159]Randal C. Archibold, "Illegal Immigrant Advocate for Families Is Deported," *New York Times*, August 21, 2007; N. C. Aizenman and Spencer S. Hsu, "Activist's Arrest Highlights Key Immigrant Issue," *Washington Post*, August 21, 2007.

184 *Nevertheless, We Persist*

moral problems with the US immigration system, exemplified by US immigration raids from Boston to Los Angeles that detained, displaced, and threatened deportation of parents without regard to their rights.

The NSM constitutes an interfaith coalition that spans locations from Los Angeles to New York; it provides sanctuary and hospitality in participating houses of worship in the form of legal, financial, humanitarian, and spiritual aid to immigrant families, especially in high-profile cases of women resisting deportation and family displacement.[160] The NSM is grounded in Christian sacred texts that contain multiple moral imperatives not to oppress but to provide individual and institutional hospitality to the accused (Exod. 21:12–14; Num. 35:10–15; Deut. 4:41–43)[161] and to the stranger, at times with identity (Exod. 22:21–23; 23:9; Lev. 19:33–34), legal (Deut. 10:17–19; 24:17–22), and salvific (Matt. 25:35–40; Luke 10:25–37) implications. Jesus' ministry of table fellowship exemplifies hospitality; Jesus' meals not only signify salvation (Luke 22:30) but also create new communities across racial, economical, religious, and other socially constructed divisive borders (Luke 7).[162] In addition, papal apostolic constitutions, pontifical councils' instructions, and national bishops conference letters since the mid-twentieth century consistently urge such hospitality to migrants as a central defining praxis of Christian discipleship.[163] To do otherwise not only contributes to unjust structures, ideologies, and actions associated with the social sins of the US immigration system[164] but also fails to recognize the *imago Dei* or the shared humanity and consequent inalienable human rights that transcend (and in this case transgress) social, political, and national borders. In modern Catholic social thought, *imago Dei*–based rights—to food, clothing, housing, state of life, family life, education, work, good reputation and conduct, conscience, respect, knowledge, privacy, and freedom—cannot be restricted by socially constructed hierarchies of race/ethnicity, gender, class, sexuality, religion, ability, politics, or nationality.[165]

---

[160]Salvatierra, "Sacred Refuge," and Antonio Olivo, "Illegal Immigrant Sanctuaries Set," *Chicago Tribune*, May 9, 2007; Grace Dyrness and Clara Irazabal, "A Haven for Illegal Immigrants," *Los Angeles Times*, September 2, 2007. Cf. James Barron, "Churches to Offer Sanctuary," *New York Times*, May 9, 2007; Saul Gonzalez, "Immigrant Sanctuary Movement," *Religion and Ethics Newsweekly*, June 15, 2007.

[161]Bau, *This Ground Is Holy*, 124–29; Cunningham, *God and Caesar*, 68–83.

[162]Groody, "Crossing the Divide," 657–658.

[163]Fonseca, "The Catholic Church's Obligation," 295–297; Groody, "Crossing the Divide," 641.

[164]Kristin E. Heyer, "Social Sin and Immigration: Good Fences Make Bad Neighbors," *Theological Studies* 71, no. 2 (June 2010): esp. 413–414, 425–429.

[165]"Pastoral Constitution on the Church in the Modern World: *Gaudium et Spes*, 7 December 1965," in *Vatican Council II: The Basic Sixteen Documents*, ed. Austin Flannery, OP (Northport, NY: Costello Publishing, 1996), para. 26. Cf. De La Torre, "For Immigrants," 82; De La Torre, *Trails of Hope and Terror*, 137; and, Groody, "Crossing the Divide," 642–648.

Ethno-nationalism, Community Organizing, and United Farm Workers   **185**

The NSM signifies the church, physically and symbolically, as a model of the public good founded on love, justice, and peace—too long denied to immigrants under the US legal system and global labor markets but mandated by scriptural ethics and parables about the reign of God (Lev. 19:33–34; Matt. 25:34–36, 41–43). The NSM's prophetic praxis of giving sanctuary expresses theologically and embodies politically a Christian-inspired vision of the public good, of a more inclusive, just, and emancipatory body politic. Giving sanctuary imagines and begins to enact the inbreaking of an alternative radical democratic space that honors human dignity and rights despite narrow legalistic and border-based nationalistic views of citizenship rights. The NSM's prophetic praxis of giving sanctuary challenges and seeks to transform dominant US notions of public/political life and thereby risks various forms of financial, legal, and religious retribution. Similar to the way the government treated the SM, the US government warned NSM congregations against interfering with federal immigration laws and enforcement,[166] but with different results. Rather than arrest, prosecution, and conviction, cities have billed or fined churches to subsidize police presence at anti-immigration protests, effectively failing to protect their rights to religious free exercise.[167] The US courts have not ruled whether sanctuary is incorporated into First Amendment rights to freedom of religion.[168] Nonetheless, the Christian gospel is centrally concerned with encountering God in the stranger (Gen. 18; Heb. 13:2; Rom. 12:9–13), with encountering Christ in providing just hospitality to the stranger (Matt. 25:34–35), and with affirming our common humanity and equal dignity. As Latina theologian Ana María Pineda states, "To welcome the stranger is to acknowledge . . . a human being made in God's image."[169]

Ethnographic studies of the NSM show that the NSM theologies and

---

[166]James Barron, "Congregations to Give Haven to Immigrants," *New York Times*, May 9, 2007; cf. Audrey Hudson, "Chertoff Warns Meddling 'Sanctuary Cities,'" *Washington Times*, September 6, 2007.

[167]Anna Bakalis, "Simi Valley, Calif., Won't Charge Church for Future Protests," *Ventura County Star*, September 25, 2007; Brent Hopkins and Angie Valencia-Martinez, "Simi Valley Bills Church for Cops' Time at Protest," *Los Angeles Daily News*, September 20, 2007; cf. Ben Daniel, *Neighbor: Christian Encounters with "Illegal" Immigration* (Louisville, KY: Westminster John Knox Press, 2010), 119–132.

[168]Bau, *This Ground Is Holy*, 90–91, 111–112; Begaj, "An Analysis of Historical and Legal Sanctuary," 151–155, 161. In the trials of SM workers in the mid-1980s, the judges either barred the defense from presenting any evidence related to the SM's religious freedom and beliefs, dismissed the defense's motion to drop the charges on the grounds that they violated Sanctuary workers' constitutional right to freedom of religion, or ruled that the US government's interests in border protection outranked the SM workers' religious principles. Begaj, "An Analysis," 155–159.

[169]Ana Maria Pineda, "Hospitality," in *Practicing Our Faith: A Way of Life for a Searching People*, ed. Dorothy C. Bass (San Francisco: Jossey-Bass, 1997, 2010), esp. 30, 34–35, 39–40, quote at 38.

186   *Nevertheless, We Persist*

churches function prophetically both as life-supporting and life-sustaining counterspaces and publics to the dominant militarist and xenophobic US public square. Faith-based sanctuary movements "compensate for the lack of public institutional mechanisms to protect human rights and care for the well-being of unauthorized journeying migrants."[170] These churches, in my view, thus constitute and offer an alternative possible model of US public life. For example, the SM substituted for the US government's failure to respect and uphold refugee rights by developing a civil initiative that crossed, sheltered, and publicized stories of Central American immigrants, in some cases lobbying for and winning US asylum hearings.[171] Similarly advocating for inclusive justice by modeling an alternative political order, the NSM assists immigrants with sustaining material, spiritual, and political resources, and thus "challenge[s] state institutions and their regulatory activities" based on narrow border-based notions of citizenship rights.[172] Forging a counternarrative and counterspace to nationalist notions of citizenship and rights,[173] US and Mexican conferences of Catholic bishops issued a joint pastoral letter in 2003, *Strangers No Longer*, that affirmed US national sovereignty but simultaneously challenged US border protection and enforcement strategies that violate human dignity and rights, particularly the right to work and to migrate for work to earn a decent living and lead a dignified life.[174] Also, annual Latino/a Catholic posada rituals performed at the San Diego–Tijuana border act as a theo-political allegory for immigrants' search for shelter—physically and politically—amid rejection, suffering, and death at the US–Mexico border.[175] This ritual commemorates border deaths and builds lived solidarity and hope between Anglo and Latino/a Americans as well as Mexican peoples through shared hands and gifts across a chain link border fence. Ritually, "symbolic racial-ethnic and denominational

---

[170]Jacqueline Maria Hagan, *Migration Miracle: Faith, Hope, and Meaning on the Undocumented Journey* (Cambridge, MA: Harvard University Press, 2008), 83.

[171]De La Torre, *Trails of Hope and Terror*, 170–175, and Coutin, *The Culture of Protest*, 107–130, 183–187; Susan Bibler Coutin, "The Oppressed, the Suspect, and the Citizen: Subjectivity in Competing Accounts of Political Violence," *Law and Social Inquiry* 26, no. 1 (Winter 2001): esp. 63–66, 67–74.

[172]Hagan, *Migration Miracle*, 83.

[173]Hondagneu-Sotelo, *God's Heart Has No Borders*, xi, 8.

[174]Conferencia del Episcopado Mexicano and United States Conference of Catholic Bishops, *Strangers No Longer: Together on the Journey of Hope*, January 22, 2003, paras. 34–39. Cf. Hagan, *Migration Miracle*, 88–92, Heyer, "Strangers in Our Midst," 433–440, and Kerwin, "Rights, the Common Good, and Sovereignty," 97–99.

[175]Hondagneu-Sotelo, *God's Heart Has No Borders*, 133–135. Cf. Pineda, *Hospitality*; Christine D. Pohl, *Making Room: Recovering Hospitality as a Christian Tradition* (Grand Rapids, MI: Eerdmans, 1999); Mary Doak, *A Prophetic, Public Church: Witness to Hope Amid the Global Crises of the Twenty-First Century* (Collegeville, MN: Liturgical Press, 2020).

Ethno-nationalism, Community Organizing, and United Farm Workers   **187**

borders are crossed."[176] Illustrating both symbolic and prophetic praxis of ekklesial work or creating community, this ritual bears religio-political significance as a locus of "a new civil society of biblically inspired social action groups . . . [that] create a momentarily sacred space that symbolically violates the divisions imposed by nation-state borders."[177] This ritual effectively reconfigures the US body politic by restoring a common *imago Dei*–based dignity to all humanity rather than reinforcing divisive nationalistic borders and attendant legal citizenship-based rights.

Binational bishops' statements and transnational border rituals, together with interfaith movements that supply humanitarian aid (food, water, and medical care) to immigrants in southern Arizona deserts (e.g., Humane Borders, the Samaritans, and No More Deaths),[178] constitute a new community that engages in prophetic hospitality, solidarity, and common humanity for the purpose of "imagining and calling for a more just future . . . a utopian vision of antiborderism, a postnational unity of humanity."[179] These movements not only incarnate a new ecclesiological model of "a borderless church"[180] that resonates with the decentralized, nonhierarchical, social justice praxis-based, and transnational ecclesiology of the earlier SM.[181] These movements also advance a more expansive notion of US religio-political public life as well as citizenship rights and responsibilities around a shared humanity and rights that consequently problematize and contest narrow nativist and ethnonationalist notions of citizenship. "One nation under God" with its exclusivist views of membership based on common race, ethnicity, religion, language, or culture is reconfigured in the NSM as "one family under God" committed to "human rights, the common good, solidarity, and cultural diversity."[182]

In providing sanctuary, NSM churches prophetically refigure religious spaces via hospitality to immigrants that embody a more expansive twenty-first-century version of the beloved community. Alexia Salvatierra, former director of Clergy and Laity United for Economic Justice

---

[176]Hondagneu-Sotelo, *God's Heart Has No Borders*, 136; cf. 157–163.

[177]Ibid., 144, 150, 161–166.

[178]Hagan, *Migration Miracle*, 103–109; Helene Slessarev–Jamir, *Prophetic Activism: Progressive Religious Justice Movements in Contemporary America* (New York: New York University Press, 2011), 140–149.

[179]Hondagneu-Sotelo, *God's Heart Has No Borders*, 167–169.

[180]Hagan, *Migration Miracle*, 93–95. Bishops in Tucson and Phoenix, Arizona, together with bishops in Hermosillo, Texas, created Diocese without Borders in 2002, to create religious coalitions of immigration ministries that offer migrant care in southern US and northern Mexican deserts.

[181]Cunningham, "Sanctuary and Sovereignty," 378–379, 383–384, and *God and Caesar*, 110–114, 130–137.

[182]Kerwin, "Toward a Catholic Vision of Nationality," 203, 206–207.

188   *Nevertheless, We Persist*

(CLUE) and co-founder of the NSM, explicitly interpreted sanctuary via the beloved community.[183] In the NSM, the beloved community serves as a theological symbol for promoting equal dignity and rights regardless of country of origin, for determining moral responsibilities in the face of suffering peoples, and for supporting groups and cities that housed "prophet families—families who are willing to tell their story publicly [as] a religious witness and a moral voice on the immigration issue."[184] Similar to other faith-based social justice movements for civil and human rights, the NSM expands the borders of the beloved community via the church into the public sphere as a means to break citizenship rights beyond the narrow box of the nation-state. In other words, civil rights activists appealed to shared humanity as a theo-political reason to justify US citizenship rights for African Americans and later human rights for all people oppressed by racism, poverty, and militarism. The NSM appeals to shared humanity as a theo-political symbol to protect and promote human rights for immigrants that transcend nationally defined rights, that confound nationalist norms for determining such rights to freedom, equality, justice, opportunity, and democracy,[185] and that express "the global citizenship enjoined on Christians."[186]

In conclusion, based on multiple waves of forced and voluntary immigration that characterize US history, the US is shaped and reshaped by displaced peoples who lack dominant racial, gender, economic, social, political, and other identity markers. The UFW and the NSM occupied and refigured economic, political, and religious spaces, in order to open up counter-narratives, symbols, and spaces in US society and politics for such displaced peoples, to expand the circle of welcome particularly to Latino/a workers and immigrants, and to advocate for broader political recognition and human rights. These movements participate in rhetorical, symbolic, and prophetic praxis—nonviolent direct action such as rallies, demonstrations, and marches/pilgrimages for economic rights and long-term hospitality for immigrants—that contest and remake political and religious spaces in an effort to model and make a more just public life.

Going beyond simple inclusion of excluded peoples in US democratic politics and daily life, both the UFW and the NSM aim through the trifold praxis of ekklesial work to remake long-standing notions of public life and political subjectivity. Rhetorical, symbolic, and prophetic praxis

---

[183]De La Torre, *Trails of Hope and Terror*, 163–170.
[184]Ibid., 164–165, 167.
[185]Kerwin, "Toward a Catholic Vision of Nationality," 201.
[186]Heyer, "Strangers in Our Midst," 439.

Ethno-nationalism, Community Organizing, and United Farm Workers **189**

in both movements carry implications for edging political belonging and membership toward cosmopolitan citizenship. As Peggy Levitt observes in a rich ethnographic study of immigrant religious groups' attitudes toward US citizenship, US political sovereignty is often interpreted from a Christian doctrinal perspective: "one land, one membership card, and one identity is a secular version of the Holy Trinity."[187] By contrast, these groups have created transcendent and transnational religious spaces. In my view, faith-based global or cosmopolitan citizenship portrays "religion [as] the ultimate boundary crosser. God needs no passport because faith traditions give their followers symbols, rituals, and stories they use to create alternative sacred landscapes. . . . [Religion helps] to trade in a national lens for a transnational one . . . [that] begins with a world that is borderless and boundaryless."[188] Both movements have claimed and promoted divinely given human rights that by definition transcend exclusionary logics and limits of the US nation-state. Rhetorical, symbolic, and prophetic praxis in both movements have reconfigured and recast political and religious spaces into alternative arenas with religio-political implications for recognizing inalienable human rights that transcend borders of race, gender, class, birth, legal residence, and so on. Feminist theorist Seyla Benhabib explores these shared basic human rights under the right of hospitality as a cosmopolitan right of respect and egalitarian reciprocity associated with our common humanity.[189] Cosmopolitan or universal rights for Benhabib evoke a new notion of political belonging, or a "postnational solidarity," that supersedes but is simultaneously embedded in the nation-state's and other political entities' respect for human qua human rights, not human qua citizen rights.[190]

Rather than disregard or negate political borders or call for borderless nation-states, cosmopolitan or universal rights require a basis for recognizing human rights, for participating in a shared humanity. Benhabib legitimates human rights by referring to UN Human Rights conventions and other supranational sources that express and embody a "context-transcending appeal" for such rights.[191] Likewise, the UFW and the NSM appeal to the nation-state to safeguard but not define human rights. Both movements question the religio-political nonbelonging of Latinx workers

---

[187]Peggy Levitt, *God Needs No Passport: Immigrants and the Changing American Landscape* (New York: New Press, 2007), 68.

[188]Ibid., 12–13, 21–22.

[189]Seyla Benhabib, *The Rights of Others: Aliens, Residents, and Citizens* (Cambridge: Cambridge University Press, 2004), 2–3, 13, 26–27, 36.

[190]Ibid., 17, 21.

[191]Ibid., 10–12, at 19.

190   *Nevertheless, We Persist*

and immigrants under US laws and policies, and thus define the rights of these groups via rhetorical and symbolic practices, that is, via religious appeals to religious texts and symbols that uphold a divinely given shared humanity. Luke Bretherton calls such an appeal Christian cosmopolitanism, which opposes narrow notions of rights coterminous with national borders and instead promotes the common as well as cosmic good against a theological horizon of the *imago Dei* (*GS*, para. 75). Following the radical ramifications of Luke 14:15–24 (a tale about inclusive table fellowship) and Galatians 3:26–28 (an early Christian baptismal ritual that creates equality in the body of Christ), a Christian cosmopolitanism emphasizes the basic human dignity and rights of all people when viewed against an eschatological horizon of hope in a future fulfillment of all creation in God's image. The *imago Dei* transgresses national or territorial borders, legal-political categories of identity, or racial/ethnic, linguistic, and social indexes of citizenship.[192] As Elie Wiesel contends, "Any person by virtue of being a son or a daughter of humanity, is a living sanctuary whom nobody has the right to invade."[193]

In keeping with these two movements toward cosmopolitan citizenship and rights, and in keeping with a feminist public theology of ekklesial work, the UFW and the NSM participate in faith-based rhetorical, symbolic, and prophetic practices to transform and transfigure religio-political spaces of our shared common life. Reconceptualized in the UFW and the NSM, the beloved community exemplifies a Christian cosmopolitanism because it questions an existing exclusionary sociopolitical order and incarnates another alternative possible way of being and living together beyond existing normalized borders. In both movements, religio-political claims and symbols cultivate a transcendent and transnational identity based on a prophetic praxis of shared humanity, solidarity, and hospitality, and thereby overcome "the sin of exceptionalism engrained in the nation's social psyche."[194] Both movements transform public and religious spaces into alternative societies that gather for the purpose of recognizing the inherent human dignity of each person, not as instrumentally valued and dehumanized commodities or objects of the market, the state, or other organizations.[195] Both movements mark and create a religio-politically

---

[192]Luke Bretherton, *Hospitality as Holiness: Christian Witness amid Moral Diversity* (Aldershot, UK: Ashgate, 2006), 121–151, and *Christianity and Contemporary Politics: The Conditions and Possibilities of Faithful Witness* (Malden, MA: Wiley–Blackwell, 2010), 126–160.

[193]In Letty M. Russell, ed., *Just Hospitality: God's Welcome in a World of Difference* (Louisville, KY: Westminster John Knox Press, 2009), 87.

[194]Heyer, "Social Sin and Immigration," 435.

[195]Bretherton, *Christianity and Contemporary Politics*, 215.

Ethno-nationalism, Community Organizing, and United Farm Workers   **191**

safe space that in turn becomes a sacramental sign of that togetherness which seeks and signifies, at least in part, the common good and common humanity. Although underwritten by and linked to a Christian theological perspective, ekklesial work and its religious rhetorical, symbolic, and prophetic practices in both movements do not require uniformity under a Christian umbrella; it does not require confessional consent to Christian beliefs about creation in the image of God. In this way public theology justifies respect for common humanity and rights from a Christian perspective, but does not preclude religious traditions or other folxs with no religious tradition from explaining and employing their transcendent supranational reasons and practices for such respect and rights. As the late Letty Russell remarked about welcoming the other in a pluralistic society, "Hospitality is an expression of unity without uniformity, because unity in Christ has as its purpose the sharing of God's hospitality with the stranger, the one who is 'other.' "[196] Exemplified in both movements, ekklesial work or community-creating praxis "will lead us to risk joining in the work of mending the creation without requiring those who are different to become like us."[197] Indeed, ekklesial work and its rhetorical, symbolic, and prophetic praxis eschews "us and them" ways of thinking and living, by instead finding religio-political ways of thinking and living about "all of us" as always already inherently interrelated with "them," whether human or other-than-human earthly life. Eco-public theology and movements explored in the next chapter, such as Catholic pacifist and green movements, amplify this ever-expanding eschatological notion of the common and cosmic good.

---

[196]Russell, *Just Hospitality*, 80; cf. 118–123.
[197]Ibid., 123.

6

Militarism, Pacifism, and the Plowshares Movement

In the landmark environmental encyclical *Laudato Si'*,[1] Pope Francis characterizes and confronts the global climate crisis in similar ways that ecofeminist theologies address and analyze the systemic exploitation of the earth intersectionally with wide-ranging racialized, gendered, classed, and other injustices that especially affect poor communities and women.

> Our common home . . . now cries out to us because of the harm we have inflicted on her by our irresponsible use and abuse of the goods with which God has endowed her. We have come to see ourselves as her lords and masters, entitled to plunder her at will. . . . The earth herself, burdened and laid waste, is among the most abandoned and maltreated of our poor. (*Laudato Si'*, paras. 1–2)

Introduced in these opening paragraphs, Francis implicitly situates ecological and social justice in struggles with kyriarchal imbalanced power relations among humans and between humans and other-than-human life that arise from and affect other kinds of socio-cultural and theological mastery. Ecofeminist theologies explicitly challenge these dominative power relations as an extension of the goals of global feminist movements to contest race, gender, and other socio-economic and political inequalities further amplified by the climate crisis.

> This movement is concerned . . . with a fundamental re-imagination of the whole of humanity in relation to the whole of reality, including non-human creation. In other words the feminist . . . agenda has

---

[1] Pope Francis, *Laudato Si': On Care for Our Common Home* (Huntington, IN: Our Sunday Visitor, 2015). Cited hereafter by paragraphs in parentheses.

Militarism, Pacifism, and the Plowshares Movement

> widened . . . to a demand for full participation of women in society and culture, to an ideal of re-creating humanity itself according to patterns of eco-justice, that is, of right relations at every level and in relation to all of reality.[2]

Similarly, in the encyclical sins against the sacramentality of creation as the incarnation of divine love and hope (paras. 84–86) occur, for instance, in rising and more acidic oceans, decreasing biodiversity and species extinction, increasing climate change with intensifying storms, droughts, and glacier melt, deforestation, desertification, destruction of wetlands, increasing pollution of water, soil, land, and air (with attendant diseases) by corporate manufacturing, agriculture, nuclear energy, extractive industries, and unsustainable rates of production and consumption (paras. 8, 12, 20, 23–24). Eco-catastrophes are thus construed as sins of eco-injustice against a creator God and against environmental and public health, that is, against low-income communities and communities of color, especially Indigenous peoples (para. 146) and women who suffer from environmental racism (paras. 48, 56, 75). Here, the Pope echoes but does not cite Brazilian liberation theologian Leonardo Boff when he contends that "a true ecological approach always becomes a social approach; it must integrate questions of justice in debates on the environment, so as to hear both the cry of the earth and the cry of the poor" (para. 49; cf. para. 93).[3] An integral ecology embodies "an integrated approach to combating poverty, restoring dignity to the excluded, and at the same time protecting nature" (para. 139). Eco-justice ties together poverty and ecological degradation, and empowers resistance to environmental racism and other enfolded eco-injustices.

As this chapter will show, *Laudato Si'* especially exemplifies rhetorical, to a certain degree symbolic, and somewhat prophetic practices of a feminist public theology, of ekklesial work. Francis's eco-public theology bridges multiple fields of public discourse, and communicates effectively about religious responses to eco-crises using economic, scientific, and other discourses. The letter is addressed to all people (para. 3) and encourages international political, economic, religious, and scientific dialogue (chapter 5). Moreover, the letter provides a cogent and compelling perspective about various environmental crises (chapters 1 and 3) and emphasizes how Christian claims and practices might wrestle with those crises (chap-

---

[2]Sandra M. Schneiders, *With Oil in Their Lamps: Faith, Feminism, and the Future* (New York: Paulist Press, 2000), 8.

[3]Leonardo Boff, *Cry of the Earth, Cry of the Poor* (Maryknoll, NY: Orbis Books,1997).

194   *Nevertheless, We Persist*

ter 2). However, the Pope offers mixed religio-political messages about reimagining religious symbols—especially God-talk—that in turn only somewhat transform status quo US conservative public discourse, politics, and economics in the pursuit of eco-justice, due to those discourses' long-standing ties to transnational technocratic power relations. Some of the encyclical's symbols prompt a religio-political prophetic praxis of ecological virtues and education (chapter 6) that enable political attitudes and actions for enhancing the common public and ecological good.

Drawing on ecofeminist and eco-public theologies, this chapter analyzes some salient global and US Catholic social justice movements in terms of how their practices of ekklesial work energize an integral ecology, that is, attend to and address intersections of ecological, socio-political, and gender justice. Beyond recent papal statements, these movements such as the Plowshares Movement and US eco-activist nuns mobilize public support for eco-justice via dramatic rhetorical, symbolic, and prophetic acts, and thereby offer and open new theo-political possibilities for understanding different Catholic theological and activist responses to our enduring ecological crises. For example, Plowshares Movement activists initially burned draft cards to protest the Vietnam War but are more internationally renowned for their efforts to disarm nuclear weapons (especially the means of storing or delivering them) by performing anti-militarist eco-rituals that advocate for peace. Ecofeminist and eco-public theologies stemming from green nuns' eco-ministries also illuminate how Catholic practices of public engagement for eco-justice in these movements envision and perform ekklesial work, or in ecological terms, better incarnate an integral ecology, that articulates, witnesses to, and builds more just, solidaristic, and biocratic community among humanity, other-than-human life, and the Earth.

Doing Eco-public Theology in *Laudato Si'*

Elaborated by Celia Deane-Drummond and Heinrich Bedford-Strohm, eco-public theology reconstructs religious traditions into more publicly accessible views to persuasively demonstrate across religious and in other ways pluralistic worlds the role of religious peoples and traditions in facing the ecological exigencies of our time and addressing pressing public questions about how to shift public discourse and policy from technocracy toward biocracy, toward a new social, economic, political, and environmental order founded on ecological justice.[4] Effective eco-public

---

[4]Celia Deane-Drummond and Heinrich Bedford-Strohm, Introduction to *Religion and Ecol-*

theology requires theologians to develop a polyglot ability and agility to engage in global public discourse and in doing so envision and recognize new possible worldviews and public policies about ecological issues in ways that illustrate religion's credibility and relevance across multiple communities with their own specialized systems of communication.[5] For example, as Peter Beyer contends, "Religious speaking for the environment . . . invariably translates environmental questions into specifically religious idioms and symbolic clusters. . . . These translations allow one to express ecological matters in religious terms and thereby permit the connectivity with religious remedies."[6]

As demonstrated by US Catholic conservative backlash to *Laudato Si'*, discussed below, dominant economic systems contextualize environmental concerns in relation to a free market-based economy that aims at generating capital and prosperity amid uneven, unequal development and unsustainable patterns of consumption and growth, given the planet's carrying capacity. Similarly, prevalent political systems consider environmental issues in terms of how to foster national interests and preserve the Global North's dominance in transnational relations. In contrast to climate-change deniers, scientific systems measure, interpret, and publish data, which contribute to a growing global scientific consensus about the impacts of climate change and its attendant crises that disproportionately affect Global Southern peoples, especially poor women of color, among vulnerable global populations such as climate refugees. Therefore, eco-public theology needs to bring religio-linguistic flexibility and theo-political savvy to bridge these particular and seemingly incommensurable ways of communicating about our eco-crises, as well as grapple with religion's differential and at times marginal power to address these crises alongside global economics, politics, and science.[7]

In addition, effective "public theology is liberation theology for global civil society"[8] that opposes oppressive socio-political, economic, or religious powers and that prophetically challenges those same powers to reorient socio-political, economic, and religious institutions and structures

---

ogy in the Public Sphere, ed. Celia Deane-Drummond and Heinrich Bedford-Strohm (London: T & T Clark International, 2011), 4–5; Peter Beyer, "Who Shall Speak for the Environment? Translating Religious, Scientific, Economic, and Political Regimes of Power and Knowledge in a Globalized Society," in *Religion and Ecology in the Public Sphere*, ed. Deane-Drummond and Bedford-Strohm, 25.

[5]Beyer, "Who Shall Speak for the Environment?," 22–24; Heinrich Bedford-Strohm, "Public Theology of Ecology and Civil Society," in *Religion and Ecology in the Public Sphere*, ed. Deane-Drummond and Bedford-Strohm, esp. 46–48.

[6]Beyer, "Who Shall Speak for the Environment?" 29.

[7]Ibid., 35.

[8]Bedford-Strohm, "Public Theology of Ecology and Civil Society," 46.

196   *Nevertheless, We Persist*

toward social and ecological solidarity,[9] toward biocracy. Thus, eco-public theology needs to be intertwined with social movements, including environmental movements, to implement and sustain prophetic change: "Lack of dialogue and cooperation between liberation theology and new social movements may thus result in liberation theologians' lack of credibility in major contemporary social issues . . . all relevant for women, Indigenous, and African-American people."[10] As my analysis of *Laudato Si'* shows, Pope Francis fails to fully articulate an eco-public theology, because his faith-rooted eco-advocacy is fundamentally grounded in global bishops' statements, not in global religious environmental movements. Subsequent to my analysis of *Laudato Si'* below, this chapter engages with selected salient examples of US Catholic eco-justice movements to more effectively do eco-public theology as ekklesial work, or the work of building biocratic community.

In this 2015 letter, Pope Francis introduces and articulates an integral ecology that interweaves environmental crises together with social and gender justice, grounded in a creation-centered theology. Francis calls for an ecological conversion to our common home by interlinking social, economic, and ecological problems, especially with attention to the Global South. For example, he analogizes between the earth's climate and water, on the one hand, and the common good, on the other hand, that enables and supports the flourishing of all life, human and other-than-human, and that requires equitable distributive justice for the respect of basic rights, which in turn create the condition for other rights (paras. 23, 28, 30, 95, 156–157). Global marginalized communities are most gravely affected by climate change and its deteriorating or disappearing ecosystems, which cause and amplify further disasters for these communities such as refugees from climate crisis–based conflicts (paras. 25, 28, 48, 57). Rapid climate change and increasingly limited as well as unsafe water detract from and damage civil society, or our mutual interdependence and obligations to one another for bolstering and building up the common good (paras. 25, 42). Indeed, Francis symbolically portrays the world itself as a common good. An integral ecology thus foregrounds and fosters our obligations to intergenerational sustainability and solidarity (paras. 159, 162).

Employing rhetorical practices of eco-public theology, *Laudato Si'*

---

[9]Ibid., 52.

[10]Elina Vuola, "Latin American Liberation Theologians' Turn to Eco(theo)logy—Critical Remarks," in *Religion and Ecology in the Public Sphere*, ed. Deane-Drummond and Bedford-Strohm, 96.

Militarism, Pacifism, and the Plowshares Movement 197

names anthropocentric sins of eco-injustice, underscores anthropogenic causes of climate change, emphasizes personal and inter/national moral failure to recognize and fulfill social, economic, political, and ecological responsibilities, and replaces prevalent notions of global technocratic power with intergenerational and ecological solidarity. Ongoing environmental crises reveal polarizing contrasts between technocratic and biocratic power, stated in eco-public theological terms between de-creation and co/re-creation,[11] or what I analyze as world-destroying work and world-making or ekklesial work. Christian eco-public theology resists and seeks liberation from hegemonic power, which Francis describes as the techno-economic or technocratic paradigm. Technocracy is characterized by the collusion of modern individualism and consumerism, un/underregulated capitalist and corporate exploitation of environmental resources aided and abetted by rapid technological progress, and Western imperialist, neocolonialist, and exceptionalist consumption of those resources to the world-destruction or de-creation of global peoples and ecosystems.[12] The letter centers and relies on worldwide Catholic bishops' statements to effectively locate climate and other eco-crises within these global contexts and patterns of economic injustice and inequality between the Global North and South. For example, African bishops urge human-planetary solidarity regarding aquifers (paras. 14, 38). Latin American bishops resist the internationalization of the Amazon rainforests to not only protect national sovereignty from transnational economic interests but also to preserve forest ecosystems and Indigenous economies from the increase in ranching (para. 38). Filipino Catholic bishops lament pollution from deforestation, agriculture, fishing, and other industries that deplete marine life, particularly coral. "Underwater cemeteries" no longer foster and regenerate the million species undergirding world majority peoples' economies (para. 41).

Consonant with this chorus of global Catholic bishops and inspired by

---

[11]Colleen Carpenter, "Rushing Winds and Rising Waters: Seeking the Presence of God in a Radically Changing World," in *Confronting the Climate Crisis: Catholic Theological Perspectives*, ed. Jame Schaefer (Milwaukee: Marquette University Press, 2011), esp. 326–327, 330–334.

[12]Geologian Thomas Berry, together with physicist Brian Swimme, encouraged earth's evolutionary history toward an Ecozoic era that values planetary and cosmic life as an organic communion of subjects-in-relation, in contrast to the Technozoic era which pathologically prizes individual, economic, and national growth at the expense of ecocide. Celia Deane-Drummond, *Eco-Theology* (Winona, MN: Anselm Academic, 2008), 40–42; Peter Ellard, "Thomas Berry as the Groundwork for a Dark Green Catholic Theology," in *Confronting the Climate Crisis*, ed. Schaefer, esp. 302–303, 310; and Daniel Scheid, *The Cosmic Common Good: Religious Grounds for Ecological Ethics* (New York: Oxford University Press, 2016), 64–81.

this integral ecology, Francis proposes new international relations that recognize the ecological debt that the Global North owes the Global South for its disproportionate consumption of and consequent harm to both natural resources and local cultures (paras. 51, 95, 143–144). Argentine bishops emphasize that this harm occurs primarily because Global Northern economic interests have fueled the deregulation of multinational corporations who operate in the Global South in ways that weaken international climate agreements, but also cause unemployment and leave unsustainable infrastructure as well as polluted and depleted resources in their wake (paras. 51, 54, 56). In keeping with and invoking an eco-justice framework, Latin American and Caribbean bishops reiterate the earth's and the poor's lament by expressing deep concerns about how Global North economic interests offset and outweigh growing ecological sensibilities (paras. 54, 56), at times demonstrated in global environmental summits that lack socio-political force and efficacy (paras. 166–167, 169). Aligned with the US bishops, Francis commits to "differentiated responsibilities" and practices to restore the public, common, and eco-good in an economic and ecological way: limited consumption by the Global North (paras. 52, 104–105), sovereignty as well as sustainable development in the Global South (para. 172), and robust legally binding norms and regulations to protect ecosystems as well as curb the "techno-economic paradigm" or the globalized logic of control, consumption, and ultimate erasure of the world's resources, including water, forests, terrestrial life, marine life, ocean life, and peoples and cultures (paras. 14, 28, 30, 38, 41), for mainly the Global North's immediate interests and infinite profits at the eclipse and expense of the poor (paras. 53, 95, 106, 109, 145, 170, 210).

Pope Francis's US visit in fall 2015 included invited addresses to a US congressional joint session and the UN General Assembly, in addition to visits to the White House, Independence Hall, and the World Meeting of Families. Pope Francis offered homilies and reflections at masses, memorial services, schools, and prisons in Washington, New York, and Philadelphia. His addresses to the US Congress and the UN General Assembly during that visit resonated with his environmental encyclical. Yet this encyclical together with this papal visit establish the limited influence of papal rhetorical practices of public engagement on conservative American bishops and US political leaders who incorporate Catholicism in reproductive, sexual, and gendered bio-politics but denounce Catholic social and eco-justice teaching. Reactionary responses from the US political and religious right to Pope Francis and *Laudato Si'* demonstrate US Catholic eco-political failure to face and embrace eco-concerns and solutions.

Militarism, Pacifism, and the Plowshares Movement   199

In Congress,[13] Pope Francis redefined politics in defense of the transcendent dignity of all life in the *imago Dei* and directed politics to play an important part in the pursuit of the common good. To reinforce this religio-political grounding and goal of common life, Pope Francis participated in a theo-politics of storytelling and drew on the "historical memory" and "deepest cultural reserves" that in his view shape fundamental US values. He took a cue from exemplary leaders of the Civil Rights Movement and Catholic pacifist movements to show that religion fosters solidarity and the common good, and contributes to "new policies and new forms of social consensus" about civil rights for African Americans, First Nations, immigrants, and refugees. Building on these historical exemplars, religion also helps develop solutions to the current climate crisis to promote the common good, which expands to encompass our common social, political, and earthly life.

At the UN General Assembly,[14] Pope Francis recalled the UN's role to significantly shape international humanitarian law and promote human rights, justice, and peace, and thereby effectively limit as well as distribute power, whether political, economic, military, or technological. Nonetheless, the Pope added that global ecosystems and marginalized peoples inhabiting them stand as contemporary "victims of power badly exercised. . . . The sectors are closely interconnected and made increasingly fragile by dominant political and economic relationships. That is why their rights must be forcefully affirmed, by working to protect the environment and by putting an end to exclusion." For Pope Francis, theological claims about the intrinsic value, interdependence, and sacredness of all life endowed and sustained by the Creator foster eco-justice, integrating environmental and human rights. While global governments have pursued concrete political steps to ensure integral human development through access to basic goods (e.g., education, housing, work, food, and water), Francis mobilized a creation-centered theology to resist "a selfish and boundless thirst for power and material prosperity [that] leads both to the misuse of available natural resources and to the exclusion of the weak and disadvantaged . . . [who] are part of today's widespread and quietly growing culture of waste."

Preceding the Pope's visit, US bishops urged Catholic politicians to

---

[13]Stephanie Kirchgaessner, "Pope Francis's Message to Congress," *The Guardian*, September 24, 2015.

[14]Holy See Press Office, "Address to the United Nations General Assembly," September 25, 2015.

200 *Nevertheless, We Persist*

cease their climate change denial.[15] Many US bishops enacted strategic plans to implement the encyclical through sermons and summer events prior to the Pope's visit, especially to spotlight the 2014 National Climate Assessment which identified ecologically endangered US cities.[16] Moreover, Catholic social teaching promotes and upholds the dignity and flourishing of all life, human and other-than-human, as created, loved, and declared intrinsically good by God. Sharpened in the Vatican II Pastoral Constitution on the Church in the Modern World and in subsequent papal as well as episcopal statements, Catholic social teaching pivots precisely on the principle of integral development. This principle provides both theological and political impetus for the church's public engagement, which engenders and enhances solidarity with marginalized peoples affected not only by workers' rights, war and peace, the death penalty, racism, immigration, sex trafficking, and so on, but also disproportionately by the global climate crisis.

Nonetheless, political partisan interests collided with and undermined Catholic social teaching. Conservative US Catholic protest and backlash against the encyclical framed Pope Francis's visit. As historian Martin Marty poignantly observes, "For a century Vatican social documents have been repudiated, neglected, misrepresented, or unrecognized, often by precisely the same set of politicians and interest groups who most ostentatiously wear the insignia and bear the banners of papal authority on some other topics."[17]

Similar to the majority of US Catholic conservative politicians,[18] leading US Catholic Republicans ignored, denounced, or aggressively challenged the letter and the Pope as a religio-political figure, thereby delegitimizing religion's public role in US common life. For example, Rick Santorum, then a US presidential candidate, rebuffed and discredited the Pope, recommending that the Pope restrict his public witness to theology and morality, particularly the five non-negotiables for US Catholic voters.[19] Jeb

---

[15]Brian Roewe, "Iowa Bishop to Presidential Candidates: It's Time to Talk Climate Change," *National Catholic Reporter*, July 2, 2015.

[16]Coral Davenport, "Pope's Views on Climate Change Add Pressure to Catholic Candidates." *New York Times*, June 16, 2015.

[17]Martin E. Marty, "Encyclical," *Sightings*, July 13, 2015.

[18]Climate change creates religio-political and partisan divides among Catholics. A Pew Research Center poll shows that 62 percent of Catholic Democrats agree with anthropogenic climate change, whereas only 24 percent of Catholic Republicans do. Suzanne Goldenberg, "Pope Francis Faces Challenge Persuading US's Catholic Leaders on Climate Change," *The Guardian*, September 16, 2015.

[19]Christopher Hale, "Rick Santorum Wants Pope Francis to Leave Science to Scientists Only When It's Convenient for Him," *Washington Post*, June 4, 2015. "Climate change continues to

Militarism, Pacifism, and the Plowshares Movement

Bush, another US presidential candidate at the time, contested the Pope's eco-public theological strategies that situated ecological problems within the global economic structures of (1) unchecked free market capitalism that controls and exploits people and resources for profit, and of (2) individualist consumerism that drives our desire to objectify, commodify, possess, and ultimately master others, including nature. Taking a religio-political tactic from former President John F. Kennedy's campaign, Bush explicitly resisted the Catholic leader's influence on US economic policy and stressed that religion should humanize not politicize issues.[20] Some congressmen pledged to boycott the Pope's address due to its politically leftist leanings.[21]

Pope Francis's rhetorical failure to reach and persuade US Catholic conservative politicians about global climate change illustrates a counter-hegemonic theological strategy with an eschatological edge: an inbreaking, fleeting, and far from fully realized possibility for imagining, proclaiming, and mediating alternative ways of being and living together in a biocratic rather than technocratic worldview at the intersectional interdependence of social, political, and earthly life: "The new heaven and the new earth that Christians are expecting can certainly not be reduced to earthly ecological healing, but such . . . healing is equally a clear sign of the very visible consequences of this great vision."[22] In other words, countering technocracy requires more than rhetorical practices of re-telling, or better re-placing, the earth story in an evolutionary, ecological, embodied, and ultimately holistic cosmic context that, collectively, stresses the co-original, co-evolutionary, interrelated, interdependent, intersubjective, intergenerational, and integrated nature of all embodied life involved in co/re-creation in order to overcome human-nature objectification and oppression and all its multiple attendant aggressive forms (racism, sexism, poverty, ableism, religious xenophobia).[23] Eco-public theologians

---

be seen as a justice issue, and not a life issue, like abortion and marriage. Reframing climate change as a life issue would command more resources, according to some within the church. Until then, climate change takes second place to abortion and same-sex marriage for many in the US church leadership." Goldenberg, "Pope Francis Faces Challenge."

[20]Christopher Hale, "Jeb Bush's Response to Pope Francis's Climate Change Encyclical Is Hogwash," *Time*, June 17, 2015; Suzanne Goldenberg and Sabrina Siddiqui, "Jeb Bush Joins Republican Backlash against Pope on Climate Change," *The Guardian*, June 17, 2015.

[21]Mike DeBonis, "Catholic Congressman Says He Will Boycott Pope Francis Over Climate Change Stance," *Washington Post*, September 18, 2015.

[22]Bedford-Strohm, "Public Theology of Ecology and Civil Society," 54.

[23]Elizabeth A. Johnson, *Quest for the Living God: Mapping Frontiers in the Theology of God* (New York: Continuum, 2007), 181–201; Anne Marie Dalton and Henry C. Simmons, *Eco-theology and the Practice of Hope* (Albany: State University of New York Press, 2010), 44–47,

202 *Nevertheless, We Persist*

also need to engage not only rhetorical but also symbolic and prophetic praxis. For example, in contrast to technocracy, eco-liberation theologian Leonardo Boff elaborated a biocratic socio-political order in which social and ecological intrinsic interconnectedness and interdependence spur on attendant rights—personal rights (social and economic rights, including rights to cultural respect, diversity, and positive reciprocity), national rights (economic and political rights to equality and citizenship to contribute freely, creatively, and responsibly to the common good), planetary rights (the option for the poor is situated within an option for the planet), and cosmic rights (the kinship of all life in its origins and its destiny, which mitigate negative effects on present and future generations).[24] Religious symbols of God, found in *Laudato Si'* and amplified in ecofeminist theologies, situate these biocratic rights in a co/re-creative context as well as urge prophetic ethics and action.

As a symbolic practice of eco-public theology, *Laudato Si'* highlights creation-centered theologies to revive the biocratic links between religious convictions and ecological commitments "that everything is interconnected, and that genuine care for our own lives and our relationships with nature is inseparable from fraternity, justice, and faithfulness to others" (para. 70). Francis particularly stresses the universal goodness, interrelatedness, and mutual responsibilities of all creation, too often disregarded, disrupted, distorted, and violated by the sins of dominion and anthropocentrism (paras. 65–67). To counteract these social sins against our created and Trinitarian web of relationships with God, one another, and all life (para. 240), Francis reinterprets biblical Sabbath traditions as well as theologies of work to restore relational balances for the fulfillment and flourishing of all life (paras. 71, 125–128). Likewise, encouraging the contemplation of creation's sacramentality or suffusion with divine presence, Brazilian bishops align with Francis's eco-theology of creation by linking the Spirit's indwelling in all life with ecological ethics (para. 88).

Eco-pneumatology is clarified and deeply cultivated in Catholic ecofeminist theologian Elizabeth Johnson's constructive theology of the Spirit, which she innovates by combining evolutionary theory and Christian theology to affirm both scientific evolution and religious belief in a creator God. For Johnson, the ineffable but active indwelling of the Spirit points to divine love that creates and continues to give life, that stands

---

74–75, 79–80, and, 99–100 on ecofeminist theories of place.

[24]Deane-Drummond, *Eco-Theology*, 46–49. Scheid summarizes theocentric and cosmocentric rights and responsibilities as the cosmic common good (*The Cosmic Common Good*, 23–44).

Militarism, Pacifism, and the Plowshares Movement

in compassionate solidarity with all suffering and extinct life, and that empowers and enables all living and dying life toward a future eschatological transfiguration.[25]

> The Creator Spirit calls the world into being, gifts it with dynamism, and accompanies it through the by-ways of evolution, all the while attracting it forward toward a multitude of "endless forms most beautiful." We glimpse here . . . empowerment of a creation that is transient and vulnerable yet resilient and generative. . . . The Spirit of God unleashes autonomy in the beloved rather than seeking to control the other by any form of power-over, even if benevolently exercised.[26]

In his encyclical, the Pope apparently translates this tacit ecofeminist pneumatology into a practice of ecological citizenship and its associated political virtues of loving care, responsibility, and solidarity (paras. 210–211, 219–220, 229, 231), out of which a new "shared identity" and "social fabric emerges" (para. 232).

Among the letter's symbolic practices, Pope Francis proposes Jesus as a theological paradigm to reject all sorts of anthropocentric dualisms and domination between heaven/earth, spirit/matter, soul/body, etc. (para. 98), which fuel both ecological degradation and the subjugation of oppressed peoples, including women. Against the Christological backdrop of the incarnation, which unifies divinity and humanity and thus reconciles all sorts of false dualisms (para. 100), Pope Francis opposes subject-object relations between human and other-than-human life (para. 11). Objectifying other-than-human life for its instrumental value trades on a flawed Christian anthropology of human dominion and mastery (para. 116), thrives on a "throwaway culture" (para. 22), and treats marginalized peoples as disposable (paras. 82, 106).[27] Treating earthly life as resources only facilitates and furthers objectification and engenders global patterns of inequality (paras. 33, 81–82), such as environmental racism, modern-day slavery, and sexual exploitation (paras. 45–46, 123).

---

[25]Elizabeth A. Johnson, *Ask the Beasts: Darwin and the God of Love* (London: Bloomsbury, 2014), 1–13, 16–17.

[26]Ibid., 178–179.

[27]"The biopolitics of disposability" invisibilizes socially and politically any struggling-to-survive community that threatens the image of Global Northern or American privilege and prominence. Henry A. Giroux, "Reading Hurricane Katrina: Race, Class and the Biopolitics of Disposability," *College Literature* 33, no. 3 (Summer 2006): esp. 174–175, 181–182, 186.

204 *Nevertheless, We Persist*

By contrast, Francis recognizes the radically incarnational, sacramental, and interrelational subjectivity of all life, that is, the intrinsic worth of all life, inhabiting social ecologies or natural ecosystems (para. 140). Such eco-subjectivity is more fully elaborated in ecofeminist theological symbols of a biocratic worlview.

In a similar ecofeminist vein that is unstated and unengaged in the encyclical, "technological control, a Western-oriented model of development, and patriarchy form an 'unholy trinity' dominating the lives of marginalized women," as Kwok Pui Lan contends.[28] US ecofeminist theologian Sallie McFague criticizes from an incarnational perspective globalization and its attendant economic systems that legitimize and reinforce gender and social injustices along with ecological degradation. McFague takes the incarnation, or the embodiment of God in Jesus' feeding and healing ministry with poor, oppressed, and other marginalized peoples, as a theological starting point for an evolutionary ecological worldview that urges an intrinsic love of nature as well as a universal love of all earthly bodies, human and nonhuman alike, as subjects in their own right, not objects for exploitative economic or other means of control. McFague analyzes how theological symbols and particularly models of a transcendent, imperial, and judgmental God shape and structure human-nature/subject-object relations. She demythologizes medieval mechanistic, modern consumerist, and globalized corporate capitalist views of the earth and of progress that objectify, operationalize, and commodify the world's allegedly limitless resources to serve and satisfy certain privileged human desires and needs for profits. Rather than a hierarchical, dualist, and instrumentalist view of the triangulated God-human-world relationship in which kyriarchal Christianity and capitalism combine to manipulate nature for our own purposes and as a vehicle to the divine, McFague's metaphorical God-talk for the world as the body of God reveres nature as a sacramental sign of the divine without collapsing God and the world and consequently treats all bodies as sacramental subjects, rather than manipulable or disposable objects, within a panentheistic view of God.[29]

Extending embodiment from the personal to the political to the earthly

---

[28]Kwok Pui Lan, "Ecology and the Recycling of Christianity," in *Ecotheology: Voices from South and North*, ed. David G. Hallman (Eugene, OR: Wipf & Stock, 1994), 108.

[29]Sallie McFague, *Super, Natural Christians: How We Should Love Nature* (Minneapolis: Fortress, 1997), 1–9, 12–16, 20–25, 32–39, 164–175. Cf. Dalton and Simmons, *Ecotheology and the Practice of Hope*, 61–63, and Kari-Shane Davis Zimmerman, "God, Creation, and the Environment: Feminist Theological Perspectives," in *Green Discipleship: Catholic Theological Ethics and the Environment*, ed. Tobias Winright (Winona, MN: Anselm Academic, 2011), esp. 256–261.

Militarism, Pacifism, and the Plowshares Movement 205

and ultimately to the cosmic context, Brazilian ecofeminist theologian Ivone Gebara, also absent from the encyclical but central to its theological symbols, supports a similar eco-holistic worldview, what she calls a biocentric unitary worldview, through God-talk. For Gebara, all life is embraced by, dwells within, and co-constitutes one same Sacred Body of the divine.[30] Within this Sacred Body, relatedness encompasses and characterizes our earthly, human (including sex/gender, ethnic, social/cultural, and sexual), ethical, religious, and even cosmic condition. For Gebara, "we are all both created within and creators of this relatedness. We are of its substance and it is of our substance. . . . Within that rediscovery we are reborn in God; we are reborn to the earth, to the cosmos, to history, and to service to one another in the construction of human relationships grounded in justice and mutual respect."[31] In these ecofeminist theological symbols, solidarity in a biocratic worldview includes the biosphere as well as different bioregions, and incorporates endangered species as well as degraded ecological systems.[32] Further, Gebara underscores earthly and cosmic citizenship to overcome all sorts of sexist, racist, and nationalist exclusions as well as other prevalent forms of xenophobia in our world.[33]

As a prophetic practice of eco-public theology, *Laudato Si'* identifies and opposes the idolatry of current economic models as sins against a creator God as well as against vulnerable peoples and environments (paras. 56, 75) but does not grapple sufficiently with how ecological crises—anthropogenic climate change and other eco-injustices wrought by the Global North—most negatively affect global poor and Indigenous women. In other words, this encyclical fails to realize an integral ecology with respect to gender justice for various theological reasons. The encyclical's blind spot to fully elaborating its own eco-public theology and to do the ekklesial work of eco-community building emerges primarily in its lack of prophetic God-talk and praxis.

Different models of God emerge within *Laudato Si'* that encourage or not intersections of gender, social, and eco-justice. The letter employs God-talk in ways that challenge and reinforce kyriarchal systems of imbalanced power relations among humans and between humanity and all life, to the detriment of women. For example, the letter foregrounds

---

[30]Ivone Gebara, *Longing for Running Water: Ecofeminism and Liberation* (Minneapolis: Fortress, 2002), 82, 91, 94, 97, 105, 155.

[31]Ibid., 103, 151; cf. 75, 84–92, 140–141.

[32]Jame Schaefer, "Solidarity, Subsidiarity, and Preference for the Poor: Extending Catholic Social Teaching in Response to the Climate Crisis," in *Confronting the Climate Crisis*, ed. Schaefer, 389–425, esp. 410.

[33]Gebara, *Longing for Running Water*, 158.

paternal language for an all-powerful absolute creator father God (paras. 73, 77, 96, 220, 226) as a theological symbol to reject anthropocentric domination and dualisms and simultaneously to create common bonds among humans and between humans and other-than-human life (para. 89). However, the interrelational interdependence of all life in God is ensured by a dominating father God "who alone owns the world" (para. 75), which thereby reinscribes and prescribes kyriarchal theologics of social, political, economic, and even ecological structures of hierarchical power and dualism that are both bolstered by and perpetuate long-held oppressive God-human-earthly relations—all of which ironically the encyclical aims to undercut and undo.[34] Kyriarchal anthropologies justified by such religio-political God-talk still significantly shape our eco-crises. As Elina Vuola claims, "To move away too fast from reworking this *anthropos* from the perspective of colonized, racialized, and gendered subjects also makes it difficult to reconceive human beings' relation to nature in radically new terms."[35]

An ecofeminist public theology rooted in pneumatology, Christology, and embodied sacramentality resists such kyriarchal models of God and of the person: "The Spirit of God moves . . . to create and sustain the conditions that have enabled the biodiverse community of life to become so interesting and beautiful . . . for nature's emergent freedom to work."[36] Prioritizing Jesus' paternal God-talk not only erases numerous scriptural feminized metaphors for the divine, but also, and more importantly, replicates as well as reproduces kyriarchal theologies of God as monarchical sovereign king and lord of creation as well as their concomitant social, political, economic, and ecological implications for a technocratic worldview and its structures. As Catholic ecofeminist theologian Rosemary Radford Ruether argued, kyriarchal God-talk with its underlying hierarchical dualisms functions to theologically legitimate unjust religious, socio-political, economic, and ecological structures of dominance.[37] God-talk and its associated hierarchical gender, race, class, and other power dualisms provide the theological symbolic and cultural system that justifies, perpetuates, and reifies technocratic human-earthly

---

[34]Catherine Keller, "Encycling: One Feminist Theological Response," in *For Our Common Home: Process-Relational Responses to Laudato Si'*, ed. John B. Cobb Jr. and Ignacio Castuera (Anoka, MN: Process Century, 2015).

[35]Vuola, "Latin American Liberation Theologians' Turn to Eco(theo)logy," 108.

[36]Johnson, *Ask the Beasts*, 179.

[37]Rosemary Radford Ruther, *Sexism and God-Talk: Toward a Feminist Theology* (Boston: Beacon, 1983), 85.

Militarism, Pacifism, and the Plowshares Movement 207

relations. Tackling a technocratic anthropology, Ruether synthesized feminist, liberationist, and ecological theologies in order to illuminate and challenge how globalization is premised on a hierarchical dualistic worldview and socio-political order of race, class, and kyriarchal power and privilege that instrumentalizes (ab/uses and discards) rather than intrinsically values women, subjugated and other vulnerable peoples, and nature.[38] The encyclical's kyriarchal God-talk—even when a dominating father God is characterized as affectionate and compassionate (paras.73, 77, 96, 220, 226)—contradicts and therefore cannot prophetically inspire and galvanize the ekklesial work or world-making of an integral ecology.

More effective eco-public theology involves rhetorical, symbolic, and prophetic praxis to reimagine a more eco-just theological anthropology—that deconstructs kyriarchal dualisms or false separation and alienation from the divine, one another, and all life, and simultaneously reconstructs divine symbols that foster active mutual healing and reciprocal, interdependent relations as well as responsibilities to all creation. As analyzed above, ecofeminist theologies turn to incarnational or body theology, specifically the panentheistic metaphor of the world as the body of God; to Sophia, particularly to the personification of God as Woman Wisdom incarnate in Jesus the Christ who co-creates, unifies, and sustains the diversity and destiny of all life;[39] or to the Spirit whose creative and vivifying power inspires and renews all life, who confounds dualisms with mutuality, and who permeates or indwells in all life, the world, and the universe as a radical sign of its sacrality.[40] These ecofeminist theologies reappraise God-talk to announce a theocentric and biocentric, rather than egocentric and technocratic, theological anthropology that affirms *both* the inherent equality and sacramentality of all life to reveal the divine presence *and* the relational subjectivity of all life within the *imago Dei*. Biocratic rather than technocratic power needs such a theo-politically grounded theological anthropology, that, as Celia Deane-Drummond contends, shows "the glory of God [as] the cosmos fully alive."[41]

---

[38]Rosemary Radford Ruether, *Gaia and God: An Ecofeminist Theology of Earth Healing* (San Francisco: HarperCollins, 1992); Dalton and Simmons, *Ecotheology and the Practice of Hope*, 48–49, 63–66.

[39]Celia Deane-Drummond, "Sophia: The Feminine Face of God as a Metaphor for an Ecotheology," *Feminist Theology* 16 (1997): 11–31.

[40]Elizabeth Johnson, *Women, Earth, Creator Spirit* (New York: Paulist, 1993); Carpenter, "Rushing Winds, 330–334.

[41]Deane-Drummond, *Eco-Theology*, 185.

The Plowshares Movement

In the concluding chapter of *Laudato Si'*, Pope Francis acknowledges that "Christian spirituality proposes an alternative understanding of the quality of life, and encourages a prophetic and contemplative lifestyle" (222). Indeed, US Catholic men and women, both lay and religious, engage in creative ritual protest and prophetic eco-activism that confront our increasingly militarized world and its growing threats of total annihilation and ecocide, more deeply theologize an integral ecology, and interlink social justice with ecological solidarity via nonviolent civil disobedience. These movements aim "to re-create the political order" characterized by a demilitarized "regeneration of the human family" for love and justice.[42]

Philip Berrigan (1923–2002), a World War II veteran, a Josephite order priest dedicated to anti-racist and social justice work, and a leading US Catholic peace activist, participated in over one hundred nonviolent anti-war protests and direct actions of the Plowshares Movement, which he co-founded to creatively, dramatically, and religiously challenge the world-destroying realities of militarism and its weapons of mass destruction, racism, and poverty.[43] After witnessing racial injustice in US society and in the military, and after earning a bachelor's degree from College of the Holy Cross in Worcester, Massachusetts, Berrigan joined the Josephite seminary in New York, then finished his seminary education in Washington, DC, which culminated in his ordination into the order and his first assignments in parishes and schools in Washington, DC, and New Orleans, Louisiana. His incisive criticisms of militarism, racism, poverty, and religion emerged from his reflections as a veteran and from his educa-

---

[42]Philip Berrigan with Fred A. Wilcox, *Fighting the Lamb's War: Skirmishes with the American Empire: The Autobiography of Philip Berrigan* (Monroe, ME: Common Courage Press, 1996), 211.

[43]Major scholarly studies of the Plowshares Movement include Kristen Tobey, *Plowshares: Protest, Performance, and Religious Identity in the Nuclear Age* (University Park: Pennsylvania State University Press, 2016); Sharon Erickson Nepstad, *Religion and War Resistance in the Plowshares Movement* (New York: Cambridge University Press, 2008) and "Disciples and Dissenters: Tactical Choice and Consequences in the Plowshares Movement," in *Authority in Contention*, ed. Daniel J. Meyers and Daniel M. Cress (Amsterdam: Elsevier, 2004), 139–159; Jason C. Bivins, *The Fracture of Good Order: Christian Anti-Liberalism and the Challenge to American Politics* (Chapel Hill: University of North Carolina Press, 2003); Murray Polner and Jim O'Grady, *Disarmed and Dangerous: The Radical Lives and Times of Daniel and Philip Berrigan* (Boulder, CO: Westview Press, 1998); Patricia F. McNeal, *Harder Than War: Catholic Peacemaking in Twentieth-Century America* (New Brunswick, NJ: Rutgers University Press, 1992); Fred A. Wilcox, *Uncommon Martyrs: The Berrigans, the Catholic Left, and the Plowshares Movement* (Reading, MA: Addison-Wesley, 1991).

Militarism, Pacifism, and the Plowshares Movement 209

tion by Black Catholics about systemic racism. Berrigan demythologized and exposed war as "the big lie" by gazing "into the mirror of my own violence." For Berrigan, US militarism hinged on and subscribed to several myths to undertake war. Militarism represented and reinforced a "warrior mentality" and "society" that entangled patriarchal gender norms of toxic masculinity (a "rite of passage for turning boys into warriors") with "brutal poverty" and "racist violence."[44] Militarism also fused with religion to sanitize and rationalize war, amplify patriotism (a noble "crusade"), eclipse any ambiguity or silence dissent about military decisions, and ultimately dehumanize and demonize the enemy.[45]

Furthermore, Berrigan's education, ordination, and early parish, educational and activist work with Black Catholics in the 1950s and 1960s coincided with major US events that collectively influenced his religio-political anti-racist and pacifist views, namely the US House Un-American Activities Committee hearings, the Korean War, the Civil Rights Movement, the Cuban Missile Crisis, and the US entry into the Vietnam War.[46] At the same time, he criticized a troubling "cultural syncretism" or an anti-Catholic alliance of church and state, epitomized by his seminary education and fellow priests that conformed to, bolstered, and mediated "the power pyramid," or rationalized the US military-industrial complex and its other power structures of racial, economic, and political domination or "institutionalized terror and death," rather than question American politics that "poisons the environment, imprisons and executes the poor, and thrives on war," show their accountability to Gospel imperatives, and "apply the Gospel to everyday life."[47]

Berrigan articulated a critical radical call for a socially responsible and transformative church grounded in gospel-based imperatives for social justice, and turned that ecclesiological call for "costly witness," for "the church in chains" to oppose "dehumanization in . . . self, in others, in structures,"[48] into his own pilgrimage to nonviolent prophetic activism for the abolition of war, exemplified by the virtues of Christ, which involved "poverty, freedom in responsibility, the politics of community, willingness to risk jail and death for the exploited person."[49] His early

---

[44]Berrigan, *Fighting the Lamb's War*, 13, 15–16, 19, 22–24.

[45]Ibid., 17–18, 21–24.

[46]Ibid., 32–34, 48–52, 56, 58–65. Berrigan almost participated in the Freedom Rides as well as the March from Selma to Montgomery, but was prevented both times by religious leaders and by police. Berrigan witnessed the impacts of both white flight and anti-Black racism in Florida, Louisiana, and Mississippi during the Cuban Missile Crisis.

[47]Ibid., 33, 36–37, 141–142, 145.

[48]Ibid., 140, 144.

[49]Ibid., 143.

religio-politically motivated nonviolent acts of anti-war protest during the Vietnam War incorporated in my view rhetorical, symbolic, and prophetic practices. Berrigan's autobiography chronicles these early acts of what I identify as ekklesial work against a militarist and racist US society—he preached sermons against racism and war, opened a faith-based community center to mobilize grassroots resistance movements, and was arrested while delivering an anti-war letter.[50] Berrigan's nascent revolutionary Christology[51] grounded and sharpened his commitments to later acts of nonviolent civil disobedience, which interrupted the prevailing political order to offer a symbolic act of prophetic hope in what Berrigan termed "the kin-dom of God," or the theo-political possibilities for a more loving, just, life-giving, and anti-imperial liberative future to flourish.[52] As Berrigan elaborated, "Jesus Christ was a nonviolent revolutionary; therefore, Christians have a duty to subvert society in order to create a world where justice prevails."[53]

The Plowshares Movement centers on practices of prophetic protest, which express both an abolitionist position and a disarmed, pacifist world. Plowshares grew from two previous nonviolent direct actions of civil disobedience against the Vietnam War, in which Berrigan participated, namely the Baltimore 4 in 1967 and the Catonsville 9 in 1968, which involved nonviolent direct actions at a Maryland customs house and draft board office where Berrigan and fellow activists poured their own blood on or burned with homemade napalm selective service records and other files in order to demonstrate nonviolent civil disobedience to war and at the same time to educate symbolically that war signifies death.[54] Although these two actions garnered national attention and ignited more than fifty such dramatic actions of anti-war protest, these protests and their carefully crafted messages were dismissed.[55]

Berrigan continued to envision and enact a "desire to communicate"[56] and embody hope in another possible abolitionist and pacificist world through critical and constructive nonviolent direct actions, rather than through traditional but ineffective practices of public engagement to boycott, conscientiously object to, and in other ways oppose war and

---

[50]Ibid., 80–82, 85, 86.

[51]Ibid., 98, 109, 143.

[52]Ibid., 96.

[53]Ibid., 109.

[54]Ibid., 87–91, 93–96; Polner and O'Grady, *Disarmed and Dangerous*, 195–198; McNeal, *Harder Than War*, 173; and, Lynne Sachs, *Investigation of s Flame* (New York: First Run / Icarus Films, 2001).

[55]Berrigan, *Fighting the Lamb's War*, 89; cf. 108.

[56]Ibid., 107; cf. 87, 94.

Militarism, Pacifism, and the Plowshares Movement　　　　*211*

military industries that prepare for war, especially nuclear war (e.g., petitions, letter-writing campaigns, vigils, seminars, marches, rallies, demonstrations). The Plowshares Movement inaugurated its nonviolent direct actions of nuclear inspection and symbolic disarmament tactics on September 9, 1980, when the Plowshares Eight entered General Electric in King of Prussia, Pennsylvania, poured blood on nuclear blueprints "to proclaim the sin of mass destruction" intended by these weapons, and hammered on nuclear missile nose cones to dramatically dismantle and disarm such state symbols of violence, death, and war.[57] More than one hundred Plowshares nonviolent protest and symbolic disarmament actions have taken place at US and global nuclear and other weapons manufacturing and military sites, leading to trials, fines, and jail sentences for activists, often stereotyped as ecoterrorists.[58]

The Plowshares Movement centralizes the intersectional struggle for peace as a major feature of Christian discipleship. US Catholic nuns and laywomen within the Plowshares Movement have charted alternate peaceful paths to the death-dealing convergence of US militarism and nuclearism, the exploitation of land and labor, and religious, sociocultural, and economic oppression, including the feminization of poverty and ecocide.[59] Women in the Plowshares Movement incisively combined anti-militarist, anti-kyriarchal, and anti-ecocide analyses, and thus are largely credited with expanding the Plowshares agenda and actions beyond anti-nuclear war protests. For example, in July 1969, women antiwar activists called the New York 5 staged and led a draft board raid in midtown Manhattan to explicitly link militarism and patriarchy/kyriarchy. The New York 5 challenged women's roles in patriarchal/kyriarchal militarist societies and in anti-militarist movements. According to their statement, Plowshares leaders called out a patriarchal pacifism and an anti-feminist Catholicism, which ostracized women in the movement and from its goals.[60] Their

---

[57]Ibid., 183–185, 191.

[58]Arthur J. Laffin, "A History of the Plowshares Movement," St. Athanasius Episcopal Church in Brunswick, Georgia, October 22, 2019; Paul Magno, "The Plowshares Anti-Nuclear Movement at 35: A Next Generation?" *Bulletin of the Atomic Scientists* 72, no. 2 (2016): 85–88; Ardeth Platte and Susan Crane, "Plowshares Movement History 1980–2009," YouTube video, August 1, 2012; Arthur J. Laffin, *Swords into Plowshares: A Chronology of Plowshares Actions, 1980–2003* (Marion, SD: Rose Hill Books, 2003); Arthur J. Laffin and Anne Montgomery, *Swords into Plowshares: Nonviolent Direct Action for Disarmament* (San Francisco: Harper & Row, 1987).

[59]Sister Jane Ingalls on the hit series *Orange Is the New Black* renewed attention to Plowshares activist nuns. Jamie Manson, "The Nun and the Actress behind 'Orange is the New Black,'" *National Catholic Reporter* June 10, 2015.

[60]Marian Mollin, "Communities of Resistance: Women and the Catholic Left of the Late 1960s," *Oral History Review* 31, no. 2 (2004): 29–51, and *Radical Pacifism in Modern America: Egalitarianism and Protest* (Philadelphia: University of Pennsylvania Press, 2006).

212   *Nevertheless, We Persist*

pioneering protest slowly shifted the gears in the movement. On Thanksgiving Day 1983 in Rome, New York, Elizabeth McAlister and six other activists entered a hangar on the Griffiss Air Force Base. As the Griffiss Plowshares, they poured blood on the hangar floor and on B52 bombers outfitted with cruise missiles, taped photos of children to the planes, and hammered on the missile doors.[61]

More than thirty years later on October 6, 2002, three Dominican nuns, Carol Gilbert, Jackie Hudson, and Ardeth Platte, broke into a Minuteman III missile silo in Colorado, where recently reactivated first-strike nuclear missiles lay beneath thousands of miles of farmland. Dressed in white hazmat suits labeled "Disarmament Specialist" and "Citizen Weapons Inspections Team," the nuns exercised their Dominican charism as a religious order of preachers and engaged in trifold practices of ekklesial work, of creating community amid threats of nuclear war. According to Gilbert, they intended to expose and symbolically disarm this weapon of mass destruction through prophetic nonviolent direct action. They cut through two sets of gates, poured their blood in the shape of crosses on and around the silo entrance, and hammered on the silo's 110-ton concrete lid. Then they performed a liturgy of prayers for peace and awaited arrest. They called their symbolic disarmament action Sacred Earth and Space Plowshares II to show, according to Gilbert, that nuclear weapons kill not only people "but also Mother Earth herself," that is, all living things. Moreover, as Platte observed, "We are all part of a loving nonviolent circle, the family of God. . . . We are one, one body, one blood, and . . . we must learn how to live on Planet Earth together."[62] As this action indicates, Plowshares activists break into nuclear and other military facilities, hammer on and pour their own blood on nuclear and other conventional weapons or their components, delivery, or storage systems, and risk serving jail sentences along with paying steep fines (for example, between 2.5 and 3.5 years for the nuns along with over $3,000 fines for injury to and obstruction of national defense) to expose the all-too-often invisible and normalized immorality and illegality of nuclear war and to witness to an alternative political reality—to the always in-breaking but not yet fully instantiated alternative world without war.[63]

Contemporary Plowshares activists and actions in the US further

---

[61]Berrigan, *Fighting the Lamb's War*, 192–193.

[62]Brenda Truelson Fox, *Conviction* (Boulder, CO: Zero to Sixty Productions, 2006).

[63]In May 2015, an appellate court overturned the conviction of Sister Megan Rice and two other activists similarly charged with sabotage for performing the Transform Now Plowshares action in 2012 at the Y-12 National Security Complex in Oak Ridge, Tennessee. William J. Broad, "Sister Megan Rice, Freed from Prison, Looks Ahead to More Anti-Nuclear Activism," *New York Times*, May 26, 2015. On the "politics of moral witness," see Nepstad, "Disciples and Dissenters," 144, 157.

Militarism, Pacifism, and the Plowshares Movement

expand and complexify an intersectional witness against the injustices of militarism, racism, and poverty in relationship to ecocide. On April 4, 2018, the 50th anniversary of the assassination of civil rights activist Rev. Dr. Martin Luther King Jr., Kings Bay Plowshares 7 including Elizabeth McAlister (Phil Berrigan's spouse and cofounder of Jonah House), Martha Hennessy (Dorothy Day's granddaughter), and Clare Grady (who participated with Liz in the Griffiss Plowshares in 1983) challenged the triple evils of racism and white supremacy, militarism, and poverty fueled by a war economy when they nonviolently and symbolically disarmed weapons of mass destruction that threaten not only genocide and ecocide but omnicide. At the Kings Bay, Georgia, naval base that houses Trident submarines equipped with first-strike nuclear weapons, these activists read a statement and then performed a symbolic disarmament action.

> We repent of the sin of white supremacy that oppresses and takes the lives of people of color here in the United States and throughout the world. We resist militarism that has employed deadly violence to enforce global domination. We believe reparations are required for stolen land, labor, and lives. . . . The weapons from one Trident have the capacity to end life as we know it on planet Earth. Nuclear weapons kill every day through our mining, production, testing, storage, and dumping, primarily on Indigenous Native land. . . . As white Catholics, we take responsibility to atone for the horrific crimes stemming from our complicity with "the triplets." Only then can we begin to restore right relationships.

After reading this statement about their intersectional ethics of anti-racist, anti-war, and anti-poverty solidarity, they poured blood at the facility's entrance signs and logos, pasted posters about genocide and omnicide as well as spray-painted messages about the abolition of nuclear weapons and hammered on the missile monument at the entrance, and created a crime scene at one facility building by pouring blood and pasting both poster and spray-painted messages "repent," "love one another," and "the ultimate logic of Trident is omnicide," which echoed and expanded on King's claim that racism means genocide. These activists were convicted in October 2019 on charges of conspiracy, trespass, and destruction and depredation of property. Although these charges correspond with approximately twenty years in jail, all activists completed their sentences, including home confinement, by late 2021.

Plowshares actions, in my view, constitute a form of community building, of world-making, of ekklesial work. They seek to upend a kyriarchal militarist socio-economic and political order and at the same time to create an alternative community to it through symbolic protest actions and through new communities. Jonah House, a nonviolent faith-based resistance and pacifist community founded in 1973 and located in Baltimore, Maryland, signifies small-scale glimpses of an alternative community, of the kin-dom of God.[64] Plowshares community building takes place through voluntary poverty, common meals, scripture study, and activism at Jonah House, because it provides material, affective, and spiritual support for activists whether in or out of jail via its original and organizing values of community, spirituality, stewardship, and activism (direct action and incarceration).[65] It embodies world-making because it also carves out and cultivates a hope-filled space for such alternative community to exist, resist, and persist: "We work at hope, together, as a community. Without community, resistance is impossible. We gather from our community hope, strength, commitment, and the courage to continue."[66] On its website, Jonah House broadens these community-building values to sponsor a food pantry; caretake and harvest the gardens and fruit trees on the grounds of St. Peter's cemetery; and stand in solidarity with Black Lives Matter, resist police brutality, and advocate the defunding and the demilitarization of police departments.

Community building or the ekklesial work of public theology also emerges in the Plowshares movement's distinct but interrelated practices, namely in Plowshares rhetorical, symbolic, and prophetic practices to publicly perform, educate about (through court testimony), and religio-politically justify a theology and praxis of nonviolent protest. Nonviolent direct actions of symbolic disarmament and prayer collectively encompass public voice, theological symbols, and prophetic work. As Catholic Worker and Plowshares activist as well as historian Art Laffin argues, "In my view, the basic hope of the Plowshares actions . . . is to communicate from the moment of entry into a plant or base—and throughout the court process and prison witness—an underlying faith that the power of nonviolent love can overcome the forces of violence; a reverence for all life and creation; an acceptance of personal responsibility for the dismantling and the physical conversion of the weapons; and a spiritual conversion of the heart to the way of justice and reconciliation."[67] Moreover, these actions

---

[64]Berrigan, *Fighting the Lamb's War*, 166–168, 170–171, 175. Many communities disbanded in New York, New Jersey, and Washington, DC, due to failure to enact and effect their visions.

[65]Ibid., 166–167, 219. Cf. Sharon Erickson Nepstad, "Persistent Resistance: Commitment and Community in the Plowshares Movement," *Social Problems* 51, no. 1 (2004): 43–60, esp. 50–59; and Bivins, *Fracture of Good Order*, 128–139, 145–151.

[66]Berrigan, *Fighting the Lamb's War*, 219.

[67]Laffin, "A History of the Plowshares Movement."

Militarism, Pacifism, and the Plowshares Movement 215

are grounded in rich theological views about God, love of neighbor and of enemy, and nonviolence. As Berrigan claimed, "We Christians forget (if we ever learned) that attempts to redress real or imagined injustice by violent means are merely another exercise in denial—denial of God and her nonviolence towards us, denial of love of neighbor, denial of laws essential to our being . . . our humanity, our daughtership or sonship in God."[68] In my view, rhetorical practices synergize and synchronize with symbolic and prophetic practices—Plowshares activists' statements prior to, during, and after trials explain and defend their actions, express their theological imaginary, as well as offer extended opportunities beyond symbolic disarmament actions for ongoing religio-political performative prophetic witness *against* the nuclear national security state and *for* life.[69]

During their trials, which charged the activists with trespassing on and damaging federal property with intent to injure and obstruct the national defense, Plowshares activists utilized and expanded a broad repertoire of rhetorical practices, such as courtroom testimony. Testimony provided a rhetorical means to justify Plowshares actions on legal and theological grounds as well as to gain a public voice for dissenting activists and marginalized peoples. Testimony educated about war, about faith-based anti-war resistance, and a pacifist world also embodied in their prophetic protest actions. Their testimony interrupted a prevailing irrational public discourse about war and reasserted as well as reclaimed religio-political resistance actions as a legitimate form of political participation.[70] Plowshares activists articulated and invoked an ever-broadening range of defenses for their disarmament actions, relying on historical, legal, and religious defenses. On historical grounds, the Catonsville 9, for example, situated nonviolent direct action within a long-standing US democratic tradition of gaining public voice through prophetic protest politics.[71] On legal grounds, in later trials they referred to international anti-nuclear proliferation treaties to object to nations who prepare for mass destruction as well as argued a necessity defense, which outlines the responsibilities of any citizen to protect life and preserve peace, to take action that neutralizes, avoids, or prevents any greater imminent harm.[72] On religious grounds, Plowshares activists recounted their own identity-based religio-political resistance to war.[73] Elizabeth McAlister

---

[68]Berrigan, *Fighting the Lamb's War*, 204.
[69]Tobey, *Plowshares*, chaps. 4–5.
[70]Bivins, *Fracture of Good Order*, 139–145.
[71]Berrigan, *Fighting the Lamb's War*, 106; cf. 85.
[72]Ibid., 187–188.
[73]Polner and O'Grady, *Disarmed and Dangerous*, 87–141; Philip Berrigan, *Prison Journals*

216　　　　　　　　　　　　　　　　　　　　*Nevertheless, We Persist*

at the Griffiss Plowshares trial proclaimed nuclearism (nuclear weapons and their associated national security, military, economic, legal, and other structures) an established civil religion, which not only verged on idolatry but also infringed on constitutional disestablishment of religion as well as obstructed religious free exercise.

> The religion of national sovereignty or nuclearism is alive and flourishing, and its existence, its pre-eminence, its rituals, gods, priests, and high priests make serious encroachments on all of us. . . . This state religion not only compels acts that are prohibited by the laws of God but the state religion itself prohibits the free exercise of religion. . . . Weapons we are expected to pay for, adulate, thank God for, become sacred objects of worship. And such worship is prohibited by the laws of God.[74]

Similarly, Berrigan portrayed nuclearism as "the National Security State's idols" and Plowshares actions as countercultural stances against its "atomic temples."[75]

Drawing on a wide range of these and other rhetorical practices in their defenses, Plowshares activists repeatedly resisted the law of the state, which authorizes and legitimates violence (especially nuclear war and its threat of total planetary annihilation), with the law of God and Christ, which promotes nonviolent resistance, love, and justice.[76] Courtroom testimony afforded Berrigan and Plowshares activists a rhetorical practice to give voice to global suffering as well as to critically engage in and reshape US public discourse about war. After the 9/11 terror attacks, the nuns involved in Sacred Earth and Space Plowshares II intended to curtail and check the US government's threats to use first-strike nuclear weapons against Iraq or other so-called Axis of Evil nations. Similar to prior trials, the judge disregarded or placed extensive gag rules on such defenses in the nuns' trial, effectively eliminating thirty categories of testimony derived from appeals to God, religion, morality/ethics, political policy, and wisdom regarding the MinuteMan III missile system, international treaties and laws pertaining to nuclear non-proliferation since 1968, war crimes, UN charters, the Geneva Convention, and so on. Despite the judge's limits on

---

of a Priest Revolutionary (New York: Holt, Rinehart and Winston, 1970), 21–26; Daniel Berrigan, SJ, *The Trial of the Catonsville 9* (Boston: Beacon Press, 1970).

[74]Berrigan, *Fighting the Lamb's War*, 193–194; Philip Berrigan and Elizabeth McAlister, *The Time's Discipline: The Beatitudes and Nuclear Resistance* (Baltimore: Fortkamp, 1989), 133.

[75]Berrigan, *Fighting the Lamb's War*, 185.

[76]Ibid., 202, 209–210, 212, 214.

Militarism, Pacifism, and the Plowshares Movement 217

the nuns' defenses, Platte affirmed that they were led by the Spirit of God to this work to make a better world for future generations, which Hudson considered a call to be the people of God, to do service for the world, a service that Gilbert interpreted as fidelity to the gospel of nonviolence and to intergenerational solidarity. Even this limited testimony enabled Plowshares activists to communicate and educate about the atrocities of war and their faith-based reasons for their anti-war actions—thereby creating and enacting, even if briefly, a counter-rhetoric and counter-public to militarism, poverty, and ecocide.

With regard to symbolic practices, religious symbols figure centrally in and explicitly enhance the theological grounds for Plowshares practices of public engagement. Plowshares activists invoke symbolic practices as a theological basis for their nonviolent direct actions and active interference with the US military- and prison-industrial complex. Activists also draw upon theological symbols to show the immorality of war and clarify an alternative theological vision of disarmed pacifist unity. Berrigan reinterpreted and applied key gospel imperatives of love and justice to guide Plowshares nonviolent resistance: not to kill and to love God, self, and neighbor, especially enemies. For example, Jesus' parable of the Good Samaritan and the Sermon on the Mount together with Jesus' crucifixion exemplify countercultural Christian ethics rooted in love of enemy and expressed in nonviolent resistance to a militarist state.[77] Moreover, a Plowshares theology of political activism rethinks and extends major Christian symbols, especially hammers and blood. Their nonviolent direct actions take their theological directive to disarm and destroy weapons of war-making and mass destruction from Isaiah 2:4: "to beat their swords into plowshares, and their spears into pruning hooks; nation shall not lift up sword against nation, neither shall they learn war anymore."[78] Blood signifies the death-dealing purposes of the weapons as well as sharply contrasts militarist societies and the new society, the new family of God initiated in the life-ministry, death, and resurrection of Jesus and remembered as well as reconstituted through the Eucharist. Pushing this symbol of blood beyond solely anti-war protest, Sacred Earth and Space Plowshares underscored that militarism means the end of all earthly life. Beyond resistance to nuclear war and its impending peril of eco-disaster, the nuns also used blood to resignify the missile silo and the surrounding farmland as a site for sustaining rather than annihilating

---

[77]Ibid., 169, 177–180.

[78]Daniel Berrigan, SJ, *Testimony: The Word Made Fresh* (Maryknoll, NY: Orbis Books, 2004), 3–22.

218 *Nevertheless, We Persist*

earthly flourishing. As Hudson claimed, "Our interconnectedness with all of creation means that our every thought, word, and action determines the direction of the universe." Sacred Earth and Space Plowshares thus enabled an imitation of Christ and emulated the purpose of Jesus' life and ministry—to establish a more interdependent, interconnected sense of community with all of life.

With regard to prophetic practices, the Plowshares Movement engages in nonviolent direct actions of civil disobedience and protest which reflect a twofold dynamic: to denounce and indict an oppressive war-making state and its death-dealing supportive structures, on the one hand, and announce and prefigure an alternative possibility to it, on the other hand, the kindom of God.[79] Nonviolent direct action performs "divine disobedience" to a militarist state and enacts as well as embraces divine obedience to a gospel of life, epitomized in the life, ministry, death, and resurrection of Jesus that preaches "a vision of life by which to interpret and to confront the works of death."[80] Nonviolent direct action then places an explicitly prophetic spin on protest as a religious means to challenge the world-destructive works of racial and economic injustice, militarism, and their supporting structures, as well as to create an alternative life-giving culture of love, equality, freedom, and just community. Nonviolent direct action provides a major "means for making this vision real" and for "recreat[ing] the political order."[81] In other words, Plowshares protest actions together with the activists' subsequent prison terms embody prophetic practices, because they evoke and engender an alternative possibility for common life, that is, a more just counterpublic to a militarist state and society.

In my view, jail is considered among the repertoire of Plowshares prophetic practices to resist, subvert, disarm, and build a pacifist counterpublic to a racist war-making state and society, to link their political resistance with a public theology of community that prevails over jail, that sustains activists, and that emerges from the gospel witness of resistance to empire through jail itself.[82] While prison is designed to undermine community through alienation and isolation, Plowshares activists leverage jail to express and embody what I call world-making or ekklesial work; they tried to create and forge community through jail.[83] Jail aptly demonstrates how Plowshares activists confront and resist the law of the state with

---

[79]Sharon Erickson Nepstad, "Disruptive Action and the Prophetic Tradition: War Resistance in the Plowshares Movement," *US Catholic Historian* 27, no. 2 (2009): 97–113.

[80]Berrigan, *Fighting the Lamb's War*, 175, 180, 188.

[81]Ibid., 211.

[82]Ibid., 220, 224.

[83]Ibid., 164–167, and Nepstad, "Persistent Resistance," 49.

Militarism, Pacifism, and the Plowshares Movement 219

the law of Christ, because jail offers a counterspace or counterpublic to empire, in which to advocate for and begin to build an alternative just and pacifist society within an unjust and war-making society. Thus, Plowshares activists accept jail as a consequence of their countercultural witness to gospel-based nonviolent beliefs and direct actions of nonviolent resistance. They "risk jail without of course seeking it," and at the same time appeal to jail as a signature praxis of discipleship and solidarity with Christ by advocating for the dignity and rights of incarcerated persons.[84] Also, Berrigan interprets jail as prophetic witness to another possible world, based on biblical and Christian themes of the desert and the wilderness as salient sites of marginality and change. He compares jail to contemporary wilderness: "Mark declares at the beginning of his gospel that social change comes from 'the wilderness.' John the Baptizer emerges from that unlikely setting, as did Jesus. . . . 'Wilderness' also includes the jails and prisons across the land; there resisters appeal to the hearts and minds of others, whether in or out, and testify against the criminality of public authority."[85] Both Jonah House and jail combine rhetorical and prophetic practices to build a transformative and just community through small-scale efforts with inter/national impact.

Symbolic and prophetic practices fuse in Plowshares public engagement for ekklesial work, for creating community. Reinterpreted Christian symbols inform and influence Plowshares prophetic practices, in that the movement relied on religious symbols to criticize the predominant socio-political order as well as to propel collective action that imagined and attempted to actualize a new vision of a more just and peaceful this-worldly order. Nonviolent direct action is linked in the Plowshares movement to Christian discipleship. Plowshares protest actions imitate in a performative, praxis-based way a nonviolent revolutionary Christ, a Christ whose subversive public acts (such as ministering among the ostracized and oppressed, overturning the money changers' tables, dying a criminal's death on the cross) confronted and confounded all forms of social, religious, cultural, and imperial domination.[86] For example, the Good Friday Plowshares of Holy Week 1995 in Washington, DC, politically reenacted or dramatized Christ's last days that spanned Holy Thursday, Good Friday, and Holy Saturday, "to reject denial, to put up the sword, to identify with Christ the victim, to embrace the Cross, and

---

[84]Berrigan, *Fighting the Lamb's War*, 90, 96–97, 223–226; Rosalie G. Riegle, ed., *Doing Time for Peace: Resistance, Family, and Community* (Nashville, TN: Vanderbilt University Press, 2012).

[85]Berrigan, *Fighting the Lamb's War*, 225.

[86]Ibid., 98, 109, 169.

220

to stand at its foot with the women."[87] Plowshares activists poured blood at the World Bank logo and in the lobby encircled a picture of a starving child which they anointed with blood to draw attention to world hunger on the day Catholics commemorate the Eucharist. They drew attention to the fatal consequences of the World Bank's investment policies, which they directly opposed to a theology of the Eucharist, the bread of life. At the Pentagon, they enacted the way of the cross or Jesus' walk to Calvary and nonviolent resistance to empire by pouring blood on the logo, entrance, and walkways. Finally, they performed street theatre and staged die-ins dramatizing the entombment of Christ at a cordoned-off zone of the White House sidewalk to symbolically oppose then-imposed sanctions on Iraq, all of which resignified how Christ defied Roman imperialism, colonialism, and militarism with nonviolence.[88]

To envision and enflesh a counter-public space to a racist and militarist society that is bent on de-creative work or destroying life, Plowshares activists draw on theological symbols from Christian anthropology and eschatology to articulate in theological terms an alternative life-giving, affirming, and sustaining pacifist or disarmed vision of the human person and the good society that rests on love, justice, equality, and peace, or the "kin-dom" of God.[89] The Plowshares symbol of kin-dom needs to be situated within a Latinx *mujerista* theological perspective to better grasp its anti-imperial meanings and its guiding vision. As previously discussed, the kin-dom of God in *mujerista* theology, much like the theological image of the body of Christ (1 Cor. 12) invoked by the Dominican nuns, underscores the interrelated interdependence of all life in the reality of a nonviolent, loving, compassionate God that lures us toward a community without racism, sexism, militarism, or any form of oppression, domination, and violence. This symbol of the future embraces persons in the image of a relational God and as a result envisions particularly but not only Latinas in multiple intersecting communal contexts and relations in which they actively struggle for and eschatologically hope in the ever unfolding this-worldly vision of the kin-dom of God, of its theological vision of right, just, and flourishing relations. Within Plowshares theology, the God of life and nonviolence does not will an apocalyptic destruction of the planet (to usher in a new kingdom) but aims and desires through the kin-dom of God "to humanize us to become children of God; we are

---

[87] Ibid., 204.
[88] Ibid., 205.
[89] Ibid., 96, 209–211.

Militarism, Pacifism, and the Plowshares Movement 221

daughters and sons, sisters and brothers of one another."[90] Nonviolent direct action thus embodies and engages in realizing the kin-dom, in such ekklesial work; these actions testify to and enflesh an alternative disarmed way to re-imagine human relations in community. Berrigan continues:

> A Plowshares action insists on the primacy and sacredness of life. A Plowshares action states that we are all sisters and brothers, one race, one people, one family. . . . That's what God made us, what we are attempting to realize through our lives. A disarmament action states the truth, makes it incarnate, makes it real.[91]

In this way, Plowshares actions thematize, theologize, and dramatize an emancipatory anthropology, Christology, and eschatology. As Art Laffin explains, "This abiding faith in the God of Life leads us to commit our lives to making God's reign of love, justice and peace a reality by doing the works of mercy, accompanying the poor and the victims, embracing the way of nonviolence and community, actively resisting the forces of death and trying, trying to build a new world within the shell of the old."[92] Plowshares actions get and give a this-worldly glimpse of humanity and of this good society in their witness, so that the kin-dom of God and its interdependent just community might become an intra-historical reality—especially for women and the earth.

Green Nuns

"World-making politics and emancipatory religion" fuse in US eco-justice movements to imagine and articulate theological and practical responses to climate change and its associated eco-catastrophes but also to utilize nonviolent direct actions akin to Plowshares to educate about, repair, and envision a planetary worldview and ethics that supports and sustains the integral dignity and sacrality of all life, including the earth.[93] An eco-public theology emerges from these diverse movements which combine an at times inter/faith-based approach to nonviolence, social justice, grassroots democracy, and various forms of eco-justice activism—which collectively aim to revision and rebuild a healed ecosystem

---

[90]Ibid., 210–211.
[91]Ibid., 188.
[92]Laffin, "A History of the Plowshares Movement."
[93]Roger S. Gottlieb, *Joining Hands: Politics and Religion Together for Social Change* (Boulder, CO: Westview Press, 2002), 153, 155, 157, 162–168.

and ecological way of life grounded in "a new kind of social solidarity" alongside "a comprehensive vision of human identity and of how that identity is interrelated with the universe as a whole."[94]

Green nuns—who have ecologically reinterpreted their vows, spiritual practices, and communities to reflect their witness to the web of life—play a spiritual as well as effective eco-public role in these movements. These nuns reinhabit and express "lived practices of hope" because they join the personal, the political, and the planetary to "continue to reshape an ecologically conscious social imaginary."[95] These nuns profess and practice an experiential and ecological knowledge of the sacramental reality of God which infuses and suffuses all life. Building on the richly detailed ethnographic study of Roman Catholic women religious in the US and Canada by Sarah McFarland Taylor, green nuns interweave, in my view, rhetorical, symbolic, and prophetic practices in their varied rural and urban earth ministries (which consist of learning centers, wildlife sanctuaries, organic gardens, sustainable farms, housing, alternative renewable energy, etc.) to express, theologically support, and perform this ecological imaginary via various practices, or what Taylor portrays as the sacred agriculture of "contemplation and cultivation."[96]

In terms of rhetorical practices, green nuns rearticulate more ecologically oriented vows and reinvent their associated commitments to poverty, chastity, and obedience in green ways and in ecologically specific spaces, places, and contexts of their order's mission and vision. As Taylor observes, these nuns "reinhabit the vows of religious life in ecologically conscious ways," including living sustainably and engaging in eco-repair and eco-justice practices.[97] Through their vows, they simultaneously renounce and embrace the world, critically engaging with and seeking to remake a more eco-just world. Poverty embodies an anti-capitalist, anti-consumer culture way to live simply, interdependently, and sustainably in solidarity with the poor and marginalized as well as within the earth's limits in their particular ecological contexts. Chastity enables interrelationality with the sacrality of all life and is portrayed as a gift to the earth, curtailing in small-scale ways humanity's overpopulation within the planet's carrying capacity. Obedience energizes active listening to the needs of all life and

---

[94]Ibid., 168, 169, 173.

[95]Sarah McFarland Taylor, *Green Sisters: A Spiritual Ecology* (Cambridge, MA: Harvard University Press, 2007), 73; Dalton and Simmons, *Ecotheology and the Practice of Hope*, 105.

[96]Sarah McFarland Taylor, "The Tractor Is My Pulpit," in *Religions and Environments: A Reader in Religion, Nature, and Ecology*, ed. Richard Bohannon (London: Bloomsbury, 2014), 183.

[97]Taylor, *Green Sisters*, 61, 62.

Militarism, Pacifism, and the Plowshares Movement   223

responding with their gifts and talents to realize the reign of God.[98] For example, Sr. Gail Worcelo at Green Mountain Monastery in Greensboro, Vermont, claims "the tractor is my pulpit."[99] In other words, the nuns' reinterpreted vows signify and symbolize an ecological imaginary, and their earth ministries are analogized to their mission and vision, or their charism, and to their sacramental, liturgical, and ritual acts "to engage prayerfully with the land; to serve others through its gifts; to create gentler ways to work with the land to meet human needs; and to be deepened, delighted, and spiritually renewed in the process."[100] Green nuns infuse, communicate, and educate about this revitalized mission and vision in their own and surrounding communities, describing the role of farming as a sacramental and a communally sustaining act. Sr. Miriam MacGillis of Genesis Farm in New Jersey explains how their community rearticulates the vocation of farmers: "We need to see farmers as entering the sanctuary of the soil and engaging the mysterious forces of creation in order to bless and nourish the inner and outer life of the community they serve."[101]

In terms of theological symbols, farming, gardening, and other earth and eco-justice ministries reveal how green nuns view the inextricable interconnection of all life—sunshine, soil, bugs, air, water, plants, trees, animals, people, planet, and cosmos. The nuns and those visiting or collaborating with their communities are urged "to seek a deeper connection with creation and with the Creator of all. Spiritual renewal here [at Michaela Farm in Oldenburg, Indiana] is as important as organic food production, ecological education, and community building."[102] Also, as Taylor explains, these agricultural ministries develop a theology of creation, and revisit the revelatory nature of the landscape and ecosystems in which their communities live, move, and have their being when designing and planting their farms and gardens.[103] For example, Sr. MacGillis elaborates how their farms recognize and nurture the vitality of the soil, take a broad perspective on the multiple impacts on planting, growing, and harvesting, read the book of nature, and attend to the cosmic rhythms for both revelatory knowledge of God and ecological insights producing quality and vitally nutritious food, so that all may enjoy abundant life, including the earth.[104]

---

[98]Ibid., 64, 67, 70, 72–73.
[99]Taylor, "The Tractor Is My Pulpit," 185.
[100]Ibid., 185.
[101]Ibid., 185.
[102]Ibid., 184.
[103]Ibid., 184.
[104]Taylor, *Green Sisters*, 198–200.

224   *Nevertheless, We Persist*

According to Taylor, "the power of the prophetic imagination for effective positive planetary transformation pervades the work of green sisters."[105] In terms of prophetic practices, these green nuns' agricultural and other ministries link ecological concerns and social justice issues; they cultivate land and build community.[106] Their community-organized small sustainable farming and gardening practices as well as habitat conservation, whether in urban, suburban, or rural settings, interrelate with their vowed solidarity with the poor, hungry, and homeless, with other small farming communities, and with all earthly life.[107] They grow and provide fresh local organic produce not only to reduce the footprint of their own self-sufficient communities but also to share their harvests in distributive justice with the surrounding communities and food banks to combat both food insecurity and food apartheid. These ministries serve as significant sites to mobilize rural and sub/urban community organizing about social and eco-justice issues.[108]

In sum, this chapter aimed to explicate the strengths and shortcomings of magisterial and US Catholic eco-public theologies based on the community-creating practices of ekklesial work informed by women's liberation theologies. On my reading, the Vatican's venture into global eco-public theology through the encyclical *Laudato Si'* succeeds in terms of rhetorical practices. The encyclical converses with multiple different voices from the Global South especially to chronicle our current environmental crises as well as to offer concrete religio-political strategies to alleviate them. However, the letter does not critically reimagine or reconstruct Christian symbols to support social and gender justice. Pope Francis's God-talk as an absolute dominating father retains and reinscribes a kyriarchal theology of power, which consequently creates a theological lacuna that leads him to tackle social and gender justice insufficiently as well as undermines the promising eco-pneumatology that enlivens the encyclical's integral ecology. Pope Francis's ecological theology of the Spirit completely disregards and therefore invisibilizes innovative salient and salutary feminist theological work in this field, foregrounded in the works of ecofeminist theologians Rosemary Radford Ruether, Sallie McFague, Ivone Gebara, and Elizabeth Johnson to better actualize the symbolic practices of a global Catholic eco-public theology and illuminate and challenge the ways in which kyriarchy functions as the taproot of our world's ecological crises. In terms

---

[105]Ibid., 19.
[106]Ibid., 20.
[107]Ibid., 196.
[108]Taylor, "The Tractor Is My Pulpit," 183, 185.

Militarism, Pacifism, and the Plowshares Movement 225

of prophetic practices, the Plowshares movement articulates, envisions, and enacts a US-based, eco-public theology that strives to sever the links between religion, militarism, and kyriarchal power, on the one hand, and in doing so highlights women's groundbreaking Christian theological praxis in Catholic pacifist traditions, on the other hand. Plowshares activists, nuns, and women in the movement employ prophetic nonviolent direct action, courtroom testimony, and jail time to ensure that multiple different voices are heard, including the voices of children, future generations, different earthly creatures, and the earth itself, in ongoing religio-political debates about warfare. These activists struggle for an equal voice in the US military-industrial complex, which also controls and limits their courtroom testimony, thereby supporting American exceptionalism to humanitarian as well as environmental inter/national laws, treaties, and accords, including the US withdrawal from the Paris Climate Agreement of 2015 and the EPA's diminished ability to enforce environmental regulations and safeguards.[109] Moreover, their struggles against American imperialism and militarism reached new heights under US President Donald Trump, bolstered by a critical and creative reinterpretation and reconstruction of Christian theological claims, symbols, and practices that only catch a glimpse of the ever-present, ever-coming kin-dom of God.

My analysis of Plowshares actions and Green Nuns has held these practices of ekklesial work, of public engagement for recreating community, in creative and dynamic tension—without reifying or drawing sharp distinctions among them—to demonstrate multiple ways in which religious resources propel participation in and transformation of US public life, to perform what I am calling ekklesial work. They carve out a counterpublic space with these distinctive yet interrelated practices, so that alternative religious, political, and ecological visions and realities might be imagined and ever transformed in a critical and constructive way to build community for the kin-dom of God. Philip Berrigan and Plowshares activists testified among other rhetorical practices and employed their symbolic as well as prophetic protest politics to educate in their words, symbols, and deeds about US militarism as well as an alternative life-giving sociopolitical order. They articulated and attempted to live out a Christian symbol of the good society, the kin-dom of God. By seeking to realize the kin-dom of God through various forms of nonviolent direct and collective action, they did not coerce conformity to Christian doctrine or moral-

---

[109]Nadja Popovich and Tatiana Schlossberg, "Twenty-Three Environmental Rules Rolled Back in Trump's First 100 Days," *New York Times*, May 2, 2017; Michael D. Shear, "Trump Will Withdraw US from Paris Climate Agreement," *New York Times*, June 1, 2017.

ity and thereby eschew religious pluralism. Rather, they, along with the concluding case study about Green Nuns, have reconstructed and revitalized central Christian symbols for their socio-politically transformative meanings, in order to reshape, reconfigure, and remake a more just, more emancipatory and flourishing body politic, which includes honoring all bodies of Mother Earth.

7

Doing Ekklesial Work
in Intersectional, Interfaith Ways

> I hunger to use my gifts
> of poetry and practicality,
> of language and law to engage
> part of the aching world.
> —Sr. Simone Campbell, "Mysticism Matters"

> We live as one this fragile gifted life—for
> We are the Body of God!
> —Sr. Simone Campbell, "Incarnation"

Thus far, critically reclaiming key texts and insights from Vatican II has served as a starting point to elaborate a feminist public theology, particularly about who and what characterize and constitute the Catholic Church's role and representatives in US public life. Sacramentality, prophetic praxis, and solidarity stand as fundamental features in elaborating ekklesial work, and thus situate women's religio-political subjectivity, agency, and practices on firmer theological footing. A feminist and womanist rereading of *Gaudium et Spes* through the lens of Wisdom Christology sheds new theological light on the purpose of public theology and its practices of public engagement, treated in *Gaudium et Spes* as a sacrament or an albeit incomplete and imperfect sign of an abiding, this-worldly divine presence that lures the world toward greater justice, love, and peace. Public theology, and relatedly the public church, is more aptly described in terms of its sacramental significance in the US public sphere, that is, its ability to signify and evoke a new more just world, to do ekklesial work through prophetic and solidarity-based praxis for the kingdom of God. Catholic feminist and womanist theologies of sacramentality can further develop doing public theology as ekklesial work. Feminist and womanist reflections on sacramentality expand who and what constitutes the church's public actors and activism for community-creating praxis. Weaving together these resources from Vatican II theologies about the church's public role and from feminist and womanist theologies of sacramentality, this chapter analyzes the Nuns on the Bus tours and argues that the ekklesial work of the US public Church bears sacramental significance when it re/creates the public, when it prophetically testifies and witnesses to an alternative political reality or creates (or births) a new world that better signifies a more interconnected, interdependent US body politic rooted in solidarity that seeks love, justice, and peace.

Theologizing about women, sacramentality, and practices of public theology from a feminist and womanist perspective enlarges who and what constitute the face and practice of the US public Catholicism, and enables, empowers, and religio-politically enfranchises women's public engagement via a common human capacity for creativity, broadly understood. Women's contributions to US public theology and the public church through the recent religio-political praxis of US women religious show that what makes public theology public goes beyond institutional church representatives who introduce faith-based views into current debates about gender or bio-politics, about so-called non-negotiable beginning and end of life issues. Rather, effective public theology consists in the ability to remake the public, that is, to imagine and create communities of justice and peace, and to generate through a rich array of democratic practices new possibilities for solidarity amid a deeply fractured society.

The Vatican, the Nuns, and the US Bishops

As feminist theologian and New Testament scholar Sandra Schneiders has well documented, US Catholic sisters foreground the church's prophetic praxis, by living the Gospel in various educational, health care, and community-based social and gender justice ministries as well as by participating in nonviolent protests for economic and ecological justice and peace.[1] The sisters' practices of public engagement contest and critically transform US public life to do ekklesial work, that is, to forge soli-

---

[1] Sandra Schneiders, *Finding the Treasure: Locating Catholic Religious Life in a New Ecclesial and Cultural Context* (New York: Paulist Press, 2000), and *Prophets in Their Own Country: Women Religious Bearing Witness to the Gospel in a Troubled Church* (Maryknoll, NY: Orbis Books, 2011). See also Mary Fishman, *Band of Sisters* (Chicago: Band of Sisters, 2012); Margaret M. McGuinness, *Called to Serve: A History of Nuns in America* (New York: New York University Press, 2013).

Doing Ekklesial Work in Intersectional, Interfaith Ways 229

darity with marginalized groups and thereby better embrace and begin to enhance our shared common life. As Sr. Simone Campbell states, "What we sisters are doing is the enculturating of faith into democratic culture" in the US pluralistic culture of we the people.[2] These practices also reveal theo-political tensions and fault lines about who constitutes the public church, who expresses its religio-political agency in doing public theology.

On the heels of its three-year apostolic visitation of US sisters, the Vatican's Congregation for the Doctrine of the Faith (CDF) reprimanded US Catholic women religious in 2012, particularly the Leadership Conference of Women Religious (LCWR), for advancing social justice issues, and focusing too little attention on reproductive and sexual issues, such as abortion and same-sex marriage.[3] Women religious stood at the forefront of shaping US public policy, and thus risked this kind of religio-political backlash.[4] More specifically, US sisters' support for the Affordable Care Act (ACA) contributed to the Vatican's investigations and subsequent LCWR doctrinal assessment, reprimand, and reform mandate.[5] Former Executive Director of NETWORK Sr. Simone Campbell's letter supported the ACA, and the LCWR as well as Sr. Carol Keehan, then head of the Catholic Health Association, were listed among the letter's fifty-nine signatories. In gratitude, President Obama invited Sr. Simone to the ACA's signing into law.

The Vatican's disciplinary action—reaffirmed in mid-April 2013 by Pope Francis—announced the LCWR's supervision by an archbishops' advisory team, with episcopal approval or veto of LCWR conferences, speakers, and publications.[6] In its official statement, the Vatican equated the LCWR—which represents more than two thirds of US women religious—with radical feminism, explicitly identified and criticized NET-

---

[2]Simone Campbell, *A Nun on the Bus: How All of Us Can Create Hope, Change, and Community* (New York: HarperCollins, 2014), 111, 117, 126.

[3]Congregation for the Doctrine of the Faith, "Doctrinal Assessment of the Leadership Conference of Women Religious," April 18, 2012; Mary E. Hunt, "We Are All Nuns," *Religion Dispatches*, May 2, 2012; Margaret Cain McCarthy and Mary Ann Zollmann, eds., *Power of Sisterhood: Women Religious Tell the Story of the Apostolic Visitation* (Lanham, MD: University Press of America, 2014).

[4]Ivone Gebara, "The Inquisition of Today and US Women Religious," *Feminism and Religion*, April 27, 2012. The Nun Justice Project mobilized global grassroots actions to the apostolic visitation and the Vatican's LCWR mandate, consisting of petitions, demonstrations, a Tumblr blog, as well as other press and media events. For example, Dan Stockman, "Petitioners Ask Francis to Drop Call for USUS Sisters' Reform," *Global Sisters Report*, September 18, 2014.

[5]Marian Ronan, *Sister Trouble: The Vatican, the Bishops, and the Nuns* (North Charleston, SC: CreateSpace Independent Publishing Platform, 2013); Annmarie Sanders, IHM, ed., *However Long the Night: Making Meaning in a Time of Crisis* (LCWR, 2018).

[6]Joshua J. McElwee, "Pope Francis Reaffirms Critique of LCWR, Plan for Reform," *National Catholic Reporter*, April 15, 2013.

WORK's political lobby and advocacy work, and thus effectively dismissed women as the face of US public Catholicism, that is, as a "harbinger" (*Gaudium et Spes*, para. 92) or sacramental sign of the already inaugurated but not yet fully realized good society.[7] The Vatican abruptly concluded its three-year oversight of the LCWR in mid-April 2015 by accepting a final report during a meeting in Rome between the LCWR, Archbishop Sartain, and the CDF.[8] Although Pope Francis rescinded this mandate, the report stressed that LCWR annual conference speakers and publications would be vetted for consistency with church doctrine. In my view, this ongoing oversight not only eviscerates Catholic women's baptismal and religio-political rights to political participation (*Gaudium et Spes*, paras. 26, 29, 30–31, 43), but also increases theo-political tensions about what consists of public theology, of responsible faith-based citizenship in US public life.

Simultaneous with the Vatican visitation, reprimand, and report on American nuns, the US Conference of Catholic Bishops (USCCB) sponsored its inaugural Fortnight for Freedom from June 21 to July 4, 2012, to signal the US bishops' opposition to the ACA on the grounds that providing reproductive health care infringes on Catholic institutions' religious liberty.[9] Recently renamed Religious Freedom Week, this event illustrated Catholic polarity between sexual morality and social justice issues.[10] The US bishops framed both their statement and the Fortnight as a faith-based lobby for ACA's repeal, which contrasts with most US court precedents about US constitutional religious liberty cases. In their statement, titled "Our First, Most Cherished Liberty," the USCCB opposed the ACA contraception mandate by appealing to civil rights era traditions of conscientious objection to and civil disobedience of unjust laws. Moreover, the USCCB utilized the Fortnight to reassert their moral authority in the wake of growing American and Catholic consensus about contraception as matters of women's and public health. During the closing mass at the National Shrine of the Immaculate Conception in Washington, DC, Archbishop Charles Chaput remarked in his homily that the USCCB acted as divinely appointed sentinels, as described in Ezekiel,

---

[7]"Pastoral Constitution on the Church in the Modern World: *Gaudium et Spes*, 7 December 1965," in *Vatican Council II: The Basic Sixteen Documents*, ed. Austin Flannery, OP (Northport, NY: Costello Publishing, 1996).

[8]Joshua J. McElwee, "Vatican and LCWR Announce End of Controversial Three-Year Oversight," *National Catholic Reporter*, April 16, 2015.

[9]Robert Pear, "Bishops Reject Birth Control Compromise," *New York Times*, February 7, 2013; Cathleen Kaveny, "The Bishops and Religious Liberty," *Commonweal*, June 15, 2012, and "Is the Government Defining Religion?" *Commonweal*, January 25, 2013.

[10]Campbell, *A Nun on the Bus*, 107.

Doing Ekklesial Work in Intersectional, Interfaith Ways   **231**

to preach and protect religious liberty as the basic context for authentic freedom rooted in the dignity of the human person as the *imago Dei*. Chaput interpreted current political and juridical battles about religious liberty in light of scripture-based contrasts between rendering taxes to Caesar and rendering ourselves, as bearers of the *imago Dei*, to God. Chaput linked authentic freedom in God with baptismal-based loyalty to a transcendent authority, and concluded with a Christian triumphalist and theocratic point that true freedom demands both seeking God and living as evangelical missionaries of Christ.

The annual Fortnight for Freedom continued through 2015 and partly inspired high-profile cases of state-sponsored religious liberty laws like the one in Indiana in March 2015.[11] Cardinal Timothy Dolan, head of the USCCB during the first Fortnight, argued in an Eastertide 2015 interview that America's founders, not the bishops, centralized religious liberty in America's ethos. He further called for more rational discourse to protect both the LGBTQIA+ community's rights and religious rights. However, Patricia Miller has shown that the USCCB "made the words 'religious liberty' flesh by attaching them to the specific issue of the contraceptive mandate, drawing parallels with same-sex marriage, and then rhetorically inciting panic that fundamental religious freedoms were under attack."[12] Passed or pending bills in nearly thirty states gained further traction after the US Supreme Court ruled in favor of legalizing same-sex marriage in the *Obergefell v. Hodges* case in June 2015. Indeed, several state-sponsored religious liberty bills appeared across the US in the wake of the USCCB's actions to promote religious freedom as a means to resist federal health care or marriage laws. Consequently, religious liberty legislation has amounted to religiously supported discrimination, allowing individuals and organizations to cite federal and state laws as a theo-political justification for refusing supportive services to women and to LGBTQ+ folxs.

In the era of President Trump, the Fortnight for Freedom continued but moved well beyond the ACA and reproductive health care. Trump engaged with, applied, and imposed conservative Catholic positions on both US domestic and foreign policy, including defunding international aid organizations that provide reproductive health care, enabling churches to engage in partisan political campaigning, appointing three conservative

---

[11]Garrett Epps, "What Makes Indiana's Religious Freedom Law Different?" *The Atlantic*, March 30, 2015.

[12]Patricia Miller, "USUS Bishops (Who Lit Religious Liberty Fuse) Urge Civility," *Religion Dispatches*, April 8, 2015.

justices to the US Supreme Court to overturn *Roe v. Wade*, and establishing a religious liberty task force in the Department of Justice that undermined many civil rights through related religious liberty legislation. Religious liberty increasingly links Catholicism with US culture wars to undermine reproductive health care and same-sex marriage, epitomized by Donald Trump's appearance at the March for Life in 2020. In these culture wars, religious liberty functions as a partisan symbol or electoral weapon.[13] The USCCB utilizes rhetorical practices and discursive strategies that stoke "a siege mentality" to "constitute an existential or apocalyptic threat to fundamental freedoms."[14] However, the USCCB campaign failed to focus on religious liberty and life issues in a pluralistic democratic society ever more endangered by a rising racist and nativist Christian nationalism, symbolized by the increasing Islamophobia reflected in and abetted by Trump's anti-Muslim immigration and refugee ban, the incarceration camps, family separations, and other horrid abuses at the US–Mexico border, and the white supremacist groups who mobilized the Unite the Right Rally in Charlottesville, Virginia, on August 11–12, 2017, and co-ordinated the insurrectionist riot at the US Capitol on January 6, 2021. Even during America's racial reckoning with systemic racism after the murder of George Floyd in Minneapolis, and the COVID-19 pandemic, which amplified health care, economic, and other inequalities, the US-CCB pressed and pursued a religious liberty agenda further, claiming in high-profile lawsuits in New York and Michigan that church closures and vaccine or mask mandates infringed on religious freedom to worship and to recognize the image of a Trinitarian, relational God in one another.[15]

More than a polarizing divide between social justice and right to life Catholics,[16] the US nuns and the USCCB illustrate an ongoing debate about prevailing agents and practices in doing public theology. In my

---

[13]John Gehring, "Reclaiming Religious Freedom from the Culture Wars," *National Catholic Reporter*, January 16, 2020.

[14]John Gehring, "Religious Liberty Should Unite Us, Not Divide Us," *National Catholic Reporter* July 1, 2017; Jamie Manson, "Trump's March for Life Appearance Calls into Question Bishops' Motives," *National Catholic Reporter*, February 4, 2020.

[15]Andrew Seidel, "Sacrificing Children on the Altar of Religious Freedom," *Religion Dispatches*, July 23, 2021; Adam Liptak, "Splitting 5 to 4, Supreme Court Backs Religious Challenge to Cuomo's Virus Shutdown Order," *New York Times* November 26, 2020, updated April 5, 2021, in contrast to Adam Liptak, "Supreme Court, in 5–4 Decision, Rejects Church's Challenge to Shutdown Order," *New York Times* May 30, 2020, updated June 15, 2020, and "Split 5 to 4, Supreme Court Rejects Nevada Church's Challenge to Shutdown Restrictions," *New York Times*, July 24, 2020.

[16]Ruth Braunstein, "Strategic Storytelling by Nuns on the Bus," in *Religion and Progressive Activism: New Stories about Faith and Politics*, ed. Ruth Braunstein, Todd Nicholas Fuist, and Rhys H. Williams (New York: New York University Press, 2017), 289.

Doing Ekklesial Work in Intersectional, Interfaith Ways 233

view, feminist and womanist reflections on sacramentality—on who and what express, embody, and signify an eschatological orientation to an alternative possible future common life—shed light on and sharpen the church's public actors and activism for ekklesial work, for doing community-creating praxis.

The Sacramentality of Ekklesial Work

Sacramentality in its broadest meaning applies to the sacrality of the world, and involves discerning the divine presence within (but not identical with) all earthly life. In Catholic traditions, the divine presence is signified in central communal celebrations such as the seven sacraments, and is encountered primarily in the incarnation, of God taking flesh in Jesus the Christ.[17] Beyond this intra-ecclesial ritual experience of sacraments, sacramentality in recent Catholic feminist and womanist theologies acts, in my view, as a theological catalyst to advance doing public theology as ekklesial work, as community-creating praxis, and to assist women in reclaiming their critical prophetic role as representatives of the Catholic public church as well as regaining their full humanity. Yet sacramentality carries an ambiguity; we cannot easily equate certain political actors or movements with the good society, framed in theological terms as the kingdom of God. Any religio-political activism recalls or points toward, but is not totally identified with, that kingdom which was inaugurated in the incarnation of the divine in the life, ministry, death, and resurrection of Jesus the Christ. Therefore, we can only propose some moderate feminist theological criteria to discern the sacramental presence of the kingdom, reign, or family of God in public life. Theologizing about the public church from a sacramental, prophetic, and solidarity-based standpoint eschews magisterial anthropologies that idealize and politicize women's bio-physical ability to birth, and instead emphasizes all humanity's capacity for creativity, for being what Vatican II called "molders [artisans] of a new humanity." Drawing key insights from Catholic feminist and womanist theologies of sacramentality, public theology and the public church recovers its sacramental significance when it re/creates the public, when it creates community, when it witnesses to an alternative political reality, when it generates or births a new world that better signifies justice, love, and peace.

---

[17] Susan A. Ross, *Extravagant Affections: A Feminist Sacramental Theology* (New York: Continuum, 1998), 33–34, 36–38, 138–42.

In *For the Beauty of the Earth*, Susan Ross outlines a feminist theological aesthetics of beauty, identifying its existential, ethical, political, and epistemological features. Beauty is integrated with and co-constitutes self-identity, models and motivates both generosity and self-love rather than greed and egoism, is manifested in praxis, plays an intrinsic part in the survival and flourishing of others, and deepens self-understanding in relation to others and to God.[18] Synthesizing these features, Ross highlights an integral link between beauty and the world's sacramental quality: "The beauty of the world gives us a sense of the care with which God holds us, a care that is attuned to our senses, and to our, and God's, delight."[19]

Women are either overly identified with beauty or coerced to perform imposed kyriarchal beauty norms and constructs, which significantly diminish women's agency in religious and political spheres. Ross argues that, although marginalized from leading roles in sacred spaces and in US public life, "women's experiences . . . tell us some important things about God's sacramental presence in the world. Yet this presence is not a static one: we are all called to make the world a better place, and, yes, a more beautiful place. For beauty and justice are indeed connected."[20] Women, in Ross's view, instill sacramentality into domestic, religious, and socio-political life via various forms of work or alternative altars and liturgies.[21] Women's work in the arts and various associated fields carries sacramental characteristics by imagining life-giving and life-enhancing links between self, community, and world in creative and transformative ways.[22]

M. Shawn Copeland in *Enfleshing Freedom* elaborates a womanist theology of the body that builds on African American humanity as a basis for theological reflection on sacramentality. Copeland uplifts Black women's bodies as a "basic human sacrament" or site of divine revelation and incarnation of the mystical body of Christ.[23] The mystical body of Christ signifies the radical interrelationality and equality of all life in God, glimpsed now and fully realized in the future.[24] Sacramentality in this anthropological and eschatological perspective inspires solidarity

---

[18]Susan A. Ross, *For the Beauty of the Earth: Women, Sacramentality, and Justice* (New York: Paulist Press, 2006), 7, 14, 30, 65–67, 72, 74–75, 77, 79–80, 86.

[19]Ibid., 5–6.

[20]Ibid., 4.

[21]Ibid., xi, 46–47, 50–51, 53, 59.

[22]Laurie Cassidy and Maureen H. O'Connell, eds., *She Who Imagines: Feminist Theological Aesthetics* (Collegeville, MN: Liturgical Press, 2012).

[23]M. Shawn Copeland, *Enfleshing Freedom: Body, Race, and Being* (Minneapolis: Fortress Press, 2010), 24; cf. 8.

[24]Ibid., 103; cf. 81–84, 90, 102–103.

Doing Ekklesial Work in Intersectional, Interfaith Ways 235

because it "pose[s] an order, a counter-imagination, not only to society but also to any ecclesial instantiation that would substitute for the body of Christ."[25] For example, US slavery obscured the sacramentality of Black bodies. Slavery commodified and objectified Black women as property and as perfomers of servile and sexual labor,[26] and thereby denied the common humanity of the Black community, but especially of Black women, with all creation in the image of God.

In contrast to multiple dehumanizing legacies of US slavery, which Black women continually confront and confound, religiously, politically, and sexually,[27] Copeland recovers and reveres Black women's bodies as a sacrament, as a way to "make the mystical body of Christ publicly visible"[28] by attending to various practices of enslaved and emancipated Black women for "enfleshing freedom." Copeland writes, "Escaping to freedom, purchasing one's own freedom or that of a loved one, fighting for freedom, offering up one's body for the life and freedom of another, and dying for freedom were acts of redemption that aimed to restore Black bodily and psychic integrity."[29] Copeland interprets these women's practices Christologically: "Theologically considered, their suffering, like the suffering of Jesus, seeds a new life for the future of all humanity. Their suffering, like the suffering of Jesus, anticipates an enfleshment of freedom and life to which Eucharist is linked ineluctably. Eucharist, then, is a countersign to the devaluation and violence directed toward the Black body."[30] For Copeland, Christology promotes intimate interconnection and interdependence with one another, God, and a more liberative future through performing liturgical acts like the Eucharist and socio-political acts of solidarity as "a countersign" to racism and other structural evils, such as war, incarceration, torture, rape, queer-bashing, transphobia, and other abuses of power.[31]

Feminist theologians and ethicists have long employed the notion of generativity to reinterpret sacramental practices in light of women's work (Ross) and embodied experiences (Copeland) of giving and sustaining

---

[25]Ibid., 125.

[26]Ibid., 38.

[27]Bernadette J. Brooten, ed., *Beyond Slavery: Overcoming Its Religious and Sexual Legacies* (New York: Palgrave Macmillan, 2010), and emilie m. townes, *Womanist Ethics and the Cultural Production of Evil* (New York: Palgrave Macmillan, 2006).

[28]Copeland, *Enfleshing Freedom*, 105.

[29]Ibid., 46, particularly the story of Lavinia Bell, 115–116, and the implications of her story for anthropology and Christology, 124–125.

[30]Ibid., 124.

[31]Ibid., 83, 107–110.

life. In keeping with the prophetic and solidarity praxis-based features of feminist and womanist theologies of sacramentality, public theology, in my view, serves as a site of women's sacramental work, because that ekklesial work makes community, that work contests and critically transforms US public life to better embrace and begin to enhance this common earthly life together. Resonant with a more expansive political understanding of the church as sacrament in *Gaudium et Spes*, a feminist and womanist theological perspective on sacramentality in public life—on what constitutes being a sign of the transformative presence of God in the world—foregrounds prophetic political praxis for solidarity and justice as a means of embodying that divine presence, and thus emphasizes a broader socio-political notion of creativity, of generativity, of community-building ekklesial work beyond the gender or bio-politics of maternity.

Synthesizing these women's liberation theologies of sacramentality opens up a new vista for the theo-political imagination, and shows that the Catholic public church is public when it bears sacramental significance, that is, when it creates community, when it makes or births a new world, an alternative political reality that better signifies some of the political conditions for a more just, loving, and peaceful US body politic. Rather than limit the Catholic Church's political actors and agency to institutional church representatives who speak about certain political issues from a religious perspective, a feminist approach to the US public church stresses prophetic and solidarity-based praxis that imagines and seeks to realize a more inclusive and just common life. It sheds light on the kind of society that is generated, that is, imagined and sustained, through that praxis. Women's socio-political praxis to create community, not their non-clerical or maternal status, enables and empowers them to do public theology via their sacramental quality as a sign of the body of Christ amid a deeply divided US body politic.

Being the public church and doing public theology entails a praxis of imagining and seeking to realize a more just, participatory common life as envisioned in Jesus' ministry for the kingdom of God. In other words, a feminist public theology understood as ekklesial work entails a hope-filled or eschatological praxis for building the common good, for reweaving a more just social fabric. When the life-ministry of Jesus serves as a model for the church's socio-political engagement, when discipleship takes the form of socio-political praxis for justice, then all people—institutional church leaders and everyday Catholics—emulate Jesus, participate in the eschatological work of Christ, strive to re-imagine and at least partly realize a just and justice-oriented common life. Most importantly for

Doing Ekklesial Work in Intersectional, Interfaith Ways   237

women, being the public church and doing public theology as ekklesial work is associated with a performative imitation of Jesus' ministry for the kingdom, rather than an ontological signification or biological replication of the historical human nature of Jesus Christ. Based on their praxis of incarnational solidarity rather than their physical bodies and biological reproductive capacities, women—and all nonordained people—stand *in persona Christi*, thus offering a far more expansive rather than mainly clericalist kyriarchal understanding of the church's public actors and agency.

In contrast to both US episcopal theo-politics and magisterial theologies, a feminist theological understanding of the public church and of public theology as ekklesial work empowers contemporary women and visibilizes women's leading roles in the church's political participation. As argued previously, a performative theology of discipleship grounded in praxis for the kingdom of God certainly resists both dominant Christologies that limit the church's political actors to ordained and other prominent male spokespersons, and magisterial theologies that frame women within maternity, whether domesticized or politicized. Resisting the theo-political limits of their nonordained or maternal status, women do public theology via their multiple forms of praxis of and for justice. In my view, US Catholic women's public engagement exemplifies ekklesial work, both its world-making potential and its sacramental significance, especially through rhetorical, symbolic, and especially prophetic practices to criticize an unjust US public life, on the one hand, and to actualize an alternative more just, solidaristic, and liberative world, on the other hand.

NETWORK and Nuns on the Bus

Interpreted from this feminist and womanist-informed perspective of ekklesial work, US Catholic sisters reaffirmed and reasserted their religiopolitical credibility. The LCWR did not let the Vatican censure their praxis "to embody the Gospel in a radical way."[32] Instead, the Nuns on the Bus tours reinforce the prophetic praxis of US Catholic women religious for social justice. NETWORK's Nuns on the Bus road trips act as a refreshing resource to construct a feminist public theology, to centralize what I have called ekklesial work or a religio-political praxis of community building. As recent Presidential Medal of Freedom honoree Sr. Simone Campbell

---

[32]Campbell, *A Nun on the Bus*, 109.

238 *Nevertheless, We Persist*

explains, these tours reclaimed and restored that "we in creation are one body. All are important in this body even though we might have different functions. . . . It is a matter of being in right relationship with all of creation and in that way we will create a community that comes closer to being the KIN-DOM of God."[33] The Nuns on the Bus tours from 2012 to 2018 illustrate the prophetic political praxis of US Catholic women religious, firmly founded on theological commitments to solidarity, the option for the poor, and the common good—all fundamental features of shared humanity.[34] The nuns' activism prophetically testifies and witnesses to an alternative reality; the tours lift up sisters' ministries, lobby key congressional representatives, run media events, hold "friend-raisers," and re/imagine and re/create a more interdependent community, or generate and bring to birth possibilities for renewed common life.[35]

In keeping with scriptural prophetic traditions, prophets perennially edge our seemingly intransigent racist, global capitalist, heterosexist, and kyriarchal religious and political institutions toward right, loving, and just relations with multiply minoritized, marginalized, and disenfranchised peoples. "We need the prophets to cry out. And we need the people to respond," claims Sr. Simone Campbell. The encounter between Jesus and the Samaritan woman (John 4:4–42), cited by Sr. Simone, models women's innovative and prophetic intercultural and interreligious religio-political engagement that moves toward right and just relations.[36] As a multiply disadvantaged foreign woman with a complex sexual history hailing from a minoritized cultural and religious community, the unnamed Samaritan woman transgresses these socio-cultural, religious, gender, and sexual borders and addresses Jesus' basic needs by drawing water from Jacob's well. Alone in public, their conversation progresses, as Mary Catherine Hilkert describes, from reflections about personal identity and differing religious practices to theological debates about the presence of God.[37] She announces this good news of God's presence in Jesus to her neighbors, who also come to see and believe through her witness. She is energized by this encounter to rhetorically and prophetically testify to what she has seen and heard and is empowered to act upon it to change others' lives.

---

[33]Ibid., 180.

[34]Ibid., 126.

[35]Ibid., 129.

[36]Ibid., 119, *Hunger for Hope: Prophetic Communities, Contemplation, and the Common Good* (Maryknoll, NY: Orbis Books, 2020), 29, 85–86, and "Politics, Faith, and Prophetic Witness," Annual Evelyn Underhill Lecture in Christian Spirituality, Boston College, July 12, 2014.

[37]Mary Catherine Hilkert, "On the Strength of Her Testimony," Annual Magdala Lecture, Boston College, July 22, 2015.

Doing Ekklesial Work in Intersectional, Interfaith Ways 239

Similarly, NETWORK's Nuns on the Bus tours relied on a theo-politics of (1) storytelling and other rhetorical practices of sharing narratives, (2) rethinking central religious symbols and claims, and (3) civil rights era-inspired prophetic practices to more adequately address a fraught and fractured US public life and attempt to model, build, and regenerate community within it.

Launched by NETWORK, a non-profit Catholic social justice lobby started in 1972, the inaugural Nuns on the Bus tour, Nuns Drive for Faith, Family, and Fairness, traveled through nine states and logged 2,700 miles en route to Washington, DC, in two weeks, from June 18 to July 2, 2012. This initial tour questioned the devastating effects of congressional budget proposals—articulated by Wisconsin Representative Paul Ryan's Path to Prosperity plan—on middle-class, working-class, and low-wealth people (figuratively to walk among the dry bones described in Ezekiel), but also to rebuild relationships.[38] The nuns' hearing and sharing of stories from the most directly affected peoples by the proposed federal budget cuts at "friend-raiser" events during the tour bear much theo-political efficacy not only for the policymaking process but also for creating community, or building relationships and a sense of solidarity with marginalized peoples via a praxis of "theological reflection and storytelling."[39] These stories gathered on the tour showcase the nuns' theo-political credibility in the public square and in congressional contexts, highlight the harm of budget proposals on struggling people and thus cultivate empathy across complex polarizing divides in US public life between elite Washington politics and everyday citizens, and ultimately create a kind of prophetic and epistemic power for these stories to gain visibility and change the policymaking process and debates.[40] As Sr. Simone explained in press releases and interviews, the tour both highlighted multiple social justice ministries and amplified the harm of the budget proposals on "the reality of our nation," that is, on nationwide low-wealth working people.[41]

"Storytelling potentially serves as a multivocal form of moral communication that transcends specific religious divisions."[42] It bridges multiple gaps that cause "othering" in US society. As Sr. Simone observes, religious litmus tests do not apply to this activism: "You do not have to be Christian

---

[38]Laurie Goodstein, "Nuns, Rebuked by Rome, Plan Road Trip to Spotlight Social Issues," *New York Times*, June 5, 2012; Mary E. Hunt, "Nuns on the Bus: 2700 Miles, Nine States, and a Rock Star DC Welcome," *Religion Dispatches*, July 5, 2012.

[39]Campbell, *A Nun on the Bus*, 103, 137.

[40]Braunstein, "Strategic Storytelling," 293–294, 296.

[41]Ibid., 297–298.

[42]Ibid., 303.

240   *Nevertheless, We Persist*

or Catholic for this journey. You just have to be open to a story that is bigger than your own," especially in divisive times wracked with racism, anti-Semitism, and Islamophobia.[43] Arriving on Capitol Hill, Sr. Simone Campbell greeted grassroots supporters with a speech that contrasted the immoral congressional budget (allegedly rooted in Catholic social teachings) with NETWORK's self-described faithful budget, captured in the phrase "reasonable revenue for responsible programs." While congressional budget proposals cut social safety-net programs and services and cut taxes on corporations as well as the wealthiest Americans, NETWORK's budget situated rights and responsibilities in the context of communities, rooted in the stories of many economically and in other ways marginalized people the Sisters saw, met, and heard on the tour. In terms of symbolic practices, the Sisters' budget was grounded in Catholic theological commitments to solidarity, to the option for the poor, and to the common good. Recalling the US bishops' landmark 1986 statement on the economy, which marked its 25th anniversary at that time, crowds in DC greeted the sisters with signs that read, "Thank you sisters for using your freedom to witness to *Economic Justice for All.*"[44] Further embodying such rhetorical practices, in September 2012 Sr. Simone addressed the Democratic National Convention to act on her religious community's Pentecostal charism and speak en-Spirited truth to power, to sustain accountability to the people's stories she encountered on the tour, to reframe the religio-political narrative toward justice, and to share NETWORK's vision with inter/national communities—"to stand with struggling families and to lift up our Catholic sisters who serve them."[45] Sr. Simone's speech centralized the narratives of folxs she met on the tour, which resonated with the political and economic marginality experienced by the majority of Americans. Her speech not only influenced public conversation and debate about poverty and justice by foregrounding the voices and views of minoritized peoples, but also created the conditions to significantly influence the convention's political policy platform as well as President Barack Obama's acceptance speech and policy agenda.[46]

Since the initial tour, other NETWORK-organized bus tours have taken place in Ohio in October 2012 and in Colorado in November 2012; they

---

[43]Campbell, *Hunger for Hope*, 8.

[44]Lauren Feeney, "Nuns on the Bus Brings Light to Capitol Hill," Moyers & Company, July 4, 2012. Cf. Mark J. Allman, ed., *The Almighty and the Dollar: Reflections on Economic Justice for All* (Winona, MN: Anselm Academic, 2012).

[45]Campbell, *A Nun on the Bus*, 145, 148–149, 151, 154.

[46]Ibid., 154–158.

Doing Ekklesial Work in Intersectional, Interfaith Ways 241

called attention to nun-run social services for poor families most negatively affected by congressional budget proposals. In the next year, the Nuns on the Bus tour from May 28 to June 18, 2013, traveled 6,800 miles during three weeks and through fifteen states from Ellis Island, New York, to Angel Island, California, to spotlight immigration reform and successfully lobby for public policy change at the time in the House of Representatives. With the message Comprehensive Immigration Reform Now, this tour received nationwide acclaim as well as support from Catholic parishes and bishops. This tour also followed a similar pattern—to meet with sisters and multifaith groups advocating with and for immigrant communities, lobby elected officials about immigrant rights, hold press events, and host friend-raisers.[47] The inaugural event for this tour was organized as an interfaith event at Ellis Island to mutually appreciate and advocate for the rich diversity of immigrants and immigration reform groups.[48] Future events on the tour in Scranton, Pennsylvania, and Camden, New Jersey, similarly contextualized immigration reform in light of multilingual, multicultural, multigenerational peoples who co-constitute immigrant advocacy groups in American democracy.[49] The tour opened up opportunities for immigrant teenagers, students, families, laborers, and activists in Georgia, Florida, Louisiana, Texas, Arizona, and California to publicly tell their stories, build community support and advocacy, and influence the public conversation about immigrant rights.[50] Sr. Simone attested to the theo-political implications of such storytelling as "a process of becoming who we really are. Each issue, each battle, each stop on the bus, each story we heard, and each story I retell here, is part of our ongoing pilgrimage together. . . . We are all one."[51] After this tour, Sr. Simone testified before the House Budget Committee, relaying the stories of struggling Americans, indicting the broken systems that perpetuate their marginality, and urging Congress to eschew any policies that further this othering.[52]

In the subsequent year, Nuns on the Bus embarked on the We the People, We the Voters tour, an eleven-state pilgrimage from September 17 through November 4, 2014, to encourage and increase voter turnout around issues related to the economy, health care, immigration, and conflict resolution. Coinciding with the US congressional midterm elections, the tour took

---

[47]Ibid., 164.
[48]Ibid., 167.
[49]Ibid., 168–169.
[50]Ibid., 171–177.
[51]Ibid., 177.
[52]Braunstein, "Strategic Storytelling," 302.

242   *Nevertheless, We Persist*

place amid much nationwide fanfare.[53] In alignment with Pope Francis's visit to the US in 2015, the Nuns on the Bus organized a Bridge the Divide, Transform Politics tour. The nuns discovered at some tour events that they could not find or forge common ground with faith-based anti-LGBTQ+ and anti-progressive groups based on shared religious or political principles.[54] Nonetheless, the nuns continued to articulate and demonstrate their vision, fighting prophetically and proactively for a theological vision of the inherent dignity and interdependence of all life, rather than a reactive resistance against others' toxic views and policies that degrade human rights.[55] The nuns encountered community-based organizing projects, such as Mothers to Mothers in St. Louis which formed after the police killing of Michael Brown, who resist racist policing and related socio-political structures by sponsoring collaborative conversations between Black and white mothers that as a result live into alternative anti-racist communities.

These six tours over seven years tackled pressing public issues and concerns, such as the federal budget, immigration reform, tax policy, voting rights and laws, and bridging divides in political conversations. Subsequently, NETWORK hosted in 2019 roundtable listening sessions with rural communities that experience these intersecting crises more intensely,[56] and continues to advocate for "mending the gaps" in income inequality, taxes and wages, worker benefits (such as paid family leave), voting, health care, housing, and so on.[57] As a member of the Sisters of Social Service, Sr. Simone theo-politically enacts in these tours a Spirit-centered and Pentecostal praxis of creating community.[58] In addition to pneumatological symbols, Sr. Simone invoked and interpreted prophetic symbols, such as Moses' transformative encounter with the divine in the burning bush and Ezekiel's prophecy among the valley of dry bones.[59] Campbell framed and envisioned these tours in a theological context— "we are called to be this bush, where God can flame up in our lives, and we can set our people free . . . this . . . bus trip gives breath, it gives hope," akin to the ways Ezekiel's prophetic speech and breath of the Spirit re-vivify a people.[60] These tours also stemmed from a prophetic Christology and ecclesiology: "The journey of a pilgrim people, always on the road,

---

[53]Simone Campbell, "Nuns on the Bus Hit the Road Once Again, to 'Reclaim our Democracy,' " *National Catholic Reporter*, September 15, 2014.

[54]Campbell, *Hunger for Hope*, 38–39.

[55]Ibid., 41, 120–121.

[56]Ibid., 31–33.

[57]Ibid., 109.

[58]Campbell, *A Nun on the Bus*, 122, and *Hunger for Hope*, 2, 6, 27, 96.

[59]Campbell, *A Nun on the Bus*, 127.

[60]Ibid., 178.

Doing Ekklesial Work in Intersectional, Interfaith Ways 243

always moving ahead. Jesus sends us together into the world to bring good news to the poor, sight to the blind, freedom to the captives. This news is brought in joy and, occasionally, on a bus."[61] Moreover, Sr. Simone coupled this distinctly Christian theological worldview with US constitutional solidarity—rooted in a recovery of we the people to breathe and hope together in community—in ways that resonated interreligiously. At the inaugural tour, for example, Catholics, Protestants, Unitarians, Jews, and Buddhists attended the send-off vigil for the sisters. That same tour as well as future tours visited and highlighted interreligious collaborations, projects, and ministries, too.[62]

In my view, a feminist/womanist approach to public theology as ekklesial work, as creating community in the present and the future, fosters and foregrounds how Sr. Simone situates the Nuns on the Bus tours and NETWORK's subsequent advocacy within a prophetic imagination. Sr. Simone draws pathbreaking lessons for prophetic community building from Walter Brueggemann's work on the topic, highlighting memory, pain, active hope, intergenerational and intercultural discourse, and countercultural vision "to imagine a new way forward."[63] "To be a community that can have a revitalized imagination to respond in our time, we need to be rooted in history."[64] Together with Christian scriptures and a continually evolving Catholic social teaching, remembering the origins of the Sisters of Social Service and their religio-political action for women's suffrage, economic justice, education, and multiple social justice issues among marginalized Eastern European peoples after World War I galvanized and sustained the social justice activism of the Sisters worldwide.[65] Deeply listening to the pain of others in the world promotes truth-telling, empathy, and solidarity: "letting our hearts be broken by the stories of those around us creates true community and connection"[66] for healing the suffering and harm in our society imposed on immigrant and low-wealth groups in the US and Latin America.[67] At times, Sr. Simone embraced a ministry of public weeping to demonstrate such pain and solidarity politics especially to mobilize for immigrant rights and justice in 2018, at a courthouse-based press conference and prayer vigil at a child detention facility in El Paso,

---

[61]Ibid., 179.
[62]Ibid., 128, 133.
[63]Campbell, *Hunger for Hope*, 46–47, 95.
[64]Ibid., 57.
[65]Ibid., 55.
[66]Ibid., 59.
[67]Ibid., 60–64, 66.

Texas.[68] Hope is actualized by and emerges from such story-based and heartbreaking encounters, leading toward empathy that intimately interconnects all of us and that inspires religio-political collective struggle.[69] In keeping with pneumatological symbols of Pentecost, public discourse plays an influential role in critically re/shaping a prophetic imagination, especially across generations, peoples, and cultures, to ensure and enact mutual dignity and respect as well as shared purpose. Such discourse continually exposes and dismantles white privilege and its systemic racism, sexism, classism, US exceptionalism, nationalism, and so on, that produce an exclusionary society.[70] Thus, a prophetic imagination cultivates a creative religio-political tension in fashioning ever more just policies for an imagined more inclusive and just world that overcomes racial, social, economic, gender, religious, and many other divisive disparities.[71]

Synthesizing these rhetorical, symbolic, and prophetic practices, Sr. Simone described the tours as "a hymn to the American sisters . . . to further the mission that the women religious have always pursued—standing with those who have been left behind, lifting up those who have been oppressed, gathering in those who have been pushed to the margins."[72] These tours, in my view, also do the ekklesial work of community-creating praxis. As Sr. Simone describes, "We are called to take in the mystery of others and weave community into the fabric of our time. We are called to be one organism, one body in this very challenging moment. . . . We are woven into one family when we can bring our broken hearts, our curiosity, our sense of history, and our willingness to engage. Together, we constitute the prophetic imagination for which we hunger."[73]

What, then, distinguishes the Nuns on the Bus tours as more efficacious sacramental, prophetic, and solidarity-based praxis of doing public theology and being the public church, or what I am calling ekklesial work, for community building in US public life? In my view, both the nuns and the USCCB claimed prophetic traditions as the basis of their religio-political action. Also theological symbols propelled both the nuns' and the USCCB's transformation of US public life. They leveraged theological symbols to criticize the predominant socio-political order and to envision an alternative possible order that sustains life. The nuns appealed

---

[68]Ibid., 67–68.
[69]Ibid., 75–76.
[70]Ibid., 80–84.
[71]Ibid., 94–96.
[72]Campbell, *A Nun on the Bus*, 135–136.
[73]Campbell, *Hunger for Hope*, 143–144.

Doing Ekklesial Work in Intersectional, Interfaith Ways 245

to solidarity, the common good, and the option for the poor to question and criticize the disastrous effects of federal policies—whether about the economy, immigration, or voting—on poor people. The Nuns on the Bus tour itself stopped at and spotlighted social justice ministries, and thereby underscored what federal policies forgot: an interdependent, interconnected sense of community with all of life. The tour as a prophetic praxis engendered an alternative possible political order grounded in those same symbols. The USCCB, too, invoked Christology, the *imago Dei*, and discipleship, to emphasize the transcendent unity of all life in the reality of God, which counters unjust political realities. As Jamie Manson has observed, the magisterium and the nuns "share a deeply sacramental understanding of their calling to serve those on the margins of our world. They agree that it is in ministering to the poor, the sick, and the vulnerable that they touch the wounded body of Christ. Where they seem to disagree sharply, however, is in their understanding of religious life as a prophetic life form."[74] In Sr. Simone's view, Christology undergirds such prophetic praxis: "Jesus is also present in the people assembled there, and in the word proclaimed, as well as in the celebration of the sacrament."[75]

More than introducing faith-based views about religious liberty into current civic debates, what makes the US Catholic public church and its public theology public, in my view of this case study, consists in the ability of the Nuns on the Bus tour to re/imagine and re/create community, to generate and bring to birth new possibilities for a US shared common life. In contrast to religious liberty laws that further polarize community, the Nuns on the Bus bear sacramental significance because the nuns' prophetic praxis—the bus tours themselves and the solidarity that they built—exposed and interrupted the prevailing irrational and immoral public discourse that "others" multiple groups in US society. In addition, the inaugural and subsequent tours educated about and engendered another possible political world by partially creating and enacting, albeit briefly, a more just body politic rooted in recovering an interdependent, interconnected sense of community and responsibility—of solidarity—between privileged Washington lawmakers and marginalized everyday peoples. The tours exemplify what I am advancing as a feminist public theology of ekklesial work, by emphasizing the role of the Catholic Church in constructively modeling or performing through its social justice

---

[74]Jamie Manson, "Time to Face Facts: Pope Francis Agrees with the Doctrinal Assessment of LCWR," *National Catholic Reporter*, May 13, 2014.

[75]Campbell, *A Nun on the Bus*, 110.

246   *Nevertheless, We Persist*

praxis—rhetorical, symbolic, and prophetic—some of the religio-political conditions for the possibility of justice, love, and peace to be created and sustained in the US body politic.

Theologizing about women's prophetic praxis via the Nuns on the Bus tours not only helps advance a feminist theology of the public church as ekklesial work but also assists women in reclaiming their full humanity. A sacramental, prophetic, and solidarity-based perspective on doing public theology and being the public church sidesteps magisterial anthropologies that forefront women's maternity as the basis of women's political engagement. Instead, this perspective aligns with theological anthropologies of creativity, illustrated in the Vatican II pastoral constitution on the public church and in feminist theologies of the *imago Dei*. According to *Gaudium et Spes*, the goal of the Catholic public church is to create or make a more just common life, which all persons as artisans co-create or co-generate with God and with one another. As feminist theologian Mary Catherine Hilkert reminds us, the doctrine of the *imago Dei* is so imbricated with sexist, racist, colonialist, and other oppressive legacies, that "the fullness of human life . . . lies ahead of us, not behind us. . . . [T]he image of God describes not a primordial state from which the first human beings fell, but the destiny toward which the human community is called. . . . In a real sense, the full meaning of what it means to image God or image Christ remains in the future."[76] Creativity, thus, challenges a conventional Christian chasm in human–divine relations. As Brazilian ecofeminist theologian Ivone Gebara claims, "To reflect on the meaning of the human person is to accept the challenge of becoming creators of ourselves and of the entire living world."[77] When living testimony to the gospel serves as the index of living into the *imago Dei*, women are thus enabled to reclaim their right to do public theology, to be the public church, and to enact their full humanity, too—through their theo-political praxis of creating communities of justice and peace, and not solely through their maternity. A sacramental, prophetic, and solidarity-based (rather than biologically determinist) anthropology of creativity widens the theological notion of the public church in feminist and womanist ways to incorporate all who stand according to Vatican II as a "harbinger" of the good society

---

[76]Mary Catherine Hilkert, "Cry Beloved Image: Rethinking the Image of God," in *In the Embrace of God: Feminist Approaches to Theological Anthropology*, ed. Ann O'Hara Graff (Maryknoll, NY: Orbis Books, 1995), 195–196. Cf. Michelle A. Gonzalez, *Created in God's Image: An Introduction to Feminist Theological Anthropology* (Maryknoll, NY: Orbis Books, 2007) esp. chap. 5.

[77]Ivone Gebara, *Longing for Running Water: Ecofeminism and Liberation* (Minneapolis: Fortress Press, 1999), 67; cf. 57, 81.

Doing Ekklesial Work in Intersectional, Interfaith Ways 247

already inaugurated but awaiting to be more fully realized. Testifying and witnessing to as well as eschatologically glimpsing that more just common life takes place through the sacramental, prophetic, and solidarity-based praxis for justice in the Nuns on the Bus tours and many other social justice movements, analyzed in this book and persistently emerging in and beyond US public life.

PERMISSIONS

Earlier publications that shape and are significantly modified in parts of this book are gratefully used with permission from presses and publishers.

Chapter 1 adapts parts of my prior publications in the method of public theology and a feminist and womanist-informed intervention in that method:

"The Relational Turn in Theological Anthropology," in *T&T Clark Handbook of Theological Anthropology*, edited by Mary Ann Hinsdale and Stephen Okey (London and New York: Bloomsbury, 2021) 71–85;

"Public Theology: A Feminist Anthropological View of Political Subjectivity and Praxis," in *Questioning the Human: Toward a Theological Anthropology for the 21st Century*, edited by Lieven Bove, Yves de Maeseneer, and Ellen van Stichel (New York: Fordham University Press, 2014), 148–163;

"Turning to Narrative: Toward a Feminist Theological Understanding of Political Participation and Personhood," *Journal of the American Academy of Religion* 78, no. 2 (June 2010): 375-412;

"'Artisans of a New Humanity': Revisioning the Public Church in a Feminist Perspective," in *Frontiers in Catholic Feminist Theology: Shoulder to Shoulder*, edited by Susan Abraham and Elena Procario-Foley (Minneapolis: Fortress Press, 2009), 173–192;

"Ekklesial Work: Toward a Feminist Public Theology," *Harvard Theological Review* 99, no. 4 (October 2006): 433–455.

Chapter 2 reworks parts of my prior publications related to practices of religio-political engagement:

"Religious Studies Classrooms as Counterpublic Spaces: A Feminist Theological and Theatrical Perspective," *Journal of Feminist Studies in Religion* 28, no. 1 (Spring 2012): 141–156;

"Turning to Narrative," as cited above; and "Claiming and Imagining: Practices of Public Engagement," in *Prophetic Witness: Catholic*

250 *Nevertheless, We Persist*

Women's Strategies for Reform, edited by Colleen M. Griffith (New York: Crossroad, 2009), 176–185.

Chapter 3 modifies parts of my prior publications, especially about Christological praxis and the Revolutionary Love Project:

"Women's Religio-Political Witness for Love and Justice," in *The Rowman & Littlefield Handbook of Women's Studies in Religion*, edited by Helen T. Boursier (Lanham, MD: Rowman & Littlefield, 2021), 281–298;

"'Artisans of a New Humanity',," as cited above.

Chapters 4 and 5 revise parts of my prior publications about the Civil Rights Movement and the New Sanctuary Movement:

"Placards, Icons, and Protests: Insights into Antiracist Activism from Feminist Public Theology," in *The Gift of Theology: The Contribution of Kathryn Tanner*, edited by Rosemary P. Carbine and Hilda P. Koster (Minneapolis: Fortress Press, 2015), 313–344;

"The Beloved Community: Transforming Spaces for Social Change and for Cosmopolitan Citizenship," in *Women, Wisdom, and Witness: Engaging Contexts in Conversation*, edited by Rosemary P. Carbine and Kathleen Dolphin (Collegeville: Liturgical Press, 2012), 237–258.

Chapter 6 expands on my prior publications about the Plowshares Movement and about ecofeminist public theology:

"Rival Powers: U.S. Catholics Confront the Climate Crisis," in *Theologies of Failure*, edited by Roberto Sirvent and Duncan B. Reyburn (Eugene, OR: Cascade Books, 2019), 197–215, www.wipfandstock. com;

"Imagining and Incarnating an Integral Ecology: A Critical Ecofeminist Public Theology," in *Planetary Solidarity: Global Women's Voices on Christian Doctrine and Climate Justice*, edited by Grace Ji-Sun Kim and Hilda P. Koster (Minneapolis: Fortress Press, 2017), 47–66;

"Claiming and Imagining," as cited above.

Finally, Chapter 7 draws on and adapts parts of my prior publication about the Nuns on the Bus, especially:

"Creating Communities of Justice and Peace: Sacramentality and US Public Catholicism," *Journal for the Academic Study of Religion* 29, no. 2 (2016): 182–202.

Index

ACA. *See* Affordable Care Act
Affordable Care Act (ACA), 229–31
agribusiness, 160, 164–65, 171–73
Agricultural Labor Relations Act
(ALRA), 162, 170
Agricultural Workers Association,
169
Agricultural Workers Organizing Com-
mittee (AWOC), 161, 169
ALRA. *See* Agricultural Labor Rela-
tions Act
Angelou, Maya, 111
anthropocentrism, 28n91, 31–32, 202,
206
apartheid. *See* segregation
Aquino, María Pilar, 109–10, 156–57
Arbery, Ahmaud, 148, 151
Arellano, Elvira, 183
Arendt, Hannah, 51
AWOC . *See* Agricultural Workers Or-
ganizing Committee

Baker, Ella, 132–44
activism, 140
and beloved community, 137, 140
religiosity, 142
rhetorical practices, 141–42
speeches, 141
Barber, William J., 111, 113, 144–46,
148, 150–51
Bedford-Strohm, Heinrich, 194–95
beloved community, 109
Dorothy Day, 70
Ella Baker, 137, 140
Martin Luther King, Jr., 120, 128–32
and NSM, 158, 180, 187–88, 190
and People's Inauguration, 105
and PPC, 153
and RLP, 112

Valarie Kaur, 108
Benedict XVI, Pope, 86–87
Benhabib, Seyla, 189
Berrigan, Philip, 208–10, 213–17, 219,
221, 225
"Beyond Vietnam", 152
biblical prophetic traditions, 32, 80,
113, 125, 130, 146
biological determinism, 87, 246
bio-politics, 198, 228, 236
birthright citizenship, 149, 181n147
Black Church, xxvi, 109, 114, 119, 123,
126, 130, 139n101
Black Freedom Movement, 132, 135,
143, 153
Black Lives Matter, 116–17, 119, 121,
214
Blackmon, Traci, 107
Black Social Gospel tradition, 126
Black women
bodies as sacrament, 234–35
and intersectionality, 34, 62, 94
and labor, 133
objectification of, 235
and SNCC, 138
and storytelling, 46–48
and womanist theology, 93
Blessed Are the Organized, 11
Bloody Sunday, 121–22, 140
Boff, Leonardo, 193, 202
Bonilla-Silva, Eduardo, 115–16
Boyle, Eugene, 163
Boyle Heights, 68
breath
practice of breathe and push,
100–102, 106, 110–11
as ritual, 105, 111
as symbol, 242
Brock, Rita Nakashima, 36–37

251

252   *Nevertheless, We Persist*

Brown, Michael, 107, 116–18, 242
Butler, Judith, 2, 120, 126

Cady, Linell E., 18, 35–36
Campbell, Simone, 108, 229, 237–45
Catholic Agitator, The, 68
Catholic Health Association, 229
Chaput, Charles, 231
Chavez, Cesar
  and CSO, 161
  and Dolores Huerta, 158–59,
    169–70, 172
  early work, 160
  and faith-based change, 164–65
  and fasting, 161–62, 167–68, 177
  and Luis Olivares, 179
  and nonviolence, 161, 164, 167–68
  pilgrimage, 166
  religious practice, 175
  rhetorical practice, 165
  and US bishops, 163
  Wrath of Grapes Campaign, 162
Chopp, Rebecca, 14, 45
Christology
  and Benedict XVI, 87
  and Dorothy Day, 70, 74, 79, 81–82,
    101
  and feminism, 89–90, 206
  and *Gaudium et Spes*, 29–30, 90–91
  and justice, 27
  and Martin Luther King, Jr., 126, 128
  patriarchal/kyriarchal, 89
  performative, 91
  physicalist, 95
  and Plowshares Movement, 221
  political, 101
  and PPC campaign, 148
  praxical, 85, 96
  prophetic, 242
  as theological guidepost, 29n93
  as theological symbol, 86
  and USCCB, 245
  Mark Taylor on, 61
  Michele Saracino on, 36
  M. Shawn Copeland on, 94, 235
  Wisdom, 92, 227
Christomorphism, 77, 90, 92–93
citizenship rights, 130, 133, 185–87
civic debate, xv, 8–9

civil disobedience
  and Black Lives Matter, 117
  and Dorothy Day, 79–80, 84
  and Ferguson protests, 107
  and LACW, 69
  and Martin Luther King, Jr., 125,
    127, 129
  and Philip Berrigan, 210
  and Plowshares Movement, 210,
    218
  Pope Francis on, 208
  and PPC, 146
  and UFW, 166, 178
  and USCCB, 230
civil rights
  and Confererate emblems, 123
  and Martin Luther King, Jr., 130–31
  and PPC, 144
  and Second Reconstruction, 149
  and Vatican II, 32n100, 90
  and voter suppression, 16
Civil Rights Act, 126, 136, 149
civil society, 2, 7, 13, 196
Clergy and Laity United for Economic
    Justice (CLUE), 187–88
climate change, xi, 115, 195–97,
    200–201, 221
climate crisis, 192, 196, 199
Commonweal, 73
Community Service Organization
    (CSO), 161, 169, 171
compassion, 10–11, 46, 108–9. *See also*
    empathy
Cone, James H., 111, 127
Congregation for the Doctrine of the
    Faith, 87, 229–30
Constitution on the Church in the
    Modern World. See *Gaudium et*
    Spes
Copeland, M. Shawn
  on personhood, 39, 94–95
  on political agency, 16, 20, 101
  on rhetorical practices, 48
  on sacramentality, 34, 234–35
  on sex and gender, 34
COVID-19 pandemic, xii, 69, 102, 106–
    7, 111, 147–48, 152, 156, 232
CSO. *See* Community Service Organiza-
    tion

Index   253

Cuban Missile Crisis, 209
Cultural Days of Action, 147

Day, Dorothy
  and beloved community, 70
  and Catherine Morris, 69
  Christology, 101
  conversion to Catholicism, 72–73, 76
  and Ella Baker, 134
  and houses of hospitality, 76
  and journalism, 71–74, 82, 101
  and nonviolence, 80, 84
  and poverty, 77–78
  protest politics, 70, 79–83, 85
  rhetorical practice, 73–74
  and self-love, 102
  symbolic practice, 74–75
  and works of mercy, 76–77
Deane-Drummond, Celia, 194, 207
Declaration of Revolutionary Love, 99
de-creation, 94, 197, 220
Democratic National Convention
    (DNC), 139–40, 240
determinism, biological, 87, 246
Dionne, E.J., 123
discipleship, 20, 92, 95, 184, 211, 219,
    236–37, 245
distributive justice, 59, 71, 82, 196, 224
divine accompaniment, 47, 94
divine intervention, 47–48
divine justice, 129, 132
DNC. *See* Democratic National Con-
    vention
Doak, Mary, 52
Domestic Workers bills, 103

earth ministries, 222–23
Ebenezer Baptist Church, 119, 136
eco-justice, 7, 98, 155, 193–94
  and activism, 193, 197, 205, 221
  and farmworker rights, 163, 168, 224
  and green nuns, 222–23
  Pope Francis on, 193–94, 198–99,
    205
ecology, integral, 193–94, 196, 198,
    205, 207–8, 224, 250
Economic Justice for All, 162, 240
El Malcriado, 162–63
empathy, 11–12, 44, 46, 51–52, 60,

239, 243–44. *See also* compassion
environmental justice, xviii, 173–74. *See
    also* eco-justice
eschatology
  Diana Hayes on, 47
  and ekklesia of wo/men, 21–22
  and imago Dei, 25–26, 40
  and Martin Luther King, Jr., 131
  mujerista, 50
  Peter Phan on, 30n98
  realized, 131, 164
  and theatre, 61
eschatopraxis, 30, 35
Eucharist, 117, 217, 220, 235
Evers, Medgar, 141

Familia Latina Unida, 183
fasting, as protest, 80, 147, 165,
    167–68, 174, 177
Feminist Wisdom Christology, 92, 96
Ferguson, 107, 116, 118–20, 122
Fiorenza, Francis, 9
Floyd, George, xvii, 106, 148, 232
Fortnight, 230–31
Francis, Pope
  2015 UN/US Congress address, 85,
    198–200
  and eco-justice, 193–204, 224
  and *Laudato Si'*, 192–208
  and LCWR, 229–30
  and World Meeting of Popular Move-
    ments, 155–56
Freedom Riders, 125
freedom rides, 125, 209n46
Freedom Schools, 138
Freedom Summer, 119, 138–39, 143

Gandhian nonviolence, 126, 161, 176
Ganz, Marshall, 165–66
Garner, Eric, 116, 118
Gaudium et Spes
  and Christology, 90–92, 95–96
  and eschatology, xix, 17, 26, 30
  and imago Dei, 28–29, 40, 190, 246
  and public participation, 17, 86, 200,
    227, 230, 236
  and theological anthropology, 27,
    31–32
  and womanist theology, 25

Gebara, Ivone, 205, 224, 246
gender
  and Christology, 86
  and injustice, 142
  John Paul II on, 87
  and *Laudato Si'*, 205
  norms, 86, 135, 165n48, 169, 209
  in religious spheres, 87–89
  and women's liberation theologies,
    34
generativity, 95–96, 235–36
Genesis Farm, 223
Gilbert, Carol, 212, 217
Global North, 195, 197–98, 205
Global South, 195–96, 198, 224
Grady, Clare, 213
grape strikes, 161–63, 172, 176, 178
Great Migration, 133
green nuns, 194, 221–26
grief, 106–7
gritos, 173
Guadalupe, 166, 174–75

Hamer, Fannie Lou, 138–41, 143, 145
Harper, Lisa Sharon, 109
Hayes, Diana, 47
Hennessy, Martha, 213
Hilkert, Mary Catherine, 30, 91, 238,
  246
Himes, Michael, 54–55
Holmes, Barbara, 62
hooks, bell, 101, 110
houses of hospitality, 76–77, 79–81, 83,
  101
Hudson, Jackie, 212
Huerta, Dolores
  and agribusiness, 171–72
  and Cesar Chavez, 158–59, 161–62
  and Dorothy Day, 80
  early work, 169
  experiences of violence, 179
  and grape boycotts, 170
  and LGBTQ+ rights, 159n10
  and nonviolence, 173–74, 176
  prophetic practice, 176–78
  rhetorical practice, 170–71, 173
  symbolic practice, 174
  theological praxis, 175–76
  use of gritos, 173
Hunger March, 73

Ifill, Sherrilyn, 109
imago Christi, 25, 89, 101, 164
imago Dei
  Ada María Isasi-Díaz on, 35
  and Cesar Chavez, 164
  Charles Chaput on, 231
  and Dorothy Day, 81, 101
  in *Gaudium et Spes*, 27–28, 31
  John Paul II on, 87
  and Martin Luther King, Jr., 126, 131
  Mary Catherine Hilkert on, 246
  M. Shawn Copeland on, 34
  and NSM, 184, 190
  Pope Francis on, 199
  and PPC, 149
  and public life, 40, 55, 187
  Rosemary Radford Ruether on, 32
  and social teaching, 25–26
  and theological anthropology, 207
  and USCCB, 245
  used to contest theologies, 31n99
  William J. Barber on, 151
immigrant rights movements, 59, 98,
  155, 159, 172, 174, 179–80, 182,
  241, 243
immigrants
  and asylum, 98, 181
  crossings, 182
  discrimination against, 75, 94, 100,
    180, 182
  and ministries, 187n180
  and NSM, 185–88
  Peggy Levitt study on, 189
  rising deportation rates, 114n3
incarnational theology, 207
Indigenous communities
  and environmental racism, 193
  and racial justice, 68, 148
  religious traditions, 106
  and sovereignty, 103–4
  women, 111, 205
injustice, systemic, 28, 63, 109, 111,
  143, 156, 166–67
Institute on Nonviolence and Social
  Change, 129
integral ecology, 193–94, 196, 198, 205,
  207–8, 224, 250
intersectional injustice, xiv, 3n5, 62, 66,
  83, 98, 104, 144–47, 152, 156
intersectional justice, 32, 106

Index

interstitiality, 37–38, 179
Isasi-Díaz, Ada María, 34–35, 48–50, 157

Jackson, Jesse, 151, 162
Jesus Christ
  as Bridegroom, 88
  as craftsman, 30
  imitation of, 30, 61, 78, 89–90, 92, 218
  kingdom of God, 92, 109
  maleness, 90
  and ministry, 29–30, 33, 40, 77, 90, 92–93, 101, 184, 218, 236–37
  mystical body as symbol, 72, 81–82, 85, 234–35
  and rage, 107
  resignifying, 86, 89
  as revolutionary, 61, 78
  soteriological significance, 91
John Paul II, Pope, 86–87
Johnson, Elizabeth, 90, 202, 224
Johnson, Lyndon, 121
Jonah House, 213–14, 219
Jubilee Platform, 148

Kaur, Valarie, 97–103, 106–12
Kennedy, Robert F., 173
kin-dom of God, 35, 49–50, 95, 149, 210, 214, 218, 220–21, 225, 238
King, Martin Luther, Jr.
  anti-war activism, 131
  and beloved community, 120, 128–32
  "Beyond Vietnam", 152
  citizenship rights, 130
  and Elizabeth Warren speech, xxviii
  and Ella Baker, 136–37
  eschatology, 131
  "Letter from a Birmingham Jail", 124
  nonviolence, 118–19, 127, 129, 132, 176
  prophetic traditions, 125
  symbolic practices, 126, 128
  kingdom of God, 29, 31–32, 35, 82–83, 90, 92, 95, 109, 111, 130, 132, 164, 233, 236–37
Kwok, Pui Lan, 38, 204
kyriarchy
  Elisabeth Schüssler Fiorenza on, 3
  and feminism, 36

M. Shawn Copeland on, 39
  and political life, 4, 14, 20–24, 213
  Pope Francis on, 192
  and racism, 113
  Rosemary Radford Ruether on, 206
  Sallie McFague on, 89, 204

LaCugna, Catherine Mowry, 53
LACW. *See* Los Angeles Catholic Worker
Laffin, Art, 214, 221
LaPorte, Roger, 80
Lara, María Pía, 51–52
Latina feminism, 22, 48–50, 156, 179, 220
Laudato Si', 192, 192–208, 224
LCWR. *See* Leadership Conference of Women Religious
Leadership Conference of Women Religious (LCWR), 229–30, 237, 245n74
Leo XIII, Pope, 72
"Letter from a Birmingham Jail", 124
Levitt, Peggy, 189
Lewis, Jacqui, 107, 123
LGBTQ+ rights, 59, 126, 159, 231
liberation theology, 176, 181, 195–96
liberative justice, 4, 19
Life-in-community, 28
Lorde, Audre, 110
Los Angeles Catholic Worker (LACW), 68–69
low-wealth people, 145, 147–48, 152, 239
lucha, 49, 156, 164, 170

MacGillis, Miriam, 223
Majority Leader's Task Force on Poverty and Opportunity, 149
Make Good Trouble Rally, 150
Manson, Jamie, 245
March for Life (2020), 232
March on Washington for Jobs and Freedom (1963), 129–30, 132, 150
Markey, John, 29
Marsh, Charles, 129
Maurin, Peter, 70, 73, 81–82
McAlister, Elizabeth, 213
McConnell, Mitch, xxviii
McDade, Tony, 148

McFague, Sallie, 204, 224
McLaren, Brian D., 109
MFDP. *See* Mississippi Freedom Democratic Party
militarism
  and border walls, xvi, 180, 182
  and kyriarchy, 211
  LACW protests, 69
  Martin Luther King, Jr. on, 131
  and nationalism, xv–xvi, 186, 225
  and nonviolence, 217–18
  Philip Berrigan on, 208
  and white supremacy, 213
Miller, Patricia, 231
Mississippi Freedom Democratic Party
  (MFDP), 139–40
Mitchem, Stephanie, 20, 131
Montgomery bus boycott, 129, 135
Moral Marches, 147, 149–50
Morris, Catherine, 69
Movement Declaration to Reconstruct
  American Democracy, 153
mujerista theology, 18, 22, 32, 34, 38,
  45, 48, 50, 95, 156–57, 220

NAACP, 134–35, 137, 141
National Civil Rights Museum, 151
National Climate Assessment (2014),
  200
National Domestic Workers Alliance,
  103, 107
National Farm Workers Association
  (NFWA), 161, 172
nationalism
  and Christianity, xv–xvii, 232
  and hate crimes, 99
  and militarism, xv–xvi, 186, 225
  religious, 111, 145–46, 148
  and white supremacy, xvi
nationalist movements, and white
  supremacy, 67
National Moral Monday (2021), 150
National Poor People's and Low-Wage
  Workers' Assembly, 149
nativism, 181n147
New Sanctuary Movement (NSM), 158,
  180–88, 190, 250
NFWA. *See* National Farm Workers Association (NFWA)
nonviolence

Art Laffin, 221
Cesar Chavez, 161, 164, 167–68
Dolores Huerta, 173–74, 176
Dorothy Day, 80, 84
Martin Luther King, Jr., 118–19, 127,
  129, 132, 176
Philip Berrigan, 215, 217
Noyola, Isa, 107
NSM. *See* New Sanctuary Movement
nuclear weapons, 69, 84, 194, 211–13,
  216–17. *See also* militarism
Nun Justice Project, 229n4
Nuns on the Bus, 108, 228, 237–39,
  241–47

Obama, Barack, xvi, 113–14, 121–23,
  158, 240
Olivares, Luis, 179–80
original sin, 33
  racism as, 113–14

Palmer Red Raids, 75
Paris Climate Agreement, 225
Parks, Rosa, 135–36
Parliament of the World's Religions
  (PWR), 99
Pastoral Constitution of the Church in
  the Modern World. See *Gaudium
  et Spes*
People's Inauguration (2021), 102–5
in persona Christi, 89, 237
personal sin, 28, 33
personhood, xvi, 3n5, 18, 33–36, 38,
  94–95, 113, 153, 180
Pfleger, Michael, 117–18
Phan, Peter, 30n98
Pinckney, Clementa, 122–23
Platte, Ardeth, 212
pluralistic society, 6–7, 10, 191
police violence, 107, 116, 118, 178, 242
political subjectivity, 9, 11, 13–14,
  17–18, 20, 23, 31–32, 38, 43, 49,
  180
Poor People's Campaign (PPC), 98, 111,
  120, 124, 144–53
Poor People's Pandemic Report, 152
poverty, 111
  Dolores Huerta, 172, 174
  Dorothy Day, 73, 77–78, 83–85
  and eco-justice, 193, 222

Index

voluntary, 77–78, 165, 168, 176, 214
PPC. *See* Poor People's Campaign
prisons, 218–19
prophetic activism, 58, 73
prophetic protest, xxvii, 67, 74, 81, 101, 119, 125, 151, 210, 215, 225
PWR. *See* Parliament of the World's Religions

racial justice, 123–24, 128, 130, 132, 134, 148
racism
  anti-Black, 123, 209n46
  Barack Obama on, 113–15, 122
  Black Lives Matter, 116, 119
  Eduardo Bonilla-Silva on, 115
  environmental, 111, 193, 203
  James Cone on, 127
  as original sin, 33, 113–14, 131
  systemic, 115, 117, 144, 146, 148–49, 209, 232, 244
  and white supremacy, xvi
rage, 107–8
Ratzinger, Joseph. *See* Benedict XVI
Reagon, Bernice Johnson, 142
refugees, 94, 179, 181–82, 196, 199
reign of God, xxvii, 26, 29–30, 61, 96, 185, 223
religio-political engagement, xii–xiii, xxvi
  and Dolores Huerta, 159, 164
  Dolores Huerta, 174
  and ekklesial work, 63
  Gaudium et Spes, 26
  and NSM, 158
  Simone Campbell, 238
religio-political subjectivity, 42, 48, 52, 156–57, 227
religio-political symbols, 64, 120, 128, 130
Religious Right, xi, xiv–xv
  religious symbols
  Laudato Si', 202
  and protest, 120
  reinterpreting, 55, 174, 194, 219
  and theological critique, 53–54, 128
reproductive rights, xi, 170, 201, 229
Republicanity, xvi
Rerum Novarum, 72, 163

revolutionary love, 97–99, 106–7, 110–11
Revolutionary Love Project (RLP), 70, 96–99, 101–2, 112, 250
rhetorical practice
  and Black Freedom Movement, 153
  Cesar Chavez, 165
  and Civil Rights Movement, 126
  defining, 43–45
  Dolores Huerta, 170–71, 173
  Dorothy Day, 73–74
  green nuns, 222
  and kin-dom of God, 50
  Laudato Si', 196, 224
  María Pía Lara on, 51
  M. Shawn Copeland on, 48
  Nuns on the Bus, 239
  Paul Ricoeur on, 51
  Plowshares Movement, 215–16
  and prophetic practice, 59
  and public theology, 2, 4, 8, 24, 63, 103
  Simone Campbell, 240
  and storytelling, 106, 115
  USCCB, 232
  Valarie Kaur on, 99
rhetorical practices function, 44
rhetorical practices of informed rational inquiry and debate, 4
Rice, Megan, 212n63
Ricoeur, Paul, 51–52
RLP. *See* Revolutionary Love Project
Ross, Fred, 161, 169
Ross, Rosetta E., 48n26, 133n63, 142
Ross, Susan, 143, 234–35
Rue, Victoria, 60
Ruether, Rosemary Radford, 25, 32, 206, 224

sacrament
  Black women's bodies as, 235
  church as, 26, 236
  public theology as, 40, 95, 227
  and sacramentality, 233
sacramentality, 30n95, 193, 207, 227–28, 233–36, 250
Sacred Body, 205
Sacred Earth and Space Plowshares, 212, 216–18
Saito, Brynn, 103

Salcedo, Bamby, 104
Salvatierra, Alexia, 187
salvation, 28, 76, 78, 88, 134, 184
Sanctuary Movement (SM), 179–81,
    183, 185–87
Saracino, Michele, 36, 115n6
Schneiders, Sandra, 228
Schüssler Fiorenza, Elisabeth, xiii, 3, 10,
    19–21, 23, 62
SCLC. *See* Southern Christian Leader-
    ship Conference
Second Reconstruction, 149
Second Vatican Council. *See* Vatican II
segregation, 129, 160
self-love, 33, 100, 102, 110, 234
Sermon on the Mount, 73, 83–85,217
Sexism and God-Talk, 25
Sikh communities
    joy as spiritual practice, 111
    and People's Inauguration, 104
    violence against, 98
sin
    original, 113–14
    personal, 28, 33
    social, 184, 202
slavery, 47, 75, 93, 111, 114–15, 166,
    203, 235
SM. *See* Sanctuary Movement
SNCC. *See* Student Nonviolent Coordi-
    nating Committee
social Trinitarian theology, 57, 94
solidarity
    as central social praxis, 34n107
    and Christomorphism, 93
    and ekklesia of wo/men, 21, 24–25
    incarnational, 30, 237
    Judith Butler on, 120
    and liberation theology, 176
    and personhood, 39, 95
    political, 106–7, 115–16
    and prophetic practice, 58
    and religious symbols, 55, 66
    and rhetorical practice, 43–44,
        50–51, 59, 115
    and sacramentality, 234
    and testimony, 46, 52
    through storytelling, 114
    and voluntary poverty, 168
solidarity politics, 13, 145, 168, 243
Southern Christian Leadership Con-

ference (SCLC), 121, 125n29,
    130–31, 136–37
Starks, Amber, 103
storytelling
    Barack Obama on, 114
    communal, 43, 45, 49, 53
    Marshall Ganz on, 165–66
    Nuns on the Bus, 239
    and Pope Francis, 199
    and PPC, 145n129, 152–53
    as rhetorical practice, 44, 51, 106
    Simone Campbell on, 241
Stout, Jeffrey, 11–12
Student Nonviolent Coordinating Com-
    mittee (SNCC), 121, 137–40, 142,
    145
symbolic practice
    Cesar Chavez, 165–67
    defining, 53
    Dolores Huerta, 174, 176–77
    Dorothy Day, 74, 78
    Ella Baker, 142
    fasting, 168
    Himes and Himes on, 55
    Laudato Si', 202–3
    Martin Luther King, Jr., 126
    and People's Inauguration, 105
    and PPC, 146, 150, 152
    and prophetic practice, 58, 60
    and reinterpretation, 64
    and RLP, 102
    Simone Campbell, 240

Tanner, Kathryn, 57, 65
Task Force on 21st Century Policing,
    122
Taylor, Breonna, 148
Taylor, Mark, 61
Taylor, Sarah McFarland, 222–24
telos, 22, 25
testimony
    Diana Hayes on, 47
    and PPC, 145
    and public discourse, 46
    Rebecca Chopp on, 45
    as rhetorical practice, 44, 52, 215
    Rosetta Ross on, 48n26, 113
theatre, 60–62, 138
Theoharis, Liz, 111, 144–45, 147,
    151–52

Index

theological anthropology
  and Civil Rights Movement, 126
  Ella Baker, 143
  feminist, 33, 35, 64, 97, 207, 246
  Gaudium et Spes, 26–27, 31
  mujerista, 32
  Vatican II, 16
theological symbols
  and anthropocentrism, 206
  beloved community as, 188
  and Christology, 86, 89
  Christology, 86
  ecofeminism, 205
  ecofeminist, 204
  and green nuns, 223
  purpose, 55
  Sallie McFague on, 204
theo-praxis, 1, 176
Thiemann, Ronald F., 9–10
Third Reconstruction resolution, 149, 153
Tracy, David, 8–9, 57
Trinitarian theology, 57, 94
Trinity, 53, 87, 95
Trump, Donald, xvi–xvii, 231

Unite the Right Rally (2017), 232
USCCB. *See* US Conference of Catholic Bishops
US Conference of Catholic Bishops (USCCB), 230–32, 244–45
US Supreme Court, 122, 231–32

Vatican, and LWCR, 229–30
Vatican II
  and anthropocentrism, 28n91

and feminist theology, 95, 227–28, 233, 246
Gaudium et Spes, xix, 17, 25–26, 31, 90, 92, 246
and political participation, 86
theological anthropology, 16
Dorothy Day, 79
Vietnam War, 80, 83, 131, 172, 194, 209–10
voluntary poverty, 77–78, 165, 168, 176, 214
voting rights, 98, 121, 149, 151–52, 242
Voting Rights Act, 16, 121–22, 126, 149

Warren, Elizabeth, xxviii, 145, 152
white supremacy, xvii, 93, 111, 146, 213
Wiesel, Elie, 190
williams, angel Kyodo, 110
Wisdom Christology, 92, 227
witnessing, 48n26. *See also* testimony
wo/men, ekklesia of, xiii, 1–4, 19–24
works of mercy, 76–78, 81, 85, 101, 221
World Meeting of Popular Movements, 155
World War I, 76, 79, 243
World War II, 83, 182
Wrath of Grapes campaign, 162
Wright, Jeremiah, 113–14

Young, Iris Marion, 15
Young People's Forum, 133